EVERYBODY
BEHAVES BADLY

EVERYBODY
BEHAVES BADLY

The True Story Behind
Hemingway's Masterpiece
The Sun Also Rises

Lesley M. M. Blume

An Eamon Dolan Book
Houghton Mifflin Harcourt
BOSTON NEW YORK

For information about permission to reproduce selections
from this book, write to trade.permissions@hmhco.com or to
Permissions, Houghton Mifflin Harcourt Publishing Company,
3 Park Avenue, 19th Floor, New York, New York 10016.

www.hmhco.com

Library of Congress Cataloging-in-Publication Data
Names: Blume, Lesley M. M., author.
Title: Everybody behaves badly : the true story behind
Hemingway's masterpiece The Sun Also Rises / Lesley Blume.
Description: Boston : Eamon Dolan/Houghton Mifflin Harcourt, 2016.
Identifiers: LCCN 2015037016 | ISBN 9780544276000 (hardback) |
ISBN 9780544237179 (ebook)
Subjects: LCSH: Hemingway, Ernest, 1899–1961. Sun also rises. |
Hemingway, Ernest, 1899–1961 — Homes and haunts — Spain. |
Hemingway, Ernest, 1899–1961 — Homes and haunts — France—Paris. |
BISAC: BIOGRAPHY & AUTOBIOGRAPHY / Artists, Architects, Photographers. |
LITERARY CRITICISM / American / General.
Classification: LCC PS3515.E37 S9216 2016 | DDC 813/.52 — dc23
LC record available at http://lccn.loc.gov/2015037016

Book design by Rachel Newborn

Printed in the United States of America
DOC 10 9 8 7 6 5 4
4500614474

Text permission credits appear on page 321.
Photo credits appear on page 323.

For G. R. M.

Contents

Author's Note

The letters and other documents quoted in this book appear exactly as they were written, including the writers' original spelling and grammar.

Introduction

I N MARCH 1934, *Vanity Fair* ran a mischievous editorial: a page of Ernest Hemingway paper dolls, featuring cutouts of various famous Hemingway personas. On display: Hemingway as a toreador, clinging to a severed bull's head; Hemingway as a brooding, café-dwelling writer (four wine bottles adorn his table, and a waiter is seen toting three more in his direction); Hemingway as a bloodied war veteran. "Ernest Hemingway, America's own literary cave man," declared the caption. "Hard-drinking, hard-fighting, hard-loving—all for art's sake."

Throughout his life, additional personas would attach themselves to him: rugged deep-sea fisherman; big-game hunter; postwar liberator of the Paris Ritz; white-bearded Papa. He relished all of these identities and so did the press. When it came to selling copy, Hemingway was one of America's most versatile leading men, and certainly one of the country's most fascinating entertainers.

By then, everyone had long forgotten one of his earliest roles: unpublished nobody. It was one of the few Hemingway personas that never really suited him. In fact, in the early 1920s—strapped for cash, ravenous for recognition—he was frantic to rid himself of it. Even in the earliest days of his career, his ambition seemed limitless. Unfortunately for him, the literary gatekeepers proved uncooperative at first. Hemingway was ready to dominate the world of letters, but its citizens were not yet willing to succumb. Mainstream publications turned down his short stories; his rejected manuscripts came back to him and were shoveled through the mail slot in his apartment's front door.

"The rejection slip is very hard to take on an empty stomach," Hemingway later told a friend. "There were times when I'd sit at that old wooden table and read one of those cold slips that had been attached to a story I had loved and worked on very hard and believed in, and I couldn't help crying."

During such moments of despair, it is unlikely that Hemingway realized that he was actually one of the luckier writers in modern history. Circumstances often seemed to conspire in his favor. All of the right things made their way to him at the right moment: motivated mentors, publisher patrons, wealthy wives—and a trove of material just when he needed it most, in the form of some delectably bad behavior among his peers, which he promptly translated into his groundbreaking debut novel, *The Sun Also Rises,* published in 1926. In the book's pages, those co-opted antics—benders, hangovers, affairs, betrayals—took on a new and loftier guise of their own: experimental literature. Thus elevated, all of this bad behavior rocked the literary world and came to define Hemingway's entire generation.

Everyone knows how this story ends: to say that Hemingway eventually became famous and successful is a gross understatement. A Nobel laureate, he has been widely called the father of modern literature and for decades has been read in dozens of languages around the globe. More than half a century after his death, he still commands headlines and crops up in gossip columns.

What follows is the story of how Hemingway became Hemingway in the first place—and the book that set it all in motion. The backstory of *The Sun Also Rises* and that of its author's rise are one and the same. Critics have long cited Hemingway's second novel, *A Farewell to Arms,* as the one that established him as a giant in the literary pantheon, but in many ways, the significance of *The Sun Also Rises* is much greater. As far as literature was concerned, it essentially introduced its mainstream readers to the twentieth century.

"*The Sun Also Rises* did more than break the ice," says Lorin Stein, editor of the *Paris Review.* "It was modern literature fully arrived for a grand public. I'm not sure that there was ever another moment when one novelist was so obviously the leader of a whole generation. You read one sentence and it doesn't sound like anything that came before."

Not that there weren't other tremors before this earthquake. A small movement of writers had been trying to shove literature out of musty Edwardian corridors and into the fresh air of the modern world. It was a question of who would break through first—and who could make new ways of writing appealing to the mainstream reader, who, for the most part, still seemed to be perfectly satisfied with the more florid, verbose approaches of Henry James and Edith Wharton. James Joyce's radical novel *Ulysses,* for example, had blown the minds of many postwar writers.

But at first the work was hardly a mainstream sensation: it wasn't even released in book form in the United States until the 1930s. Paris-based experimentalist Gertrude Stein had resorted to self-publishing her works, which were often deemed incomprehensible by those who actually did read them. One of her books reportedly sold a mere seventy-three copies in its first eighteen months of existence. F. Scott Fitzgerald had also been striving to reinvent the American novel and felt that he had succeeded with the publication of *The Great Gatsby* in 1925. Yet while the content of his novels was thoroughly modern—flappers, bootleggers, and other exotic urban creatures—his style remained decidedly old-school.

"Fitzgerald was a nineteenth-century soul," says Charles Scribner III, a former director at Charles Scribner's Sons, which published both Fitzgerald and Hemingway for the majority of their careers. "[He] was wrapping up a grand tradition; he was the last of the romantics. He was Strauss."

Hemingway, by contrast, was Stravinsky.

"He was inventing a whole new idiom and tonality," explains Scribner. "And he was completely twentieth century." As one prominent critic noted around that time, Hemingway succeeded in doing for writing what Picasso and the cubists had been doing for painting: after the debut of the "primitive modern idiom" of cubism and Hemingway's stark, staccato prose, nothing would ever be the same again. Modernity had found its popular creative leaders.

The Sun Also Rises immediately established Hemingway not only as the voice of his generation but as a lifestyle icon as well. Before the novel's debut, Fitzgerald had been doing most of the talking. In those days, novelists had quite a national platform. Movies were still a relatively new medium; TV was decades away. Novels and stories were a major form of popular entertainment. Fitzgerald had become a national celebrity; his new works were devoured and discussed as the finale of a beloved television show — such as *The Sopranos* or *Mad Men* — might be rhapsodized about today. Yale students flocked to the New Haven railroad station when trains bearing magazines with his latest stories were due to arrive.

From Fitzgerald's point of view, however, that generation was a decadent, champagne-soaked constituency. *The Great Gatsby* became the bible of the Jazz Age—which Fitzgerald himself had done much to invent. If he was seen as an apt chronicler of his times, he also prompted life to imi-

tate art: many fashioned themselves after Fitzgerald's racy characters—
and after Fitzgerald and his flapper wife, Zelda, themselves.

"Scott gave the era a tempo," Zelda wrote years later, "and a plot from
which it might dramatize itself."

Hemingway's debut novel changed that tempo considerably. With
the publication of *The Sun Also Rises,* his generation was informed that it
was not giddy after all. Rather, it was simply lost. The Great War had ruined everyone, so everyone might as well start drinking even more heavily—and preferably in Paris. Back in America, the college set gleefully
adopted the label of the "Lost Generation," a term that Hemingway borrowed from Gertrude Stein and popularized with his novel. *The Sun Also
Rises* essentially became the new guidebook to contemporary youth culture. Parisian cafés teemed with *Sun* character wannabes: the hard-drinking Jake Barnes and the studiously blasé Lady Brett Ashley were suddenly
trendy role models. Many generational movements would follow—the
Beats, Generation X, the Millennials—yet none has been as romanticized
as this pioneering youth movement, which for many still shimmers with
dissipated glamour.

And at the time, no one seemed a better representative of that chic
lost world than Hemingway himself, thanks to the public relations machine that plugged him as a personality along with *Sun.* Those charged
with marketing Hemingway's work were aware of their good fortune: in
a sense, they were getting two juicy stories for the price of one. It quickly
became apparent that the public's appetite for Hemingway himself was
as great as that for his writing, and he and his team were quite happy to
oblige them. Here was a new breed of writer—brainy yet brawny, a far
cry from Proust and his dusty, sequestered ilk. Almost immediately upon
the release of *The Sun Also Rises,* at least one press outlet noted the emergence of a Hemingway "cult" on two continents.

NO ONE WAS a better promoter of Hemingway than Hemingway. He
had more commercial savvy than most of his competitors, and was almost savagely determined. Only twenty-two years old when he first arrived in Paris in late 1921 with his new wife, Hadley, Hemingway already
"wanted very much to be a great, great writer and at that moment wasn't,"
as his fellow expat and close friend Archibald MacLeish put it. Not that
Hemingway expected immediate glory: at that time he knew that he had
a lot to learn, but he had a strong sense of what he wanted to accomplish
and executed his goals with precision.

"[He] wanted to be a great writer," he wrote of one of his short story characters around that time, yet he could have been writing about himself. "He was pretty sure he would be . . . He felt almost holy about it. It was deadly serious."

To those who first met him in Paris, he seemed aptly named: earnest. Eventually he would reveal his ability to achieve his noble goals through less than noble means and material. Both the author and his debut novel would be born of unrepentant ambition. Even during those first few weeks and months, for Hemingway it was never enough simply to bask in the wonders of Paris and become part of the scenery. Not only did he want to stand apart from his expatriate colleagues; he wanted to leave them in his dust.

His work ethic became famous around Paris. God help any well-wisher who "bitched" his writing sessions on the terrace of his home café, La Closerie des Lilas. He reviled creative poseurs who squandered hours drinking and gossiping at cafés like La Rotonde. He appeared to prioritize writing above all else — including Hadley and the little son they had two years into their Paris adventure. For Hemingway, "family life [was] the enemy of accomplishment," says another of his sons, Patrick. "On several occasions he said being a good husband, being a good father, . . . all of [these things were] not recognized by a reviewer when he reviewed your book."

Many expats at that time had grand literary ambitions, but beyond his good fortune, work ethic, and obvious talent, Hemingway held yet another ace that the others did not: a peculiar sort of charisma. He was gregarious, smart, and great-looking, and therefore a social prize. Because he was so opinionated, he drew the less assured like moths to a flame. Yet these are all components of a merely popular personality, not necessarily a charismatic one. Hemingway, however, could inspire slavish devotion during initial encounters, and no one has ever adequately articulated what made him so attractive to his peers. Some attribute his allure to his wicked wit and claim that he emanated an aura of excitement. Or it may have had something to do with his infectious enthusiasms, whether for icy Sancerre or heroic matadors or fish yanked from the Seine and fried on the spot. Maybe it was the way he listened to you: thoroughly, attentively.

"If you knew all about roses, he would talk to you about roses until he knew everything you knew," recalls his friend Joseph Dryer. "He'd smile at you encouragingly and ask you questions. It was very flattering to be listened to like that."

Only after the conversation ended might you realize that he now knew everything about you, yet had revealed little about himself.

Even his most ardent detractors grew obsessed with him — some of whom resented his eventual rise even when they had heartily contributed to that ascent. One of his earliest publishers took to calling Hemingway the "Limelight Kid" and a "fabulous phony," but still devoted many pages of his eventual memoir to him.

"He made men want to talk about him," recalled Morley Callaghan, a former *Toronto Star* colleague of Hemingway's.

Hemingway also proved irresistible to well-connected mentors — even before he had published a single word of fiction. Within weeks of arriving in Paris, he had enraptured two gods of the modernist movement, Gertrude Stein and Ezra Pound. They were among the first of many figures who would clamor to support him; perhaps no other writer has ever been so flush with patrons.

"When he met those people, it wasn't that they took [his] writing in isolation; they took the writing in combination with this person himself," says Valerie Hemingway, Hemingway's assistant during the writer's final years and later his daughter-in-law. "Hemingway was a charmer, [but] he wasn't an idle charmer. He was a charmer when he had a goal."

These luminaries invited young Hemingway into their homes; they taught him everything they knew and helped sculpt him into the effective modern writer he longed to be. All along he watched and listened as he drank their tea and liquor. Soon many of Paris's best-placed expat writers, editors, and literary gatekeepers were also placing their resources at his feet. He unabashedly took what he needed and usually moved quickly on — repaying most of his patrons for their generosity in unexpected ways, to put it mildly.

Yet despite their patronage and his own furious efforts, Hemingway simply could not break through. By 1923, it was driving him crazy. It seemed that practically every month, another Fitzgerald short story appeared in another major American publication, but no one would publish the stories of Ernest Hemingway. Eventually a couple of Paris-based expat boutique publishers brought out two little volumes of Hemingway poems, sketches, and stories. These booklets showcased his revolutionary new style but didn't exactly earn him a mass readership; in fact, fewer than five hundred copies of both titles combined ever went into circulation.

Yet for the few who did read them, those stories gave an enticing glimpse into what a Hemingway novel might look like. Short stories were big business for magazines in those days, but as far as publishers were concerned, the best-selling novel was still the holy grail. Hemingway's future was quietly discussed among those who might stand to profit from long-form Hemingway. Back in New York, one American publisher wrote wishfully to a friend in the mid-1920s, "Hemingway's first novel might rock the country." The time had come for Hemingway to make a bold move.

"I knew I must write a novel," he later recalled.

Frankly, he had known it all along, but it wasn't necessarily an easy feat to accomplish. Already there had been at least three false starts. One idea had died on the vine. A second book had been started but didn't make it past the twenty-seventh page of the manuscript. Another novel appears to have reached relatively mature form but was then lost in a soul-crushing mishap that would strain both Hemingway's young marriage and his will to persevere as a writer. He chose to struggle onward, but his reporting job for the *Toronto Star* took away precious time from his own writing. When he dared to give up reporting, he was rewarded with penury; his family had to wear extra sweaters indoors to keep warm. He was plagued by writer's block: sometimes it took him a whole morning just to scratch a few sentences onto a page. In the meantime, he feared that other young writers were surging past him. Then, once he managed to perfect his prose formula, there was the terrifying prospect that someone else might rip off his new style and make a splash with it before he could.

Yet Hemingway refused to force the issue. The novel would happen when it was meant to happen. "I would put it off though until I could not help doing it," he recalled later. "When I had to write it, then it would be the only thing to do and there would be no choice." Until then, there was just one way to get there, in his opinion.

"Let the pressure build."

IF YOU SHAKE a bottle of champagne vigorously enough, the cork will eventually shoot out with explosive force. Just when the pressure on all fronts had reached intolerable levels, the cosmos gave Hemingway his luckiest break. It came in the form of a sensual, dissipated English aristocrat with a penchant for men's fedoras and casual lovers. The moment Lady Duff Twysden turned up in Paris, everything changed for Hemingway.

At first he didn't know it. But in the summer of 1925, when he went to the San Fermín bullfighting fiesta in Pamplona, Lady Duff Twysden came along. Hemingway adored Spain; he eventually described it as "the country that I loved more than any other except my own." He drew deep inspiration from Spanish culture, and bullfighting in particular: sitting ringside at a fight was like being at a war, he wrote. By the time they reached the fiesta, Hemingway appeared to have grown infatuated with Twysden, but she complicated any possibility of an affair by bringing along two of her lovers on the trip. One of them — Pat Guthrie — was a perpetually drunk Scottish debtor. The other, writer Harold Loeb, was the product of Princeton and two of New York City's greatest and wealthiest Jewish families. Until Twysden entered the picture, Loeb had been one of Hemingway's tennis friends and among his most ardent supporters. Now he was Hemingway's rival.

The outing quickly degenerated into a Bacchanalian morass of sexual jealousy and gory spectacle. By the end of the fiesta, Loeb and Guthrie openly despised each other; Hemingway and Loeb would nearly come to fisticuffs in public over their entourage's resident Jezebel; Lady Duff herself materialized at lunch one day with a black eye and a bruised forehead, possibly earned in a late-night scrap with Guthrie. Despite the war wound and the atmosphere she was creating, Twysden glowed throughout the fiesta. The drama became her.

It also became Hemingway, but in a different way. Seeing Twysden there amidst all of that pagan decadence triggered something in him. He immediately realized that he had material for an incendiary story. The moment he and Hadley left Pamplona to watch bullfights throughout the region, he began transcribing the entire spectacle onto paper, writing almost in a fever trance. Suddenly every illicit exchange, insult, and bit of unrequited longing that had broken out during the fiesta had a serious literary currency. The Hemingways kept up a manic travel schedule as the story flooded out of him; parts of the story were added in Valencia, Madrid, and Hendaye.

Hemingway eventually ricocheted back up to Paris, where he finished the first draft in September 1925. Soon he was calling the finished result *The Sun Also Rises,* a phrase borrowed from the Bible. Hemingway knew that he had a hot property on his hands — and his ticket out of the literary backwater.

"It is a hell of a fine novel," he wrote to an editor acquaintance, adding that it would "let these bastards who say yes he can write very beautiful little paragraphs know where they get off at."

After years of frustration and buildup, Hemingway's debut novel had been conjured up in a mere six weeks. He was joining the novel club at last, and suddenly many stood to profit.

WHEN *The Sun Also Rises* was released a year later, those who had been translated onto its pages were incredulous that it was being marketed as fiction.

"When I first read it I couldn't see what everyone was getting so excited about," recalled Donald Ogden Stewart, a best-selling humor author who had been part of the Pamplona entourage. Hemingway repurposed him into the book's comic foil Bill Gorton. In his eyes, *The Sun Also Rises* was "nothing but a report on what happened. This is journalism." Stewart was not the only one who believed that Hemingway had shown his reporting chops, and nothing more. He had even written the whole thing as though delivering a juicy scoop on deadline.

When he began writing the novel, Hemingway failed to warn his characters' prototypes that they were about to star in his big literary coup. That said, one evening he leaked the news to Kitty Cannell, another one of the novel's unwitting real-life models. In Paris, some of the Pamplona crew had gathered for dinner to make amends. Nerves were still raw from the fiesta, which had concluded nearly two months earlier. After dinner, the group walked to a café nearby. Hemingway and Cannell were strolling together when he suddenly made a startling admission.

"I'm writing a book," he told her. "Everybody's in it. And I'm going to tear these two bastards apart," he added, indicating Harold Loeb and Hemingway's childhood friend Bill Smith, who were walking along nearby. Furthermore, Hemingway informed her, "that kike Loeb is the villain." He then reassured Cannell that because he thought she was a wonderful girl, he wouldn't put her in the novel.

"But, of course, he did put me in," she wrote woefully years later.

Cannell, Loeb, Lady Duff Twysden, and the other figures who had inspired the book's characters reacted to *The Sun Also Rises* with varying degrees of rage and dismay. Not only did the book depict in painful detail events that had transpired in Paris and Pamplona, but also vast swaths of their personal backgrounds had been blatantly used as the characters' biographies. Loeb found himself cast as the hapless, insufferable Robert

Cohn. Cannell had been translated into Cohn's aging, desperate American girlfriend, Frances Clyne. Twysden had been transformed into the glamorous but anguished Lady Brett Ashley; the caricature permanently branded her as an "alcoholic nymphomaniac," as Hemingway would later describe Twysden herself. Hemingway had depicted details of his friends' failed past marriages, college sporting activities, idiosyncrasies of speech, and assorted indiscretions.

"He had a rat-trap memory," says Hemingway's son Patrick. "Anything that he experienced was at his immediate recall. That was one of the great assets that he had."

Because Harold Loeb, Donald Stewart, Lady Duff, and some of the others were well-known figures, *The Sun Also Rises* proved a scandalous sensation in the cafés of the Left Bank, London, and New York. At first, however, the book's greater literary significance was lost on many of Hemingway's fellow expats. Some saw *The Sun Also Rises* as just another of the naughty *romans à clef* common among their crowd. Many of the Paris colony's writers regularly fictionalized, reported on, and satirized their fellow imbibers, lovers, and colleagues; the Quarter was a glass house in which everyone threw stones at one another.

Unfortunately for Hemingway's prototypes, others saw the book as a groundbreaking work, perhaps even an instant classic. At least one critic had noted that Hemingway had shown glimmers of genius with his stories and vignettes; now he was proving it. Of course some critics hated *The Sun Also Rises,* but few dismissed it as fluff. After all, it had a biblical title, and a weighty epigraph purloined from Gertrude Stein: "You are all a lost generation." It had been clever of Hemingway to add these ingredients, which immediately notified readers that *The Sun Also Rises* wasn't merely a run-of-the-mill bitchy tell-all. Rather, it was profound cultural commentary. Hemingway made it clear that he was not interested in silly little Jazz Age stories of the F. Scott Fitzgerald variety. Though both authors wrote about profligate socialites who drank too much and slept with people they shouldn't, Hemingway's work, he was quick to point out, explored death, regeneration, and the meaning of life. (And if that failed to entice readers, he added, there was "a lot of dope about high society" in it—always a reliable hook.)

Like all works that aim to please almost everyone, *The Sun Also Rises* ran the risk of pleasing no one. Yet Hemingway pulled it off. His high-low formula held fast. Elite critics bought it as a convincing exposition of postwar angst and heralded the spare new style. And as Hemingway hoped, all of that swank society, sex, and booze duly titillated the less high-minded readers. Overnight, it seemed, he went from being a promising upstart to an important provocateur.

The bewildered real-life *Sun* characters were left with little recourse in the wake of such success. Life before the book's publication "later [became] known to some of us as 'B.S.' (Before *The Sun Also Rises*)," recalled Kitty Cannell. "A.S." — after *Sun* — amounted to lives permanently altered by Hemingway's unsparing ambition. The portraits would haunt Cannell, Loeb, and the others for the rest of their lives, but for Hemingway, his one-time friends were simply collateral damage.

After all, he was revolutionizing literature, and in every revolution, some heads must roll.

NINETY YEARS LATER, the high-low siren call of *The Sun Also Rises* continues to beguile readers. Some other novels that have earned voice-of-a-generation status — Jack Kerouac's *On the Road,* for example — feel dated in comparison. But *Sun* still feels fresh and modern, and it remains a best-seller around the globe. While exact statistics are closely held by Hemingway's heirs, Scribners estimates that 120,000 copies of the book are sold domestically every year, but sales overseas could easily double that number. The publisher knows of at least eighteen translation markets; Charles Scribner III says he would be shocked if worldwide sales were under 300,000 copies a year.

The Sun Also Rises still banks on the same dual function that made it a craze the moment it was released: it remains at once a vanguard work of modernist art and also a depiction of a sexy, glamorous world rife with naughty behavior — and little of the flawed human nature depicted in the book's pages has changed.

"Everybody behaves badly," observes protagonist Jake Barnes. "Give them the proper chance."

It was true then and remains true now. Little bourgeois morality can be detected in the pages of *The Sun Also Rises.* The novel reveals a world where people aim to please themselves — even if their actions don't bring them much pleasure. For the more inhibited reader, this has long provided a voyeuristic thrill. In the *Sun* realm, accountability, fidelity, and routine seem like dowdy residents of a faraway, more puritanical country.

Of course, much of the novel's appeal lies in the specific era it depicts, although in real life, Hemingway's Paris could be even sexier and darker than the Paris of *The Sun Also Rises,* and his early 1920s excursions to Pamplona were even more debauched, rivalrous, and confused than his fictionalized retellings. Artists and bullfighters alike were willing to kill or be killed in order to rise to the top of their fields. In both realms, it was a zero-sum game. There was, after all, so much at stake—especially for Hemingway. He knew what he wanted to achieve and who he wanted to be, and no one and nothing could stand in his way.

PART I

Paris Is a Bitch

I N 1921 EVERYONE IN AMERICA was talking about a young midwestern novelist. He was everything that a thrilling new writer should be: ambitious ("I want to be one of the greatest writers who have ever lived, don't you?" he once told a friend), appallingly youthful (he was twenty-three when he published his first book), exuberant, and controversial. For his publishers, it was the happiest of arrangements: this fellow was poised to become *the* voice of the postwar generation, and a lucrative one at that. He alarmed his elders; his peers adored and imitated him. Already the social rhythms of the young decade were obediently following the strokes of his pen. His name was F. Scott Fitzgerald.

Back in the Midwest—Chicago, to be precise—Fitzgerald had some competition brewing, although he did not know it. Another feverishly ambitious would-be novelist was watching Fitzgerald's success and planning something of a coup d'état. Fitzgerald's fame was encouraging, but his stories, he thought, were frivolous, dizzy with flappers, Ivy League shenanigans, and champagne bubbles. Plus, what was new about his style? Fitzgerald might have been writing about a new generation, but he was doing so in the voice of an older one. Shouldn't the so-called voice of a generation have a genuinely fresh voice, a new way of spinning out sentences? Adjectives were so passé, so Victorian.

It was time for a revolution. At least that was the opinion of Fitzgerald's then-anonymous rival, who would soon seize the opportunity to spearhead that revolt personally. This young man was not alone in his opinion: already he had accrued a cult-like following. Admittedly that cult was rather small: it consisted of one devotee, the writer's fiancée. No one in the vaster world had heard of Ernest Miller Hemingway, the author. There was no reason for anyone to have heard of him. He had yet to publish a single short story.

Yet his fiancée, Hadley Richardson — a sturdy, relentlessly optimistic redhead eight years his senior — was sure he was destined to become a renowned writer, even a cultural icon. At first she hadn't felt an overwhelming "glorious faith in his future," but he had swiftly changed her mind. Their life together quickly became geared toward launching his career. She wrote worshipful missives to him, validating his ambitions and practically begging to be his "helper."

No one was more assured about the magnitude of his future than Hemingway himself. Not only did he believe he was capable of creating masterly modern stories; he likely knew that he himself was a masterly modern story. He was undeniably charismatic. His handsome features were chiseled but sensual: there was that full mouth and pleasing symmetry, and an intense stare that implied a certain shrewdness. He had "the kind of eyes that can stare straight into the sun," as Fitzgerald would later write of one of his own characters.

Extraordinary things happened to him. Even when those things were terrible, they made a hell of a story. Spotlights sought him out as though by magnetic attraction. Three years earlier, just short of his nineteenth birthday, he had fallen victim to shelling and enemy fire while distributing chocolate and cigarettes to soldiers on the front lines in Italy. As the first American casualty in Italy, he had garnered press attention across the country. The *New York Sun* reported the number and quality of shrapnel pieces that had savaged his legs: "227 marks, indicating where bits of a peculiar kind of Austrian shrapnel, about as thick as a .22 caliber bullet and an inch long, like small cuts from a length of wire, smote him." The Chicago papers were also filled with Hemingway news. A coterie of gift-bearing admirers surrounded him as he recovered in a Milan hospital.

"Men loved him," recalled his nurse Agnes von Kurowsky.

And he loved the attention; in fact, it was, he wrote to his parents, "the next best thing to getting killed and reading your own obituary." But a few headlines and the adoration of a few comrades in arms was not the sort of destiny Hemingway had in mind. His ability to inspire devotion in his peers would prove an essential ingredient in his success, but he craved attention of a loftier caliber. One did not simply lurch out of nowhere, however, and become a world-renowned revolutionary author. He still actually needed to pen the work that would make him famous and establish him as the *true* literary voice of the modern world. It was an inconvenient but unavoidable stepping-stone.

He was working on it. By the summer of 1921, he had an idea for a novel. Hadley was beside herself with excitement.

"It'll be *wonderful* to have you writing a novel," she informed her twenty-two-year-old fiancé. She was willing to do whatever she could to help bring it to fruition. "I'll be as happy as happy to be with you thru it all or be kicked out or slid into a corner or anything you like," she assured him. She could tell already that Hemingway's first novel would be a wholly modern work, stripped down and lean. His approach "eliminated everything except what is necessary and strengthening," she complimented him. It was all wonderfully simple, "but as fine as the finest chain mail."

She and Hemingway were then living in different cities as they planned their wedding. Hadley was anticipating the event from her native St. Louis; Hemingway had set up shop in Chicago, where he was scraping together a meager living as a reporter at a magazine called *The Cooperative Commonwealth* and penning freelance pieces for the *Toronto Star*. He had been training himself to become a reporter since high school in Oak Park, Illinois, where he wrote for his school paper, *The Trapeze*. During those early years he had also been trying his hand at writing fiction and had already acquired a bit of literary bravado.

"Cicero is a pipe," he wrote in 1915. "I could write better stuff with both hands tied behind me."

Hemingway wasn't drawing on a grand family literary tradition, although a streak of creativity did run through his clan. His mother had once been an aspiring opera singer and often took her children to concerts, plays, and art exhibits in nearby Chicago. Yet by the time he was a teenager, it was evident that his talent lay in writing, not in the visual or performing arts: his English teachers praised him, and his themes were often read aloud in class. *The Tabula,* his high school literary magazine, printed some of his earliest short stories — which, like some of his later work, involved subjects such as boxing, woodland living, and suicide. Back then, his work was more imitative than original; he frequently wrote in the style of Ring Lardner, a popular sports and humor writer. Yet when Hemingway graduated in 1917, he was nominated Class Prophet — a designation that could be seen as prophetic in its own right, considering that he would later help envision and usher in the era of modern literature.

The literary encouragement, however, had more or less ended after he left Oak Park High School. Hemingway's doctor father wanted him to attend Oberlin College; but the First World War was then raging in Europe, and Hemingway, like countless other young men of his generation, was determined to see action instead. He later admitted to having viewed the entire war as something of a sporting event, and dubbed his younger self an "awful dope." Defective vision prevented Hemingway from enlisting in the military, but in 1918 the Red Cross Ambulance Corps deemed him good enough for service and promptly dispatched him to Italy, where he was wounded within weeks of his arrival.

When he returned to America, Hemingway found work as a reporter, but magazines were not interested in his short stories. Some experts have deemed Hemingway's earliest surviving stories dull and derivative; he was then, they say, a far cry from the grand innovator of the English language that he would become. Therefore this early spate of rejection was perfectly reasonable. Yet others have faulted magazine editors of the early 1920s for lacking vision.

"I saw some of [Hemingway's] work [in] 1920 and I thought it was very good," recalled Hemingway's childhood friend Bill Smith, who spent a good deal of time with him during this period. "The only trouble is he was sending it to the wrong magazines," he said, adding that a publication like the *Saturday Evening Post* — then a hugely popular vehicle for fiction — "would never have used that experimental writing of his, . . . and it was experimental even before he went to Paris."

Still, everyone had shunned Fitzgerald's first short stories too. At one point during his early career, he had artistically arranged over a hundred rejection slips on his bedroom walls. It had required the firepower of a first novel, *This Side of Paradise,* to help him stage a breakthrough. When crafting that all-important debut novel, both Fitzgerald and Hemingway started out by writing what they knew. Fitzgerald's novel was a somewhat country-clubified account of life at Princeton University, which he had attended before the war. When Hemingway began his starter novel, he apparently set it in northern Michigan, where he'd spent his boyhood summers, and filled its pages with stories of fishing and hunting. It is unclear how well developed this novel might have been in 1921; he may even have had more than one in the works. He appears to have been bandying about a few ideas with Hadley, for she wrote to him that she was "all treading on air about these novels!" It was criminal, she added, that "we aren't free yet to put your best time and tho't [into] them."

Still, if Hemingway was to turn out the requisite magnum opus, he was going to need to situate himself in a more muse-friendly atmosphere. At the moment, he was camping out in the apartment of Bill Smith's adman older brother, Y. K. Smith, then home to a passel of boarders. Hadley had also stayed there while visiting Chicago; it was here that she first met Hemingway. The attraction between them had been immediate, despite the difference in their ages. He liked her red hair and the way she played the piano; she deemed him a "hulky, bulky something masculine." Nicknames were exchanged. Among their crowd of mutual friends, Hemingway went by "Oinbones," "Nesto," "Hemingstein," and "Wemedge." Hadley dubbed Hemingway "Erniestoic"; she was christened "Hash." Even the apartment itself had a nickname: "the Domicile."

Soon afterward, Wemedge and Hash became engaged and began planning a wedding—not a grand affair, as had been portended by the St. Louis society press, but rather a small country wedding in Horton Bay, Michigan, where Hemingway had spent his childhood summers. The church where the ceremony eventually took place on September 3, 1921, stood next to the town's general store. The nuptials were to be followed by a voyage to Italy—perhaps for as long as a year or two—starting with Naples.

The trip would be a homecoming of sorts. Hemingway was proud of his personal history there. He'd had, for example, a bit of the shrapnel removed from his leg set into a ring; it was a wearable reminder of his dramatic brush with death and first exposure to international fame. Eager to show the country off to Hadley, he began buying Italian lire. Hadley had long assured him that she was not in the market for a conventional existence; she too began to prepare to make a "bold penniless dash for Wopland."

Such a dash would indeed have been bold, but not penniless: Hadley had a trust fund, bestowed upon her by a banker grandfather; she called it "my sweet little packet of seeds." It would give the Hemingways $2,000 to $3,000 a year to play with. Hemingway retired his affiliation with *The Co-operative Commonwealth,* whose future he deemed unpromising. Hadley's "filthy lucre," as he called it, would now be the main engine powering their overseas adventure.

"There are those who think Hadley's name became Hash because she had a small inheritance and thus became Hem's meal-ticket but that is untrue," stated Bill Smith later. "Hash was simply a corruption of Hadley."

Whether or not "Hash" meant "cash," Hadley was undeniably a meal ticket. It was a relatively modest meal, but nourishing enough. Her money would get them over to Europe, and for the next half decade her trust fund would be their sole consistent source of income. Hemingway was already worried that his reporting work was forcing him to relegate his other writing to "on the side" status; his frantic work schedule was making him "busy and tired and done in." He needed to leave the tug-of-war behind. Italy — funded by St. Louis dollars — might provide the necessary respite.

"Think of how in Italy there won't be anything but love and peace to form a background for writing," Hadley wrote to Hemingway. "Why you'll write like a great wonderful sea breeze bringing strong *whiffs* from all sorts of strange interior places."

Even at this early stage, Hadley knew that she was being outshone by Hemingway and she did not seem to care. She was content — even ecstatic — to become the woman behind the nascent genius. All of her resources were at Hemingway's command. He was poised to write "the best things you've ever done in your life," she told him. "Honest, you're doing marvels of stirring, potent stuff . . . Don't let's ever die. Let's go on together."

They planned to leave for Europe that November.

THE SUBSTANTIAL INDUSTRY now known as Hemingway's Paris might have been Hemingway's Naples if not for the intervention of a regular visitor to the Domicile.

Today writer Sherwood Anderson has fallen into obscurity, but in the early 1920s he was well known. Not household-name, mega-best-seller famous, but certainly well regarded. He had come to authorship through a circuitous route. For a while he had headed a mail-order paint firm, but — according to legend — he suffered a nervous breakdown at the office in 1912, during which he stalked out and never returned. He chose literary pursuits as his cure-all, and by 1914 was publishing stories in magazines.

When he met Hemingway in 1921, Anderson was having an Icarus ascent-to-the-sun moment; his recent collection of stories — *Winesburg, Ohio* — had sold well, and that year he would receive the inaugural *Dial* award for his contribution to American literature. Short stories were considered his forte; his novels appear to have been tolerated cheerfully by critics and the public. In the 1930s he would spiral into obscurity, but in 1921, Sherwood Anderson was a celebrity. He knew Y. K. Smith through the Chicago advertising world and lived nearby; his visits to Smith's apartment were considered exciting events.

There was no reason for Anderson to have heard of Hemingway when they first met, but Hemingway knew about Anderson. Like everyone else, he approved of Anderson's short stories but found his novels "strangely poor"—an early assessment that would take on great (and from Anderson's point of view almost sinister) significance a few years later.

When Anderson first ambled into the apartment—probably in a state of disrepair, for he usually resembled a disheveled professor with a carefully selected wardrobe of ill-fitting jackets—Hemingway treated him with polite, quiet attentiveness. This would become his customary approach to would-be mentors with stellar connections. Hemingway claimed later that he and Anderson "never spoke of writing" at that time, but even if this was true, he still managed to make a powerful impression on the veteran writer. Like Hadley, Anderson became quickly converted to the idea that Hemingway was a man with a future.

"Thanks for introducing me to that young fellow," Anderson told Smith and his wife after his first meeting with Hemingway. "I think he's going to go some place."

It was an expert bit of casual matchmaking by Y. K. Smith, who "knew Hem was a genius even then," recalled his brother Bill. Did Bill think Hemingway was a genius at that time? "Of course not," he admitted later. "Your buddy is never a genius." Yet Y.K. was pleased that the connection had been made, and saw its immediate effect on Hemingway. "At this point Ernest began to take seriously his own talent as an alluring possibility," he wrote later. "I think this was his first contact with a big-time artist and it gave him as it were a chance to measure himself."

In measuring himself against Anderson, Hemingway seems to have deemed himself in a position to surpass the veteran writer—or at the very least, he felt he was in a position to critique. During return visits, Anderson occasionally read his work aloud to the Domicile entourage. Hemingway evaluated every word. He may have been polite to Anderson in person, but he was said to be have been, in private, "thoroughly hostile" to Anderson's approach.

"You couldn't let a sentence like that go," he announced after Anderson left the apartment after one reading session.

Anderson also irritated Hadley by comparing Hemingway to Victorian writer Rudyard Kipling. "That's foolish," she fussed in a letter to Hemingway. "Why I don't want to compare you to anybody . . . you're Ernest Hemingway."

Anderson did manage to redeem himself for these unwitting offenses in a significant way. During his visits, when he wasn't reading aloud from his own manuscripts, he extolled the wonders of Paris to the Domicile crowd; the city was now a magnet for creative types from all over America.

Earlier that year Anderson had made the transatlantic voyage to Paris and there encountered the redoubtable Gertrude Stein, an American heiress and experimental writer who had famously settled there decades earlier. He had also met the Irish writer James Joyce, who had been busy scandalizing readers with installments of his book *Ulysses* in the American literary magazine *The Little Review*. Anderson had had to wangle the introductions; after all, one didn't just materialize in Montparnasse and receive an invitation to Stein's legendary salon or to a Joyce family dinner.

To gain entrée, Anderson had descended upon Shakespeare and Company, a new but already renowned English-language bookstore on the Left Bank, founded and run by American expat Sylvia Beach, who knew many important creative figures around town. One day Beach noticed an intriguing-looking man lurking outside on the store's doorstep. Eventually he bustled inside and expressed his admiration for a book Beach had featured in her window. No other bookseller in Paris had the good sense to carry *Winesburg, Ohio,* he told her, and then revealed that he was the book's author.

Beach was immediately charmed by Anderson. "I saw him as a mixture of poet and evangelist (without the preaching), with perhaps a touch of the actor," she later recalled. Anderson lingered and regaled her with the tale of his defiance of the mail-order paint industry; Beach was sufficiently amused to introduce him to her lover, Adrienne Monnier, who was equally taken with him. When Monnier invited Anderson to dinner, he knew that he had been officially admitted to one of the great citadels of expat literary Paris.

This citadel was linked to another. Anderson soon pressed Beach for an introduction to Gertrude Stein, whose work had fascinated and influenced him. Beach gamely complied. They arrived at Stein's salon, where Anderson kissed the Steinian ring with gusto.

"Sherwood's deference and the admiration he expressed for her writing pleased Gertrude immensely," recalled Beach. "She was visibly touched."

The meeting set in place a literary friendship that would last for decades. Anderson probably could have stayed in Paris and happily enrolled in the elite expat scene, especially now that he had secured the devotion of two of its foremost doyennes. Yet he returned to America, where he would remain a devout non-expat for his entire career. It was a curiously untrendy stance, but he remained unmoved by the allure of living abroad. "You see, dear friend, I believe in this damn mixed-up country of ours," he explained to Stein. "In an odd way I'm in love with it."

That said, Anderson avidly encouraged other creative types to make the leap across the Atlantic. He found a receptive audience in Hemingway and Hadley. Back in Chicago, over dinner one evening, he informed them that they should immediately swap their Italian lire for French francs. Paris was definitely the place for ambitious young writers with experimental inclinations. Plus, it was cheap. And what was more, Anderson knew gatekeepers there now and could pave the way for Hemingway too.

He made a convincing case: by Thanksgiving, the Hemingways had shelved their Neapolitan foray and booked passage for France. Instead of visiting the sites of Hemingway's past glories, they had chosen a different backdrop for new and inevitably greater glories. Paris was, after all, now a laboratory of innovative writing and the supposed creative center of the universe. Yet even though the city was attracting countless would-be modern novelists—Hemingway's soon-to-be competitors—there was great opportunity there as well. No one had yet conjured up *the* Paris novel or a definitive postwar expat work, at least not one that the masses were reading. Fitzgerald was already laying claim to New York's postwar discontent and decadence. In Paris there might be more oxygen, and definitely ample material.

The night before the couple left Chicago, Hemingway stopped by Anderson's apartment and dropped off a token of his appreciation: an oversized army knapsack filled with over a hundred pounds of canned foods from his apartment. Anderson was moved by the gesture.

"I remember his coming up the stairs, a magnificent broad-shouldered man, shouting as he came," he recalled. "That was a nice idea, bringing thus to a fellow scribbler the food he had to abandon."

Anderson returned the favor with interest. When Hemingway boarded a transatlantic liner days later, he had in his possession a rare form of currency obtainable at no bank: personal letters of introduction provided by Anderson to the most influential literary figures in Paris.

THE HEMINGWAYS arrived in Paris just before Christmas—not the most auspicious time to make the city's acquaintance. It was akin to meeting a legendary and glamorous woman of the stage when she's hungover and sans makeup. Even the poorest expats made efforts to flee the damp, dreary Paris winters; the Hemingways would soon follow suit. But when they first got off the boat train, they made their way to the Hôtel Jacob et d'Angleterre in Saint-Germain and settled in. Sherwood Anderson had lodged there during his recent Paris visit and recommended it to the couple; he even sent ahead a welcome letter to greet them when they arrived. The hotel was wonderfully cheap—twelve francs a day, or just under a dollar—and notorious in expat circles. "Vicki Baum's *Grand Hotel* couldn't touch the drama and intrigue which occurred in that hotel," recalled one former Paris-based editor. A roster of colorful, creative celebrities in residence counterbalanced the drab decor.

Like all recent American arrivals, the Hemingways dropped off their luggage and dutifully beelined for the café Le Dôme, the gossip-and-Pernod-fueled nerve center of the Left Bank's expatriate colony. The Dôme was a good antidote to loneliness: everyone flocked there; its revelers seemed to promise that most newcomers eventually got their Paris land legs and joined the party. Hemingway would soon heap ire on such cafés and their expat "inmates," as he dubbed their clientele, but in those early days, the Hemingways headquartered at the Dôme as they staved off the woozy disorientation that comes with first setting foot on alien terrain. There he and Hadley sipped hot rum punches and described their earliest impressions in letters to family and friends.

"We've been walking the streets, day and night, arm through arm," he reported to Anderson. It was freezing, he complained, and added that they had been in low spirits. "I do not know what I thought Paris would be like but it was not that way," he recalled later.

The Dôme provided a temporary warm respite, but outside, the leafless trees and buses appeared slimy in the gray rain. As Hemingway and Hadley walked through the streets, they peered into the city's cold stone courtyards and store windows and watched steam rising from horses' bodies. Paris was filled with jarring sights. Expats staggering home at dawn after an all-night bender might encounter a pipe-blowing goatherd pulling a herd of black goats down the street, or even hitch a ride in a horse-drawn cart full of carrots. Both the city and many of its inhabitants bore disturbing war scars. "I watched to notice how well [veterans] were overcoming the handicap of the loss of limbs, or at the quality of their artificial eyes and the degree of skill with which their faces had been reconstructed," Hemingway later wrote. To Hadley, Paris was a "marvelous strange city, marvelous and awful."

The couple clung to modest luxuries and diversions to comfort them. The Quarter, as Montparnasse was called, was reassuringly small: its social life centered on a handful of cafés and bars that stood within a couple of blocks of one another. The newlyweds took long walks, but there was always that reassuring ground zero to welcome them back. Hadley devoured French pastries; Hemingway threw himself into scripting ecstatic, detailed reports on the low cost of food, wine, liters of various liquors, and hotel rooms. The city was almost unfathomably affordable for Americans, thanks to inflation. The American dollar was king, worth twelve and a half francs; the Canadian dollar was a mere prince at eleven francs. Even comparative paupers were courted by French business owners, from hoteliers to restaurateurs to *poules* — prostitutes. Almost every American expat might expect to be "treated like a millionaire and disliked accordingly," wrote Alfred Kreymborg, another American who arrived there in the early twenties.

Paris may have been blissfully affordable to the Hemingways, yet the city's more decadent and complex pleasures eluded them at first. They were outsiders, dazed and isolated. At that moment it would have been difficult for them to imagine that someday they would come to epitomize all that was romantic and exciting about 1920s Paris.

DESPITE HIS COMPLAINTS that his work as a reporter distracted him from serious literary pursuits, Hemingway had scored a position as a Paris-based correspondent for the *Toronto Star*. It was a freelance arrangement; atmosphere stories were prioritized, meaning that he would be paid for savvy observations of his new milieu.

Editors back home were quickly learning that there was a ravenous appetite for stories about Paris. Wealthy Americans had long been obsessed with Parisian fashion and cuisine, but the newly almighty dollar made the city's pleasures available to vast new demographics. Debutantes, starving artists, and even the midwestern bourgeoisie were starting to take a keen interest in all things French, from the social goings-on of the growing expat colony to the manifestos of the various artistic movements sparking away in the city's cafés and salons. Reporter Arthur Power began documenting the lives of Montparnasse painters in a *Paris Herald* column titled "Around the Studios." The fledgling *New Yorker* magazine tapped writer Janet Flanner for a popular fortnightly "Letter from Paris" column, in which she detailed everything from political gossip to bedroom gossip. (It was always most exciting when these spheres overlapped.) *Vogue* covered and promoted Paris with such dedication that it practically recruited Americans and shoveled them onto boats; it even offered its readers the services of a Paris-based *Vogue* information bureau. "Paris is, perhaps, the most generous city in the world and the richest in sheer delights," gushed one *Vogue* writer.

Hemingway's coverage, by contrast, was less breathless. It did not take him long to size up his contemporaries and report on their shortcomings in the pages of the *Star*.

"Paris is the mecca of bluffers and fakers," he declared in an article penned soon after his arrival. All sorts of Americans were turning up in Paris and presenting themselves as figures of greatness, from faux dancing "stars" to nonentity prizefighters. The only reason these wayward Americans were getting away with it, Hemingway declared, was because of the "extreme provinciality" of the French people. In case anyone else was thinking about turning up in Paris and posing as a luminary, he offered some instruction: "You must choose to be a champion of some very distant country and then stay away from that country."

He also shot a sharp, glinting arrow at the expats thronging the Montparnasse cafés. "The scum of Greenwich Village, New York, has been skimmed off and deposited in large ladles on that section of Paris adjacent to the Café Rotonde," he announced. (The Rotonde was another major expat destination across the boulevard du Montparnasse from the Dôme.) To Hemingway, the posturing tourists and expat residents cramming themselves into the Rotonde twelve hundred at a time "have all striven so hard for a careless individuality of clothing that they have achieved a sort of uniformity of eccentricity." They could hardly be turning out immortal creative work, he surmised. "Since the good old days when Charles Baudelaire led a purple lobster on a leash through the same old Latin Quarter, there has not been much good poetry written in cafés."

It was a shrewd choice of topic on Hemingway's part, and one likely to garner attention. Since the war's end, the cafés and bars of the Left Bank had served as backdrops for much expatriate melodrama and debauchery, and they were filled with unspoken rules. Once newcomers alighted upon Montparnasse, they picked their café affiliations carefully and were judged accordingly. The Dôme was the headquarters of the official rumor mill among American expats: anyone who wanted to broadcast a salacious bit of gossip, show off a new mistress, or brag about selling a new novel did so at the Dôme; word then ricocheted through the crowd with satisfying speed. Dôme patrons reviled Rotonde customers, and it was equally fashionable among the literary in-crowd to detest the Rotonde's owner, who was alternately called a "sour-faced, scurvy swine" or merely a "bastard." (His offense: he had decreed that ladies should neither smoke nor sit hatless at his café — unacceptable policies to Americans who were there to cut loose.) Luckily, the boulevard was too wide for Dôme and Rotonde customers to fling chairs at each other, but insults could still carry quite clearly across the din of traffic.

Behavior at these establishments often rivaled the saloons of the American Wild West. "Many [expats], really highly respected and stable citizens at home, went completely berserk the minute they hit Montparnasse," recalled one bartender of the era. Yet the drunken antics of patrons often paled in comparison to the black-hearted practices of the cafés' owners, who regularly tried to sabotage one another. For example, one day Hilaire Hiler, proprietor of a popular bar called Le Jockey, discovered a suicidal patron taking poison in the bar's washroom. Hiler pumped the fellow's stomach and heard his confession.

"Hiler, I cannot, I really cannot go on living," the customer told him. "I'll do it again, and right away, too."

"What have you got against me?" Hiler asked him. "Why do you want to hurt my business in the Jockey?"

"I don't, old man, really I don't," responded the patron.

"Well," Hiler instructed him, "the next time you want to commit suicide, go somewhere else." When asked for his recommendation on an appropriate site, Hiler paused and said, "Well, the Dôme is my big rival, you know."

The next day, the patron was found dead in the Dôme's bathroom.

Any astute writer could immediately see that expat Paris was rife with insights into the less savory aspects of human nature—and Hemingway was more astute than most. The material had an immediate use for newspaper stories that were helping to pay the bills, but it held limitless promise for an even bigger and more significant work, something literary and profound—if only the right premise would come along.

Other writers must also have sensed that Paris was a treasure trove of literary possibility, but many of them were too consumed by the frantic scene to document it with any clarity. Some expats likened their Paris experiences to an extended, drug-fueled party. Poet Hart Crane described life as a spree of "dinners, soirees, poets, erratic millionaires, painters, translations, lobsters, absinthe, music, promenades, oysters, sherry, aspirins, pictures, Sapphic heiresses, editors, books, [and] sailors." For the American writer Malcolm Cowley, Paris was like cocaine, and just as debilitating a habit when it came time to pull himself together and work. Some expats quickly learned that it was wise to distance oneself from Paris's less wholesome charms.

"[At first] I was always in a fever of excitement," wrote expat editor

Robert McAlmon, whose path was about to cross Hemingway's. "But I knew all too well that Paris is a bitch, and that one shouldn't become infatuated with bitches, particularly when they have wit, imagination, experience, and tradition behind their ruthlessness."

Hemingway was among the wise: he never wholly succumbed to the bitch—not even during his days as a Paris novice. Later, as dissipation gradually brought less resilient writers to their knees, he instead blithely described Paris as "the town best organized for a writer to write in that there is." In holding back, Hemingway gave himself a distinct advantage as a clearheaded, removed observer. Later, many of his fictional protagonists would share this attribute.

Until he could make serious literary use of the Quarter's atmosphere and characters, Hemingway chronicled them in at least a dozen life-in-Paris articles. Some of those *Toronto Star* stories had the feel of literary test runs and even included dialogue. One story detailed an amusing overheard conversation between two Frenchmen whose wives had insisted on administering their haircuts:

> *"Your hair, Henri!" said one.*
> *"My wife, old one, she cuts it. But your hair, also? It is not too chic!"*
> *"My wife too. She cuts it also. She says barbers are dirty pigs, but at the finish I must give her the same tip as I would give the barber."*

Through his dispatches, readers were introduced to jewel-pawning Russian aristocrats exiled by their country's revolution, who now occupied themselves by "drifting along in Paris in a childish sort of hopefulness that things will somehow be all right." They met failing European politicians, incurably dishonest Arab rug merchants, French hatmakers who festooned their wares with sparrows, and a career executioner with two guillotines—one large model, and a small one for traveling jobs.

But over and over again, Hemingway returned to tales of the American in Paris. He simply could not empty that well. He made it clear that he was adept at detecting phonies and hypocrites among his self-exiled compatriots—which apparently included pretty much everyone besides himself. Among his targets: the ugly American tourist who demanded that "Paris be a super-Sodom and a grander Gomorrah" and was "willing to pay for his ideal"; a dumpy woman with fake blond hair slumped in a chair at the Rotonde, her teeth clamped around a two-foot-long cigarette holder; and a Connecticut housewife footing a café bill for an assortment of young male gigolo types. They were a repellent, worthless bunch, Hemingway reported, especially those who insisted on posing as artists.

"They are nearly all loafers," he wrote in one *Star* story. "The trouble is that people who go on a tour of the Latin Quarter look in at the Rotonde and think they are seeing an assembly of the great artists of Paris. I want to correct that in a very public manner, for the artists of Paris who are turning out creditable work resent and loathe the Rotonde crowd."

Hemingway was clearly allying himself with the real artists who scorned the fakers. He wasn't publicly among the band of recognized true artists yet, but there was an implicit promise in those early stories that he would be joining their ranks soon.

H E WAS AN ERRATIC and obviously brilliant young man," recalled one of Hemingway's fellow Paris-based journalists years later. Another American reporter thought of him as "some sort of genius in a garret," although he noted with faint contempt that Hemingway ran with the same café crowd that he skewered in his stories. No one in the Paris press corps had neutral feelings about Hemingway—throughout his career he would inspire either adoration or revulsion—but everyone seems to have sensed that he had an exceptional life ahead of him.

Though he was making a big impression on his colleagues, by spring 1922 Hemingway had already wearied of the foreign correspondent lifestyle. While it was more glamorous than his reporting work at *The Cooperative Commonwealth,* it was no less exhausting.

"I've been earning our daily bread on this write machine," he informed Sherwood Anderson, not mentioning the fact that they were largely sustained by his wife's trust fund. He complained to another friend that he'd been working so hard that he had nearly worn through his typewriter ribbon.

Not only was he worried that journalism left him little time to create revolutionary fiction; he had even begun to fret that all of the reporting was impairing his ability to write decent prose. His travels were giving him great potential material, and journalism was teaching him a thing or two about communicating ideas effectively on paper: "On the *Star* you were forced to learn to write a simple declarative sentence," he conceded. But otherwise, all of the reporting work was just destructive interference.

"This goddam newspaper stuff is gradually ruining me," he wrote to Anderson. "But I'm going to cut it all loose pretty soon and work for about three months."

Unfortunately, his editors at the *Toronto Star* were also now impressed by Hemingway and started assigning him increasingly prestigious and time-consuming stories. They sent him all over Europe, which was then still roiling from the aftereffects of the last world war and busily setting the stage for the next one. Shortly after making his pledge to "cut it all loose," Hemingway departed on a nearly month-long reporting trip to Genoa, thus launching a year of intensive, lengthy assignments that ping-ponged him from Milan to Geneva to Frankfurt; the *Star* ran at least twenty-three stories and items by him from the Genoa excursion alone. In Constantinople he profiled a refugee procession of 250,000 "slow, rain-soaked, shambling, trudging" Thracian peasants, "plodding along in the rain, leaving their homes behind . . . just keeping their feet moving, their eyes on the road and their heads sunken," all scraping their way toward Macedonia. In Milan he interviewed Mussolini and warned his readers about the rise of fascism there, calling Il Duce's followers "black-shirted, knife-carrying, club-swinging, quick-stepping, nineteen-year-old potshot patriots." He bestowed upon Mussolini himself the title "Europe's Prize Bluffer," adding that the dictator had a weak mouth, noting his capacity for "clothing small ideas in big words," and asserting, "There is something wrong, even histrionically, with a man who wears white spats with a black shirt." Hemingway's confidence seems astonishing given his youth (he was now twenty-three years old) and relative inexperience, but no one seems to have dismissed him as a rookie.

In fact, the *Star*'s editors often devoted considerable front-page real estate to his dispatches and — realizing that the reporter himself was becoming a point of interest — began creating an exciting public persona around him. At one point that year, the paper printed a lengthy column titled "Something About Ernest M. Hemingway, Who Is Taking the Lid Off Europe," a profile of the man who'd been turning out all of those "intensely interesting articles" lately. Not that these biographies were always accurate — one informed readers that Hemingway had "fought with the Italian army in the great war" — but that was beside the point. The reporter was now becoming a part of the story.

WHEN HEMINGWAY AND HADLEY first arrived in Paris, he wrote to Sherwood Anderson and told him that he planned to send out those golden-ticket letters of introduction to the literati as soon as the couple was properly settled in. It would be like "launching a flock of ships," he added. Yet at first, he kept the letters to the most important figures under wraps.

Most aspiring writers would have given anything for such introductions to the expat literary gods of Olympus, as writer Malcolm Cowley dubbed the creative inner circle of 1920s Paris. Sylvia Beach referred to this hallowed collective as "the Crowd." They were "sort of royalty, almost infallible, with a sort of magic around [them]," as one F. Scott Fitzgerald character would later summarize their position.

Many Americans were streaming into town and vying for introductions, but in the eyes of the Paris Olympians, most of them "didn't count, except for incidental amusement," decreed pioneering expat journalist and in-crowd editor Harold Stearns. The Crowd communed largely in private homes and salons, not on public café terraces. Many would-be creatives and patron types who wanted desperately to "count" were snubbed, diligently used, or merely ignored. Sherwood Anderson had gained access to the inner sanctum via Sylvia Beach, but she was not always so generous with her connections: she once even declined to introduce novelist George Moore to James Joyce when the two were standing only feet from each other in her store. Intrepid visitors approaching Gertrude Stein's apartment, hoping to be admitted to her salon, were greeted at the door with the curt salutation "De la part de qui venez-vous?" or "Who is your introducer?"

The Crowd knew they were gods, or at least comported themselves as such, even though some of their leaders were not exactly on intimate terms with commercial success. Yet the press on two continents often cast them as vanguards of modernity. If you wanted to see what the future was going to look like, you would watch what Miss Stein, Pablo Picasso, Man Ray, and others of their ilk were up to. Clearly aware of their place in history, Crowd members incessantly documented their shared world and one another during this time. Picasso famously painted Gertrude Stein. Gertrude Stein interpreted her peers in "word portraits," a form she claimed to have pioneered. Man Ray and Berenice Abbott photographed all of the major players. "To be 'done' by Man Ray and Berenice Abbott meant you were rated as somebody," recalled Sylvia Beach, whose bookstore doubled as an informal yet intimidating gallery of these photographs.

Curiously, even though the Crowd had chosen Paris as the backdrop for their various revolutions, theirs was largely an American movement. The community was essentially "America in Europe," as one expat writer put it. They published their own Paris-based English-language magazines and books, usually backed with American financing, often to make impressions on American publishers who might then give them a major American platform. "I never met an American who wasn't, in Paris, busy with American plans and purposes and material," recalled Archibald MacLeish.

Like many other American writers, Hemingway had landed at the heart of the rebellion against stuffy Victorian prose. "There was no grandly experimental, furiously disrespectful school of writing in America, and we were going to create it," recalled writer and editor Kay Boyle, who first arrived in France in 1923. "'Down with Henry James! Down with Edith Wharton!' . . . the self-exiled revolutionaries cried out." Of course, part of the plan in deposing long-reigning monarchs like James and Wharton involved claiming their thrones. Ambition and sharp-elbowed competition coursed through the community. "Fame was what they wanted in that town," wrote MacLeish in a poem documenting the feverish atmosphere in Paris back then.

Of course, there was fame, and then there was *fame*. Gertrude Stein was famous; James Joyce was famous. Joyce's radical novel *Ulysses,* for example, had rocked the world of many postwar writers. "In 1922 it burst over us, young in Paris, like an explosion in print those words and phrases fell upon us like a gift of tongues," recalled expat *New Yorker* writer Janet Flanner.

But the novel—with its racy sexual content, ranging from masturbation to adultery—was considered so scandalous that it was banned in book form in the United States until 1934. (It was ironic, mused the *New York Times* upon the book's release, that the ban was lifted "just when Joyce [was] losing his influence on young writers.") Experimentalist Gertrude Stein had her admirers, but no American commercial publisher would touch her gargantuan manuscripts.

F. Scott Fitzgerald, by contrast, had become truly *famous*. Tens of thousands of people bought his books, published by Charles Scribner's Sons, one of the most prestigious major publishing houses back in New York. He and his insouciant golden-haired wife, Zelda, were already pop culture icons; Zelda was said to epitomize flapper culture. The latter category of fame was more what Hemingway had in mind. But he intended to have it all: both the snob appeal *and* the mass following.

It was an unapologetically ambitious goal, but Hemingway saw the opportunity and he certainly had the will.

BY LATE WINTER, Hemingway felt it was time to send out Sherwood Anderson's letters of introduction. Hemingway first approached writer Lewis Galantière, an erudite, bespectacled American then working for

Paris's International Chamber of Commerce. Sherwood Anderson had written to Galantière before the Hemingways had set sail for Europe; Hemingway was delightful, Anderson assured him, and "a young fellow of extraordinary talent."

Galantière kindly found Hemingway and Hadley a starter apartment: a small $18-a-month fourth-floor walk-up at 74 rue du Cardinal Lemoine on a hilltop in the Latin Quarter. Each landing featured a smelly pissoir. Downstairs, next to the entrance, stood a noisy *bal musette,* or workers' dancehall. Beggars lined the street's rambling decline to the river. It was a tough, poor neighborhood, but the price was right and the street had a literary atmosphere: James Joyce had worked on *Ulysses* at number 71; French poet Paul Verlaine had lived at number 2. Hemingway returned Galantière's favor by inviting him to box a few rounds back at the Hôtel Jacob and then punching Galantière in the face while his guard was down. Hadley thought it was a near-miracle that neither Galantière's eyes nor his face had been cut by his shattered glasses.

Hemingway then contacted Gertrude Stein and Ezra Pound, both enemies of frilly, old-fashioned writing. Pound was "the acknowledged leader of the modern movement," according to Sylvia Beach. He often sported a scarf stitched with the words MAKE IT NEW; the garment billowed out behind him as he bicycled around town. As larger-than-life characters, Stein and Pound probably intimidated meeker souls. That said, for those with strong constitutions, serious intentions, and sufficient talent, Stein and Pound were willing mentors.

Hemingway approached Pound first. Pound was known as something of a literary midwife. He had already had a hand in bringing to fruition some of the twentieth century's most seismic modernist literary works; he had, for example, edited T. S. Eliot's 1922 poem "The Waste Land." He could also get talent published, and often proved a hard-hitting advocate on behalf of his protégés. Since 1920 he had acted as an agent and material scout for *The Dial,* a New York–based literary magazine that called itself "the leading review in the English language." He fought ardently to get *Dial* editor Scofield Thayer to publish "The Waste Land," which ultimately ran in the magazine in November 1922. He had helped James Joyce by getting some of Joyce's early stories and his debut novel, *A Portrait of the Artist as a Young Man,* published in literary magazines. Pound also was responsible for introducing Joyce to Sylvia Beach, who was brave enough to publish his scandalous novel *Ulysses* in book form in Paris in 1922. In addition, Pound happened to be a foreign editor for *The Little Re-*

view, an important magazine devoted to showcasing experimental writing and new international art; it had serialized *Ulysses* and published works by Sherwood Anderson, Gertrude Stein, and Wyndham Lewis.

Anderson's endorsement earned Hemingway an invitation to tea at Pound's studio on the winding rue Notre-Dame-des-Champs, where he lived with his wife, Dorothy. The Hemingways found the studio poignant: lovely light bathed Pound's collection of Japanese paintings and those created by his wife.

At first glance, Pound, then forty-six, was not exactly an obvious candidate to become a Hemingway confidant. Thanks to a childhood spent fishing, hunting, and camping, Hemingway reeked of the great outdoors and manly pursuits. Pound, by contrast, took dandyism to an almost operatic level. He was often heavily costumed in velveteen ensembles and romantic Byronic shirts. An untamed mop of hair billowed from the top of his head. His most emphatic accessories included a spearlike mustache, a pointed goatee, and a walking stick — all of which he used to accentuate his words.

Their first meeting was long and resembled Hemingway's first encounter with Sherwood Anderson back in Chicago. Dorothy fluttered around, serving tea. Hemingway listened quietly and attentively as Pound spoke at length; he must have downed at least seventeen cups of tea, Hadley thought. This would be the first of many meetings: after all, there was much to discuss. Pound had a great deal to teach Hemingway in the matter of creating spare language. He was known for his stern opinions on the subject of adjectives: namely, they were to be distrusted. He also insisted that writers should never use superfluous words, and should never be descriptive. "Don't be viewy" was classic Pound advice.

He also liked to compare writing and music. "Behave as a musician, a good musician, when dealing with that phase of your art which has exact parallels in music," he later wrote. "The same laws govern, and you are bound by no others." These were all tenets that Hemingway would take to heart.

Following their first meeting, Pound gave Hemingway access to his vast book collection. He had a general reading list for up-and-coming writers. One must read the ancient authors: Homer and Confucius in particular were to be read "in full." Dante and Voltaire must also be studied — but in the case of the latter, one could reasonably steer clear of his "attempts at fiction and drama." And, of course, any serious aspiring writer should read and take to heart the genius of Pound's protégés T. S. Eliot and James Joyce.

Hemingway offered himself up as a willing pupil to Pound, yet he walked away from that first meeting filled with scorn. Shortly afterward, he showed Lewis Galantière something new that he had written: a nasty little satire about Pound, skewering his goatee, his coif, his garb—his whole bohemian demeanor.

Galantière looked at Hemingway and asked him what he intended to do with it.

Hemingway informed him that he planned to send it directly to *The Little Review* for consideration.

This probably wasn't such a great idea, Galantière advised him. Had Hemingway forgotten that Pound was the publication's longtime foreign editor? The editors at home probably wouldn't appreciate the outlandish attack. Hemingway ripped up the parody.

Pound soon visited the Hemingways' new home on rue du Cardinal Lemoine. Soon the men began to be seen around town together socially. They seemed an odd couple to other Left Bankers, who observed them with keen interest and amusement. "Ernest was always the champion sportsman in every café he entered and Pound, with his little beard, looked and was conscientiously aesthetic," recalled Janet Flanner.

Yet the relationship flourished, and Pound began to step into Hemingway's world as well. Hemingway soon reported to Sherwood Anderson that he was teaching Pound to box. Not that he was making great headway: Pound may have been a brilliant poet, but he had all the grace of a crawfish, Hemingway wrote. That said, he added with due respect, Pound was a good sport to "risk his dignity and his critical reputation at something that he don't know nothing about."

Pound had other virtues too, in Hemingway's opinion—including his admirably bitter tongue. Apparently Pound felt similarly about him, for he immediately started marketing some of Hemingway's poems and a story to his editors at the magazines. Hemingway had snared his first Olympian champion.

HEMINGWAY'S NEXT Crowd conquest led him into the realm of Sappho, a seemingly unlikely destination for a man who would soon be known around the globe for his pronounced masculinity and penchant for blood sport. Sherwood Anderson had provided an especially complimentary introduction letter to Gertrude Stein. Here, Anderson assured Stein, was "an American writer instinctively in touch with everything worth-while going on here."

Many vied for invitations to Stein's regal apartment at 27 rue de Fleurus. The grand entranceway to the building's courtyard stood in stark contrast to the Hemingways' walk-up with its squalid pissoirs. When Hemingway and Hadley turned at Stein's doorstep, a maid in a white cap and apron ushered them in. A small woman then stepped forward to greet them; she looked like a "little piece of electric wire," Hadley recalled, "small and fine and very Spanish looking, very dark, with piercing dark eyes." This was Alice B. Toklas, Stein's longtime lover and partner. (Hadley's description was one of the more charitable ever offered up by one of Toklas's contemporaries; others were inspired to giddy heights of cruelty when describing her hooked nose and broom-like mustache.) In the far corner of the salon, near a fireplace, sat Gertrude Stein, who was as substantial as Toklas was stringy. After the visit, Hemingway would ponder the weight of each of her breasts.

"I think about ten pounds, don't you, Hadley?" he asked his wife.

Stein's commanding physique and outsized persona earned her an array of nicknames around the Left Bank: "the Sumerian monument," "the great god Buddha," and perhaps most amusingly, "the Presence." She was usually as distinctively turned out as Ezra Pound (who, incidentally, had been banished from Stein's apartment after he'd accidentally crushed one of her favorite chairs while delivering an especially enthusiastic monologue). Typical Steinian garb included floor-length burlap gowns; Hemingway later described her wardrobe as having a distinct "steerage" motif.

Securing a private audience with Stein was an honor. Her admirers, wrote Sylvia Beach, "would come to me, exactly as if I were a guide from one of the tourist agencies, and beg me to take them to see Gertrude Stein." Most guests at the salon had to share her with other gawkers; callers would often enter such gatherings and behold Stein perched in a large, high chair in the center of the studio, preparing to deliver a sermon. Soon she would begin to "monologue, and pontificate, and reiterate, and stammer," recalled a former guest. Attendees were advised to maintain a reverential hush as she spoke.

"Don't frighten her or she won't talk," one visitor was warned. "She is shy, very unsure of herself."

"Shy," however, was not the first word most people would have used to describe Gertrude Stein. "Megalomaniac" and "mythomaniac" were more accurate, according to one fellow Crowd member. "Genius" was Stein's own preferred term when describing herself.

"Nobody has done anything to develop the English language since

Shakespeare, except myself," she once asserted. "And Henry James perhaps a little," she generously added.

There were variations on a theme: she also once maintained that "the Jews have produced only three originative geniuses: Christ, Spinoza, and myself." When, in her book *The Autobiography of Alice B. Toklas*, Stein wrote—speaking in Toklas's voice—"I may say that only three times in my life have I met a genius," this time the trinity included Gertrude Stein, Pablo Picasso, and the philosopher Alfred North Whitehead.

As the Hemingways made their way into the salon during that first visit, a well-rehearsed dance was set in motion. As Stein gestured to Hemingway to sit in a chair near her, Toklas swooped in, steered Hadley to the other side of the room, and regaled her with distracting chat about current affairs. Artists' wives were persona non grata as far as Stein was concerned, piddling intruders on her conversations with great men. Toklas's efficient "wife-proof technique," as Sylvia Beach put it, had become famous among veteran Paris residents.

Hemingway gamely took a seat near Stein. Dozens of large modern paintings covered the walls around them, all the way up to the ceiling: Picassos, Braques, Cézannes. It was like being in a private museum. He and Stein began to talk shop.

As he had done with Anderson and Pound, Hemingway gazed at Stein intently and listened closely as she spoke. He struck Stein as "rather foreign looking, with passionately interested, rather than interesting eyes." While Ezra Pound was instructing Hemingway to strip language down, Stein would illuminate the value of the intentional stammer. Her style was predicated on free association and word repetition, as depicted by her 1913 poem "Sacred Emily":

> Rose is a rose is a rose is a rose.
> Loveliness extreme.
> Extra gaiters.
> Loveliness extreme.
> Sweetest ice-cream.
> Pages ages page ages page ages.

No one felt neutral about Stein's experiments with the English language, just as few people felt neutral about Miss Stein herself. Her writing style had been drawing attention on two continents since before the war, yet neither publishers nor readers were in a hurry to get their hands on her books. Back in 1908, Stein had had to self-published her first book, *Three Lives;* it is said to have sold fewer than seventy-five copies during its first year and a half on the market. She was, as one chronicler of the Paris scene put it, "nobody's idea of a popular author."

Hemingway, however, saw a distinct opportunity in aspects of her style. He must have sufficiently impressed her during their first meeting, for soon there was a return visit from Stein and Toklas to the Hemingways' cramped flat on the rue du Cardinal Lemoine. Stein dutifully climbed up the four flights of stairs to the apartment and, once there, heaved herself up onto the Hemingways' bed, where she patiently thumbed through all of Hemingway's early writing. She read and considered, and then delivered her verdict: there was a lot of work to be done.

First of all, he would have to give up journalism, Stein told him. It was a necessary sacrifice if he was going to get anywhere as a real writer. Here she was preaching to the choir.

Second, some of his subject matter was too dirty. "You mustn't write anything that is *inaccrochable,*" Stein admonished him — meaning anything too salacious. She took particular offense at his short story "Up in Michigan," which concluded with a drunken, fumbling date rape. Hemingway cheerfully tolerated the advice but would in due course reject it.

They moved on to the subject of his starter novel — more Michigan fare. Stein had nothing good to say about it.

"There is a great deal of description in this," she informed him, "and not particularly good description. Begin over again and concentrate."

If Hemingway was discouraged, he didn't lash out at Stein — not yet, anyway. There was too much to be learned from her. He made more visits to her salon, during which they sipped tea and fruit liqueurs. While they sipped, he stared at her Cézanne paintings. There was something to be gleaned from Cézanne's thick, methodical brushstrokes, he thought, something in their repetition that would help his writing — something profound. Stein herself had been deeply influenced by the painter while writing her book *Three Lives*. She saw his influence on Picasso's work too, in certain landscape paintings — especially the "cutting up the sky not in cubes but in spaces." Picasso once called Cézanne "my one and only master," and added that "Cézanne came closer than anybody else when he said, 'Painting is something you do with your balls.'" Soon Hemingway was visiting the Musée du Luxembourg daily to examine the Cézannes on display there as well. "I was learning very much from him but I was not articulate enough to explain it to anyone," he wrote later. "Besides," he added, "it was secret." That said, it pertained to the crafting of "simple true sentences."

During his early visits to Stein's salon, Hemingway's hostess talked ceaselessly. They often discussed other writers, and Stein's opinions were soaked in competitiveness. She refused, Hemingway later claimed, to speak well about any writer who hadn't publicly supported her work. Sylvia Beach echoed this sentiment: "She took little interest, of course, in any but her own books."

Yet Stein became interested in Hemingway; she even admitted to developing a "weakness" for him. He was just so attentive when she talked about the general principles of her writing, she later explained. It was flattering to have such a good pupil, someone who took training so eagerly. Champion number two had been added to his arsenal.

"Gertrude Stein and me," he reported back to Sherwood Anderson, "are just like brothers."

THAT WINTER Hemingway rented a garret on the top floor of a hotel at 39 rue Descartes. Like rue du Cardinal Lemoine, the building had its own literary history: poet Paul Verlaine had died there. Reaching the icy room required a climb up many flights of stairs; Hemingway usually carted with him bundles of twigs to heat the space. If the chimney wasn't in the mood to draw properly, smoke filled the room; he would then have to stomp down all of those flights of stairs again and seek refuge in a nearby café.

Yet the room had its redeeming qualities: there was a modest view over the rooftops of the surrounding buildings, with smoke from other chimneys unfurling up into the gray Paris sky. Maybe more important, it was Hemingway's own private room at last: a place to put the lessons of Pound and Stein into practice on paper, a backdrop for him to push and jab at the English language and, perhaps, even create a modernist magnum opus.

When he wasn't marching all over Europe for the *Star,* Hemingway devoted himself almost wholly to his fiction. When he wasn't actually writing, he was thinking about writing, recovering from writing, or preparing to write. He dictated that breakfasts were to be silent — "please, without speaking," he told Hadley — so he could clear his head for the day of work before him. And even when he wasn't involved in his own writing, he was dutifully reading someone else's. Sometimes when Hadley was snuggling with her husband, she would hear a rustling sound and look up to find that he was reading something behind her back.

His nascent novel was on his mind, but instead of diving back into it,

Hemingway worked on short pieces. He was trying to find his voice and craft the style that he had started to conceive even before arriving in Paris. Some of this early work — both fiction and articles — contained the seeds of what would later become quintessential Hemingway, such as a paragraph he wrote about roughneck *bal musette* culture for the *Star:*

> *The people that go to the Bal Musette do not need to have the artificial stimulant of the jazz band to force them to dance. They dance for the fun of it and they occasionally hold someone up for the fun of it, and because it is easy and exciting and pays well. Because they are young and tough and enjoy life, without respecting it, they sometimes hit too hard, or shoot too quick, and then life becomes a very grim matter with an upright machine that casts a thin shadow and is called a guillotine at the end of it.*

On the whole, his new pieces were indeed beginning to resemble Cézanne paintings with their blunt brushstrokes. His work was leaner, simpler, and more rhythmic. Yet as far as Pound and Stein were concerned, he was still just a promising novice. Hemingway submitted work for review to Pound, who could be unsparing: often the pages came back to Hemingway covered with blue-penciled amendments and slashes through the adjectives. Yet Pound encouraged Hemingway too, even sending six Hemingway poems to Scofield Thayer at *The Dial* and a story to *The Little Review.*

"Pound thinks I'm a swell poet," Hemingway wrote to Sherwood Anderson. He added that it was unclear how much "drag" Pound had with Thayer, but whatever the case, Hemingway wished to hell that Pound's influence would help get him published.

Thayer did not, however, take the poems; nor did he solicit further material. *The Little Review* also rejected Hemingway's story. Yet Pound's support did not flag.

Hemingway had Stein's lessons to follow too, and it was difficult work.

"Isn't writing a hard job though?" he asked her. "It used to be easy before I met you."

Not only did Stein lecture him in her salon, but she also lent him many of her manuscripts that demonstrated her approach. He took her work with word repetition seriously; right away some of his writings began to bear signs of her influence — including the *inaccrochable* short story Stein had found so objectionable.

"Liz liked Jim very much," Hemingway wrote. "She liked it about his mustache. She liked it about how white his teeth were when he smiled. She liked it very much that he didn't look like a blacksmith."

He started doing little stream-of-consciousness exercises on the pages of blue notebooks used by French schoolchildren, another habit he picked up from Stein. "Down through the ages," went one such effort. "Why is it down through the ages? Down through the ages. Down and out through the ages. Out through the ages . . ."

During this time, Hemingway carefully observed his mentor. By Stein's own admission, she was becoming bitter about "all her unpublished manuscripts, and no hope of publication or serious recognition." It was becoming extremely important to her to get published. Eventually he would help her meet that goal, but in the meantime, he was seeing obvious applications for her style in work that he knew *he* could get published. Just because she hadn't made a success of her writing style didn't mean that he couldn't. Hemingway had, since before arriving in Paris, been concerned with "rhythm and tones and lines," as Hadley had once put it, and Stein's ideas about cadence advanced his thinking. He openly borrowed from her, but began to Hemingway-ify her ideas, making them all subtler, more appealing, more accessible. After all, what was the point of writing something brilliant and fresh and new if no one was going to read it? With every stroke of his pencil up in that icy garret on rue Descartes, Hemingway was quietly turning Stein from his Pygmalion into a mere forerunner.

Sooner or later, Hemingway knew, he would have to channel these lessons and new exercises into a significant work. Perhaps he could rewrite his starter novel, as he had rewritten the story "Up in Michigan." True, Stein had told him to throw the novel away and start anew, but he had no intention of obeying *all* of her instructions.

At that moment he had no way of knowing that soon he would be forced to take Stein's advice and start from scratch — whether he wanted to or not.

3

Fortuitous Disasters

N THE FALL OF 1922, Hemingway left Paris to cover the evacuation of Greek troops from eastern Thrace. After the end of the world war, Greece had attempted to expand its territorial holdings in what had been the Ottoman Empire; Turkey voiced its objection with a counterattack that expelled the would-be conquerors. The repulsion amounted to, Hemingway informed his *Star* readers, "the end of the great Greek military adventure."

He was then rerouted to Lausanne, Switzerland, where a conference was being organized to settle the Greco-Turkish situation. There Hemingway ran into investigative journalist Lincoln Steffens—or, rather, Hemingway "dawned upon me one night," Steffens remembered, adding that, among the foreign correspondents covering the conflict, Hemingway had impressed him as having "the surest future over there."

Hemingway showed Steffens a cable he had written. He had grown fascinated with the art of "cablese"—the ultimate adjective-free expression. One couldn't get much further away from Victorian frippery. Even while on assignment, Hemingway was finding ways to instruct himself in the art of spare communication. For example, he later explained, a cable that read "KEMAL INSWARDS UNBURNED SMYRNA GUILTY GREEKS" could be translated by his editors back home to read: "Mustapha Kemal in an exclusive interview today with the correspondent of the Monumental News Service denied vehemently that the Turkish forces had any part in the burning of Smyrna. The city, Kemal stated, was fired by incendiaries in the troops of the Greek rear guard before the first Turkish patrols entered the city."

The cable he shared with Steffens described the exodus of Greek refugees from Turkey, a "vivid, detailed picture of what he had seen in that miserable stream of hungry, frightened, uprooted people," recalled Steffens. "I was seeing the scene and told him so."

"No," Hemingway chided him. "Read the cablese, only the cablese. Isn't it a great language?"

Steffens wanted to see more. "I asked him to read all his dispatches, for the pictures," he wrote later.

Hemingway also had with him a copy of "My Old Man," a dramatic racetrack short story. Steffens read it and liked it; this, along with the cables, made him feel certain that Hemingway was the real deal. "He could, he would, do it some day," he recalled thinking. Eager to play a role in launching him, Steffens sent Hemingway's short story off to an editor at *Cosmopolitan,* in New York, which published fiction at the time.

Meanwhile, Hadley was back in Paris, nursing a nasty flu. Hemingway implored her by cable to join him as soon as she felt "travelly" again. She soon felt sufficiently recovered to make the trip. As she prepared to leave, she made a curious decision: in a valise she packed Hemingway's manuscripts, including his short stories, poetry, the starter novel, and all of the carbon copies of these works. Nearly his entire literary output to date would be making the trip alongside her clothes and toiletries. Hemingway had been sending her letters "singing high praises" of Steffens, she later explained, and she had been certain that her husband would want Steffens to see more of his work. What happened next would haunt the Hemingways for the rest of their lives.

Hadley arrived at the Gare de Lyon train station, stashed her bags in a compartment of the Paris-Lausanne Express, and then got off the train to buy some water and a newspaper. She had a little time to kill, so she lingered on the platform, chatting with a few correspondents who were also heading to the conference. When Hadley finally got back to her compartment, the small bag containing Hemingway's manuscripts had vanished.

She made the trip anyway, soaked with panic and despair. In Lausanne, Hemingway was waiting for her at the station. Lincoln Steffens stood at his side. Hadley got off the train, sobbing.

"She had cried and cried and could not tell me," Hemingway later recalled. "I had never seen anyone hurt by a thing other than death or unbearable suffering except Hadley when she told me about the things being gone."

Hemingway hired someone to cover for him at the conference and went back to Paris. At first he was in denial that Hadley had brought along everything, all of his work, but he soon got to their apartment and realized that she had indeed packed nearly his entire opus. "I remember what I did in the night after I let myself into the flat and found it was true," he wrote later. Yet he apparently never revealed what the mysterious, possibly scandalous activity had been.

"No amount of sleuthing ever brought the valise to light," Hadley later recalled. "And so deeply had Ernest put himself into this writing that I think he never recovered from the pain of this irreparable loss." The disappearance of his starter novel—which she described as "sacred"—had been an especially tough blow for him, she added.

If this was true, Hemingway was almost incomprehensibly nice to Hadley about what his friend Bill Smith dubbed "the Great Train Robbery"—at least on paper, as he recounted the ghastly incident in later years. Poor Hadley was, Hemingway wrote, a "lovely and loyal woman with bad luck with manuscripts." He had never really blamed her, he claimed in another account. After all, "she had not hired on as a manuscript custodian," he went on, adding that "what she had hired on for—wife-ing—she was damn good at." (To be fair, these magnanimous words were uttered after he'd had more than a quarter century to cool down.)

Gallows humor helped Hemingway pull through. When *Cosmopolitan* rejected and returned "My Old Man," he began to refer to the story as "Das Kapital," claiming that it had suddenly become his total "literary capital." This wasn't exactly true: the *inaccrochable* "Up in Michigan" had also survived; for some reason it had been stuffed "in a drawer somewhere," apart from the other manuscripts.

Hemingway also sought the sympathies of his new mentors but received little coddling. "I suppose you heard about the loss of my Juvenilia?" he wrote to Ezra Pound a few weeks after the theft. "You, naturally, would say, 'Good' etc. But don't say it to me. I aint yet reached that mood. I worked 3 years on the damn stuff." It was an "act of Gawd," Pound replied, adding that Hemingway should perhaps try to re-create the lost writings. After all, memory was the best editor anyway, he added. Gertrude Stein hadn't liked his novel in the first place.

Eventually Hemingway grudgingly came to believe that "it was probably good for me to lose the early work." For him there was no question of re-creating the entire portfolio from scratch; he was having a clean slate forced upon him. Yet whatever came next would almost inevitably be an improvement on what had been lost. After all, it would be created against the backdrop of intellectual Paris, infused with all that Hemingway had learned from Pound and Stein. Now his earliest works—far from smacking of "Juvenilia"—would instead make him appear as something of an Athena springing fully formed from Zeus's forehead. In fact, not only were these powerful influences now in place; Hemingway was already prepared to surge past them and write in a bold new voice of his own.

"I know what I'm after in prose," he wrote to Ezra Pound. "If it is no fucking good I'll know it."

By the end of January 1923, he informed Pound that he was already working on new material.

Years later, Hemingway created a character in an unpublished short story titled "The Strange Country" whose wife lost all of his early works. The character, Roger, desperately misses the lost stories. Yet, he says, "I could see already, as you begin to see clearly over the water when a rainstorm lifts on the ocean as the wind carries it out to sea, that I could write a better novel."

THAT FEBRUARY, the Hemingways traveled to Rapallo, Italy, where Ezra and Dorothy Pound had taken up residence. It seemed a promising recuperative backdrop: there would be fresh figs and good wine and warm Italian bread, and long walks and tennis matches with the Pounds.

There would, however, also be the daunting prospect of creating an entirely new body of work. It was painful going at first, and Hemingway pressed Pound and Stein for encouragement. He was working hard, he informed Stein, and had a couple of new pieces finished. He had been bearing her lessons in mind while writing, but added that if she had any additional advice, he wished she would put it in a letter to him. In the meantime, at least he had reached a détente with Hadley: at the moment, he was happiest in bed with her, he wrote privately.

That is, until Hadley informed Hemingway that she was pregnant. She had arrived in Lausanne not only sans manuscripts but also sans contraception; she'd duly warned Hemingway, but they had taken their chances anyway. The development still apparently shocked Hemingway. Once back in Paris, he sought refuge at Stein's salon.

"He came to the house about ten o'clock in the morning and he stayed," recalled Stein. "He stayed for lunch, he stayed all afternoon, he stayed for dinner and he stayed until about ten o'clock at night and then all of a sudden he announced that his wife was enceinte."

"I am too young to be a father," he told them—with great bitterness, according to Stein.

Stein and Toklas consoled him "as best we could and sent him on his way." Yet Stein's sympathies ran only so deep: she found the incident entertaining and relayed her amusement to Hadley, who presumably found it less comical.

In any case, it was the second time in about as many months that Hadley had served up some deeply unwelcome news. Plans were soon made for a late-summer return to Canada, where Hemingway would take up a position as a home-based reporter for the *Toronto Star* to give the new family some additional security during the baby's first year. He seemed to view fatherhood and a return to full-time journalism as a dual prison sentence. Nor was he particularly thrilled at the prospect of swapping Europe for Toronto. At least the *Star* offered him a prestige weekly salary of $125.

Yet no amount of adversity could entirely sidetrack his literary ambition. He worked relentlessly that winter and spring of 1923, drafting vignettes and short stories in his new spare, intense, and rhythmic style.

"I want, like hell, to get published," he wrote to one editor.

And as luck would have it, a publisher came along who soon wanted, like hell, to publish him: Robert McAlmon, an acid-tongued expat writer and editor based in Paris. McAlmon had founded the Contact Publishing Company, an elite boutique press dedicated to publishing, in very limited editions, the work of experimental writers "who seem not likely to be published by other publishers, for commercial or legislative reasons." His list eventually boasted works by Ezra Pound, William Carlos Williams, Gertrude Stein, Edith Sitwell, and Mina Loy, among many other of that generation's literary luminaries.

McAlmon materialized in Rapallo during the Hemingways' winter stay. He had never heard of Hemingway before, and his early impressions of the young writer were less than favorable. He had a "small-boy, tough-guy swagger," McAlmon recalled later. "And before strangers of whom he was uncertain a potential snarl of scorn played on his large-lipped, rather loose mouth."

Like Pound, McAlmon, then twenty-seven, was an unlikely champion for Hemingway. A former model who sometimes wore a turquoise earring, McAlmon was openly bisexual—and thought to be more than a little bit self-obsessed. "When Bob McAlmon had had a drink or two he seemed to believe every good-looking citizen, man or woman, postman or countess, wanted to make a pass at him," recalled a writer who ran in the same circles.

McAlmon had married a British heiress who most in the expat colony believed was a lesbian, and they served as each other's beards. As a result of the union, he was relatively flush; his nickname around town became "Robert McAlimony."

Even though McAlmon and Hemingway seemed socially mismatched, they got together in Rapallo and drank in the evenings. For Hemingway, a potential publisher was still a publisher, no matter what his tendencies. He showed McAlmon the remains of his earlier work and his new efforts. McAlmon didn't love the style; he deemed it the self-conscious approach of "an older person who insists upon trying to think and write like a child." Also, "My Old Man" — one of the older short stories that had survived the Great Train Robbery — sounded too much like Sherwood Anderson's style to him. But the newer work seemed fresh and un-derivative. McAlmon decided that Hemingway might just make a good addition to Contact's list.

Meanwhile, Hemingway told Pound that he found McAlmon's company enjoyable, and in addition the publisher had "given us the dirt on everybody." So happy was the initial union that a few months later, in June 1923, the two men decided to take a trip to Spain together. McAlmon pledged to foot the bill. They would be accompanied by expat journalist and publisher Bill Bird, co-founder of the wire service the Consolidated Press, whom Hemingway knew from the press corps. Unlike McAlmon, who sometimes inspired "sneers and open hostility," the amiable Bird was universally liked in the Paris colony — no small feat given the tempestuous nature of the Crowd. And Bird also happened to own a new little book press in Paris. For an ambitious new writer in search of publishers, these were most promising travel companions.

Thanks in part to Gertrude Stein, Hemingway had been nursing a growing fascination with bullfighting and was eager to behold the spectacle in person. Stein had seen her first Spanish bullfight two decades earlier with her brother Leo; she had gone back to Spain again a decade later with Alice Toklas, who wore a demure bullfight-attendance costume that involved a black feathered hat, black satin coat, black fan, and gloves. ("I called [it] my Spanish disguise," Toklas recalled in the autobiography she actually *did* write.)

The ladies of 27 rue de Fleurus imparted tales of their experiences to Hemingway, who was engrossed in the subject. As part of his recovery effort from the valise theft, he penned a stylized vignette about a bullfight gone horribly wrong, drawing on secondhand accounts:

The first matador got the horn through his sword hand and the crowd hooted him. The second matador slipped and the bull caught him through the belly and he hung on to the horn with one hand and held the other tight against the place, and the bull rammed him wham against the wall and the horn came out, and he lay in the sand, and then got up like crazy drunk and tried to slug the men carrying him away and yelled for his sword but he fainted.

Hemingway clearly had a feeling for the material, but it was a spectacle he had to see for himself. As he would soon find out, it would be like having a front-row seat at a bloody battle.

He could hardly wait.

ON THE FIRST of June, 1923, McAlmon and Hemingway left Paris for Spain by train.

"Beery-poppa (Hemingway) said a loving goodbye to Feather-kitty (Hadley)," recalled McAlmon, citing the latest nicknames Hemingway and Hadley had bestowed on each other. "And he and I, well lubricated with whisky, got on the train."

Bill Bird planned to meet them in Madrid. By the time he got there, McAlmon was on Hemingway's blacklist. Once anyone earned a spot on this roster, it was nearly impossible to receive a pardon.

They found themselves at odds before their train even crossed the Spanish border. At one point, while still in France, the train stopped. On the track beside their car, on top of a flatcar, lay a festering, maggot-eaten dog corpse. McAlmon blanched and looked away—a gesture that immediately earned Hemingway's disdain. He had seen similar scenes in war, he advised McAlmon; one simply had to be detached and scientific about it.

"He tenderly explained that we of our generation must inure ourselves to the sight of grim reality," McAlmon remembered. "I recalled that Ezra Pound had talked once of Hemingway's 'self-hardening process.'" McAlmon was proving to be too soft for Hemingway's taste.

Once in Spain, the men prepared to see their first bullfight. After downing a few drinks to steel themselves, they took their seats in the stands, bringing along more whisky in case their nerves needed further steadying. The very first bull charged a horse, lifting the animal over its head on its horns. Later, another horse was gored and galloped "in hysteria around the ring, treading on its own entrails," McAlmon recalled. He was repulsed—and not just by the goings-on in the ring. The crowd was also brutal and vulgar, he thought. Bill Bird was less horrified, according to McAlmon. "But neither he nor I were putting ourselves through a 'hardening process.'" Hemingway, however, was immediately seduced. "It's a great tragedy—and the most beautiful thing I've ever seen," he wrote to a friend. Bullfighting, in his eyes, took "more guts and skill and guts again than anything possibly could." It was like, he added, "having a ringside seat at the war with nothing going to happen to you."

He immediately began acting like someone newly admitted to a secret society, Bill Bird observed, and set about making himself an instant expert. ("If there's ever anything you want to know about bull fighting ask me," he wrote to his father a few weeks later, adding that the trip would provide material for "some very fine stories.") At the same time, Hemingway's patience with McAlmon was running thin, and he insulted him unsparingly, even though McAlmon was funding the entire enterprise. McAlmon's inability to stare down brutality—whether a rotting dog or a gored horse —repelled Hemingway; plus, Hemingway felt that McAlmon considered him a poseur. Nothing could be further from the truth. His bullfighting *afición* was real, and he was going to prove it.

Yet astonishingly, by the time the trio returned to Paris, Hemingway had earned not one but two new publishers: both Bird and McAlmon decided that they were going to publish his works via their respective presses. McAlmon planned to beat Bird to the punch, publicly announcing soon after they got back from Spain that he would be the first to publish a book by Ernest Hemingway. Talent was talent, after all, whether it kissed the ring or bit the hand.

THAT FIRST BOOK would be a slim affair, as one could intuit from its eventual title: *Three Stories and Ten Poems*. Two of those three stories were survivors of the Great Train Robbery: "My Old Man" and "Up in Michigan."

The third story was one that Hemingway had written that spring after his Rapallo trip, while skiing at Cortina with Hadley. "Out of Season" was a stylistic breakthrough for him. Not only was it clipped and rhythmic, but also it showcased a new "iceberg theory" that he'd been kicking around. He was not just intent on stripping down language itself; he was now stripping down his material and prompting readers to infer events not explicitly spelled out. When it came to story lines, a gifted writer could get away with showing only the tip of the iceberg. "If the writer is writing truly enough, [the reader] will have a feeling of those [omitted] things as strongly as though the writer had stated them," he explained later. This approach would involve the reader more deeply in the story and make him or her more of an active participant.

"Out of Season" would be a case study of sorts. It was, Hemingway later admitted, a near-literal translation of something that had happened to him and Hadley during their Cortina foray. At the story's center is a fraught marriage between a young man and a young woman named "Tiny"—one of Hadley's nicknames for Hemingway. The characters are on holiday; they are bickering. Amidst this discord, they allow themselves to be taken on an illegal out-of-season fishing expedition by a drunken old guide named Peduzzi. The unpleasant little voyage unravels, thanks to Peduzzi's ineptitude, and at the story's end, the reader is left speculating about the cause of the quarrel between the couple and what becomes of the hapless Peduzzi.

In real life, the Hemingways had gone on a similar excursion, and afterward Hemingway had complained about the "drunk of a guide" to their hotel manager, who promptly fired the old villager. The "very desperate" old man then hanged himself in a stable. When he later recounted the incident, he expressed no remorse about his possible role in prompting the man's suicide; he only matter-of-factly explained why the suicide did not work as a literary device in the story that stemmed from the events. He simply "didnt think the story needed it." Clearly his self-hardening process was working.

Also, here Hemingway's reporting skills were coming in handy. The "Peduzzi" affair was one of many real-life events that he would treat as a fiction scoop. Over and over again, he would recognize the literary currency of an event and then practically race to the closest flat surface on which he could translate that event onto paper—usually in faintly fictionalized, highly stylized form. He had written "Out of Season" in a frantic reporter-on-deadline rush, starting as soon as he returned from his own ill-fated fishing trip. He claimed to have written it so fast that he didn't even use punctuation.

"Your ear is always more acute when you have been upset by a row of any sort," he explained later.

Hemingway also needed to come up with new material for his book project with Bill Bird. Like McAlmon's press, Bird's newly founded Three Mountains Press was an independent publisher dedicated to limited editions of experimental writing. Yet unlike McAlmon's books—which one expat described as "uglyish wads of printing"—Bird's were tactile, artisanal objets d'art, printed on an eighteenth-century handpress; the whole operation was crammed into a tiny former wine vault. He had recently teamed up with Ezra Pound to publish a six-volume series titled *The Inquest into the state of contemporary English prose*. Bird asked Hemingway to contribute the sixth and final book. He suggested a series of vignettes like Hemingway's 183-word gored-matador passage. Luckily, Hemingway had already been laboring over a series of them, six of which had been published in *The Little Review* earlier that spring. One of them, a war story, consisted of a mere seventy-five words:

> *We were in a garden at Mons. Young Buckley came in with his patrol from across the river. The first German I saw climbed up over the garden wall. We waited till he got one leg over and then potted him. He had so much equipment on and looked awfully surprised and fell down into the garden. Then three more came over further down the wall. We shot them. They all came just like that.*

Hemingway agreed with Bird; they called the resulting volume of vignettes *in our time*. It was a declarative title, implying that readers might find the literary zeitgeist within its rough-hewn pages.

The slenderness of the book made it appear diminutive, yet it was anything but. A mere 3,500 words long, it contained eighteen "chapters" — most of which were no longer than the "garden at Mons" passage. Yet those words had been painstakingly selected and arranged. Each of the *in our time* vignettes — many of which drew on material that Hemingway had picked up on reporting assignments around Europe — conjured up its own engrossing little world. Robert McAlmon was about to have the honor of being Hemingway's first publisher, but *Three Stories and Ten Poems* was largely repurposed material from Hemingway's largely lost "Juvenilia" era.

Bill Bird, by contrast, got the real goods. *in our time* hinted at what the future would hold: not just Hemingway's future but the future of literature. The new Hemingway formula was falling into place, saturated with Pound-inspired spareness and Steinian repetitive stream-of-consciousness elements. Yet the vignettes were unique too — as action-driven and engrossing as any Hemingway article; as literary as anything that Pound or Stein might have created yet more accessible.

To Bird and the other early *in our time* readers, they felt like something new under the sun.

. . .

AMIDST ALL of this building momentum, Hadley's belly began to grow moon-big: the baby was due sometime in October 1923. The couple was due to depart for Canada soon—just as Hemingway was putting literary Paris on notice. He was not happy about it. Other expat hopefuls were coming to Paris in droves to pursue the very goal he was poised to achieve, and now he was exiling himself from the literary center of the universe. He complained bitterly about the situation to friends, even though the Canada move was voluntary.

Despite his initial jitters, Hemingway did find ways to get into the spirit of his wife's pregnancy. The couple went to Spain together in July for the weeklong San Fermín festival in Pamplona: it was an annual pilgrimage site for bullfighting aficionados. Hemingway felt the experience would be a good prenatal influence on his child. The fiesta proved to be more than that. For Hemingway, it was a life-changing, intoxicating revelation. He was giddy when describing it to others: "5 days of bull fighting dancing all day and all night," he wrote to one friend. "Wonderful music—drums, reed pipes, fifes—faces of Velasquez's drinkers, Goya and Greco faces, all the men in blue shirts and red handkerchiefs circling lifting floating dance."

What was more, from a reporter's point of view, it was a hell of a scoop. Here was essentially an untapped trove of material, a world filled with decadence, high art, ceremony, frivolity, and profundity all at once—and he and Hadley had been, he claimed, the only foreigners there. (The spectacle had a less profound effect on Hadley, who cheerfully sat at Hemingway's side during the bullfights, stitching clothes for their baby and "embroidering in the presence of all that brutality," as she later put it.)

This first fiesta immediately inspired him: nearly a quarter of *in our time*'s chapters would feature bullfighting scenes. He worked passionately on the material all summer, consulting with Ezra Pound on the edits. Yet now the student had also begun instructing the mentor: Hemingway gave stern, detailed guidance on how the material should appear in the final version of the book. He gave equally strict guidance to Robert McAlmon about the proofs for *Three Stories and Ten Poems,* enlisting firepower from Gertrude Stein about aesthetic matters along the way. He even submitted a cover he had designed himself with input from Bill Bird. "I like the look of it. Maybe you don't," he wrote to McAlmon. "You are the publisher," he added magnanimously, but it was clear whose opinion Hemingway valued most.

McAlmon released *Three Stories and Ten Poems* on August 13, 1923. Ernest Hemingway had officially become a published author.

Two weeks later, he and Hadley left for Canada. Within days of their arrival, Hemingway's darkest fears had been confirmed.

"It couldn't be any worse," he wrote to Pound. "You can't imagine it."

BY THE END of the summer, excitement had begun to build in the *Toronto Star's* newsroom amidst rumors of Hemingway's imminent arrival. When he materialized in September, he immediately commanded the spotlight. He spoke almost casually of his friendships with Gertrude Stein and Ezra Pound—who must have seemed like mythical creatures to many of the staffers—and was candid about his intention to join them in the literary pantheon.

Hemingway became a hot topic around the newsroom; rumors often circulated about him. According to Morley Callaghan, then a young *Star* reporter: "He couldn't walk down the street and stub his toe without having a newspaperman who happened to be walking with him magnify the little accident into a near fatality. How he was able to get these legends going I still don't know."

Hemingway may have filled some young staffers with a sense of awe, but the older men were less than impressed, for example, when Hemingway—clutching proofs of *in our time,* came to work one day and announced, "I've discovered a new form." To Callaghan he added, "Ezra Pound says it is the best prose he has read in forty years."

Staffers quietly began passing around a copy of *Three Stories and Ten Poems* among themselves. Callaghan—who worshipped Hemingway and his writing—asked two colleagues for their thoughts on the tome. "I can still remember the patient smile of the older one as he said, 'Remember this, my boy. Three swallows never made a summer,'" said Callaghan.

No one appeared less impressed by Hemingway than his managing editor, Harry Hindmarsh—also the son-in-law of the paper's publisher. Hindmarsh had a reputation as a ruthless newsman, a general who was "driven to break [the spirit of] any proud man" who challenged him, according to Callaghan. He took a passionate dislike to Hemingway and immediately went to great lengths to humble his new reporter, sending him on far-flung yet menial assignments. Soon Hemingway was "busy galloping around the country in the Hindmarsh harness." Gone were the prestige days of interviewing Mussolini and covering international conflicts; the new stories Hindmarsh gave Hemingway were "piddling, just junk assignments," recalled Callaghan, who gaped at Hemingway's story lineups in the newsroom assignment book with disbelief. Hadley was equally appalled, and reported to Hemingway's mother that he was "greatly over-worked" and rarely slept.

Hemingway made no effort to disguise his misery to his friends back in Paris. His missives to France grew increasingly desperate. He begged Pound to write to him. "You may save a human life," he pleaded. (Pound, who allegedly "hated all things American," was apparently gently scornful about Hemingway's Canadian adventure; his letters from Paris were mockingly addressed to "Tomato, Can.") Furthermore, he was tormented over his suddenly halted creative trajectory; he told one colleague that his stint in Toronto had already killed off ten years of his literary life.

The tension between Hemingway and Hindmarsh neared explosion when the editor sent his reporter on assignment to New York just before Hadley was due to give birth. Sure enough, on October 10 — while Hemingway was away — their son was born. Hemingway returned at once and went straight to Hadley's bedside; Hindmarsh in turn reprimanded Hemingway for failing to bring his material to the newsroom first. Hadley commiserated wholly with her husband: she feared that the new job would "kill my Tiny if we stay too long," she wrote to a friend. Hemingway was furious that Hadley had had to "go through the show alone" and pledged to Ezra Pound that all future work delivered to Hindmarsh would be done with "utter contempt and hatred."

Hemingway and Hadley named their seven-pound baby John Hadley Nicanor Hemingway. In more than one letter, Hemingway jokingly noted the child's resemblance to the king of Spain. Hadley explained to her mother-in-law that "John Hadley" was one of Hemingway's reporting pen names. "As it includes me," she added, "he is really named for us both." "Nicanor" honored the Spanish matador Nicanor Villalta, whom the couple had seen in Pamplona that summer. The baby would soon acquire some nicknames as well. To his parents, he was "Bumby" — a Hadley invention which reflected his roly-polyness; two of his new godparents, Gertrude Stein and Alice Toklas, called him "Goddy."

To their friends, both Hemingway and Hadley described Bumby's progress with typical new-parent giddiness and pride, but Hadley reported that they had heavy hearts "just when we ought to be so happy." Hemingway complained of a shot stomach, nervous fatigue, and insomnia. Their existence in Canada was a waking nightmare, he wrote to Stein and Toklas. For the first time, he added, he understood how a man could be driven to suicide.

There were, however, indications that his fighting spirit had not been extinguished, just pummeled temporarily into submission. "I'll get on your shelves yet," he pledged to Sylvia Beach. He wrote a few spirited articles about bullfighting and also found time to dash off several nasty little sketches of his co-workers, whom he described as "all *merde*" to Beach. One colleague, he wrote, was "dry inside his head like the vagina of an old whore."

He even thought about developing a revenge novel skewering Hindmarsh; it would be titled *The Son-in-Law*. It is unclear how much progress he ever made on this book; he apparently gave the project up quickly, telling a colleague that a writer shouldn't premise a novel on someone he despised because hatred distorted one's perspective.

Yet nothing could distract him enough from the daily agonies of his routine. Soon a decision was made to give it all up: not just his position at the *Star* but journalism in its entirety. There would be no more freelancing, no more deadlines, and no accepting tempting faraway assignments. There would be only the writing — real writing. Hemingway and Hadley began making plans to flee back to France, which, they realized, had become their true home over the past two years. They implored various Left Bank friends to help them find an apartment there and regain their foothold in the city. They would not be "too fussy" about their lodgings, Hadley promised Sylvia Beach; they were simply pining for "the light of day in Paris."

The move took on the tenor of a prison escape. As the Hemingways would be illegally breaking their lease, they asked friends to shuttle their possessions secretly out of their apartment. When the transatlantic liner *Antonia* set sail for France from New York in mid-January 1924, the Hemingways — now numbering three — were aboard.

Hemingway was now officially a published author, a retired journalist, and a free agent. Until he began to earn income from his fiction, the family would rely entirely on Hadley's trust fund. They would soon learn the meaning of poverty, but those material deprivations would be nothing compared to the anguish they had just lived through. It had been a turbulent year, filled with trials and upheaval. As with the Great Train Robbery and Hadley's "surprise" pregnancy, however, the silver lining of the Canadian debacle would soon reveal itself. As Morley Callaghan later pointed out, "if it hadn't been for Hindmarsh, Hemingway might have remained a year in Toronto," and the events that set the stage for his first real novel — not an amateur effort or a petulant satire — might never have taken place.

4

Let the Pressure Build

THE HEMINGWAYS seem to have had a talent for finding Parisian flats above raucous ground-floor businesses. This time around, they swapped the background noise of *bal musette* accordion music and stamping feet for the persistent gasp and wheeze of a wood saw: their new flat at 113 rue Notre-Dame-des-Champs overlooked a lumberyard and sawmill that specialized in making doors and window frames. The mill opened at 7 a.m. each day, and the courtyard below quickly filled with workmen and dogs.

The prospect of living upstairs from this cacophony might have driven others to despair, but the Hemingways managed to wreath their circumstances in a romantic haze. There was only a "very gentle buzzing noise," Hadley assured Hemingway's mother, and the lovely scent of freshly cut wood wafting up from below.

However gently administered, the sound of the buzzing saw — combined with the cries of a newborn — continually drove Hemingway out of the apartment to write. He began to frequent La Closerie des Lilas on boulevard du Montparnasse and guarded the outpost with territorial ferocity. Each day he set up a de facto office at one of the café's marble-topped tables, armed with pencils, a pencil sharpener, and French school notebooks.

"The marble-topped tables, the smell of *café crèmes,* the smell of early morning sweeping out and mopping and luck were all you needed," he contended. Those things, and a horse chestnut and worn-down rabbit's foot as good-luck talismans. A writer could easily loiter at the Closerie for hours. "Nobody ever threw you out or said, 'If you're going to stay here, you'd better order another,'" recalled expat poet Archibald MacLeish. "That's not the way the French do things." This was a godsend arrangement for someone with semi-private office needs but limited resources.

Savvy acquaintances knew to steer clear of Hemingway as he sat on the Closerie's terrace, his pencil skittering across the small notebook pages. He was like a "blind pig" when he was working, he later joked. It helped that the Closerie had not yet become populated with the same expat riffraff who besieged the Dôme and Rotonde at all hours. Unfortunately, however, both of those cafés were within walking distance of the Closerie on the same boulevard, and Hemingway occasionally had to contend with their spillover. To most people, such intrusions would be considered an occupational hazard of public-café-based writing, but Hemingway considered any interruption that "bitched" his work a hostile act. One had to be "ruthless" with interlopers, and anyone who interrupted the scripting of a spare, rhythmic sentence could expect a greeting along these lines: "You rotten son of a bitch what are you doing in here off your filthy beat?"

These were not leisurely outings. For Hemingway, the pressure was on. He had committed to being a full-time writer; his fiction needed to become a profitable venture sooner rather than later, and he still had a rather slender body of work to his credit. In Paris, as in the *Toronto Star* newsroom, it seems that no one felt neutral about Hemingway's style. Some found his new writing "marvelous," while others "held their noses," recalled writer Malcolm Cowley. Either way, he was becoming something of a junior god on Olympus. The right people were backing him and he was clearly ambitious.

However exciting and promising his little books with Robert McAlmon and Bill Bird had been to insiders, they didn't do much to shore up the dwindling Hemingway treasury, which was strained to the limit now with the addition of the baby's expenses. Nor did Hemingway's Paris books create a furor among major American publishers and reviewers. When *in our time* debuted in March 1924, Bird had planned to publish 300 copies of the book; but somehow he botched over a third of his print run, meaning that only 170 copies were available for sale. (Bird was, to be fair, the first to admit that publishing was only a hobby for him.) This meant that Hemingway now had two artisanal books in print, with a grand combined inventory of 470 copies in circulation—a pittance by anyone's standards, but especially for someone with grand aspirations for commercial success. Few reviewers back in the States even noted the books' existence. A critic for the *New York Herald Tribune* deemed both books to be largely derivative with a few glimpses of originality, which was perhaps worse than being wholly ignored.

"Burton Rascoe said In Our Time showed the influence of who the hell do you think?—Ring Lardner and Sherwood Anderson," Hemingway complained to Ezra Pound. It was not the first time his style had been likened to Anderson's. The comparison annoyed Hemingway: after all, even back in his Chicago days he had been critical of Anderson's writing.

As if the pressure to succeed wasn't already high enough, disaster struck the Hemingways once again—this time taking aim at Hadley's modest trust fund that spring. The couple had concluded that their trust company was too conservative, and instead handed over management of the fund to the husband of a friend of Hadley's. This wizard not only managed to halve the fund's capital but also even left the Hemingways without an income for several months. Hemingway squandered precious hours trying to trace the trail of the lost funds, but the couple was ultimately left bewildered and nearly destitute.

"It was my 'complete poverty' period," Hemingway reportedly told a friend later. The Hemingways didn't even have enough money to buy milk for the baby, he swore. "I hit everyone for cash. I even borrowed a thousand francs from my barber. I accosted strangers. There wasn't a sou in Paris that hadn't been nailed down that I didn't solicit."

He began to skip meals. Paris was torture for a hungry man, especially one who liked to work in cafés. He claimed later that he had even ambushed pigeons in the Luxembourg Gardens and brought them home to the family cookpot.

News of their poverty got around town. A rumor circulated that Bumby slept in a dresser drawer. Hadley trudged all over the city, scouting out places to buy cheap food—a daily chore probably made more dispiriting by the holes in her shoe soles; resoling was a luxury they could not afford. The family used a public bathhouse by the river. Guilt plagued Hemingway, who could have alleviated their situation by going back to journalism, but he stuck with his game plan. Hadley never complained, which made Hemingway feel worse. "The one who is doing his work and getting satisfaction from it is not the one the poverty is hard on," he later wrote.

The couple refused to accept gestures of charity. Bill Bird's wife had her dressmaker create a dress for Hadley, whose clothes were falling into tatters. Hadley burst into tears of embarrassment and would not wear the new garment. Yet she and Hemingway did not acknowledge themselves as poor or inferior; he later wrote that they actually felt superior to their wealthier counterparts, who could be stupidly oblivious to the simple pleasures in life. The Hemingways, by contrast, found luxury in necessities, savoring hearty peasant food and reveling in the warmth of their bodies at night under the covers.

Yet for Hemingway, a feeling of hunger plagued him at all hours. Even after he and Hadley had eaten dinner, the feeling lingered. It was still there after the couple made love in the dark. It kept Hemingway awake at night as Hadley slept quietly in bed next to him, bathed in moonlight.

His was a hunger that had little to do with food, and it would not abate until he broke through.

LIKE BOUTIQUE PUBLISHING HOUSES, literary reviews were becoming quite a fad among expats in Paris. Most of these publications were, as Sylvia Beach put it, "short-lived, alas! but always interesting." A new one joined the roster in January 1924: the *transatlantic review,* administered by British novelist and literary editor Ford Madox Ford, who had come over from London.

Ford and Ezra Pound had been longtime acquaintances and fellow crusaders in the name of modernism, and now Pound helped ease Ford's entry into the Paris Crowd as they prepared to launch the publication. "I had never read [Ford's] works," recalled Robert McAlmon, "but was prepared to believe Ezra Pound that he was 'one of us.'" News of the publication's imminent debut had reached Hemingway the previous fall while he was still toiling away in Toronto. He wrote to Pound and posited the idea of pitching a work titled "Oh Canada." (The theme of the proposed piece: how Canada was "shit.") Pound in turn implored Hemingway to come back to Paris and become the publication's editorial director. When Hemingway returned, Pound invited him to his studio and introduced him to Ford. Hemingway made a poignant first impression on Ford by shadowboxing his way through their first encounter, Ford recalled, while Pound informed Ford that Hemingway was the finest prose stylist in the world. Duly impressed, Ford made Hemingway his second in command at the *transatlantic.*

It was a fraught collaboration from the start. First of all, Ford didn't pay Hemingway, an arrangement almost guaranteed to brew resentment. Second, while Ford was a highly esteemed writer, he could also be distinctly ridiculous. He seemed almost predestined for a wicked Hemingway parody. Thanks to his rotundity and a fringe of blond hair that drooped from his upper lip, Ford was frequently likened to a walrus. Being embraced by him was like being "the toast under the poached egg," said one writer.

None of this ridicule seems to have had an adverse effect on Ford's self-esteem. Like Gertrude Stein and Ezra Pound, Ford saw himself both as a director of modern literature and a mentor to the new generation. "He was always generous, particularly to young writers, often too generous," recalled Sherwood Anderson. And like Stein, Ford was quick to espouse his own genius. He had an incorrigible penchant for self-aggrandizement. "Publishers and editors would clamor for his work," added Anderson. "When he awoke in the morning there would be a dozen of them camped on his doorstep. Indeed, in Ford's imagination they did camp there."

Ford's "imagination" was the source of great debate within the Crowd. He quickly became known around town as an unremitting liar. "Ford was blessed with total unrecall: he remembered nothing as it actually happened," recalled one expat. For the most part, Ford's fabrications seemed whimsical and innocuous. Sherwood Anderson recalled that Ford once invited him to visit a house of his in Pennsylvania. "He described the house, the view from the terrace at the front, the garden, the apple trees that grew on a nearby hillside . . . [It] was beautifully furnished and there was a retinue of servants." The only hitch: the house didn't actually exist—or if it did, it did not belong to Ford. That same evening, Ford offered Anderson a stay at two more fictional homes, one in Florida and one in California.

Ford's new deputy editor was less amused by Ford's fibs. Hemingway later claimed that Ford lied about money matters, which, for an aspiring writer living hand to mouth, was no small consideration. That tendency, according to Hemingway, scarred their relationship, although he did concede that not all of Ford's stories were injurious—such as one tale in which Ford tried to convince Hemingway that he had once crossed the American Southwest in the company of a puma.

The *transatlantic review* office occupied a cramped gallery in Bill Bird's Three Mountains Press quarters on the Quai d'Anjou. The ceiling in Ford's area hovered only five feet above the floor; he and his secretary constantly whacked their heads. Hemingway rarely wedged himself into the workspace—not necessarily because it was so tiny, but rather because of Ford's breath. It was "fouler . . . than the spout of any whale," Hemingway complained; he instead edited manuscripts down on the banks of the Seine. This was apparently fine with Ford, who had grown wary of his adjunct. "He comes and sits at my feet and praises me," he reported back to Gertrude Stein. "It makes me nervous."

Yet he loved Hemingway's writing. "I did not read more than six words of his before I decided to publish everything he sent me," Ford wrote later. He duly included a new Hemingway short story — "Indian Camp" — in the April 1924 issue of the *transatlantic*. The volume also contained reviews of *in our time* and *Three Stories and Ten Poems* — penned by Ford's secretary — which applauded the spareness of Hemingway's prose.

With his new position and acquisition of yet another enthusiastic patron-publisher, Hemingway had become, as writer John Dos Passos later put it, "a figure in the top Valhalla of literary Paris." Yet he was becoming increasingly desperate to conquer new territory. Major publications back home were still declining to publish him. "I was finally doing all the good writing I had promised myself," he later recalled. "But every day the rejected manuscripts would come back through the slot in the door." He admitted to crying as he read the rejection slips, and complained to Ford that it took a man years to build a reputation.

"That attitude is nonsense," Ford reassured him. "You will have a great name in no time at all."

"No time at all" was still too long a prospect for Hemingway. He knew that he had something to say, and he believed he was saying it differently and better and more accessibly than everyone else. Now he just needed to reach a vast audience. So far his vignettes and short stories — as brilliant as they were — had not been opening the right doors. It was time to step up his game.

"I knew I must write a novel," he later recalled.

He had known it for a long time. After all, he had planned to help kick off his career with a novel, but after Hadley lost his starter novel at the Gare de Lyon, he had apparently made little effort to re-create it or start a new one. In the meantime, everyone else his age had written one, Hemingway told himself — and here he was, practically over-the-hill at twenty-four, still without a major work to his name.

Yet the prospect of starting a full-length book was daunting. Just a few years earlier, Hemingway had regaled Hadley with ideas for novels; now, suddenly, the form seemed excruciating. Writing had become so much more complicated since he had come to Paris. He could no longer rely on naïve giddiness to propel him; his approach had become deeply considered and laborious. It was difficult enough laying down paragraphs each day, much less stringing together hundreds of them into a major work of modernist fiction.

"I would put it off," he decided, "until I could not help doing it. When I had to write it, then it would be the only thing to do and there would be no choice."

In other words, he simply planned to "let the pressure build."

LIKE GERTRUDE STEIN, Ford Madox Ford quickly became one of the Crowd's great hosts, although his parties were decidedly more raucous than hers. Sylvia Beach turned up at one party thrown by Ford and his wife at a big studio; a feast of beer and cheese had been laid out and an accordionist played noisy tunes. Ford bounded over to her barefoot; he made Beach take off her shoes and swept her up in a dance—although with Ford, she said, "it was more bouncing and prancing than dancing." He also hosted evenings at *bals musette,* including the one housed beneath the Hemingways' raffish first Paris apartment on the rue du Cardinal Lemoine.

On Thursdays, Ford hosted teas at the *transatlantic*'s little office. These gatherings had a more literary tenor than his dances, and were well attended by the starving artist contingent. "Famished beginners were sustained by the lavish crumpets and sandwiches, nut bread and plum cake, possibly their only meal that day," recalled one former attendee. Ford dispensed literary advice along with the delectables: "Observe, listen, cut, polish, place," he instructed.

Hemingway rarely attended the teas, even though Hadley liked Ford and got a kick out of his painter wife, Stella Bowen, who once created an amusing portrait of Ford passed out upright in a chair, his mouth hanging open. That spring, however, Hemingway made a tea party appearance, at which he first encountered expat editor and writer Harold Loeb. This meeting would alter the course of both men's lives.

Hemingway "had a shy, disarming smile and did not seem interested in the other guests," Loeb remembered years later. To him, Hemingway looked cool and unpretentious. "I thought never before had I encountered an American so unaffected by living in Paris," he added.

Loeb had every intention of becoming affected by living in Paris. Now thirty-two, he had come to France in an ongoing yet half-hearted bid to reinvent himself. The descendant of two of New York City's richest and most prominent Jewish families, the Loebs and the Guggenheims, he had for several years been playing at being a "poverty-stricken Bohemian," as he put it. Years earlier, as a child, he had had a conversation with his father, a Wall Street broker, which haunted him. One evening after work, his father marched into Loeb's nursery and gathered the boy up. He had some serious advice to impart.

"Harold," he said, "keep off Wall Street . . . Make something. Create something. Don't be a broker. We're nothing but parasites.'"

Loeb could not forget these words. Instead of marching straight into New York's Jewish society circles after finishing at Princeton, he worked as a day laborer in a Canadian construction camp. After abandoning this adventure, Loeb joined the army during the war and became a first sergeant, although he never made it overseas; after that, he backed a New York City–based avant-garde bookstore called the Sunwise Turn. By this time he had also acquired a wife, a wellborn woman from his New York social circle, who became increasingly dismayed by her husband's *vie bohème* fantasy once there were two new little Loebs to consider.

Yet Loeb was not ready to surrender the guise. He sold his share of the bookshop; the proceeds "seemed to burn a hole in my pocket," he recalled. He had also received a $50,000 inheritance while still at Princeton. After parting ways with his unhappy wife and children, Loeb departed for Europe, and with those funds launched a new literary magazine called *Broom*. As the name indicated, he was making a clean sweep of things.

By the time Hemingway met Loeb at that fateful 1924 tea party, Loeb was once again at liberty. Financial difficulties had just doomed the magazine after a twenty-one-issue run, but it had been a surprisingly impressive addition to the literary landscape. Loeb had launched it as a counterpoint to the more established literary magazines of the day and aimed to feature some new voices. Even *The Dial* "tended to repeat the same names over and over," he complained, adding, "No longer was there novelty in publishing T. S. Eliot or James Joyce, Mina Loy or Marianne Moore." With *Broom* he had intended to bring together young American writers whose common trait was "disapproval of the generation that preceded them." The list of contributors ended up being more varied, and included Dostoyevsky, Virginia Woolf, Robert Graves, Gertrude Stein — and a writer who called himself "H.A.L.," otherwise known as Harold Loeb.

Like practically everyone else in town, Loeb was trying his hand at being modern on paper. In his contribution to the experimentalism of the times, Loeb had decided to omit most of the "a's" and "the's" from the manuscript of his first novel; the publisher would demand their return before agreeing to let the book roll off his presses.

Socially, he got mixed reviews within the colony: certain Crowd members may have vied for publication in *Broom,* but that didn't necessarily mean that they had to like its editor. The obviousness of his wealth seems to have been off-putting. Loeb's relatives regularly traveled across at least two continents swathed in luxury; his mother once arrived in Paris "with a newly acquired husband, a Packard, and a present . . . so generous that it enabled me to live comfortably for quite some time," Loeb recalled. Uncle Daniel Guggenheim would materialize and treat Loeb to dinners at the Ritz. Loeb's younger cousin Peggy Guggenheim had also become an electric presence in the city as a young heiress in a tempestuous, gossip-generating marriage to the surrealist painter and writer Laurence Vail. Loeb and his clan were, in other words, laden with the trappings of privilege; his daughter called him a "spoiled man [who] always had everything he wanted."

He was not, of course, the only independently wealthy literary patron type in town: Gertrude Stein also had money to burn, but she was obviously dead serious in her commitment to modernism, and besides, she ran a semi-public bar at which all of the drinks were gratis. Yet Loeb appears to have had a reputation as a comparative lightweight, despite the intelligence and serious-mindedness of *Broom*. To one fellow expat, Loeb had "no more personality than a clean, expensive blanket lying folded across [a] café chair." And unlike Hemingway, Loeb didn't actively cultivate the Olympians. Expat writer Morrill Cody remembered Loeb as a vain person who "did stupid things," which included being rude to James Joyce and annoying Sylvia Beach.

Still, the literary life and literary men had great allure for Loeb, and he could tell, he later said, even during that first encounter at Ford's tea that Hemingway was the real deal. The two men also discussed hunting and fishing, and soon there were further meetings.

"The more I saw of Ernest the more I liked him," Loeb wrote later. He was especially impressed that Hemingway could be so tough and sporty, yet so sensitive and devoted to the art of writing. "I had long suspected that one reason for the scarcity of good writers in the United States was the popular impression . . . that artists were not quite virile," he added, offering up Oscar Wilde as a culpable example. "It was a good sign that men like Hemingway were taking up writing."

Predictably, Hemingway invited Loeb to face off in the boxing ring. Loeb had briefly boxed at Princeton but had swapped the sport for wrestling; Hemingway outweighed him by forty pounds, but Loeb pulled on the gloves anyway. The men began to spar. Luckily, Loeb quickly learned that Hemingway telegraphed his punches by "a jiggling of the pupil"—a discovery that gave Loeb a shot at survival. The two men also became tennis pals. For their first match, Hemingway invited Loeb to play on courts "near the prison where the guillotine was kept."

When they weren't bludgeoning each other or whacking balls across a net, Hemingway and Loeb frequented cafés and bars together, drinking and trading stories. Loeb told Hemingway details about his upbringing and adult life. He had many powerful advantages that Hemingway lacked — an Ivy League education, seemingly unlimited resources — and the inequity soon created tension between the men. But from Hemingway's point of view, Loeb had one particularly intolerable advantage: he was about to publish his first novel, *Doodab,* with Boni & Liveright, a major American publisher.

The tension built and eventually boiled over. Years later, Loeb recounted the probably inevitable confrontation. One rainy evening, the two men were eating oysters and drinking Pouilly-Fuissé at L'Avenue in Montparnasse. After a couple of bottles of wine, Loeb made a serious misstep. He had been thinking lately about why Hemingway was having such a difficult time breaking through, and decided to offer some constructive criticism.

"What you've got to do is bring in women," he advised. "People like to read about women and violence. You've got plenty of violence in your stories. Now all you need is women."

"Women?" asked Hemingway, who was likely staring at Loeb with murderous intensity.

It would probably be hard for Hemingway to understand, Loeb went on. After all, "a happily married man misses so much," he said. "Such as misery."

He then noticed that Hemingway's face had gone "stiff and dark" and that his teeth were bared.

"So I haven't had misery," Hemingway began. "So that's what you think."

Loeb tried to backpedal. "How about another bottle," he suggested desperately. "To hell with misery!"

But the damage had been done. Hemingway spent the rest of the evening punishing Loeb with details of his life's miseries. Loeb fiddled with the wineglasses and listened obligingly, not knowing what else to do.

"Sure," he said, somewhat feebly. "I should have known it."

The incident blew over, but there was another. In October of that year, the men traveled together to the medieval town of Senlis, just north of

Paris. One evening they were playing poker in their hotel. Loeb won hand after hand, yet Hemingway refused to stop. He ran out of cash and started writing IOU's. Loeb didn't want his money and "certainly didn't want his IOU's," but the pile kept growing. Finally, Hemingway wrote out an IOU for a hundred francs, raised Loeb, and won a hand.

The tables turned. Suddenly Loeb's luck ran out, and eventually his money ran out as well. He stood up from the table and tried to quit, "but Hem wanted to continue, [and] even tried to shame me into going on," Loeb recalled. The incident shifted the dynamic between them. Loeb felt that a "shadow seemed to come between us."

Still, the men continued to socialize, and Loeb's early delight in Hemingway evolved into blind adoration. Despite the undercurrent of resentment and competition, Loeb "relish[ed] his spontaneity [and] his zest for living."

Above all, Loeb admired what he called Hemingway's "great capacity for friendship." The more he saw of him, the more he liked him. The relationship became so important to Loeb that when Hemingway left town for a holiday, Paris suddenly felt empty.

AT LEAST ONE person had a sense of foreboding about Hemingway: Loeb's girlfriend, Utica, New York–born Kathleen Eaton Cannell, who went by "Kitty."

In 1924 Cannell was a thirty-three-year-old expat fashion correspondent and popular girl-about-town. She was also a lady of the stage, having danced, sung, and acted professionally, sometimes as a mime. More recently, Cannell had taken up writing; it was, she felt, a good break from the rigors of the stage and a much less exhausting discipline than singing.

Cannell knew everyone in Paris, especially those in the artistic set, and was therefore a great asset to any deserving arriviste to the colony. She had been helpful to Loeb during the *Broom* days, introducing him to Ford Madox Ford and wrangling talent and submissions for the magazine. Some suspected that she had been the brains behind the operation.

"The mistress of the editor," Malcolm Cowley, a former consultant to the *Broom* team, confided by letter to a friend, "[has taste that is] sounder than Loeb's, and I believe much stronger."

The Cannell-Loeb liaison likely made for great people-watching down at the Dôme. As a flashy heir to a fortune, Loeb always drew attention, but Cannell was said to be prone to jealous rages and apparently did not wait to conduct all of them in private. At that time their relationship was in limbo: Cannell was waiting for her divorce from Imagist poet Skipwith Cannell to come through, and was therefore a member of the prominent demographic known around town as the "alimony gang." (Paris was apparently a popular destination for the soon-to-be-divorced as well as the recently emancipated.) This state of limbo was perfectly fine with Loeb; he had since become divorced from the wife he had left behind in New York, and was in no hurry to return to the shackles of matrimony. Once Cannell's divorce case was due to come up in French court, he started to feel anxious.

"There is a security in having a sweetheart with a husband," he admitted.

Up to that point, their romance had had a certain church-and-state feel to it. Loeb and Cannell even occupied adjacent apartments, separated by a flimsy wall. Like his relationship with Hemingway, his arrangement with Cannell seemed potentially explosive.

Loeb and Cannell began visiting Hemingway and Hadley at their home above the sawmill; the two couples saw each other several times a week, sometimes dining out, sometimes playing tennis. Unlike her boyfriend, Cannell was not susceptible to Hemingway's charms.

"I instantly felt that Ernest was undependable and unpredictable," she later reported, adding that she could detect "weakness slant[ing] out of his wrists and ankles." She was mystified by Loeb's hero worship of Hemingway. "Doubtless Hem represented some sort of ideal to him," she ventured.

Yet Cannell liked and respected Hadley, even though she was appalled by the Hemingways' living conditions. Her own insistent glamour made Hadley's poverty stand out even more starkly.

"Her clothes are falling off," Cannell told Loeb. "She can't even show herself on the street." Hemingway may have been able to wreathe their life in the carpenter's mill flat with a certain purist romanticism, but Cannell was having none of it. It was Hemingway's fault that Hadley was clad in rags, she insisted, and Hadley was a "perfect fool to take it." After all, she pointed out, they were living on Hadley's money — or what was left of it, anyway.

Cannell promptly made Hadley into a pet project, taking her shopping and on antiquing outings. "All the in-girls were collecting earrings," she recalled, a trend that probably had as much relevance to Hadley as a vogue for hunting Siberian tigers. These jaunts were also a mischievous jab at Hemingway. It gave her pleasure to hold herself up as a "bad example to a submissive wife."

Hemingway did have one redeeming quality in Cannell's eyes: he loved cats. She eventually gave one to the Hemingways; they named it "Feather Puss." A little while later, Cannell ran into Hemingway at a café. He was looking depressed.

"I have just one consolation in life," he informed her.

She waited, expecting him to say Hadley or Bumby. Instead he told her, "My kitty."

Hemingway may simply have been punning on her nickname, but Cannell apparently took the incident as evidence of what she saw as Hemingway's selfish and inconsiderate nature. She complained about him to Loeb repeatedly over the next year, but her opinions made no difference. Unlike his feelings for Kitty, Loeb's affection toward Hemingway seems to have been unconditional. He would soon lay his resources at his friend's feet—including entrée to his powerful publisher in New York. This was a most welcome development. Hemingway was exhausting his publishing opportunities in Paris, and it was time to begin cultivating the big guns back home. Loeb would soon prove an invaluable asset in bridging the gap.

5

Bridges to New York

NO MATTER HOW BROKE the Hemingways were, they always seemed to have enough money to go to Spain. In May 1924, Hemingway wrote to his family that he and Hadley were planning a June trip to that "wonderful and beautiful country." They would be going trout fishing in the Pyrenees and also planned to hike from Pamplona to Saint-Jean-Pied-de-Port; Hemingway was keeping his fingers crossed that they wouldn't be mistaken for smugglers and shot. He began buying pesetas in anticipation of the trip.

In the meantime, Paris continued to offer up both frustrations and pleasures. In addition to weathering his publication blues, Hemingway was now at loggerheads with Ford Madox Ford. He had begun to suspect that Ford was praising his own work under pseudonyms in the *transatlantic* (he was correct); he reported this to Ezra Pound, adding that Ford was running the magazine as a "compromise." All of the work that Ford was publishing could just as easily be found in other magazines already; why didn't he take some risks? Hemingway wondered. After all, he had barely any subscribers or advertisers to offend.

"The thing to do with Ford," Hemingway wrote, "is to kill him."

Nor did Hemingway appreciate edits that Ford had made to a short humor piece he had whipped up. He complained to Pound, but also implored him not to mention anything to Ford, as he didn't want to start a kerfuffle — at least not yet.

Around this time, Hemingway connected with humor writer Donald Ogden Stewart, who had alighted in Paris that spring. Stewart was one of the era's premier satirists, then an extremely popular genre. His first book, which bore a thirty-word title — *A Parody Outline of History Wherein May Be Found a Curiously Irreverent Treatment of American Historical Events Imagining Them As They Would Be Narrated By America's Most Character-*

istic Contemporary Authors — had become a best-seller and made him famous. A year or two earlier, when Stewart was about to make a trip to Europe, an editor friend advised him to look up Hemingway in Paris, even though Stewart was an established heavyweight and Hemingway still just an aspirant. By chance, Stewart had run into Hemingway at Madame Lecomte's, a restaurant on the Île Saint-Louis.

"I didn't know anything about him as a writer, but he seemed to be my kind of guy," Stewart recalled. This meant, he explained, that they both liked to eat and drink heavily, and that Hemingway proved an appreciative audience who "understood my kind of humor."

They became fast friends. Hemingway even lent his apartment to Stewart after that first meeting; as he was about to go to Switzerland for a few weeks with Hadley and Bumby, Hemingway "insisted, with characteristic enthusiasm, that I occupy his rooms until he brought them back," Stewart wrote later. "I woke up the next morning in his room, very happy, with a note from him telling me where I could get eggs and milk."

For Hemingway, it was another serendipitous acquaintance. Stewart was even richer in New York literary contacts than Loeb. Not only did he know influential editors and publishers across town, but also he was an insider at that city's own literary Olympus, the Algonquin Round Table, an informal yet exclusive lunchtime club attended by two dozen or so of the town's sharpest wits. Food was beside the point; rather, martinis were the essential fuel as the Algonquinites gathered to dazzle and decimate one another with banter.

"Conversation in the early twenties had to be one wise-crack after another," recalled John Dos Passos. "Cracks had to fly back and forth continually like the birds in badminton." Stewart was, he added, "one of the most skilled at this exhilarating sport." In his memoir, *By a Stroke of Luck!* Stewart professed that this "dog-eat-dog" world always made him feel ill at ease — "most of my ripostes occur to me three or four hours after I have been attacked," he claimed — yet he was still a welcome presence at the table.

In the year since his first encounter with Hemingway, Stewart had taken some blows. Both he and booksellers nationwide had harbored high hopes for his sophomore effort, a satirical time-travel manifesto titled *Aunt Polly's Story of Mankind* — but much to the chagrin of all, the book had flopped. In the wake of this disappointment, in April 1924 Stewart absconded to Paris, where he and Hemingway crossed paths once again.

The dynamic between them had shifted somewhat. Stewart's *Aunt Polly* failure had temporarily put him on his back foot. Hemingway was by now a respected literary figure in Paris, and Stewart shared with him the manuscript of a new novel he was working on. He was delighted when Hemingway asked to publish some of it in the *transatlantic*. (Some of that delight seeped away when Stewart learned that contributors to the *transatlantic* were uncompensated.) Regardless, he was happy to accept Hemingway's invitation to join him in Spain that summer, along with a group of other writers and editors.

"Bring plenty of pesetas," Hemingway advised, adding that Stewart could expect both the *plage* (beach) and the *poules* (prostitutes) to be of the highest caliber.

Stewart accepted Hemingway's hospitality and encouragement without reserve.

"I was to learn later that when Ernest was enthusiastic about something it was extremely dangerous to resist anything, especially friendliness," he wrote years later.

THE HEMINGWAYS' FIRST FORAY to the San Fermín fiesta in Pamplona had been an adventure for two. But in July 1924, leaving Bumby in the care of his nanny, they brought along a large entourage, which included both of Hemingway's Paris book publishers, Bill Bird and Robert McAlmon; Bird's wife, Sally; Hemingway's wartime friend Eric Edward "Chink" Dorman-Smith; and John Dos Passos, whom Hemingway had first met during the war. A fever pitch of excitement was a prerequisite for attending guests.

"[Hemingway] had an evangelistic streak that made him work to convert his friends to whatever mania he was encouraging at the time," recalled Dos Passos.

Pamplona still felt as pure and insular as it had the summer before, untainted by influxes of Americans and other tourists.

"[The town] was ours," Stewart wrote later. "No one else had discovered it . . . It was vintage Hemingway. It was a happy time . . . it was a masculine time."

Spaniards in blue berets danced in the town's squares as small bands of natives streamed through the city, playing drums and blowing whistles. Hundreds of peasants from the nearby mountains crowded the streets, wearing garlic necklaces and spurting wine into their mouths from goatskin wine bags. Fifteen-foot papier-mâché giants were paraded through the town. At night, fireworks exploded in the sky, and revelers danced in the streets until dawn.

"From every alley [came] the rhythms of Basque fife and drum or the bleating of Galician bagpipes or the rattle of castanets," wrote Dos Passos. "As a show the San Firmímes are terrific. Bands. Processions. *Cohetes* [rockets]."

The heat was almost savage; it "sweated through one's flesh and bones," McAlmon recalled. Once the fiesta took off, it was a surreal, sleepless, adrenaline-and-alcohol-fueled marathon. The Hemingway entourage started each day by slugging black coffee; they then moved on quickly to Pernod. They lost each other in the bacchanal and found each other again — sometimes not until the following day. One might be engulfed by a roving crowd of musicians or dancers or peasants at any moment. Every night, the drinking continued until the sun came up or one passed out, whichever came first. The expats couldn't even keep up with themselves: Hemingway later claimed that Donald Stewart had thrown up all over Pamplona.

When he wasn't vomiting, Stewart got deep into the fiesta spirit. One night he danced in the main plaza with around two hundred *riau-riau* dancers swirling around him; they then carried him off on their shoulders. For the rest of the fiesta he was an adored mascot among the peasants.

The festival truly began on July 7 with the running of the bulls, or the *encierro,* a dramatic ritual in which the bulls for that day's fights were driven from their corrals at the town's edge through barricaded streets into the bullring at Pamplona's center. At dawn, small bands began circling through the town, playing ancient reedy oboes and beating drums. The sound woke up the hundreds of people sleeping in the streets: bodies carpeted the town's squares, benches, and sidewalks. By six o'clock in the morning, thousands of people lined the bull run and crowded onto balconies to see the spectacle.

Suddenly, at seven o'clock, a rocket shot into the sky, announcing that the bulls were being released. Then a second rocket was launched into the air: the bulls were coming. Down the corridor, a crowd of men scrambled ahead of the animals. The bulls thundered after them in a cloud of dust. If no one tripped and fell, the half-mile dash took only a few minutes — but tramplings were common occurrences. When the bulls reached the ring, more rockets were fired. Amateur hour had begun: anyone with enough *cojones* could leap into the ring with the animals and play toreador.

Hemingway was ready to join them. If he had been undergoing a "self-hardening" process during his Spanish voyage a year earlier, this year there was a new variation on the theme.

"[He] had been talking a great deal about courage, and how a man needs to test himself to prove to himself that he can take it," recalled McAlmon.

Naturally, this now meant goading a two-thousand-pound animal into charging him in front of thousands of people. That week in Pamplona, he jumped into the ring many times. During one of his forays, he tried to get the attention of a steer by waving his coat; when the distracted animal ignored him, Hemingway caught the steer's horns and tried to throw it. The crowd cheered. The steer "ran away bellowing a bewildered moo," McAlmon remembered.

McAlmon had no intention of following Hemingway into the ring, but Donald Stewart did. He later stated that although he was usually a "practicing coward," he had been compelled into the ring because "Hemingway shamed me into it." He didn't want to lose Hemingway's regard, which had become precious to him.

"Ernest was somebody you went along with, or else," he noted.

Stewart drank some wine and dropped into the bullring. In due course a bull charged him full force and knocked him "ass over teakettle." He went after the bull again; this time it promptly tossed him into the air. When he got up off the ground, Hemingway came over and clapped him on the back.

"I felt as though I had scored a winning touchdown," Stewart wrote later.

He had, instead, scored a few broken ribs. Once again he was hoisted up on the shoulders of enthusiastic Spaniards, who carried him out of the ring.

The bullring antics of the Hemingway entourage were captured by local photographers and immortalized in souvenir postcards. News of the Hemingway-Stewart heroics quickly spread back to Paris and even to the States. Hemingway was again proving himself to be great copy. The *Chicago Tribune* ran an item proclaiming BULL GORES 2 YANKS ACTING AS TOREADORES.

The story cited the afflicted parties as one "MacDonald Ogden Stewart" and Ernest Hemingway, a "Hero of World War." According to the *Tribune*'s account, a bull gored Stewart, who had pledged to "leap on the bull's back, blow smoke in his eyes, and then beat him down." When Hemingway attempted a rescue, the bull gored him as well. He was spared a grisly demise, the article announced, only because the bull's horns were bandaged.

Stewart denied that either he or Hemingway had been the source of the original reports ("They must have come from Bird or McAlmon or Dos Passos"), although Hemingway wrote a letter to the *Toronto Star,* clarifying facts the paper had gotten wrong in its own separate account. He also boasted to his former colleagues that he and Stewart had accrued a following that materialized daily to watch them. He clearly had a strong sense of how he wanted to be showcased in the press. It had also become clear that the exotic, dangerous world of bullfighting—and accounts of expat antics within that world (the *Tribune* article noted that all members of the Hemingway entourage were American writers living in Paris) —were of keen editorial interest back home, just as stories about the Paris colony had enthralled readers.

A week after it started, on July 14, the festival ended with an effusion of fireworks and rockets in the main plaza. The Hemingway crew was hungover and spent. John Dos Passos's enthusiasm had completely waned by the end of the fête. Everyone had been too exhibitionistic to suit him, and the "sight of a crowd of young men trying to prove how hombre they were got on my nerves," he wrote later. The occasional bullfight was fine for him, but every day for a week was simply too much. For Hemingway, however, it had been a different story entirely.

"He stuck like a leech till he had every phase of the business in his blood," Dos Passos recalled, "and saturated himself to the bursting point." Donald Stewart had been the crowd's favorite clown; McAlmon had been the cynical but amused observer. But Hemingway had been the "cynosure of all eyes."

THE HUNGOVER ENTOURAGE repaired to a quiet, remote Basque village in the Pyrenees called Burguete. It was the perfect place to recover from the debaucheries of Pamplona. The whole party moved into the little village inn, where they dined on peasant fare: goat cheese, tortillas, black bread, and coffee with goat's milk. Sheep and goats dotted the hillsides, and the trout-filled Irati River flowed a few miles away. The crew took picnic lunches and hiked to the river.

Robert McAlmon watched his author during the outings. As they fished in the falls, Hemingway was mentally working on a short story that would be titled "Big Two-Hearted River."

"He was so intent thinking about what it was that a man who was fishing would be thinking about . . . that he didn't catch many trout, but he jotted down notes for the story," he recalled. His cynicism about Hemingway was growing. He deemed the resulting short story "a stunt and very artificial," and he would soon conclude that Hemingway was "a very good businessman, a publicity seeker, who looks ahead and calculates, and uses rather than wonders about people."

Hemingway apparently did not improve McAlmon's opinion with the tantrum he threw on one of the group's country walks. He suspected that Hadley was pregnant again (she was not), and complained so vigorously about the prospect of once more becoming a father that Bill Bird's wife, Sally, dressed him down in front of the others.

"Stop acting like a damn fool and a crybaby," she berated him. "You're responsible too. Either you do something about not having it, or you have it."

Even after the matter of Hadley's pregnancy had been resolved, Hemingway found other things to be glum about. He reported to Ezra Pound that the bullring was the only place left where valor and art still coincided. He envied the acclaim that was showered upon matadors but denied to young authors. Matadors got pointed out in the street and won ovations and respect. Writers had to wait until they were eighty-nine years old to get such accolades. Also, in the literary world, the more "meazly and shitty the guy," the more success he could wrangle, Hemingway contended, and offered up James Joyce as an example.

Money woes were back in full force, adding to his dark mindset: he told Pound that his dwindling resources meant that he was going to have to quit writing.

"I never will have a book published," he lamented.

What was bound to happen next, he feared, was that some inferior competitor would rip him off and stage the massive stylistic coup that Hemingway badly wanted to spearhead. By the following spring, he grimly joked, "some son of a bitch will have copied everything I've written and they will simply call me another of his imitators."

It was time to go back to Paris, and to the business of breaking through.

PROBABLY TO NO one's surprise, Hemingway's rupture with Ford Madox Ford and the *transatlantic review* was not far off. Like many ambitious but shakily financed lit mags before it, the *transatlantic* was soon on the ropes. While Hemingway had been planning his trip to Spain, Ford had gone back to the States to try to secure more backing, leaving Hemingway to close the magazine's July issue and pull together the August one. Hemingway took the opportunity to add to the July issue an unsigned editorial skewering several prominent surrealists, and then devoted the August issue almost entirely to his various American friends, even though the magazine was supposed to feature international content. By the time Ford came back to Paris, it was too late to make changes in the August issue. Instead, he inserted an editorial, making sure his readers knew that the issue was Hemingway's sole handiwork, and that with the next number, the review would "re-assume its international aspect." Then, in the October issue, Hemingway published an attack on T. S. Eliot, for which Ford in turn ran another apologetic editorial in November. By then the men were no longer on speaking terms. Hemingway informed Gertrude Stein that Ford was "an absolute liar" and a "crook." The partnership dissolved; the magazine folded a few months later.

In the wake of the fallout, Hemingway turned to satire. For him, writing "could be an arrow of revenge in [his] quiver," as his future daughter-in-law put it years later. He had not only been working on new short stories but also scribbling down satirical pieces about his Left Bank compatriots, including an unpublished sketch featuring Ford and his wife bickering at the Nègre de Toulouse restaurant. Another story—eventually published as "Mr. and Mrs. Elliot"—depicted the travails of a couple trying to have a baby ("They tried as often as Mrs. Elliot could stand it," ran the second line), based on the real-life conception struggles of writer Chard Powers Smith and his wife. He also wrote a story about an overweight virgin who comes to Paris yearning for romance, inspired by the woes of one of Hadley's friends. Hemingway had a little bit of poison for everyone during this time, and he was becoming quite adept at co-opting the lives and vulnerabilities of others as grist for his literary mill.

That said, this gossip-lit bender coincided with nobler writings and motives as well. Late that past summer he had finished "Big Two-Hearted River," the story he had been mulling over while fishing in Burguete. The finished product, which he eventually divided into two stories, not only showcased his formidable new style, but also contained a later-deleted passage illuminating what is widely considered to be a window into Hemingway's own thinking about his writing at the time: "[Nick] wanted to be a great writer. He was pretty sure he would be . . . He, Nick, wanted to write about country so it would be there like Cézanne had done it in paint-ing . . . He felt almost holy about it. It was deadly serious."

"Big Two-Hearted River" was the ninth completed story he had writ-ten since the Toronto debacle. Together with the three stories that had ap-peared in *Three Stories and Ten Poems,* this material seemed enough for a full-length book. Hemingway cobbled together a manuscript, lacing the *in our time* vignettes in among the short stories. Soon he was calling the book *In Our Time* — with each word capitalized to differentiate it from his slen-der Paris book. It wasn't the all-important novel he knew that he still had to write, but it was enough to court major American publishers and get his name known in New York at last.

Both old and new friends were standing by to advance Hemingway's cause. By October, Donald Stewart had gone back to New York City, where he was staying at the Yale Club. Hemingway charged John Dos Passos with bringing the *In Our Time* manuscript across the Atlantic and hand-delivering it to Stewart, who had pledged to show it to his own pub-lisher, the George H. Doran Company.

Dos Passos would also act as an ambassador. He later recalled that he had, upon reading the vignettes from the original *in our time,* "right away put [Hemingway] down as a man with obvious talent for handling the English language." He began "trumpeting it abroad" and came up with his own way of pitching Hemingway and his material. "My story was that basing his wiry short sentences on cablese and the King James Bible, Hem would become the first great American stylist," he later explained.

In addition, Harold Loeb hastened to be of assistance. If he had been fretting before about "why Hem was getting nowhere," as he put it, here was his opportunity to help his friend at last. He immediately began strat-egizing the presentation of Hemingway to his publishing house, Boni & Liveright — and to Mr. Liveright himself.

It would prove a most memorable introduction.

HORACE LIVERIGHT was not exactly a conventional publisher. A decade earlier, he had gate-crashed the clubbish publishing world and had been scandalizing his colleagues ever since.

Nothing in his early background had portended that he would become a man of letters. While many of his colleagues at other houses boasted Ivy League educations, Liveright had exempted himself from the rigors of formal education after grammar school. To earn his living as a teenager, he worked in a Pennsylvania stockbrokerage house. Yet he clearly had a more grandiose vision for his future. He eventually moved to New York and set up shop in a colonnade at the old Waldorf-Astoria Hotel, where he paid a bellboy to page him as "Lord Roseberry." He composed an opera; it got as far as rehearsals but was never officially performed. Then, in his mid-twenties, Liveright founded Pick-Quick Paper, a toilet paper concern backed by his father-in-law, a vice president at the International Paper Company. Liveright had proudly named the product himself. Only when the venture ended disastrously did he turn his attention to more cerebral paper products.

He was casting about for a new enterprise when he met Albert Boni. The latter had used his Harvard tuition money to open a bookshop in Greenwich Village, but his dream was to found a publishing house. Liveright proposed himself as Boni's partner, and in 1917 the men announced the foundation of Boni & Liveright. Boni would swiftly exit the enterprise over creative differences, but the house retained his name. The firm was often described as a "madhouse" and its proprietor alternately deemed by his fellow publishers a glamour-seeking charlatan, a reckless upstart, or an outrageous interloper. Liveright kept his checkbook on his desk next to a bottle of whisky; his waiting room boasted a highly unusual atmosphere.

"When you went to see him in his publishing house often enough the whole outer office was filled with chorus girls," Sherwood Anderson recalled. "It wouldn't have surprised me when I went there to have had one of the women jump up and, with a practice swing, kick my hat off."

It probably would have surprised no one if Liveright had commissioned the chorus girls as ornamentation, but they were usually there to audition, as the ever multi-venture-minded Liveright had also taken up theatrical producing. In the house's waiting room, dancers and authors alike could expect to keep company with Liveright's army of bootleggers as well. It was not exactly the most reverential environment.

Boni & Liveright quickly became known as the unofficial publishers of the bohemian Greenwich Village crowd, and almost as immediately became "the most noisome stench in the nostrils of the established [houses]," as Hemingway's first friend in Paris, Lewis Galantière, would put it. Boni & Liveright had posed an immediate threat to the older houses: the firm had managed to snare major talent right away; for example, it signed literary giant Theodore Dreiser in its first year. Liveright would also soon poach Sherwood Anderson from B. W. Huebsch with the lure of a substantial five-year contract and a $100 weekly allowance. These acquisitions showed that the scrappy house meant business. The established publishers could revile Liveright as much as they pleased, but they could not dismiss him.

Like other publishers, Horace Liveright had begun to scout talent among the expats in Montparnasse. One of the house's former vice presidents, Leon Fleischman, had moved to Paris and was charged with finding manuscripts suitable for the American market. Harold Loeb and Fleischman knew each other from New York, and now, as Hemingway was preparing his *In Our Time* manuscript, Loeb arranged to bring him over to Fleischman's apartment.

Kitty Cannell grew anxious in advance of the meeting. She worried that Hemingway harbored anti-Semitic tendencies and might create a terrible scene in front of Fleischman and his wife, Helen. She said as much to Loeb. He brushed her off.

"I tended at that time to ignore the gossip, current in 'The Quarter,' about Hem's temper," he wrote later. "I was aware that people exaggerated."

The evening of the meeting arrived. Perhaps out of ghoulish curiosity, Cannell came along with Loeb and Hemingway when they turned up at the Fleischmans' flat near the Champs-Élysées. Helen Fleischman answered the door.

"It's the maid's day off," she explained as she ushered them in.

Leon Fleischman then stepped forward, wearing a velvet smoking jacket. Both Cannell and Loeb could tell that Hemingway disliked Fleischman on sight.

Drinks were sipped; small talk was scrounged up. Cannell and Helen gossiped about Peggy Guggenheim and her husband. Loeb tried to liven up the atmosphere by recounting a story about "two little colored girls who had their picture taken at Coney Island."

Eventually the men began to talk business. Fleischman kicked things off with a speech: He had been hearing about Hemingway as an up-and-coming talent, he said, but one never could tell whether a new writer would actually prove popular. The public needed to be educated about new literary trends.

For Loeb, it was an excruciating monologue. "I seemed to be hearing Leon with Hem's ears," he wrote later. "Everything he said sounded precious, supercilious, affected."

Hemingway swigged impassively from a glass of scotch. When Fleischman glanced in his direction for reactions, Hemingway rewarded him with emphatic grins. Loeb grew even more alarmed.

"I want to read your stories," Fleischman finally announced. If he deemed them sufficiently impressive, he went on, he would send them to Liveright with his recommendation. "Horace knows it pays to accept my advice [but] it must be tactfully put, of course," he added. "Horace think he makes his own decisions."

Mercifully, the gathering concluded shortly afterward. Loeb, Cannell, and Hemingway left together.

"In the street I made an anodyne remark about having spent a nice evening," Cannell recalled. "Hemingway exploded into profanity: 'Double god damned kikes!'—with a lot of picturesque explicit expletives."

Later, Loeb and Cannell would give different versions of what occurred next. Loeb recalled that he and Cannell went out to dinner and discussed what had happened.

"See what I mean?" Cannell supposedly reprimanded him. "You never believe me. I'm glad he said what he did. Perhaps you'll listen to me next time."

Loeb hadn't cared for Hemingway's reaction, but he still made excuses for him. "He likes to express himself violently," he told Kitty. In another recounting of the incident, Loeb recalled telling her that Hemingway had "used the word as I might say mick or dago. It doesn't mean a thing."

Cannell remembered a pithier and more visceral exchange. In her version, Harold stood stunned on the sidewalk while Hemingway marched away.

"Well, Baby there's your future friend," she remembered saying.

"'Oh no," Harold reportedly replied. "If Hem thought of me as a Jew he wouldn't have spoken that way in front of me."

IN OUR TIME was now en route to two major American publishers— Doran and Liveright. Now Hemingway just had to sit back and sweat bullets until the responses came in.

Weeks went by. In his letters he seemed alternately nervous and confident. He implored Stewart to send updates and thanked him "ever so god damn much" for his help. A few days later he wrote to a friend that he had a book coming out in New York the following spring, although no such deal with any publisher was yet in place and he had yet to hear from either publisher.

"Doran are going to publish it I think," he told his old friend Bill Smith. "We're dickering now. Boni and Liveright want it if they dont come through but I'm all for keeping out of the manuals of the Semites as long as possible."

Yet by mid-December he still had no definitive answer from Doran, the Semites at Liveright, or any other publisher. He peddled a farcical story to *Vanity Fair*—Donald Stewart's turf—titled "My Life in The Bull Ring with Donald Ogden Stewart." It was rejected. His letters took on a less boastful tenor. He and Hadley prepared for a family trip to Austria to do some therapeutic skiing and hearty eating.

"Same old shit going on here," he reported to Robert McAlmon. "Glad to be getting away."

Just before Christmas, the little family made its way to the Hotel Taube in Schruns, a tiny mountain town in western Austria. Like Burguete that past summer, Schruns was remote and unpretentious and devoid of Montparnassians. And like France, Austria had become absurdly cheap even for struggling American writers. The entire family boarded at their pension for around two dollars a day.

Hemingway kept himself busy as he waited for word from New York. He and Hadley skied while a fetching Austrian girl took care of Bumby. The locals soon took to calling Hemingway the "Black Christ," in honor of the black beard he grew while there. (If the Austrians were feeling particularly elaborate, they promoted Hemingway to "the Black Kirsch-drinking Christ.") He spent evenings sampling the thirty-six different types of beer on tap at the Taube and playing illegal poker games behind shuttered windows. Hadley knitted wool sweaters.

Harold Loeb had originally planned to tag along on the Austrian adventure, but back in Paris he was still haggling with Horace Liveright over changes to his novel *Doodab*. He delayed his journey to Schruns—"I wanted to get the matter of my book cleared up first, for I could not really enjoy myself with that hanging fire," he later recalled—and eventually booked a berth back to the States instead, departing just after New Year's. He also took advantage of this absence to try to remove himself from his romantic entanglement with Cannell, writing her a "difficult and painful letter." It simply wasn't fair to her, he explained: "She should have a husband, and I did not want to marry anyone. For over three years we had been close friends [and] it hadn't worked." Cannell did not agree. They remained a couple after all.

Before learning that Loeb was going to New York instead of coming to Austria, Hemingway had written to him, imploring him to hurry up and bring along some good whisky, and adding, "Bring my book from Fleisch-mann will you?"—perhaps on the assumption that Doran was going to bite. A week later, however, he wrote to Loeb again, this time a profanity-laden missive full of news, ire, and strategy.

Doran had rejected *In Our Time*.

Hemingway had just received a letter from Donald Stewart with a check nestled inside. At first, Hemingway assumed the money was from Doran, but rather it was a personal check from Stewart, a morale-boosting Christmas present to help take the sting out of the rejection letter also en-closed from publisher George Doran.

"They were all agreed on the power of my stuff and what a great book it was," Hemingway reported to Loeb. "Only they didnt want to publish it."

The Doran editorial team had objected to the sexual content of some of the stories—but also, they simply didn't want to lead a new writer out of the stable with a short story collection. That said, "he would go all the way with me in a novel," Hemingway told Loeb.

Suddenly the Semites at Boni & Liveright looked more palatable. Hemingway didn't know it at the time, but initial enthusiasm for his manu-script hadn't been particularly strong at that house either. When he reached New York, Harold Loeb went to Liveright's brownstone office and asked one of the firm's readers, Beatrice Kaufman, about *In Our Time*. He was horrified to learn that it had been relegated to the slush pile. Kaufman fished it out and informed Loeb that she was just about to return it.

Loeb pleaded with her not to send it back: "You'll live to regret it. You are missing a tremendous opportunity. He can write. One paragraph will tell you that. And his next is going to be a novel."

His impassioned plea apparently did the trick: when he stopped by the office a week later, Kaufman told Loeb that Liveright had accepted *In Our Time* for publication. Sherwood Anderson had also buoyed the effort and attempted to convince Liveright of the book's importance.

"Anderson [was] then at the peak of his reputation and Liveright's star author, [and] since Liveright was anxious to hold Anderson, his best-sell-ing literary author, in our time was accepted," Loeb later recalled.

The publisher's offer: $200 against royalties. Both Loeb and Stewart cabled their congratulations to Hemingway, who received the news with mixed emotions.

"Hurray for you and the news and Horace Liveright and the whole business," he wrote to Loeb, adding that while he felt "wonderful" about the book, he also felt as if he had been "kicked in the balls." Apparently "it had taken half the population of New York" to sell the book — and to Liveright, no less.

Still, a big American publisher was a big American publisher. A week after receiving the news from Loeb and Stewart, Hemingway sent a cable to Liveright:

DELIGHTED ACCEPT
= HEMINGWAY

PART II

6

The Catalysts

WHEN THE HEMINGWAYS returned from Schruns to Paris in March 1925, the city suddenly felt overcrowded.

"Now everybody seemed to be coming to Paris," wrote Harold Loeb, who also returned from New York that month. Hordes of American tourists would have piled into Loeb's boat and the other transatlantic liners plowing across the Atlantic to France that year. The franc was once more rising against the dollar, but this did nothing to stem the flow. All of that press about the wonders of Paris was clearly having an effect. By one estimate, in 1925 some five thousand Americans arrived in Paris every week. The city trembled with an almost volcanic excitement.

"Too much advertising had turned the spontaneity of 'la vie bohème' into a huge commercial success," recalled Montparnasse bartender Jimmie Charters. For the original postwar expats, the tide had begun to turn, he felt. The Quarter was acquiring a carnival-like atmosphere, complete with an audience of gawkers eager to sample a bit of authentic bohemia.

As ever, introductions to James Joyce, Gertrude Stein, Ezra Pound, and others of their rank were hotly sought after. Hemingway was now situated firmly among them. No longer was he humbly toting letters of introduction to luminaries; rather, that spring, people of importance, interest, or possible utility were introduced to *him*. Over the past year, Hemingway had become an even more powerful attraction within the Crowd and to voyeurs alike. Word went around that he now had a big American book deal in the works. According to one of his contemporaries, he had become an "overwhelming prize" at café tables and social gatherings.

"Ernest did have that gift for attracting public homage," recalled expat writer Malcolm Cowley. "'Charisma' would be the later word for it."

Some in the Crowd watched Hemingway's ascent through narrowed eyes, including those who had once happily helped build his platform.

Robert McAlmon, for instance, had decided that Hemingway was an utter phony. "He's the original Limelight Kid, just you watch him for a few months," he ranted one day after running into Hemingway in a Montparnasse café. "Wherever the limelight is, you'll find Ernest with his big lovable boyish grin, making hay . . . He's going places, he's got a natural talent for the public eye, has that boy."

For Hemingway, there were seemingly few literary Olympians left in Paris to conquer. But then, that spring, a different group of luminaries began to flood into his life, people who could advance his ambitions in a wholly different way.

"That year the rich came," he wrote later.

A year before, he contended, they would have ignored him. He had been too obscure then, and this particular breed of "rich" — or "international birds of paradise," as one of Picasso's mistresses once put it — cultivated and collected only highly successful talents. Otherwise, it was just a waste of their time and charm. Even now, he felt, they likely were on the fence about him, because he had yet to pen the novel that would confirm his greatness.

Hemingway's entrée to these new circles may have begun with Donald Stewart. "[He] was telling us both that we ought to see more of 'people that mattered,'" John Dos Passos recalled. Stewart repeatedly mentioned one American couple in particular: Sara and Gerald Murphy.

"They were both rich," Stewart later wrote. "He was handsome, she was beautiful; they had three golden children . . . They had the gift of making life enchantingly pleasurable for those who were fortunate enough to be their friends."

Sara hailed from a midwestern fortune, and Gerald's family owned the Mark Cross Company, purveyor of fine leather goods; they now stood at the apex of Paris's creative scene. Their dinner guests on any given evening might include Picasso, Cole Porter, or Douglas Fairbanks, who would be seated alongside dancers from Sergei Diaghilev's Ballets Russes. Theirs was a "closed circle, it was privileged, but within those narrow limits it was immensely stimulating," said Stewart.

Stewart did not, however, do a great job of selling them to Hemingway and Dos Passos at first. "He almost put us off the Murphys by building them up as rich socialites," remembered Dos Passos — a frivolous category almost certain to elicit scorn from Hemingway. Yet when both men actually met the Murphys, they had to admit that they were not merely rich in a vulgar or ostentatious way. Yes, they had a beautiful apartment and entertained on a grand scale, and there was also that glorious seaside villa down on the French Riviera they had just purchased and renovated.

Yet the Murphys were curiously unpretentious. Ten years older than Hemingway and Dos Passos, they were extremely devoted to their little family. The role they assumed in Paris's social life was a mentoring one; their homes were chic but secure refuges amidst the riotous decadence outside. "They were the parents everybody wished they'd had," recalls Murphy friend Calvin Tomkins.

Their artist and writer friends often sought the couple's opinions on their latest works, yet they "wanted them to approve for different reasons," adds Tomkins. "Not for literary excellence but because they loved you." Gerald was himself a respected cubist painter, admired by the other cubist greats and top-tier artists in town. "He seemed to me to have a sort of butcher's approach to painting, violent, skillful, accurate, combined with . . . a surgeon's delicacy of touch," said Dos Passos.

The Murphys found Hemingway wondrously talented, and he was quickly admitted to the ranks of writers permitted to descend upon them at any hour to read their latest work. He and Hadley joined in the Murphys' grander entertainments as well. It did not matter that the Hemingways were as broke as ever. Their new companions offered them "all the amenities, [and] could take them anywhere for gorgeous meals," recalled Hadley. Hemingway earned their keep simply by being Hemingway. Hadley was not an especially charismatic or stylish addition to the scene, but she did her best to play along, and the Murphys were kind to her. Around this time she would listen with amusement to conversations between her husband and Gertrude Stein, in which both claimed not to care about material success. Yet after these chats, she pointed out later, Hemingway would still readily accept all of the expensive and flattering hospitality anyway. He didn't entirely want to "simply sink back and take all this," Hadley added, but he often couldn't resist the trappings of his popularity.

Hemingway would remain friends with the Murphys — especially Sara — for decades, and they were about to play a central role in his most intimate affairs, professional and personal. Yet even they were window dressing in comparison to the three upper-echelon expat luminaries who were about to happen to him. Each would act as a catalyst, accelerating his final transformation from embryonic Hemingway into legendary Hemingway. The first catalyst provided a conduit to desperately needed financial stability. The second would serve as the previously elusive idea trigger for the novel that would make his reputation at last. And the third — a dynamic but tragically self-destructive patron saint—would help usher Hemingway onto the prestigious international stage he craved.

Like Paris itself, Hemingway's life teetered on the verge of explosion.

AS SOON AS he returned to Paris, Harold Loeb visited Hemingway at his carpenter's loft, filled with excitement about their respective triumphs at Boni & Liveright. At first he was irritated to learn that Hemingway's old friend Bill Smith—whose brother Y.K. had introduced Hemingway to Sherwood Anderson in Chicago—had also just arrived in Paris and would be competing for Hemingway's attention that spring. An amusing counterpoint to the posh company the Hemingways would be keeping that year, Smith, who was resolutely broke, moved in with the couple. The arrangement was supposed to last a few weeks but stretched into months. Hemingway tried, without success, to get Smith a job as an editorial assistant on one of the expat magazines; eventually he helped install him as a business manager at Robert McAlmon's press.

Initially Loeb and Smith "eyed each other with suspicion," Loeb recalled. Hemingway had to finesse relations between the men; he assured Loeb that Smith was a swell guy and briefed Smith on Loeb's virtues, which included boxing, wrestling, and tennis skills. After their initial wariness, the men became fast friends. Loeb liked Smith's low-key manner and discretion, but also his cynical wisecracks—an attribute that Hemingway had spent years observing and would soon advertise to much of the literate world.

By this point, Loeb's relationship with Kitty Cannell had been strained beyond repair. When he returned from New York, she greeted him at the train station, filled with optimism and plans. Loeb, for his part, simply felt hollow about her. Not long after their reunion, she threw a jealous tantrum over another woman that "did not let up until the songbirds were tuning up outside the window," he claimed later. The incident led at last to their breakup, and Loeb wasted no time letting it be known around town that they were finally finished.

That said, he and Cannell still overlapped socially, including at one teatime gathering that would have profound ramifications for the Hemingway-Hadley union. One day Cannell invited Hadley to come over to her apartment to meet two American sisters who were relatively new to Paris, Pauline and Virginia "Jinny" Pfeiffer. Later that afternoon, Hemingway and Loeb bounded in, sweaty from their latest boxing round. There Hemingway beheld his wife sitting and making small talk with two bird-like, aggressively stylish strangers, both of whom resembled Japanese dolls with their black bobbed hair and heavy bangs.

The impulse to connect Hadley with the Pfeiffers — especially Pauline — was an odd one. Apparently they and Hadley had lived near each other in St. Louis but never met; this seemed a sufficient reason to Cannell for making the introduction. Yet beyond their geographical backgrounds, the ladies had little in common. In the first place, Pauline and Virginia were rich; their purses were thick with dollars regularly supplied by their doting wealthy father and an equally doting uncle. Plus, Pauline worshipped at the altar of fashion, while Hadley could not have cared less about couture. That season Pauline sported a luxe chipmunk fur coat conjured up by a top Paris designer; long emerald earrings occasionally dangled from her earlobes. According to Morley Callaghan, she considered hanging out at cafés "beneath her," and opted for the Ritz over the Dôme and the Rotonde. Even her vocabulary was trendy and luxurious: she described people and things that pleased her as "ambrosial," the chic woman's superlative du jour.

Yet, perhaps the starkest discrepancy, Pauline had a career. A year earlier, in 1924, she had come to France to assist Main Bocher, the elegant new Paris editor for *Vogue,* America's preeminent fashion magazine. Paris fashion and "the Paris look" were then big business for fashion houses and publications alike, and the Paris-based *Vogue* editors worked hard. Pauline's life as a fashion journalist centered on interviews, fashion shows, typewriters, and deadlines, while Hadley's was dedicated to caring for Bumby and scouting food bargains. Pauline reported on the Paris collections and trends tirelessly; her byline appeared regularly in the magazine. She was a clever writer; even her shortest items about fads demonstrated a brisk, coquettish wit.

"Handkerchiefs and reputations are exceedingly easy to lose," read one of her opening paragraphs. "Both are lost in about equal numbers daily. All reputations lost are very good ones — and the more irretrievably lost they are, the better they were. The handkerchiefs lost should be better."

Yet despite her sleek bob and her reporter's notebooks, Pauline was apparently traditional in at least one significant way: she was believed by some to be husband hunting. "Pauline, nearing thirty, was a virgin and a good Roman Catholic," Cannell later wrote. The ticking clock, she insinuated, was making Pauline more aggressive on the romantic front than she might have been a few years earlier — and also open to less than predictable matches.

Hemingway fell into that category. In fact, he repulsed Pauline that first afternoon at Cannell's apartment. (Her sister Virginia, by contrast, found him interesting as he regaled the group with stories about skiing and Austria.) Hemingway was as dismissive of Pauline as she was of him.

"I'd like to take Virginia out in Pauline's coat," he declared after the Pfeiffers had left.

Yet the Pfeiffers and the Hemingways must have found some common ground, for soon Pauline and Virginia visited Hadley and Hemingway in their sawmill apartment. Pauline — who lived in a posh Right Bank flat — saw no charm in the Hemingways' dingy loft. Their living conditions appalled her, and she couldn't believe that Hadley would tolerate such squalor — even in the name of art. Hemingway spent the visit cloistered away in the bedroom; Pauline caught a glimpse of him writing in bed, looking slovenly. She inwardly blanched.

Cannell ran into the ladies shortly after this visit. "They remarked with delicate shudders that they found Ernest so coarse they couldn't see how a lovely girl like Hadley could stand him," she reported.

Despite the discrepancy between her setup and the Pfeiffers', Hadley claimed that she remained unashamed; nor did her comparative personal shabbiness seem to bother her — yet. If she felt any insecurity about her husband's increasing proximity to glamorous women of means, she did not admit to feeling at a disadvantage romantically. She later claimed that Hemingway made her feel as though he was proud of her and that he was always, in one way or another, saying "See, here is this beautiful, smart, talented, charming wife of mine."

There must have been moments during this period, however, when both of the Hemingways began to see themselves through the eyes of their rich new friends. It is difficult to imagine that the veneer of bohemian romanticism never once dissolved and revealed instead a scene of cramped, dreary struggle.

If Virginia Pfeiffer was actually as repelled by Hemingway as Cannell reported, she seems to have gotten over her aversion fairly quickly. The two reportedly struck up a flirtation and possibly even an affair. Gradually the Pfeiffers went from being a novel and occasional presence in the Hemingways' lives to a constant one, and Hemingway became absorbed in stories of the Pfeiffers' privileged upbringing and lives. It appeared that a changing of the guard might be in the offing.

• • •

NEW ROMANCE SEEMED to be in the offing for Harold Loeb as well. One afternoon he had stationed himself at the Select, a Montparnasse café near the Dôme and the Rotonde, working on revisions to his *Doodab* manuscript.

"I heard a laugh so gay and musical that it seemed to brighten the dingy room," he remembered later. "Low-pitched, it had the liquid quality of the lilt of a mockingbird singing to the moon."

He glanced up and spotted a long, lean woman perched on a bar stool, surrounded by men. Her light hair had been shorn into a boyish cut; though she sometimes favored rakishly angled men's fedoras, on this day she wore a slouch hat. A simple jersey sweater and tweed skirt completed the ensemble. Her strong, spare features were devoid of makeup. All in all, it seemed a fairly chaste presentation, almost masculine, yet she was arresting and sexy. This woman had, Loeb thought, a "certain aloof splendor."

Mesmerized, he ogled her for a while and eventually ambled over to a nearby table where Robert McAlmon was holding court. As usual, McAlmon had the dirt. The mockingbird was a Brit named Lady Duff Twysden; she was in her mid-thirties. She had acquired the title by marriage, but was soon to lose it: like Kitty Cannell and others in the Montparnasse alimony gang, Twysden had come to Paris to weather a nasty divorce. Her aristocratic husband had remained back in the U.K. Though a notoriously hard drinker, she handled her liquor admirably for such a fashionably gaunt creature.

"I wondered how long she could keep it up without losing her looks," Loeb wrote.

He was merely the latest man intrigued by the charms of Lady Duff: she had been captivating men throughout the Quarter. "We were all in love with her," recalled Donald Ogden Stewart. "It was hard not to be. She played her cards so well."

Twysden was an idiosyncratic temptress. Despite the upright English title, there was said to be something feral about her; some maintained that she didn't bother to bathe regularly. Yet everything about her self-presentation worked. The tweediness of her ensembles—which might have looked dumpy on another women—seemed a symbol of good breeding. Even though she co-opted men's accessories and drank like a man, Twysden somehow managed to translate all of that appropriated masculinity into feminine seductiveness. Even her tipped fedora implied that she was taking all sorts of other masculine liberties, like the pursuit of pleasure.

She was gregarious but also exuded an air of unattainability—a necessary attribute for any successful siren.

That aloofness worked like catnip: everywhere Lady Duff went, a flock of men invariably sat at her feet, "listening to her every word, loving her looks and her wit and her artistic sensitivity," as one former expat put it. She treated her many admirers with a democratic flippancy, calling each of them "darling"—possibly unable to remember any of their names. Also, in a community forever scavenging for inspiration and material, Twysden had the makings of a possible muse—a role that could be flattering and dangerous in equal parts. Many in the Quarter and beyond believed that the commercial fiction writer Michael Arlen had based the femme fatale character Iris Storm in his 1924 novel *The Green Hat* on Lady Duff, although Nancy Cunard—another long-limbed, lithe, aristocratic British expat—was more likely the inspiration. Modernist author Mary Butts also mulled a book partly inspired by Twysden, but found that "it won't shape." It seemed only a matter of time before some other enterprising writer would figure out how to translate her onto paper in a big way. Creatively speaking, Lady Duff was low-hanging fruit.

Though other men readily flocked to her side at bars, Harold Loeb couldn't muster the courage to approach her. But he did become obsessed with her. Whenever he walked into a café or bar, he immediately scanned the room to see if she was there. When he did spot her, she was usually attended by her customary retinue of males, and Loeb would hover in the background, observing her from afar.

"She was not strikingly beautiful, but her features had a special appeal for me," he remembered. Her face made an indelible impression. "I tried halfheartedly to banish her image but was unsuccessful," Loeb wrote. "It seemed to be etched on the lens of my mind."

To his annoyance, he quickly discovered that Twysden was not completely at liberty, romantically speaking. While she had left her baronet ex-husband back across the Channel, she had imported with her from Britain another man, with whom she lived and caroused. Pat Guthrie was, like Twysden, a dissipated thirty-something Briton with a rumored aristocratic lineage: his mother was said to possess a fortune and a castle in Scotland. Guthrie came to epitomize genteel, debauched poverty within the colony. Like Lady Duff, he was a relentless drinker, although unlike her, he couldn't hold his alcohol. As expat Morrill Cody put it, "Poor Pat was maudlin at the end of the second glass." He also occasionally became belligerent, and would often have to be led away while the night was still young. On these occasions, Twysden usually "went on to other places, and other drinks with other people."

Despite the fact that he was sharing Twysden's bed, some thought Guthrie was bisexual or gay, although others were less certain. "[Duff] was really quite a dish for a fairy to have, and yet it happens all the time," ruminated Donald Stewart later. He vaguely remembered once visiting a brothel in Spain with Guthrie but conceded that it might have been some-one else. Others maintained that the Twysden-Guthrie union was roman-tic, perhaps even one of the greatest love affairs in Montparnasse.

Loeb hated his would-be rival on sight. He supposed that Guthrie was "handsome in a disagreeable Irish way," but beyond that, there was little to redeem him. "He was typical . . . of that fraction of the British upper class which chooses parasitism for a vocation," he concluded.

It was an uncharitable summary of Guthrie's position, but not an iso-lated one. Donald Stewart called him "a kind of bump on the log of Lady Duff Twysden," even though Twysden essentially relied on him financially. He was known around town as a remittance man, surviving on family al-lowance checks that sporadically made their way across the Channel. Ac-cording to legend — one eventually propagated by Loeb himself — when-ever money came in, Twysden and Guthrie would move into the Ritz and rummage up their finery (white gloves and gowns for Twysden; a pressed dinner jacket for Guthrie). They would dine on caviar and champagne un-til their pile of francs grew discouragingly low; then it was back to Mont-parnasse and pauperdom. After their Ritz benders, Twysden and Guthrie often didn't have enough money left over for food and relied on local bar-tenders for charity, whether in the form of credit, cash, or libations.

The couple frequented the same Left Bank bars and boîtes as Loeb, and their social circles began to overlap. One evening, when Loeb turned up at a friend's cocktail party, Twysden and Guthrie were there. Loeb ner-vously downed drink after drink. Rather than imbuing him with cour-age, the alcohol gave him the spins; he suddenly became fixated on the fact that he hadn't shaved that morning. He left the party and staggered out to a local barber. "I made my way gingerly until I came to a striped pole," he remembered later. Once there, he sprawled drunkenly in the barber's chair and berated himself as the barber lathered and shaved his face. This impulse to groom under duress was apparently a tic of Loeb's — one that Hemingway had noticed and would soon commemorate on paper.

Not long afterward, Loeb was back at the bar of the Select, drinking a scotch and soda. Twysden was also there, chatting with a couple of admirers. He stared at her in the mirror behind the bar until her attendants left. She was—for once—alone.

"Before I could move," Loeb recalled, "she turned to me and said, 'It is the only miracle.'"

It took Loeb a moment to realize that she was addressing him. Even if he had no idea what she was talking about, he collected himself quickly and tried to muster a suave response.

"That always makes it incredible," he replied. ("It was as if I was speaking a part," he later remembered.)

He got up and sat down on the stool next to her. They stared at each other in the mirror. Soon their hands were touching. Then plans were being made to meet up the next day at an obscure bar. Loeb left when Pat Guthrie turned up.

The next day, Lady Duff and Loeb met at Restaurant Foyot. The paneled oak walls covered with English hunting scenes seemed an appropriate backdrop for Twysden to brief Loeb on her past. This was a topic of intense speculation around Paris. Stories of her Buckingham Palace debut were making the rounds; some believed she was descended from the Stuart kings of England; Twysden did nothing to discourage this impression.

"Her early memories were of mist and heather and horses, of cliffs on the hills and the neighbors in to tea," wrote Loeb.

Yet ignoble whisperings about her past countered these regal images: that her father was a lowly proprietor of a wine store somewhere in the north of England; that her family had been broke but socially ambitious; that she was a promiscuous man-eater. She didn't seem to be mourning the imminent loss of her title. It had been a perk of her 1917 marriage to Sir Roger Twysden, tenth baronet, and from the start, it had not been a successful union. Lady Duff told Loeb that she had run away with the best man on her wedding day but ended up marrying Sir Roger anyway. They had one child together, but Sir Roger turned out to be a drunk, she said; they simply couldn't live with each other. Her aristocratic in-laws were thrilled to be rid of her and currently had custody of her young son.

"I made a mess of it," Twysden told Loeb, "but I'm not sorry."

They met again the next day, and this time they made plans to go away together. Conveniently, Guthrie was about to leave for England to try to wangle more funds out of his mother. Twysden suggested a liaison in Saint-Jean-de-Luz, a fishing port just south of Biarritz.

"I'll get the tickets," Loeb told her.

In the meantime, another American expat had also been wheedling his way into Lady Duff's affections. It's unclear how Hemingway, with a wife at home and a supposed affair with Virginia Pfeiffer on the side, might have had any spare time to devote to cultivating Twysden, but that spring they were increasingly seen in each other's company.

"I [introduced] Hemingway to Lady Duff and the title seemed to electrify him," claimed Robert McAlmon years later. After that, Hemingway was seen for weeks on end in Montmartre, somehow buying drinks for both her and Guthrie despite his own limited resources. Sometimes Hadley joined his excursions with Lady Duff, although they were not happy outings for her. She often burst into tears, and Hemingway would prevail upon McAlmon or their friend Josephine Brooks to take her home while he stayed out drinking with Twysden.

"[It] looked like love or infatuation at least," McAlmon observed. "Of course neither Jo Brooks or I DID take Hadley home, thinking if he was going to break with her that was his job, and we saw no reason [for] leaving our own drinks and companions."

Hadley's tears did little to sway Hemingway, either, who began bringing Twysden to their sawmill apartment. Now that he was gaining a modest celebrity, women of high rank were starting to lavish attention on him. As with the favors of his new rich friends, he apparently basked in the more flirtatious luxuries coming his way. Hadley may have insisted that Hemingway was still proud of her and attracted to her, but late that spring of 1925, he described the state of their union somewhat more coolly.

"We are fond of each other as ever," he wrote to Sherwood Anderson, "and get along well."

It was hardly a passionate avowal. Like the Pfeiffer sisters, Lady Duff was becoming a fixture in the Hemingways' personal life.

THAT SPRING, Hemingway sent off his signed contract for *In Our Time* to Horace Liveright. In an accompanying letter, he demanded final approval over any suggested alterations, arguing that each story in the collection was "written so tight and so hard" that tampering with a single word would render the whole work off-key. It was going to sell well, he predicted. Unlike the work of his other experimental contemporaries, his writing would have wide appeal. "My book will be praised by highbrows and can be read by lowbrows," he assured Liveright. "There is no writing in it that anybody with a high-school education cannot read."

It was a savvy but tricky approach that few experimentalists could actually master. Yet there were encouraging forerunners in the community. One of Paris's most visible artists, Pablo Picasso, was pulling it off.

"I've always felt that painting must awaken something even in the man who doesn't ordinarily look at pictures," he later told his mistress Françoise Gilot. "Just as in Molière there is always something to make the very intelligent person laugh and also the person who understands nothing. In Shakespeare too. And in my work, just as in Shakespeare, there are often burlesque things and relatively vulgar things. In that way I reach everybody. It's not that I want to prostrate myself in front of the public, but I want to provide something for every level of thinking."

Hemingway was now attempting a similar high-low approach in the realm of literature. People like Gertrude Stein and poet E. E. Cummings might craft fine, provocative books in experimental language, but "no one who had not read a good deal of 'modern' writing could read [them]," Hemingway wrote to Liveright. He would not be among that crew, and looked forward to becoming a prominent "property" for Boni & Liveright as soon as possible.

Less than a week later, Hemingway visited Sylvia Beach at her bookshop. As usual, she handed him a pile of correspondence that had arrived for him. Among the missives: two letters of inquiry from Maxwell Perkins, an editor at Charles Scribner's Sons, the prestigious publishing house in New York City. Hemingway saw with dismay that the letters had been written over a month earlier. The first one—dated February 21—told him everything he had ever dreamed of hearing from a major American publisher. Perkins had heard through the grapevine that Hemingway was doing some remarkable writing. After tracking down a copy of his little Paris book *in our time*—which had apparently taken quite a bit of effort—Perkins had been impressed by its contents. He instinctively understood Hemingway's style.

"Your method is obviously one which enables you to express what you have to say in a very small compass," he wrote.

Would Hemingway consider publishing another one of his works with Scribner's? Perkins hastened to add that *in our time* itself was too scant to be considered saleable for a commercial publisher like Scribner's—perhaps a hint that he would be interested in seeing something of novel length.

Yet this flattering missive had gone missing because of an insufficiently specific address. Luckily a mutual acquaintance saved the day by instructing Perkins to contact Hemingway via Sylvia Beach; she practically ran a post office for the Crowd. Perkins sent off another enthusiastic letter a few days later, adding that he had since heard that Hemingway "would likely have material for a book before so very long."

The timing could not have been more frustrating. Hemingway quickly replied to Perkins, explaining that while he had been excited by the inquiry, his hands were tied: he had *just* entered into an agreement with Horace Liveright for his next book—and furthermore, the terms of his contract gave Liveright the option on his next three books.

"It makes it seem almost worth while to get into Who's Who in order to have a known address," he wrote.

Yet Hemingway was clearly already eyeing loopholes: if Liveright did not accept his next book, he duly reported to Perkins, the firm would relinquish its option on the one that followed. So there was hope for future collaboration with Scribner's. He described to Perkins other projects he had in mind—including more short stories and perhaps a definitive non-fiction book about bullfighting—and went on to make a bizarre and disingenuous declaration. "I don't care about writing a novel," he wrote. It was, he added, an "awfully artificial and worked out form." Nevertheless, he waffled, some of his short stories were now reaching up to twelve thousand words, so perhaps he would get there yet.

"So that is how matters stand," he reluctantly concluded.

Neither he nor Perkins appeared willing to submit to their "rotten luck," as Perkins put it in his response. Over the next few months they kept up an affable correspondence. In these exchanges, Hemingway never asked how Perkins had heard about his work in the first place, perhaps just assuming that his name had been swirling in the ether. He may have been astonished when he learned that Perkins had first heard about him from none other than F. Scott Fitzgerald.

In the five years since publishing his debut novel, *This Side of Paradise,* with Scribner's, Fitzgerald had not only become one of the house's leading literary stars and a national celebrity; he had also been serving as an unofficial talent scout for Perkins. Popular sports columnist and author Ring Lardner—once called America's "most humorous man" by no less an authority than Groucho Marx, and an early influence on Hemingway himself—was among Fitzgerald's more prominent contributions to the Scribner's stable. Donald Ogden Stewart also credited Fitzgerald with helping to launch his career by introducing him to Frank Crowninshield, *Vanity Fair*'s editor.

Furthermore, once Fitzgerald successfully ushered a writer into Scribner's stable, he often remained closely involved in his career; Perkins even occasionally sent Fitzgerald sales statistics and reviews of his discoveries' releases. Fitzgerald's benevolence toward his fellow writers was almost startling, given the competitive nature of the field. Some wondered if he brokered careers to gratify his own ego, but most felt that his motives were pure. "[He] was selflessly generous about other men's writing," wrote John Dos Passos, who knew Fitzgerald in the early days of his career.

The previous fall, Fitzgerald had decided to help to send some of that generosity in the direction of Ernest Hemingway. He had come across *in our time* and breathlessly informed Perkins in a letter that he should look up a Paris-based American writer named "Earnest [with the "a" crossed out] Hemmingway," who had just published a remarkable book.

"He's the real thing," Fitzgerald declared.

For Fitzgerald to have billed Hemingway thus meant that he likely saw the glimmer of commercial viability in Hemingway's writing: at last, here was an experimental writer from the milieu of Gertrude Stein and Ezra Pound who could actually be appreciated by the average American reader. Barely any of Stein's book *The Making of Americans,* Fitzgerald complained, had been "intelligable at all." (Perkins agreed with him: while he found Stein's style fascinating and effective, he doubted that "the reader who had no literary interest, or not much, would have [any] patience with her method.") Hemingway was a different matter entirely.

Hemingway had actually never met his new champion, although —like everyone else in his generation—he had for years been reading Fitzgerald's books and stories. He often had less than glowing things to say about them.

"Ernest seemed on the fence about that early Fitzgerald work," recalled his *Toronto Star* colleague Morley Callaghan. "Not grudging, . . . but he did make it clear that Fitzgerald wasn't exciting him at all."

He appeared to be in the minority. In the five years since Fitzgerald had made his thunderous debut, he had only become more prolific, critically applauded, and famous than ever. He had published two short story collections and two more novels; one of them, *The Beautiful and Damned,* had been made into a film. *This Side of Paradise* had also been optioned. In 1920 and 1921 alone, three movies had been conjured up out of Fitzgerald short stories.

"[He] was making more money than anybody in Paris ever dreamed of a writer's making," recalled expat poet Archibald MacLeish.

As if all of this success wasn't intoxicating enough, Fitzgerald also appeared to have captured one of the most coveted literary prizes of all: as early as 1921, he had become, according to one press profile, "the recognized spokesman of the younger generation." Scribner's helped considerably in setting the tone for coverage of its new author, touting him in ads as "The Novelist of a Rising Generation." On paper, he was a keen observer of the postwar atmosphere and the attitudes of his contemporaries, which were so starkly different from those of their parents.

"My point of vantage was the dividing line between the two generations, and there I sat—somewhat self-consciously," Fitzgerald acknowledged later.

In *This Side of Paradise,* he wrote that his peers had grown up "to find all Gods dead, all wars fought, all faiths in man shaken." Yet he was also strongly associated with postwar frivolity and giddiness: he and his wife, Zelda, were sometimes credited in the press with single-handedly creating flapper culture. They led by example, and their champagne-soaked world received liberal coverage. According to John Dos Passos, "They were celebrities in the Sunday supplement sense of the word . . . and they loved it."

Whatever Hemingway thought of his writing, Fitzgerald must have seemed a particularly maddening and enviable presence. By his own admission, Hemingway was *still* having a hard time cranking out single paragraphs, much less three celebrated novels in five years. At least he could console himself that Fitzgerald was not deemed a stylistic innovator. "Modern" and "experimental" were words that rarely attached themselves to him. Rather, his work was often called "vivid" and "alive." Even though his subject matter—flappers, bootleggers, jazz—was strikingly modern, his writing had far more in common with Edith Wharton than with Gertrude Stein. Yet no matter what others might think, Fitzgerald saw himself as a pioneer.

"I want to write something new—something extraordinary and beautiful and simple + intricately patterned," he wrote once to Perkins.

With his new novel *The Great Gatsby*—just released that April—Fitzgerald felt that he had hit his mark. Shortly after the novel's release, he informed Perkins that he considered it "something really NEW in form, idea, structure—the model for the age that Joyce, and Stien are searching for, that Conrad didn't find." He reported that T. S. Eliot agreed with him: "[He] wrote me he'd read <u>Gatsby</u> three times and thought it was <u>the 1st step forward American fiction had taken since Henry James!</u>"

Yet for the experimentalists, this sort of step wasn't nearly big enough. A writer couldn't simply write about modern life; one had to do so in a thoroughly modern and revolutionary way. *Gatsby* had not achieved that. For example, in the opinion of Edmund Wilson, a Fitzgerald confidant and a leading critic of that era, Fitzgerald would someday be considered "one of the first-rate figures in the American writing of his period," but Wilson did not credit him with being a literary radical. This meant that there was still a major prize left to be claimed: authorship of a voice-of-a-generation novel that was both modern in subject *and* a stylistic groundbreaker.

Fitzgerald and his wife had recently traded New York for Europe; they had eventually landed in Paris, where they rented an apartment near the Arc de Triomphe. They quickly "made a special social category of themselves and their pleasures" among the rich of the Right Bank, as *New Yorker* writer Janet Flanner put it. Their recklessness and profligacy became legendary.

"Poor Scott was earning so much money from his books that he and Zelda had to drink a great deal of champagne in Montmartre in an effort to get rid of it," recalled Sylvia Beach.

To do so, they did everything short of torching cash in the lobby of the Ritz. Beach claimed that Fitzgerald spent an entire publisher's check on a pearl necklace for Zelda, who then gave it to "a Negress with whom she was dancing" in a nightclub. They reportedly left a heap of money on a tray in the foyer of their flat so bill collectors and deliverymen could help themselves. Yet despite the frivolity, Scott was immediately, even passionately, embraced by the Crowd. "We liked him very much, as who didn't?" recalled Beach, remembering with affection Fitzgerald's "blue eyes and good looks, his concern for others, . . . and his fallen-angel fascination." Given the limited roster of cafés and bars favored by literary expats, it was probably only a matter of time before Fitzgerald ran into Hemingway.

Sure enough, one day that spring Hemingway had settled in at the Dingo bar in Montparnasse with Duff Twysden and Pat Guthrie (or "some completely worthless characters," as he later put it). In the prewar days, the Dingo had been a grungy workers' café, but had since been discovered by Flossie Martin, a former Ziegfeld showgirl and informal, bawdy mascot of Montparnasse. Once she began to frequent it, the Dingo became a requisite destination dive for expats, many of whom drank themselves into oblivion at its small bar and could sometimes be found passed out up in the trees or clinging to the lamppost outside.

As Hemingway, Twysden, and Guthrie were sitting at the bar, probably already drinking, two men approached them. The first was Fitzgerald, who apparently knew Hemingway on sight. He introduced himself and his friend, Dunc Chaplin, and then ordered champagne for the group.

Fitzgerald's face unsettled Hemingway. It was too pretty, he thought, especially that delicate mouth. Fitzgerald then launched into an excited monologue, which unnerved Hemingway even more.

"It was all about my writing and how great it was," Hemingway recalled later.

It was disgraceful, he thought, to lavish praise on another writer like that. Things only got worse when Fitzgerald started interrogating Hemingway about his sex life, demanding to know whether he and Hadley had had sex before marriage. Hemingway claimed not to recall. Fitzgerald persisted.

"Don't talk like some limey," he pressed. "Try to be serious and remember."

Just then, Hemingway noticed that Fitzgerald was beginning to sweat; drops beaded his upper lip. Suddenly the color drained from his face and he blacked out right there at the bar. Hemingway was afraid that he might be dying, but Chaplin assured him that it was not a serious matter. The two men carried Fitzgerald out of the Dingo and wedged him into a taxi, instructing the driver to take him home.

At least, this was Hemingway's version of how he first met his famous benefactor. There were other versions of the story as well—Fitzgerald, for example, told a friend that he had simply "looked up Hemminway"— but Hemingway's tale has been taken more or less as fact over time.

Whatever the circumstances of that fateful first encounter, by June 1925 Hemingway wrote to Maxwell Perkins that he and Hadley had been seeing "quite a lot" of Fitzgerald and that the two writers had even taken a road trip together. Fitzgerald needed to go to Lyon to retrieve a Renault that he and Zelda had abandoned there. Zelda, in the mood for a convertible, had arranged for the car's top to be sawed off, and inclement weather had forced them to abandon temporarily the newly decapitated vehicle. Fitzgerald invited Hemingway to make the journey with him: they would take a train down and drive the Renault back.

Here Hemingway saw an opportunity. Even though he found some of Fitzgerald's work silly and badly written—and even openly accused Fitzgerald of being a literary whore when it came to tricking out short stories to make them more saleable to major magazines—if he went along to Lyon, he would have "the company of an older and successful writer" from whom he would "certainly learn much that it would be useful to know."

He accepted the invitation. According to his retelling, the trip was a debacle. Fitzgerald committed a slew of offenses, which included standing Hemingway up at the train station (they eventually connected in Lyon), taking to his bed with an acute bout of hypochondria, and subjecting them both to an endless and unnecessarily opulent hotel meal. He apparently rounded out their holiday activities by delivering an unwelcome lecture about how both he and Hemingway could learn a thing or two from writer Michael Arlen and then treated Hemingway to another passing-out episode, during which "he looked like a little dead crusader," Hemingway wrote.

Somehow their friendship survived the journey. Fitzgerald may have been a bad drunk and a literary slut in Hemingway's eyes, but he was an influential slut, and one didn't simply cast him aside.

Fitzgerald's wife soon complicated the relationship considerably. Poison immediately coursed between Zelda and Hemingway; it was "hate at first sight," as Fitzgerald's eventual mistress put it. Their first encounter took place at the Fitzgeralds' Paris apartment, a dark, airless place on the rue de Tilsitt. Zelda was weathering a nasty hangover that day, Hemingway recalled, and ceaselessly picked on Fitzgerald, who in turn made Hemingway and Hadley examine a ledger bearing details of his earnings in recent years. It was a tense, unpleasant gathering.

Zelda and Hemingway seemed hardwired to detest each other. Even her legendary beauty had little effect on him; rather, he likened her eyes to those of a predatory hawk and drew attention to what he called her thin lips. Whereas Hadley played a submissive support role in the Hemingways' marriage (she followed Hemingway around "as silently as an Indian squaw," thought one of Zelda's friends), Zelda was indomitable and opinionated. After reading *The Great Gatsby,* Hemingway decided that Fitzgerald had potential after all—but now that he had met Zelda, he realized that Fitzgerald needed protectors if he was going to be able to write an even better book. Zelda, Hemingway immediately concluded, would ruin her husband. She was obviously jealous of his work, and could not be more emasculating. She became especially happy when Fitzgerald was drinking wine, Hemingway thought.

"I learned to know that smile very well," he wrote later. "It meant she knew Scott would not be able to write."

These early assessments were damning enough, but soon Hemingway decided that Zelda was outright insane, and told Fitzgerald as much.

"Zelda is crazy," he informed Fitzgerald one afternoon, after Fitzgerald allegedly complained that Zelda deemed him insufficiently endowed. Hemingway inspected Fitzgerald's wares in the bathroom of Michaud's, a Saint-Germain restaurant where James Joyce regularly dined with his family. "There's nothing wrong with you," he concluded. "Zelda just wants to destroy you." Nor did he keep his opinions to himself. Fitzgerald "should have swapped Zelda when she was at her craziest but still saleable back 5 or 6 years ago before she was diagnosed as nutty," he wrote to Perkins later.

Zelda was equally impervious to the virile charm that had beguiled so many others; she called Hemingway a "phony he-man" and a "pansy with hair on his chest"—assessments that she would reiterate many times over the years with only slightly varying vocabulary. She knew that Hemingway was trying to undermine her marriage; the couple began to quarrel about him, just as Harold Loeb and Kitty Cannell had. Yet like Loeb, Fitzgerald apparently adored Hemingway and would not be swayed.

"Ernest . . . was an equeal and my kind of an idealist," he later tried to explain to Zelda.

His "literary crush on Hem, the sportsman-stylist, the pugilist-storyteller," as John Dos Passos put it, quickly became apparent to everyone in the Paris Crowd. Soon he was submitting to the requisite boxing rounds with Hemingway, who also took him to meet Gertrude Stein. Unlike Hemingway, Fitzgerald didn't especially care about the modern paintings lining her salon walls, but he found Stein herself intriguing and the two became friendly. Alice Toklas noted that when Fitzgerald started visiting 27 rue de Fleurus alone, he was always sober, which she took as a token of his esteem for Stein.

In the meantime, Fitzgerald resumed his advocacy on Hemingway's behalf. On May 22, he gave Maxwell Perkins a cheerful update, calling his new friend "a fine, charming fellow." Perkins had made inroads with Hemingway, Fitzgerald assured him. "If Liveright doesn't please him, he'll come to you," he pledged his publisher. "And he has a future."

7

Eve in Eden

I N THE MIDDLE OF JUNE, Hemingway sat down to write. He pulled
out a stenographer's notebook, otherwise used for list-making. The
back contained a rundown of letters he "must write"; intended recipi-
ents included Ezra Pound, Sylvia Beach, and Aunt Grace. Also scribbled
there: a list of stories he had recently submitted to various publications.

On this day, he opened the notebook to a fresh page and scrawled in
pencil across the top:

> *Along with Youth*
> *A Novel*

He began writing a sea adventure, set on a troop transport ship in 1918
and featuring a recurring Hemingway short story hero named Nick Adams. The first pages included a conversation between Adams and a few
Polish officers on the deck as someone strummed a mandolin in the background. Exactly two months earlier, Hemingway had informed Max Perkins that he considered the novel to be an artificial and played-out genre,
yet here he was, making another bid to jump-start one. It turned out to
be a false start, however: little happened in the pages that followed, and
Hemingway ended the draft abruptly on page twenty-seven. Yet it was
clear that he might be on the verge of getting back into the novel game at
last.

July was fast approaching, and for Hemingway, that month had become synonymous with Spain, beginning with Pamplona. He secured tickets and rooms at the Hotel Quintana, on the town's main square, owned by
the devoted bullfighting aficionado Juanito Quintana.

Hemingway started rounding up a fiesta entourage. It was shaping up
to be a good gang, he wrote to Horace Liveright. Donald Stewart was

slated to make a return appearance, along with a fellow Algonquin Round Table habitué, Robert Benchley, a humor writer who had also been staying in Austria near the Hemingways the previous winter and was in Europe that summer doing some reporting for *Life*. Architect Paul Fisher showed interest in coming too. Scott Fitzgerald was not mentioned in the early roster as a probable participant: he was on a "perpetual drunk" that June, Hemingway reported to Ezra Pound.

One Pamplona regular had been conspicuously left out of the plans this time around: Robert McAlmon. Not long before the group was due to leave, he dined with Kitty Cannell. Over supper they discussed "Hemingway and his sycophants," as she called the entourage. They decided to stop by the Hemingways' sawmill apartment after their meal to see how the travel arrangements were coming along.

"I wanted to see my ex-kitty, so we went," Cannell wrote.

When they got to the flat, McAlmon decided to play a little joke on Hemingway.

"I'm thinking of taking Kitty with me to Pamplona next week," he informed Hemingway in a deadpan way. Suddenly, Cannell reported, Hemingway's face turned purple and he flew into a rage.

"He lunged toward me, seized a lighted lamp from the table at my elbow and hurled it through the window into the yard piled high with boards and kindling," she claimed.

The visitors quickly scurried out. In later interviews and writings, neither of them speculated about why Hemingway had such a fierce reaction to the prank, but if the lamp-flinging incident is true, his antipathy toward both Cannell and McAlmon was finally out in the open, and it clearly ran deep. Afterward, Cannell pretended nothing had happened, but McAlmon appeared satisfied with the result of the visit, having avenged his snubbing.

Unlike Cannell and McAlmon, Harold Loeb made the Pamplona cut. Hemingway sent him a jovial note, filled with logistical guidance and promising that Pamplona would be "damned good." By then, however, Loeb was keeping a secret from Hemingway. He and Duff Twysden had gone on their clandestine Saint-Jean-de-Luz holiday. It had been wildly romantic, Loeb later claimed; they couldn't even wait to get there before consummating their union, and instead did so in a cramped Paris flat borrowed from a friend. Once in Saint-Jean-de-Luz, they moved into an *auberge* with a view of the Pyrenees and picked up where they'd left off in Paris.

"We made love furiously," Loeb wrote, "as if we were trying to squeeze a life of love-making into three short days."

They drifted between their bed and a terrace, where they dined and talked into the night. Hemingway came up in conversation. Twysden was frustratingly close-mouthed on the subject.

"[He's] a good chap," she said tersely.

Loeb pushed the subject. In his opinion, he said, Hemingway had exuberance and joie de vivre, but worked too hard for his taste.

"I have nothing against work," replied Twysden, "for those who like it." She did not discuss him further.

As their tryst drew to a close, Loeb says, Twysden implored him to go on another trip—this time to South America. ("Should we go there, darling? To a strange land, all new and different. To live as you want to live. Take a boat and go, just like that?") But he turned her down: he didn't know Spanish, it didn't rain enough in Chile, and so on. The next day Twysden asked him to buy her a train ticket back to Paris. Guthrie would be returning from London soon and she needed to meet him at the station.

Loeb also returned to Paris, and fretted about squandering the opportunity to be with Twysden. Three days later a letter arrived from her, scribbled on Dingo stationery. She was miserable without him, she reported, and loved him "with all [her] forces." That said, she had some "doubtful glad tidings."

"I am coming on the Pamplona trip with Hem and your lot . . . With Pat of course," she informed him. "Can you bear it?"

If he couldn't bear it, she promised, she would try to get out of it—but she was dying to come along. At least the trip would allow them to be near each other, albeit under the jealous gaze of Pat Guthrie.

Then a letter from Hemingway arrived, confirming that Twysden and Guthrie would now be among the fiesta crew.

"Pat has sent off to Scotland for rods and Duff to England for Funds," he wrote.

It was a chipper letter—Hemingway told Loeb three times what a "swell time" he had been having lately—but it gave Loeb a "low feeling which I could not shake off." This feeling was replaced with one of genuine foreboding when he received another missive from Twysden.

"I expect I shall have a bit of [a] time managing the situation," she wrote, adding, "Hem has promised to be good and we ought to have really a marvellous time."

Loeb was dumbfounded. Why on earth had Hemingway pledged good behavior? Was he sleeping with Duff now as well? It seemed so, he grimly concluded.

It is unclear how Twysden and Guthrie had scored an invitation to Pamplona in the first place. She and Hemingway may have met up in Paris after she returned from Saint-Jean-de-Luz, at which point he could have asked her to join the entourage; or she may simply have invited herself.

Hemingway had, in any case, learned about her liaison with Loeb. Their Saint-Jean-de-Luz secret had apparently been working its way through the Left Bank gossip mill. Bill Smith had been with Hemingway when a mutual friend told him the news. Hemingway had been furious, Smith recalled. Like Loeb, everyone around the Quarter began to wonder if Hemingway was sleeping with Lady Duff—a question that has never been answered to anyone's satisfaction.

The upcoming Pamplona trip was starting to look like a powder keg. Yet no one backed out. Hemingway, Loeb, and Twysden all put on their best poker faces.

"By all means come," Loeb replied to Twysden with affected breeziness.

He even pledged to meet her and Guthrie in Saint-Jean-de-Luz and escort them to Pamplona. In the meantime, Hemingway and Hadley dispatched Bumby to Brittany with his nanny, packed their bags, and left Paris, heading for Burguete to kick off the holiday with a week of trout fishing.

The fiesta was about to begin.

FOR WEEKS, Hemingway and the others had been looking forward to Burguete. It had proved such an untainted paradise the year before, with its rolling hills, thick forests, and silver streams and rivers. Nothing provided a better antidote to the cynical urban artifice of the Left Bank. Donald Stewart and Bill Smith met the Hemingways there; Smith had toted along a colorful array of flies to help tempt the trout out of the Irati.

The Irati trout, however, were in no position to oblige them that season: the fish had all been killed over the last year. A logging company working in the area had destroyed the local pools, broken down dams, and run logs down the river. The loggers' trash was everywhere. Hemingway was in despair over the sight. It was not an auspicious start to their excursion.

Meanwhile, Loeb skipped Burguete altogether and went to Saint-Jean-de-Luz to meet Twysden and Guthrie. He grew upset the moment Lady Duff stepped off the train onto the platform. Instead of her usual man's fedora, she was wearing a beret.

"I did not like her in a beret," Loeb grumbled. "Hem usually wore a beret."

The hat may have been an incendiary gesture on Twysden's part; it implied that she was enjoying the discord she was creating among her paramours. Like Hemingway, Guthrie had now been apprised of the Loeb-Twysden interlude. Unlike Hemingway, he had no intention of pretending not to know.

"Oh, you're here, are you?" he said, greeting Loeb on the platform.

The party immediately repaired to the train station's bar, which Loeb and Twysden had graced together just a few weeks earlier. Three martinis later, Guthrie adjourned to the pissoir. Loeb began to interrogate Twysden. Her behavior toward him had changed, he said. What had happened?

"Pat broke the spell," she reportedly told him. "He worked hard at it."

"I see," Loeb responded quietly, and that was the end of the chat.

The trio hired a car for the fifty-mile journey to Pamplona. It was a long, tense drive. When they reached the Hotel Quintana, Twysden and Guthrie went to one room and Loeb to another. The Burguete group arrived the next morning in similarly petulant spirits. Hemingway was in a black mood over the fishing disaster.

A round of absinthe, a large Spanish lunch, and a walk through the town helped alleviate the atmosphere, but already it was clear that the jubilance of the previous year was probably not going to be repeated. First of all, Pamplona itself had changed. Just as Paris had become overrun with tourists, Pamplona now also included the appalling presence of some of the group's compatriots.

"We were no longer the exclusive foreign participants in the show," Stewart later observed. "By the second trip, the establishment had caught up with the frontier."

Rolls-Royces that had carted luminaries from Madrid and France now idled outside their hotel. The American ambassador himself had materialized in a limousine; to Hemingway, his presence at the festival seemed particularly intrusive and symbolic of the shift. The town suddenly felt "cluttered and ordinary," Stewart recalled. "Pamplona seemed to be getting ready for the hand of Elsa Maxwell" — one of that era's most prominent gossip columnists.

Yet Lady Duff would prove the most disruptive intruder of all. "Someone had left the door open and Eve had walked into my male Garden of Eden," wrote Stewart. Suddenly, in her presence, "Ernest had changed," he noted. "Hadley wasn't the same . . . [T]he fun was going out of every-body."

The enmity clearly suited Twysden: that first morning, she looked especially beautiful and aloof in a broad-brimmed Spanish hat. The group hustled to the town's railroad yards to watch the unloading of the bulls. Soon wine was flowing. Guthrie procured a goatskin wine bag at a nearby tavern; he squirted the wine from his mouth, staining his face and shirt a deep blood red. Everyone laughed. Twysden demanded a swig.

"Evidently Duff was not going to be a drag on the party," Loeb observed.

The next morning, everyone in the Hemingway entourage scraped themselves out of bed in time to see the bulls driven from their corral to the stadium, with the usual crowd of men scrambling ahead of the herd. As ever, it was a thunderous, God-is-coming display, with men leaping over the barriers when the bulls got too close. One man was gored by a razor-sharp horn. No one from the Hemingway group joined the race, but when the bullring was opened for the amateur hour, Hemingway, Loeb, and Smith leaped in. The press corps was on hand, including photographers.

Hemingway, sporting a beret and white pants, got right down to the business of baiting the bulls. One bull knocked Smith down; it then turned and faced Loeb, who took off his sweater and waved it at the animal. The bull charged; its horn caught the sweater, which dangled from the bull's head as it then galloped around the arena. Loeb chased after it, hoping to salvage the garment, but it had been slashed up the middle, making it quite a souvenir of this first bullring adventure.

That afternoon the real bullfights began. In front of the Hemingway crew, a bull gored a horse, which took a death-throes run through the arena, trailing its intestines. At another point, a bull tried to escape by jumping over the wall surrounding the ring. "Perhaps he felt that it wasn't his party," Loeb grimly joked. He became increasingly dismayed by the spectacle; he even "considered *oléing* the bulls that refused to charge," he recalled. "It seemed, in some obscure way, shameful," he added.

After the fight, the Hemingway entourage reconvened on a café terrace. The fiesta was in full swing around them. Hundreds of people filled the main square, along with the relentless thump of drums and shrill piping of fifes. Several small parades did their best to march through the crowd. Guthrie had moved on from wine to absinthe and was now exploring the merits of Fundador, a Spanish brandy. Hemingway asked Loeb what he thought of his first bullfight. When Loeb replied that he was not "too keen on the theme," Hemingway was predictably unsympathetic. "We all have to die," Loeb told him, "but I don't like to be reminded of it more than twice a day."

"Balls," Hemingway said, and then turned his back on him. Loeb seemed to be adding to his list of offenses daily; being less than reverential about bullfighting was one of the surest ways to antagonize Hemingway. The only worse offense might be stealing the limelight from him.

Later, when Hemingway, Guthrie, and Stewart had been swept up in a parade streaming in an endless circuit around the square, Loeb began to quiz Bill Smith.

"Hem seems to be bitter about something," he ventured.

Smith cut to the chase. Hemingway was angry about Loeb's fling with Twysden. "You should have seen his face," he told Loeb, "when Jo Bennett told him you and Duff had gone off in a *wagon-lit*" — a reference to a train's sleeping car.

When Loeb pressed him about whether Hemingway was also in love with Twysden, Smith refused to give a straight answer. The conversation abruptly ended when Loeb realized that Twysden and Hadley — sitting together at the far end of the table — had gone silent. Loeb quickly changed the subject.

If Hadley had indeed overheard the chat and entertained her own suspicions about a possible affair between her husband and Lady Duff, she appears to have kept them to herself.

THE NEXT MORNING, Hemingway, Loeb, and Smith headed back to the bullring for amateur hour. To spare his wardrobe any further indignities, Loeb came armed with a hotel towel.

This time when a bull charged him, there was no chance to get out of the way. Loeb dropped the towel, and as the bull lowered its head to butt him, Loeb turned around, grasped its horns, and sat on the bull's head. The bull loped across the arena and eventually tossed Loeb into the air. Miraculously, he landed on his feet, as though the entire episode had been a choreographed stunt. The crowd went mad; photographers caught his moment of glory.

Hemingway then emerged from the sidelines and approached a bull from behind. He grabbed the animal and then managed to catch hold of its horns and wrestle it to the ground. The other amateur bullfighters closed in on the downed bull.

"For an instant it looked as if they would tear the animal's limbs off," Loeb reported in horror, but ring attendants came to the rescue.

Yet despite Hemingway's Herculean feat, Loeb was the king of the ring. After that, he was treated like a hero around town. Even the barber whose shop Loeb had been frequenting wouldn't take money from him. Apparently the locals were in awe of the first man (or the first foreigner, anyway) in living memory who had ridden a bull's head. His newfound fame even carried across the Atlantic: pictures of Loeb perched atop the bull, legs scissoring in the air, eventually appeared in New York publications. Hemingway had been outshone—and by a man who scoffed at the whole sport.

None of these heroics, however, was enough to lure Twysden back into his bed. She visited him in his room before lunch that day and told him that she was sorry he was having such a tough time on her account. She was worth it, Loeb replied and tried to embrace her, only to be rejected yet again. Later that afternoon, over absinthe, he asked Bill Smith if he should leave Pamplona.

"Why don't you do what you want to do?" Smith responded unhelpfully.

For years afterward, those familiar with the story wondered why Loeb did indeed stay on when Hemingway was so clearly souring against him, Twysden had proved an unreliable ally, and Guthrie likely wished that Loeb had never been born.

"Obstinacy kept me there," Loeb explained later. Guthrie's hatred only made him more determined to stay, and he still wanted to get the bottom of the Hemingway-Twysden mystery. He also reasoned that if he left now, it would look like he was running away.

That evening he cornered Twysden in the square and finally persuaded her to come have a drink alone with him. They walked off together to a small café, and then got swept into a private party in one of the buildings overlooking the square. Champagne flowed; a monocled man with a goatee played popular tunes on a piano. A crowd of men naturally formed around Twysden, who entertained her admirers with stories in French about the bullfights while Loeb stood next to a window and drank himself into oblivion. He tried to wrench Twysden away from the festivities but finally abandoned the effort. He woke up the next morning in his bed, with no memory of having come back to the Hotel Quintana.

Loeb staggered out to meet the crew for lunch. Guthrie was in an ugly mood; even Hadley had lost her kindly smile, and Smith wore a grim look. Twysden turned up later, accessorized not with a beret or a fedora but rather with a black eye and a bruised forehead. Loeb demanded to know what had happened to her, but before she could respond, Hemingway interrupted, saying that she had fallen. No one else — including Twysden — offered an explanation, and Loeb made no further inquiries. Once again he considered leaving the fiesta, but once again he was afraid of looking like a coward. He stayed put.

As usual, Loeb noted, "there was too much lunch."

THE ONE BRIGHT, joyous presence in Pamplona that week was Cayetano Ordóñez, a nineteen-year-old matador who had been thrilling aficionados throughout Spain.

"He was sincerity and purity of style itself with the cape," Hemingway wrote of him later, adding that he "looked like the messiah who had come to save bullfighting if ever any one did."

At that moment there were interesting parallels between Ordóñez — who went by the name Niño de la Palma — and Hemingway. Both men were considered potentially revolutionary prodigies who might revitalize their respective fields, but neither man had yet proven himself. Audiences and critics alike were willing Ordóñez to become one of the greats, but he still needed to build a convincing body of work and show that he belonged in the master category.

In Pamplona that week he fought in the ring along with famed matador Juan Belmonte, long one of bullfighting's heavyweights; he was now an aging champion but could still command a crowd. He and Ordóñez were a fascinating duo: Ordóñez was almost comically handsome; Belmonte was "very small and ugly," with a jutting jaw and a stammer, recalls American matador Barnaby Conrad, who later fought on the same program with Belmonte. But he had something special. "You'd see this little guy go out, round-shouldered and his feet kind of hurting," says Conrad, "and then suddenly he'd grow about five inches."

Yet it was Ordóñez, not Belmonte, who quickly became the grand attraction at Pamplona. "He did everything Belmonte did and did it better," Hemingway wrote to Gertrude Stein and Alice Toklas. "Everybody in Spain is crazy about him — except of course those that can't stand him."

Hemingway reportedly devoted much of the week to trying to cultivate Ordóñez, perhaps having been introduced by hotel proprietor Juanito Quintana, with whom Hemingway had been becoming close. "I was amazed at how quickly this man could learn," Quintana later said about Hemingway. "He had a fantastic identification with the drama of the ring and caught on immediately. By the time he left Spain he knew bullfighting as well as any of us."

The ingratiation apparently worked, for later, when Ordóñez was awarded a bull's ear after a particularly good corrida, he gave it to Hadley. "[She] wrapped it up in a handkerchief which, thank God was Don Stewarts," Hemingway reported to Stein. Hemingway, however, was probably less than delighted when Ordóñez applauded Loeb's performance in the ring. "One would have thought he had done it on purpose," he told Hemingway the night after Loeb's bull's head feat.

Ordóñez fought especially well toward the end of the fiesta. On the second-to-last evening, Hemingway informed his entourage that Ordóñez had personally assured him that the following day's bulls were going to be the best in Spain. They were sitting around a café table in the square after dinner, drinking brandy. As Loeb recalled it, Hemingway then turned to him and said, "I suppose you'd like it better if they shipped in goats."

Loeb was close to losing his temper. He responded that while he didn't dislike bullfighting, he simply sympathized with the victims.

Apparently both Hemingway and Guthrie were also spoiling for a fight after a week of pent-up tension. Guthrie snickered. "Our sensitive chum is considerate of the bull's feelings," he said. "But what about ours?"

"Harold is very considerate," Hemingway responded. "You should see him with [Kitty]. I've listened to him taking it by the hour."

Loeb still kept his cool, but the situation quickly deteriorated. Hemingway accused him of ruining their party. Encouraged by Hemingway's backing, Guthrie blurted: "Why don't you get out? I don't want you here. Hem doesn't want you here. Nobody wants you here, though some may be too decent to say so."

"I will," Loeb replied, "the instant Duff wants it."

Twysden quietly turned to him. "You know that I do *not* want you to go," she said.

This was all too much for Hemingway. "You lousy bastard," he exclaimed to Loeb. "Running to a woman."

Loeb stood and asked Hemingway to step outside. Hemingway followed him. Loeb was scared to fight Hemingway in the dark; he wouldn't be able to see Hemingway's eyes, and therefore couldn't detect when his punches were coming. But perhaps more disorienting was Loeb's realization that Hemingway had gone so quickly from being a close friend and colleague to a "bitter, lashing enemy."

The two men marched on, now side by side, through the square toward a dark side street; they reached the edge of the plaza and walked down a few steps onto an ill-lit street. Loeb took off his jacket and slipped his glasses in the side pocket. He squinted around, looking for a safe place to put the garment.

"My glasses," he nervously explained to Hemingway. "If they're broken I couldn't get them fixed here."

To his surprise, he looked up and saw Hemingway smiling at him. It was a boyish, contagious smile—and even in that moment, that grin made it hard for Loeb to dislike him. He even offered to hold Loeb's jacket. Loeb then offered to hold his. Their mutual rage had suddenly seeped away. The men unclenched their fists, put their jackets on, and walked back through the square.

When they returned to the café, the rest of the entourage acted as though nothing had happened. Everyone kept drinking. Loeb and Guthrie ignored each other. As for Twysden, Loeb realized that maybe she wasn't worth all of this antagonism after all. A line had been crossed; he felt suddenly numb about her.

"Duff," he decided, "no longer seemed to matter."

THE NEXT MORNING, Loeb received a note from Hemingway.

"I was terribly tight and nasty to you last night," he wrote. He wished that he could wipe out what had happened, he went on, adding that he was ashamed of his behavior and of the "stinking, unjust uncalled for things I said."

Loeb turned up at lunch and afterward accepted Hemingway's apology in person. He hoped they could be friends as before, he told him.

"But I knew we wouldn't be," he wrote later.

Nothing—not even a sincere apology—could undo what had been done and said. Perhaps, at that time, Loeb thought that he and Hemingway would simply go their separate ways. He couldn't have guessed that Hemingway would soon do something that would link them for the rest of their lives and beyond.

Mercifully, it was time to depart. As everyone was checking out of the Hotel Quintana, it transpired that Twysden and Guthrie couldn't pay for their room. Guthrie may have failed to procure the necessary funds during his recent jaunt to England, or else the couple just expected someone else to pick up the tab. Hemingway was enraged about the situation, according to Donald Stewart. Twysden and Guthrie were mortifying him in front of his friend Juanito Quintana, who already regarded them as drunks and a sacrilegious presence in his reverential *taurmachine* establishment. Stewart ended up paying the bill. Following this final fracas, he noted, any remaining "camaraderie fell to pieces."

Loeb, Smith, Twysden, and Guthrie hired a car to take them up to Saint-Jean-de-Luz. Hemingway and Hadley prepared to leave for Madrid. Hemingway had been in suspiciously high spirits and "overdid the heartiness," Loeb observed before they all left. On that note, the fiesta ended.

"Some fiesta," Loeb recalled glumly.

Donald Stewart departed for Antibes, where he would recuperate at Sara and Gerald Murphy's villa. On the way there, he later wrote, "it occurred to me that the events of the past week might make interesting material for a novel."

He was not the only one to think so.

8

The Knock Out

IF DONALD STEWART HAD ANY serious designs on translating the Pamplona fiasco into literature, he seems to have forgotten about them quickly. Instead, he devoted the next two weeks to, as he put it, "the intensive sun-tanning of my body" on the beaches of the Riviera and mulled a follow-up to his recently released satire.

"The success of *The Haddocks Abroad* seemed to call for a sequel to be known as 'Mr. and Mrs. Haddock in Paris France,'" he recalled, and that was apparently the end of his would-be Pamplona novel.

For Hemingway, however, the events of the previous week had become practically priceless. Here was the heaven-sent trigger he had been waiting for.

"Let the pressure build," he had told himself. "When I had to write [a novel], then it would be the only thing to do and there would be no choice."

He had now reached that point. Just as the pressure surrounding him had built to an almost intolerable level — all of those financial woes, the fears of obscurity and of being surpassed, the excruciating writer's block — Duff Twysden had saved the day. The moment she arrived at the Hotel Quintana, everything essentially came together for Hemingway at last. Back in Paris, people had suspected that she might someday make great fodder for a novel. Yet when Hemingway saw her there at the fiesta — a Jezebel in Arcadia, manipulating all of her suitors like marionettes — he knew that he had figured out the puzzle at last. A story began to shape itself in Hemingway's mind — an intense, poignant story. Suddenly every fiesta confrontation, insult, hangover, and bit of frazzled sexual tension took on a real literary currency. The story almost began to write itself.

After the fiesta, Hemingway and Hadley boarded a train to Madrid, where they would watch Cayetano Ordóñez perform in the ring again.

En route, they drank with a couple of priests and a handful of civil guards, but Hemingway may also have been busy translating the fiesta's events onto paper as the train sped south. Once he started working on the Pamplona story, he could not stop. The couple moved into the Pensión Aguilar in Madrid, where Hemingway wrote furiously in the mornings. During the afternoons, he went with Hadley to the bullfights. The next morning he would begin again. No longer would it take him half a day to scratch a single paragraph onto a page. Not even a bout of fever and suspected dysentery quashed his momentum.

"Have been working like hell," he reported to Bill Smith a week after the fiesta entourage had broken up. He soon wrote again, informing Smith that he had been turning out around 1,200 words a day since leaving Pamplona.

"Some of it's maybe bludy good," he added.

He was still referring to his new project as a "story" at this time and revealed little to Smith about its content, although he did give some hints that the tale was rooted in actual events and might feature some characters drawn from real life. He had "gotten some swell stuff on this trip," he told Smith.

By early August, however, he let it be known that he was officially about to join the novel club. Sylvia Beach was the first to get the news.

"I've written six chapters on a novel and am going great," he wrote to her.

By that time, he and Hadley had moved on to Valencia; they had seen seventeen bullfights, and he had completed fifteen thousand words of the manuscript. He had kicked it off with a thirty-three-page draft penned on loose-leaf paper. His handwriting—smooth, even, and upright—belied the urgency with which the story poured out of him. At this point, Hemingway's tale was basically a précis of dialogue and events that had just gone down in Pamplona—from his conversations with Quintana and Ordóñez, to his aversion to the American ambassador, to the affair between Twysden and Loeb: "[Harold] was in love with Duff and she had slept with him while Pat was away in Scotland and told Pat about it and it had not seemed to make any difference but now whenever he got drunk he kept coming back to it. She had slept with other men before but they had not been of Harold's race and had not come on parties afterwards."

Also included was the showdown between Loeb and Guthrie:

Pat stood wobbly. ". . . Why don't you see you're not wanted, Loeb. Go away . . . Go away for God's sake. Take that sad Jewish face away. Don't you think I'm right?"

Loeb just sat there . . . looking through his spectacles, taking it all seriously. His affair with a lady of title.

"But I won't go Pat," said Loeb.

In Hemingway's on-paper version of the fight, as in real life, fisticuffs are averted at the last minute.

All of the Pamplona entourage members appeared as themselves in this draft. Nearly everyone was badly behaved. Pat was depicted as drunk and belligerent, and repeatedly informed Cayetano Ordóñez that "bulls have no balls." Don was the resident jester who ordered ceaseless shoe shines for Pat from local bootblacks. Duff smoldered and quipped and undressed the handsome Ordóñez with her eyes; her probable corruption of the young bullfighter—and her corrupting potential in general—promised almost unlimited dramatic potential.

"I will not judge the gang who were at Pamplona," wrote Hem-as-protagonist in the manuscript, but Hem-as-author was setting everyone down on paper to be judged by readers for generations to come.

He soon put this loose-leaf draft aside—but a good deal of material from these first pages would eventually be transplanted into the official manuscript. His vision was startlingly clear from the beginning. His "highbrow-lowbrow" formula was also already in place—and it was a potent version of what he had described to Liveright earlier that spring. Like his *In Our Time* stories, this new Pamplona story already contained something for everyone. Its terse, innovative prose would titillate the literary crowd, and the simplicity of the style would make it accessible to mainstream readers. And if that deceptive simplicity didn't do the trick, the story promised to stand alone as a scandalous *roman à clef* featuring dissolute representatives from the worlds of wealth and ambition.

"There is a lot of dope about high society in it," Hemingway wryly noted in a later discarded passage of the manuscript. "And that is always interesting."

IN VALENCIA, Hemingway ditched the loose-leaf paper and began writing the rest of the story in a small sand-colored French school notebook, the first of seven. On its cover, Hemingway inscribed his name and his

Paris address, perhaps in a return-to-sender plea inspired by the Great Train Robbery. He would not be sacrificing another nascent novel.

In that first notebook, he moved the setting of his new novel to Paris. The action would eventually wind back to everything that had just happened at the fiesta, but "to understand what happened in Pamplona you must understand the Quarter in Paris," he wrote, and proceeded to pen an unsparing portrait of the scene that recalled his early spiteful *Toronto Star* stories about Montparnasse.

"There is nothing romantic about the Quarter and very little that is beautiful," he wrote. Everyone there detested everyone else, from the writers to the critics to the painters. It was a grim, unwholesome world, filled with "fairies" and women who casually racked up abortions. The only happy inhabitants of the Quarter were the drunks, and even they all inevitably succumbed to gloom. He offered up specific examples of the expat reprobates who populated the Left Bank. Anyone who had ever rankled Hemingway at the Dôme or Dingo was about to get sent up. The draft was littered with unflattering descriptions of the local color: a popular former showgirl who serves as a patron saint of the colony's cafés (this was, of course, Flossie Martin); a scampering little Greek painter and self-proclaimed duke named "Zizi" (the real-life version went by "Mitzi"; he was, as barman Jimmie Charters put it, "the best-known person in Montparnasse in its heyday"); an unwashed, alcoholic former intellectual who moons around drunkenly at the Quarter's popular cafés, accepting handouts (a character any Quarterite could easily identify as expat writer Harold Stearns). Hemingway's debut novel appeared poised to become a who's who of the colony.

Against this backdrop, he introduced the major characters who had been given their practice run in his loose-leaf preamble: Duff, Pat, and Loeb. Donald Stewart and Bill Smith would be condensed into a single character, "Bill Gorton." In the loose-leaf Pamplona story, Hemingway called the narrator "Hem"; in this notebook, he became "Jake Barnes."

At first glance, Jake has a lot in common with Hemingway: he is a young, well-connected Paris-based American foreign correspondent with bullfighting *afición*. The character wryly notes that, like all newspaper reporters, he has long aspired to write a novel, and now that he is doing it, "the novel will have that awful taking-the-pen-in-hand quality that afflicts newspaper men when they start to write their own book."

Yet there would be departures from Hemingway's personal biography in creating the character. He borrowed a line from the résumé of his *in our time* publisher Bill Bird when he made Jake the co-founder of a wire service. Also, unlike Hemingway, Jake is burdened with neither wife nor child. Hadley had appeared briefly in the loose-leaf draft but did not make the leap to his beige notebooks. (The real Hadley seems to have been un-rattled by her omission; she later claimed that she had found the finished book "magnificent" and that it made her "happy.") Jake was to be a free agent, tethered only by his longing for a certain titled lady.

As he introduced the other main characters, Hemingway revealed how much information he had squirreled away about their prototypes. He later reportedly remarked in an interview that he had "hated newspaper work" because he "was shy and didn't like to ask people questions about their private lives"; yet for someone with this professed aversion, he had a deep cache of intelligence on his various victims. "To damn people properly you must have the dope on them," he confided to Ezra Pound. All of that ac-crued dope—especially on Loeb and Twysden—was now pressed into service. No real-life detail was too gory to be barred from the pages of Hemingway's notebook.

"When you are writing stories about actual people," Hemingway later told an editor friend, "you should make them those people in everything except telephone addresses."

He kicked off the book with a lengthy introduction to his leading lady. Eventually Hemingway began to call the character "Lady Brett Ashley," but for the entire first draft of his novel, Duff would appear under her own name. She fared badly, especially in the earliest passages.

"Duff had been somebody once," Hemingway began, and then crossed out the line. He started again: "Duff had something once." But now she is a "typical Montparnasse drunk, doing absolutely nothing else except oc-casionally posing for people who flattered her by begging to paint her." Lest this imply that she is still in demand, Hemingway clarified that these painters are nobodies: first-rate artists no longer knock at her door now that she has reached the advanced age of thirty-four.

In describing the character's past, Hemingway gave a near-literal ver-sion of the real Lady Duff's turbulent romantic résumé. Already divorced from a starter husband who found her "too expensive for what he got," Hemingway's Duff has left England and is currently idling in Paris, wait-ing for a divorce from her second husband—eventually revealed to be a ninth baronet, a slight amendment from the real Sir Roger Twysden's actual designation as tenth baronet—from whom she has leveraged her title. As in real life, the couple have a son, whom the Duff character has abandoned before sashaying off to the Continent with a man named Pat.

Still, the character does have some redeeming qualities: Hemingway's early version of Duff is "clean bred, generous and her lines were always as sharp"—probably a reference to both her prototype's witticisms and her lithe build. Hemingway would later improve on this description: "Brett was damned good-looking. She wore a slipover jersey sweater and a tweed skirt, and her hair was brushed back like a boy's. She started all that. She was built with curves like the hull of a racing yacht, and you missed none of it with that wool jersey."

If anything, the real Duff Twysden got a bit of an upgrade here: while Hemingway's Lady Duff/Lady Brett certainly has a wardrobe in common with her prototype, the actual Duff Twysden's jersey look and cropped hair were in fashion at the time, not pioneering, and she was not particularly voluptuous. Yet in a mere forty-nine words, Hemingway would sculpt the real Duff into a trailblazing, Amazonian fictional version of herself, someone who inspires imitation in women and desire in men.

Pat Guthrie was up next. In the pages of Hemingway's notebook, he is a weak bankrupt and an embarrassing drunk. In addition to these offenses, he is also gay: "[He] had various habits that Duff felt sorry for and did not think a man should have and cured him by constant watchfulness and the exercise of her then very strong will."

Like the real Pat Guthrie, Hemingway's Pat subsists on an allowance that trickles in from across the Channel. On paper, he and Duff languish in bed most of the day and drink all night at cafés and parties, at which the fictional Duff regularly gets so soused that she loses her powers of sight, speech, and hearing, one after the other. Pat is, Hemingway wrote, prone to abominable behavior on these outings. That said, he is "a charming companion . . . one of the very most charming." Eventually Hemingway would give Guthrie the name "Mike Campbell."

Unlike the others, Harold Loeb was given a pseudonym in this early pass: "Gerald Cohn." It would eventually be changed to "Robert Cohn." As with Twysden, Hemingway went deep into Loeb's background and put it all on paper. "Gerald Cohn was a member through his father of one of the richest Jewish families in the east and through his mother of one of the oldest," he wrote. Cohn also happens to be a graduate of Princeton; there, Hemingway wrote, Cohn's classmates had treated him to an advanced course in anti-Semitism, and he had taken up boxing to give himself some sort of defense against his detractors.

"How that kike hated to fight and what a sweet scrapper he was," says Cohn's fictional boxing coach Spider Kelly in Hemingway's first draft. The line would be cut later.

In reality, Loeb had wrestled at Princeton, not boxed, but Hemingway's version was only a slight digression from fact. Like Loeb, Cohn has also been left $50,000 by his father and has abandoned his wife and family to start a literary magazine. Hemingway's fictionalized version of *Broom,* however, reflects none of the actual publication's sophistication, nor does it allude to the real journal's high-profile contributors. Cohn is painted as a lightweight interloper with slender credentials for running a literary magazine. Like the real *Broom,* Cohn's magazine has folded.

Loeb's fraught relationship with Kitty Cannell was also too juicy to be left out of the novel. Cannell was given a shrewish literary makeover as "Frances Clyne," a woman who "lived on gossip" and inflicts on Cohn, her noncommittal lover, "an atmosphere of abortions, doubts, . . . dirty rumors, dirtier reporters, still dirtier suspicions." Like Duff, Frances Clyne is a lady of a certain age—meaning, of course, that she is teetering on the edge of desperation. And like her prototype Kitty, Clyne has been lingering in Paris, awaiting a divorce, and angling to snare Cohn as a husband. Yet she subjects him to humiliating, emasculating jealous tirades and interrogations—once in the presence of Jake. ("Why did he sit there?" Jake wonders. "Why did he keep on taking it like that?") The portrait was guaranteed to set the Montparnasse gossip mill on fire.

The fictional relationship mirrored what had actually happened between Loeb and Cannell: Cohn rejects Clyne and falls in love with the Duff Twysden character. And in Hemingway's pages, Cohn eventually has an affair with Duff/Brett, albeit in San Sebastián instead of Saint-Jean-de-Luz. This drives a wedge between Cohn and Jake, for Jake is also in love with Duff. For Jake and Duff, however, there will never be a holiday of ardent lovemaking in a seaside village. Not because Duff doesn't desire him—in Hemingway's reimagined version of events she does, almost desperately so—but because Jake is impotent, the result of a war wound.

It was a fascinating decision to make about a male protagonist—especially one created by a writer known for goading friends and acquaintances into bullrings and boxing face-offs. Yet Hemingway didn't actually use the word "impotent" until deep into the book, and then it comes up only twice, in quick succession — and still isn't directly attributed to Jake. For the most part, Jake's condition has to be inferred through allusions in dialogue and private ruminations.

"Well, it was a rotten way to be wounded," Jake broods in one passage. He finds solace in gallows humor, recalling with grim wit a speech made to him in the hospital by a sympathetic liaison colonel: "You, a foreigner . . . have given more than your life."

The scene perfectly showcased Hemingway's tip-of-the-iceberg omission approach. Years later he discussed the exact nature of Jake's wound. "I got the idea when I was in the hospital in Italy after I had been wounded," he told an interviewer in the mid-1950s. "I too had been wounded in the groin [and] I was swollen up like footballs . . . but I was not made impotent like Jake Barnes, obviously. I was put into a so-called genito-urinary ward where there were many guys with groin wounds, and it was pretty bad." Hemingway told another friend that he had just been nicked in the scrotum by shrapnel, but some of the other "poor bastards" in the ward had had everything blown off.

It was important for readers to realize, he explained in another interview, that Jake's testicles are intact and undamaged, and that Jake is "capable of all normal feelings as a *man* but incapable of consummating them." Hemingway depicted Jake's torturous desire for Lady Duff/Lady Brett in spare, repetitive stream-of-consciousness ponderings that would have made Gertrude Stein proud: "Good advice, anyway. Not to think about it. Oh, it was swell advice. Try and take it sometime. Try and take it. I lay awake thinking and my mind jumping around. Then I couldn't keep away from it, and I started to think about Brett and all the rest of it went away. I was thinking about Brett and my mind stopped jumping around and started to go in sort of smooth waves. Then all of a sudden I started to cry."

Some scholars and Hemingway friends have speculated that Hemingway may have been channeling his frustration over the real Duff Twysden's possible refusal to sleep with him into this other form of on-page frustration. In any case, Jake's war wound relegates him — and elevates him — to the role of the perfect observer. He is the only one in the group who is incapable of behaving badly — carnally speaking, at least.

Hemingway eventually downplayed the gravitas of his choice. "Impotence is a pretty dull subject compared with war or love or the old lucha por la vida [life struggle]," he would write to Maxwell Perkins a year later.

But Jake's impotence made it clear that Hemingway was willing to take wild risks—even ones that might compromise his personal dignity, for there would certainly be assumptions that he had based Jake's condition on his own well-publicized wartime injuries. Though he had been enjoying an almost aggressively masculine image—one that was about to prove immensely bankable—he would not hesitate to challenge that image if doing so would serve his art.

Before moving the action in his novel from Paris to Spain, Hemingway gave a few other Crowd luminaries some cameos. Ford Madox Ford bumbles into the novel's pages under the name "Braddocks" (amended from the initial pseudonym "Bradox," perhaps Hemingway's skimpiest attempt at an alias), his wheezing and gloating, bad teeth, red face, walrus mustache, and buffoonery on display for all to behold. In that first draft, Braddocks patronizes a café waiter and, while sitting with Jake and a "fellow named Dos Passos," proceeds to snub a man who has no idea that he's being snubbed. Braddocks resurfaces later in the manuscript alongside his amiable but asinine wife, who grows so excited when speaking French that she is "liable to have no idea what she was saying." Like the real Fords, the Braddockses host evenings at *bals musette,* to which expats flock. The published portrait would end up being relatively innocuous, with much of the damning physical description of Ford edited out; but the omitted material portended what Hemingway would have in store for Ford in later years and subsequent books.

In that first draft, Ezra Pound and Sylvia Beach are spared appearances; Gertrude Stein is mentioned only in passing. Robert McAlmon is ignored altogether, although his exclusion may have been a greater insult than even an unflattering cameo. F. Scott Fitzgerald is name-dropped by Jake Barnes but does not materialize as a character. It appears, however, that Hemingway intended to include one of Fitzgerald's characters from *The Great Gatsby*—the polo-playing, philandering Tom Buchanan—as one of Lady Duff/Lady Brett's past lovers. In Hemingway's manuscript, when Lady Duff/Lady Brett and Pat/Mike casually discuss Duff's past conquests, they mention a fellow who seems to fit the bill:

> *"Duff's gone off with men. But they weren't ever jews and they didn't come and hang about afterwards,"* [said Mike.]
> *"Damned good chaps,"* Duff said. *"You remember Tom?"*
> *"He was an American,"* Mike said. *"Maybe you know him. Chap who plays polo."*

The passage would be cut later. Still, even though this reference was omitted, Fitzgerald would soon leave his imprint on the novel in a far more significant way.

SINCE LEAVING PAMPLONA, the Hemingways had ricocheted from Madrid to Valencia, back to Madrid, then on to San Sebastián. They finally landed in Hendaye, a small port town in French Basque country, just southwest of Saint-Jean-de-Luz. By the time they arrived, he had completed over ten chapters of his new book.

"How long is a novel anyway?" he wrote to a friend, adding that the only book he had with him — *War and Peace* — was a daunting 1,563 pages. By comparison, Hemingway had cobbled together two hundred pages over the past few weeks — but it was going to be a "Wham," he reported.

Several days later, he wrote to Ezra Pound about the novel but implored him, "Don't for Chrise sake say anything to anybody." This probably meant "Tell everyone in sight" — which is essentially what Hemingway himself had been doing. The literati on two continents had now been alerted about the imminent arrival of Ernest Hemingway's debut novel.

By August, the characters' prototypes themselves may have known that he was cooking something up: in one of his earliest post-Pamplona outreaches to Bill Smith, Hemingway asked him to greet Harold Loeb and Don Stewart on his behalf; that greeting was almost certain to accompany the news that since they all parted ways, Hemingway had been working like mad on a mysterious new tome. He soon informed Smith that the story was "going like wild fire," despite the fact that he had been weathering some inconvenient intestinal issues.

He told his former *Toronto Star* colleague Morley Callaghan about the novel in mid-August, and assured him that it "ought to be damned good." By then it was more than halfway finished — over forty thousand words had been inscribed in those little notebooks — but Hemingway showed no signs of slowing. To editor Ernest Walsh, he excitedly opined that the book was so scandalous it would be "suppressed the day they publish it." Soon Gertrude Stein and Alice Toklas were looped in: he had never worked so hard, Hemingway informed the ladies, sometimes staying up until nearly dawn. Despite his exhaustion, he often still couldn't sleep and would rise again to write.

Perhaps the most cocksure missive of all was dispatched to Jane Heap, co-editor of *The Little Review*. "It is a hell of a fine novel," he asserted, adding that it was simply written and action-packed. "I think it will be a knock out and will let these bastards who say yes he can write very beautiful little paragraphs know where they get off at."

He audaciously declared that he had avoided the pitfall that usually tripped up first-time novelists: relying on autobiographical information. Furthermore, when this book came out, no critic was going to compare him to another writer ever again. And by the way, the book also happened to be funny. How frequently did American writers happen to be funny anymore? Take Sherwood Anderson, for example: he was funny in person, but his humor dried up once it hit paper.

"Well wait for this one," he wrote.

Hemingway knew that he had a hot property on his hands, and he was not going to let it go cheap. Too long had he worked "for love," he informed Heap, adding that he was not yet in a position to talk business. He then proceeded to talk business anyway. No publisher was going to get his hands on this novel without paying a $1,000 advance: "Now when I've got something I know is valuable I'm not going to give it away." The more a publisher paid for a book, the more incentive the house would have to promote it, he reasoned.

A few weeks later, Hemingway wrote to his mother and informed her that the novel had a new name — *Fiesta* — although he was on the fence about it. He added that he had indeed been offered a $1,000 advance for the new novel — not by Boni & Liveright but rather by another publisher, he contended. "Of course [I] will stick with my contract," he told her.

None of Hemingway's other surviving correspondence from this period indicates that he actually got such an offer, but in his mind's eye, his still incomplete and unedited manuscript had already propelled him into an auction-like realm filled with hungry bidders.

HEMINGWAY originally intended to stay in Hendaye until he finished the book, but he came back to Paris on August 18, 1925. Even in that bustling city, nothing distracted him from his novel. He had been working on it for a mere month but was already nearing the endgame.

"I want to get it finished now and then put it away and come back and work it over," he informed Gertrude Stein and Alice Toklas.

Physically Hemingway was in France, but mentally he was back in Spain with Duff Twysden and the rest of the Pamplona entourage. The novel's backbone was in place and would remain essentially intact up through the published version. The book now documented the lives of a group of expats as they first coincide in Paris and then venture as an uneasy entourage to the San Fermín fiesta in Pamplona. Against a backdrop of ceaseless drinking, bullfights, and sexual jealousy over Lady Duff/Lady Brett, civility among the group members quickly spirals into a morass of insults, jealousy, and fistfights.

Along the way, some of the book's characters stop off at Burguete and the Irati River, which had proved such a disappointment to Hemingway earlier that summer. The real Irati may have been a casualty of the logging company's invasion, but Hemingway transformed its fictional counterpart back into the bucolic fantasyland of his 1924 pilgrimage with Donald Stewart, Bill Bird, and Robert McAlmon. Hemingway's portrait of Burguete was a love letter to the region, which served as the unpolluted, idyllic counterpoint to the artifice of the Quarter and its inhabitants. It could also be seen as a love letter to Cézanne, whose paintings Hemingway had admired so ardently in Stein's salon and in Paris's Musée du Luxembourg: "We walked on the road between the thick trunks of the old beeches and the sunlight came through the trees in light patches on the grass. The trees were big, and the foliage was thick but it was not gloomy. There was no undergrowth, only the smooth grass, very green and fresh, and the big gray trees well spaced as though it were a park."

As Cézanne had painted his lush landscapes with broad, thick strokes, Hemingway was doing the same with words. His new novel was becoming an exposition of everything he had learned from his mentors and taught himself over the last three years.

The new Burguete scenes also gave Bill Smith his moment in the sun. In the earlier Paris scenes, Hemingway introduces the character "Bill Gorton," an amalgamation of Bill Smith and Donald Stewart. At first Gorton is more Stewart than Smith: the character is supposed to be a successful novelist with a string of best-selling books to his credit. Yet as the book progresses, the character takes on more of Smith's attributes, especially his idiosyncratic wit. As showcased in one Burguete scene, in which Gorton and Jake share a picnic of icy wine and cold chicken while fishing, Gorton specializes in quirky monologues that smack of the pulpit: "Bill gestured with the drumstick in one hand and the bottle of wine in the other. 'Let us rejoice in our blessings. Let us utilize the fowls of the air. Let us utilize the product of the vine. Will you utilize a little, brother?'" He and Jake Barnes then "utilize" quite a bit of the wine they have brought with them on their trek to the river. Hemingway lifted the phrase directly from Smith, who had been playing around with the word during his trip to Burguete with Hemingway.

"I remember it catching on somehow," Smith recalled later. "We all have our moments I guess. You can get pretty silly when you're tight."

Yet for all of the character's comic-relief silliness, not all of his remarks are endearing. Bill Gorton also utters a handful of disconcerting anti-Semitic slurs against Cohn—referring to him as "that kike" and deriding him for acting "superior and Jewish."

Donald Stewart later shamefacedly took the blame for having been the probable inspiration for Bill Gorton's anti-Semitic remarks and exclamations. "I have no doubt that I was really basically anti-Semitic in those days, as probably also was Hemingway," he said. His was not, he clarified, a deep-rooted hatred like the variety that gave rise to Nazism, but rather "a form of social snobbishness, something that people simply took for granted" at the time. He hadn't, he recalled, been cruel to Loeb to his face, but had been "even worse behind his back."

After finishing the Burguete scenes, Hemingway sent the core characters to Pamplona, to the Hotel Quintana—dubbed "Hotel Montoya" in the novel. As he began to write about the fiesta, it seemed as though the entire centuries-old spectacle had been contrived to show off his newly fashioned rhythmic prose: "The fiesta was really started. It kept up day and night for seven days. The dancing kept up, the drinking kept up, the noise went on. The things that happened could only have happened during a fiesta. Everything became quite unreal finally and it seemed as though nothing could have any consequences . . . It was a fiesta and it went on for seven days."

As in real life, Pamplona's fictional streets are filled with *riau-riau* dancers, peasants wreathed in garlic necklaces, and sky-high puppets of Moors, kings, and queens. At one point in Hemingway's story, some dancers form a circle around the Lady Duff character, who tries to dance with them and is made to stand still: "They wanted her as an image to dance around."

Yet his anxiety that Pamplona, like Paris, was on the verge of being spoiled by expats also seeped into the text. Even in the pages of Hemingway's preamble loose-leaf draft, the American ambassador and the "haute monde from Biarritz and San Sebastián" surge into Hemingway's fictional square as they did in real life, except their presence on paper becomes almost sinister. The young purist matador Cayetano Ordóñez is particularly vulnerable to their influence. "People would wreck him to make a nymphmaniacs holiday," wrote Hemingway. A pure, fine bull-fighter like that, he added, should stay away from "this Grand Hotel business . . . until he is safely arrived." And even then, Hemingway warns, this expat crowd is poisonous. He offers up bullfighter Juan Belmonte—who appears in both the early draft and the published version of the book under his own name—as evidence of what happens when a matador allows himself to become fashionable. Belmonte is written up as a sallow, hemorrhoidal sellout who performs merely to please clueless society people, and who is willing to face off only against little bulls better suited to teaching children at bullfighting schools.

At the end of Hemingway's novel, however, the most potent poison is delivered neither by the objectionable ambassador nor by any of the Biarritz crowd. Rather, it is injected by the steady hand of the fictionalized Lady Duff, whose presence—as in real life—sets the entourage's men at one another's throats. Loeb's character Cohn tells Lady Duff/Lady Brett that she is a modern-day Circe. Amused, she relays the comment to Pat/Mike.

"He claims she turns men into swine," he tattles to the others at a café.

In Hemingway's book as in real life, the presence of Lady Duff/Lady Brett truly does bring out the pig in nearly every man in the entourage. Cohn is reduced to the most swinish state of all. As the real Twysden had done to Loeb in actuality, the fictionalized Duff rejects Cohn after their seaside holiday. After that, Cohn spends much of the fictional fiesta stalking her, even tailing her in the shadows when she takes a walk with Jake. His only relief from her siren song are trips to the local barber—for Cohn, like Loeb, is depicted as a relentless stress-groomer.

As the story poured out of him, Hemingway's notebooks piled up. Near the end of his fictional fiesta, he finally made significant leaps from fact to fiction. On paper, at last, he got to have his fight with Loeb: instead of chummily resolving their differences at the last minute, Jake and Cohn actually come to blows. (Or, rather, Cohn knocks Jake out cold at a café; Pat/Mike is also flung to the ground.) Instead of being satisfied by tinkering with the affections of her fellow expats like the real Duff, the fictional Duff embarks on a full-fledged affair with the Cayetano Ordóñez character. (In reality, the only physical contact between the two was said to be a handshake on the stairs of the Hotel Quintana.) In Hemingway's notebooks, Cohn jealously beats the hell out of Ordóñez on the eve of an important bullfight; Ordóñez withstands the blows and then fights with particular elegance the following day, giving the cut-off ear of one bull to Lady Duff/Lady Brett as a trophy.

Hemingway's Lady Duff exits Pamplona somewhat more gracefully than the real Lady Duff did earlier that summer: instead of defaulting on her hotel bill and waiting for someone else to pay it, she simply decamps to Madrid with Ordóñez, whom Hemingway refers to as Niño de la Palma, or simply Niño, in early drafts. The real Pat Guthrie's fiscal humiliations, by contrast, are recorded for posterity: not only does Hemingway depict Pat/Mike as wholly broke and a drunken wreck, but also, by the fictional fiesta's conclusion, the character is forced to admit that he has even borrowed money from Quintana, the hotelier. Jake and Bill deposit him at Saint-Jean-de-Luz (after footing his portion of the bill for the car and his drinks en route), where he plans to subsist on credit until the next installment of his allowance comes in.

At last, the fictional fiesta is over. The character Bill Gorton summarizes it best: the whole week has been "like a wonderful nightmare."

On September 21, 1925, Hemingway completed the manuscript, penning the final sentences in a seventh little notebook. He had written over eighty thousand words in at least five cities and towns in just over two months.

9

Breach Season

AFTER FINISHING HIS DRAFT, Hemingway seemed to be suffering from the melancholy of things completed, as philosopher Friedrich Nietzsche once put it. His head was "tired as hell inside," he wrote to editor Ernest Walsh, and he was restless and "damned lonesome." He swam in the Seine every day and drank heavily, but was so exhausted that even whisky couldn't make him drunk.

Italy beckoned him: he was dying to go on a recuperative walking tour and "let [his] head get normal again," but Hadley wouldn't be able to join him because Bumby had just rejoined them in Paris. It might be therapeutic, he thought, to go to Venice and "get a little romantic fucking," but fears of spawning a tribe of illegitimate offspring and getting stuck with support payments prevented him, he joked to Walsh, from taking along another girl.

The real-life Pamplona entourage had dispersed all over the world. Lady Duff Twysden had been staying at a country pub on credit; she would eventually return to Montparnasse and resume her role as resident siren. In the final passages of Hemingway's novel, his protagonist Jake Barnes goes off to Madrid to save the fictional Duff from herself: she has parted ways with the bullfighter, Niño de la Palma, having realized that he is ashamed of her. ("He wanted me to grow my hair out," she confesses to Jake. "Me, with long hair. Can you see it? I'd look so like hell.") They end the book the way they began it—in love and destined for misery:

> *"Oh, Jake," Duff said. "We could have had such a damned good time together."* . . .
>   *"Yes," I said. "It's nice as hell to think so."*

Though the fictional Duff would be bound to Jake in perpetuity, it appears that the real Duff Twysden fell out of Hemingway's life once he completed his book. Around this time he received from her a missive, addressed to "Ernest Hemingway Esq." in her languorous handwriting, imploring him to give her some cash.

"I want 3000 francs—but for Gods sake lend me as much as you can," she wrote.

It was a brazen request, considering that Hemingway was still living off his wife's trust fund. (Perhaps with this in mind, Twysden had sagely entrusted the letter to a bartender at the Dingo rather than sending it to the Hemingways' apartment.) The money matter was, Twysden added, an emergency: she owed the country pub a considerable sum and did not dare abscond without paying her bill.

"I am in a stinking fix but for once only temporary and can pay you back for sure," she promised him.

It is unclear whether he sent her the money, but in any case, their once-intense friendship seems to have more or less ended that autumn. The rift may have been an organic one, in which two people discover they have less in common than they'd originally thought—or else Hemingway may have lost interest in Twysden now that her utility had dwindled. Perhaps for Hemingway, as for Harold Loeb, she simply no longer seemed to matter. Unlike Loeb, Hemingway may never have been able to steer Twysden into bed, but she had ended up giving him something far more significant. And now that he had created a superior version of her on paper, her far more obedient fictional counterpart would be commanding his attention instead in the year to come.

Meanwhile, Donald Stewart was summoned to Los Angeles: when he got back to Paris from the Riviera, a cable from his publisher informed him that one of his books had been optioned by MGM; the studio wanted him on-site to write the script. Stewart accepted the offer warily.

"I knew that Hollywood was regarded with contempt by most of my writer friends," he recalled later, "but I argued myself into believing that it would offer me a new and much wider audience."

Any hesitation seems to have melted away once he got back to New York and saw his photo on the front page of the *Mirror*. "It was exciting to be treated as an important 'catch,'" he wrote. It was equally thrilling to inform people on the train to California that he was going to Hollywood to write a movie.

Harold Loeb and Bill Smith had also decided to return to America.

Theirs was the one friendship that emerged stronger from the ruins of the Pamplona odyssey. After the fiesta, while Hemingway was busily recording its events for posterity and Stewart was sunbathing on the Riviera, Loeb and Smith had gone on a three-week bike tour to explore the Rhine and Worms, the German ancestral seat of Loeb's father's family. They had then returned to Paris and gone together on a prolonged fiesta of a different variety, this time in the company of two club hostesses.

For Loeb, the spree was a coda. Paris was over for him. *Broom* had folded; his friendship with Hemingway had been a bust; his affair with Lady Duff had ended on a most unsatisfying note.

"It was now or never," Loeb wrote of his decision to return to New York. "My book [*Doodab*] was coming out. I was going back to a land transformed by distance into a place of shining towers and green hills." His time in Paris had taught him many lessons, including "what to expect of a friend and what not to expect."

Loeb would also soon learn that there was no such thing as a clean break. He and Hemingway played tennis once after Hemingway returned from Spain; even though the friendship had clearly run its course, Loeb claimed that he made one last effort at appeasement by allowing Hemingway to beat him. Even this concession may have provided additional material for Hemingway's new novel: in its pages, Robert Cohn's tennis game would go to hell after he falls in love with Lady Brett. Vain about his own game, Loeb took issue with Hemingway's depiction.

"The things one imagines!" he fumed decades later.

He and Smith booked passage on the same liner back to New York. As their departure date drew closer, arrangements for a small bon voyage restaurant dinner were made. The guests were to include Hemingway and Hadley, Loeb and Smith, and Kitty Cannell. Although it is unclear who organized the outing, the ostensible purpose was to bury hatchets. The animosities that had peaked during the fiesta seemed to have simmered down to their pre-festival levels; the Pamplona combatants had apparently reached some sort of wary détente.

Hemingway would not be sorry to see Loeb leave; nor was he sad about losing Bill Smith to America. Smith was, Hemingway privately complained to another friend, prone to bouts of despondency so intense that they had been a factor in Hemingway's prolonged furlough from Paris that summer. He had feared that Smith's moods might derail his writing. "I'd rather he would have bumped himself off when he first began to get that way," he wrote, adding that Smith had been "a wonderful guy" once.

Ironically, at the farewell dinner, Bill Smith was the most spirited presence, Loeb recalled. Everyone automatically assumed their usual roles. Hemingway was "full of Madrid and bullfighting," but was apparently close-mouthed about the contents of his new book. Hadley and Cannell chatted with each other. Loeb held himself back from the banter and watched. Everything went smoothly until the waiter served Hemingway a plate containing a duck's "lower anatomy" while allotting the breasts to Loeb and Cannell. Hemingway apparently glowered over this but did not create a scene. The evening limped on and eventually farewells were exchanged.

Before they parted ways, however, Cannell received a jolt of unwelcome news from Hemingway. The two had been walking together and discussing the trip-wired topic of Hemingway's writing. Cannell liked his style but found his work lacking somehow. Like Loeb, she had given the matter some consideration and felt that she had a solution for him.

"If only you'd write about life instead of moods, you'd have a sure fire best seller," she implored him.

Hemingway replied that he was taking her advice.

"I'm writing a book with a plot and everything," he told her. "Everybody's in it. And I'm going to tear these two bastards apart," he added, gesturing toward Loeb and Smith, who were walking separately.

Then he pointed at Loeb: "And that kike Loeb is the villain."

If "everybody" was in it, that surely meant Cannell as well. Hemingway may have detected a look of panic on her face.

"But not you, Kitty . . . I'm not going to put you in," he told her. "I've always said you were a wonderful girl!" Hemingway then gave her a grin —the same wide, boyish smile he had given Loeb back in Pamplona as the two prepared to square off in a dark side street.

That smile, Cannell wrote later, made "you feel like giving him an apple—or your heart." Still, it did little to reassure her.

On September 5, Loeb and Smith left for New York. The group would never sit at a table together again. Yet they would soon be permanently linked to Hemingway and one another, whether they liked it or not.

AT THE END of September, Hemingway managed to get out of town after all—not to Italy, as he had hoped, but rather to Chartres, an ancient town southwest of Paris. He had wanted to bring along a woman; instead, he towed along his manuscript and went back to work.

The novel's title needed attention. Its working title, *Fiesta,* was out:

Hemingway had decided that he didn't want to use a foreign word after all. Besides, there was the risk that *Fiesta* might misrepresent the material as frivolous. In case anyone mistook the book for a Spanish and Parisian version of F. Scott Fitzgerald's *bon ton* antics, a weightier title would help create an atmosphere of gravitas around the work.

In an eighth notebook Hemingway scribbled his name and "Chartres, Sept. 27, 1925." Inside he wrote the header:

The Lost Generation
A Novel.
Foreword.

Gertrude Stein was about to become a significant presence in the book after all. In the foreword that followed, Hemingway recounted an incident that Stein had just related to him. She had recently stopped by a garage to have some work done on her ancient Ford. Four young mechanics were assisting the garage owner; one of them impressed Stein with his skill, and she quizzed the owner about how he had managed to find such good help.

"I thought you couldn't get boys to work any more," she said.

The owner replied that one simply could not hire anyone between the ages of twenty-two and thirty.

"C'est un generation perdu," he informed her. "No one wants them. They are no good. They were spoiled."

That said, he went on, men younger than twenty-two were still a harvestable crop. Stein asked what would become of the no-good age group.

"Nothing," the owner replied. "They know they are no good."

The anecdote reminded her of Hemingway's whole circle of contemporaries.

"That's what you are," she declared. "That's what you all are. All of you young people who served in the war, you are a lost generation."

Members of this unfortunate demographic could be easily identified by their lack of respect and lethal drinking habits, she added.

This anecdote would completely change the prism through which the entire book would be seen, Hemingway reasoned. With its addition, he was about to reconceive his cast of characters as a symbolic band of lost souls. It immediately elevated their dissipation and bad behavior: it wasn't their fault that they were drunk, aimless, and destructive; they had been ruined by an ignoble war and the flawed institutions that used to give life meaning. What was left, Hemingway wondered in the foreword, to guide them? His generation had unsuccessfully sought solace in the Catholic Church, Dadaism, royalism, and the movies. Now there was a void of guidance, spiritual or otherwise. Other writers had been grappling with these seismic issues, Hemingway conceded, but he implied that his own literary examination was about to prove far more meaningful.

"This is not a question of what kind of mothers will flappers make or where is bobbed hair leading us," he wrote in the foreword, taking an obvious swipe at Fitzgerald's subject matter.

Once again, perfect material had presented itself to Hemingway at a crucial moment. With this new Lost Generation angle, not only could he position himself as a revolutionary stylist and documenter of sexy, saleable material; he was now speaking for an entire generation, as Fitzgerald had been doing. Granted, they were saying very different things about their contemporaries, but that was just as well. It would differentiate Hemingway nicely.

He later claimed that he had felt immediately hostile to the idea of a "lost generation," at least in the way that Stein had meant it. The night when she told him the story, he walked home from her rue de Fleurus studio and decided en route that all generations had been "lost" in one way or another.

"I thought of Miss Stein and Sherwood Anderson and egotism and mental laziness versus discipline and I thought who is calling who a lost generation?" he later wrote. Stein's "dirty, easy labels" and talk of a lost generation could just go to hell.

He may have reviled the label, but he co-opted it anyway. He eventually axed *The Lost Generation* as a title and even did away with the long, treatise-like foreword. But he held fast to the sentiment of the foreword, condensing it into a brief epigraph that packed an even more powerful punch:

> "You are all a lost generation."
> —Gertrude Stein

His instinct had been spot-on. In the end, it took only these six simple, borrowed words to elevate the book from a work of gossip-fueled fiction into a generation-defining event.

There was still room for more gravitas, he decided. Even as he wrote about his generation's rejection of the church, he was mining the Bible as a source of alternative titles. In the same Chartres notebook containing the excised foreword, he listed some candidates pulled from the Book of Ecclesiastes, including *River to the Sea, Two Lie Together, The Old Leaven,* and *The Sun Also Rises.* The *Sun Also Rises* option had been culled from a line in the "Vanity of Life" passage:

> One generation passeth away, and another generation cometh:
> but the earth abideth for ever.
> The sun also ariseth, and the sun goeth down,
> and hasteth to his place where he arose.

The theme of death and regeneration was as poignant as that of a devastated generation, and it fit neatly with Hemingway's belief that each generation was just as lost as any other; the concept would resonate with him for the rest of his life. He enthused about Ecclesiastes in a letter to Ezra Pound; he implored his former mentor to read it again and not let his "just disgust with the so called Christian religion" prevent him from seeing its merits. Soon he made a decision.

"[I] am calling it The Sun Also Rises," he wrote to Harold Loeb a few weeks later.

Hemingway declined, however, to describe the book's plot and characters. Loeb would simply have to learn about a certain "Robert Cohn" on his own, many months later.

AS HEMINGWAY WAS agonizing over a title for his incendiary novel, Boni & Liveright was preparing to debut *In Our Time,* which would introduce Hemingway to the wider American public. For months he had been corresponding with Horace Liveright about the proofs for the book.

"Reading it over it is even a better book than I remember," Hemingway wrote to his publisher, who appears to have been left out of Hemingway's flurry of correspondence announcing the existence and progress of his new novel.

Boni & Liveright had prepared a bullish cover for the book: nearly the entire front jacket was covered in blurbs from some of Hemingway's most powerful supporters, as though the publisher were daring critics to utter a word against the book.

"Mr. Hemingway is young, strong, full of laughter, and he can write," promised Sherwood Anderson, whose blurb hovered next to the book's title. A statement somehow cajoled out of Ford Madox Ford, despite his strained relationship with Hemingway, assured prospective readers that Hemingway was "the best writer in America at this moment . . . the most conscientious, the most master of his craft, [and] the most consummate." In the lower left corner, Donald Ogden Stewart likened the book to eating a hearty meal after being forced to subsist on literary lettuce sandwiches.

The book was published in New York around the time Hemingway was in Chartres. Just over 1,300 copies rolled off the Liveright presses — not a staggering first printing, but still more than four times that of any of Hemingway's previous books.

If his patrons had been intent on driving home the point that Hemingway was a unique new talent, reviewers were not ready to cast him as more than a talented apprentice. Several reviews linked him stylistically to Sherwood Anderson and Gertrude Stein. At least two reviews called Stein's influence on the stories "obvious," and *The New Republic*'s critic wrote that Hemingway's "fine bare effects and values coined from simplest words" had clear overtones of Anderson while lacking Anderson's warmth.

One reviewer, however, saw something profoundly exciting in the book.

"Ernest Hemingway is something new under the sun in American letters," wrote Robert Wolf of the *New York Herald Tribune*. Yes, Hemingway bore the influence of Stein and Anderson, but they were prewar writers, and there had been "more discontinuity between the literary tradition of 1920 and that of 1925 than between that of 1914 and that of 1920." Hemingway was the first representative of the postwar school of writers, who were bound to take literature in astonishing directions. Stein and Joyce may have started it all — it was "impossible to write in the old way" since they had made their mark — but Hemingway was poised to become the leader of the new guard. His style was "built after the pattern of a machine . . . reflecting our modern, stereotyped machine civilization." He finished the review with the ultimate endorsement: "Ernest Hemingway has promise of genius."

The esteem was not mutual: Hemingway later described Wolf as "stupid but well meaning." Yet the reviewer was clearly onto something: had Hemingway been published before the war, he might have been disqualified from being a postwar voice of a generation. Only a newcomer who hailed from that doomed twenty-two- to thirty-year-old category could qualify for that honor. Once again, luck had conspired to promote Hemingway's talent.

Sales for *In Our Time* proved dismal: that first season, only around five hundred copies would make their way from booksellers' shelves into the hands of readers. Yet Hemingway's name was becoming known in New York publishing circles. Publisher Alfred Harcourt sent a letter to author Louis Bromfield about Hemingway and *In Our Time* that fall; in his view, the book portended great things.

"Hemingway is his own man and talking off his own bat," he wrote, and prophesied, "[His] first novel might rock the country."

Soon enough, that property would be in play.

HAROLD LOEB, in the meantime, had arrived back in New York City. If he'd expected fanfare and adulation over the release of his own book, he too was sorely disappointed.

"I didn't get a decent review in the city + none too many outside," he reported to Hemingway that November. Sales were low. Despite the unraveling of their friendship, Loeb was still acting as an unofficial liaison between Hemingway and Liveright. Unfortunately, he had equally grim news to impart about *In Our Time*.

"They tell me in the office . . . [that] the sale of short stories in book form is next to impossible," he wrote. "Your book is no exception."

It is tempting to say that Hemingway's relationship with Boni & Liveright ended then and there. He had never been ecstatic about the house to begin with. Horace Liveright had further vexed him that past summer by asking him to scout additional authors in Paris and send them in the house's direction; Hemingway had declined. "Being a simple country boy from Chicago I dont know anything of the technique of grabbing off authors," he informed his publisher.

The firm's apparent disinclination to market his book aggressively brought out Hemingway's ire. He wrote back to Loeb that Liveright's team had obviously decided in advance that it wasn't worth their effort to sell a book of short stories. They weren't even fulfilling actual orders, he reported: over in Paris, Sylvia Beach would order a dozen and receive half that number. Unlike Liveright, *she* knew how to market Hemingway's work. She would sell out of those six copies in a single day, he claimed, and would have to cable for additional copies. By the way, he added, there had been three offers on his new novel—swell ones. He planned, at the moment, to be loyal to Liveright, but it was "up to them to keep me happy"—which meant giving *In Our Time* "a good ride" and rummaging up a sizable advance for the novel.

"They are certainly putting Sherwood over big," Hemingway added resentfully, referring to the promotional campaign surrounding Anderson's newly released best-selling novel, *Dark Laughter.* He imagined that Anderson stood to make a lot of money, and he was right. It was Anderson's first book to be published by Liveright, and the house made an enormous effort to showcase its new star. *Dark Laughter* was released around the same time as Hemingway's book; yet while *In Our Time* sold only about a third of its modest first printing, *Dark Laughter* sold over 22,000 copies by December.

"The sales climbed up and up," recalled Anderson, who seemed almost bewildered by his newfound success. "I went on a visit to New York and saw my own face staring at me from the advertising pages of newspapers, on the walls of busses and subways."

If *The Sun Also Rises* was Hemingway's postwar commentary novel, *Dark Laughter* was Anderson's. Like *The Sun Also Rises,* it had been dashed off in a sprint. "This whole novel was written in a heat last fall," Anderson had told Liveright earlier that spring. "I went through the whole thing in about two months and have never been so absorbed in a job before. It is the story of the present day, of postwar life in America now and in particular of postwar life in the Middle West." It was, he added, going to be his best novel yet.

"It walks and sings," he advised Liveright. "Bet on this book, Horace, it is going to be there with a bang."

Anderson apparently had no idea that Hemingway was stewing about his success or that he loathed the unremitting critical comparisons between their respective styles. "I dare say, more than one critic . . . intimated that I was a strong influence," Anderson wrote later. "I myself never said so. I thought . . . that he had his own gift, which had nothing particularly to do with me."

Hemingway, by contrast, was hardly in a mood to laud Anderson's creative gift. *Dark Laughter* was pretentious and fake, he wrote to his mother; the book had only a few instances of passable writing in it, he added. Others agreed with him. F. Scott Fitzgerald wrote to Maxwell Perkins that "Anderson's last two books have let everybody down who believed in him," and called the tomes "cheap," "faked," and "awful." That said, Fitzgerald did not feel the need to translate this disdain into a public rebuke.

Hemingway did. *Dark Laughter* was "so terribly bad, silly and affected that I could not keep from criticizing it in a parody," he later wrote, and that November, he began to draft a nasty little satire of Anderson's novel.

It took him only about a week to complete the nearly thirty-thousand-word novella, which he would call *The Torrents of Spring*.

In defending his decision to write the book, Hemingway would claim that it had been the noble thing to do. It enraged him that Anderson was squandering his talents: the older writer needed to be set straight, and it was up to other writers to call him out via the time-honored form of satire. Years later, Hemingway would call parody "the last refuge of the frustrated writer" and add that "the step up from writing parodies is writing on the wall above the urinal," but at that moment in 1925, when it came to rectifying Sherwood Anderson's wayward course, it was apparently a respectable weapon.

The Torrents of Spring took dead aim at Anderson's stylistic affectations. In *Dark Laughter,* the action had centered on a wheel company; Hemingway's satirical setting was a pump factory. He lampooned Anderson's fragmented language and tendency to use repetitive questions—"Could she hold him? Could she hold him?"—and peppered the book with blasé yet boastful end-of-chapter notes directly addressing the reader. In one note, the narrator informs his audience that he wrote the previous chapter in a mere two hours, then carried it to a lunch with John Dos Passos, who read it and declared, "Hemingway, you have wrought a masterpiece." Another note, insinuating that Anderson suffered from misguided impulses toward grandiosity, announced, "It is at this point, reader, that I am going to try and get that sweep and movement into the book that shows that the book is really a great book."

Anderson may have been the primary target of *Torrents,* but Hemingway also took aim at a few other writers as well. In the book's pages, he accuses novelist Willa Cather of having lifted war-related material from the 1915 film *Birth of a Nation.* F. Scott Fitzgerald staggers blind drunk into the action at one point, plunking himself down in a fireplace. Later in that passage, Hemingway addresses the reader again: "And you're not angry or upset about what I said about Scott Fitzgerald either, are you? I hope not . . . Need I add, reader, that I have the utmost respect for Mr. Fitzgerald, and let anybody else attack him and I would be the first to spring to his defense!" There was also a little poke at Gertrude Stein. Part Four of *Torrents* was called "The Passing of a Great Race and the Making and Marring of Americans," a riff on the title of Stein's book *The Making of Americans.* In one passage, a character ponders Stein's significance; the rumination was rendered in a spoof of Stein's now famous style: "Gertrude Stein . . . Ah, there was a woman! Where were her experiments in words leading her? What was at the bottom of it? All that in Paris. Ah, Paris. How far it was to Paris now. Paris in the morning. Paris in the evening. Paris at night. Paris in the morning sun. Paris at noon, perhaps. Why not?"

By December 2, *The Torrents of Spring* was complete.

Hemingway began to share the work with select members of his crowd. Literary parodies were fairly commonplace at that time: Donald Stewart's *Parody Outline of History* ribbed the styles of ten famous writers, including Fitzgerald, Edith Wharton, Sinclair Lewis, and Ring Lardner. Robert McAlmon wrote poems parodying Ezra Pound and T. S. Eliot. (Pound had reportedly not been amused.) It was a live-by-the-pen, die-by-the-pen world, and all stylists were vulnerable to ridicule.

Yet some early readers of *Torrents* found its humor unnecessarily cruel. Hadley thought it "detestable" to send up the man who had supported her and Hemingway so selflessly and made all of their Paris introductions; she urged Hemingway not to publish it. John Dos Passos—far from deeming the book a masterpiece—told Hemingway that it "wasn't quite good enough to stand on its own feet as a parody," and argued that "*In Our Time* had been so damn good he ought to wait until he had something really smashing to follow it with." He agreed with Hemingway and Fitzgerald that *Dark Laughter* had been overly sentimental and that "somebody ought to call [Anderson] on it"; he just didn't think that Hemingway was the right person to do so, given Anderson's kindnesses to him in the past.

"I suppose it wasn't any of my goddamn business, but friends were friends in those days," he wrote later.

Hemingway may have been inspired by Donald Ogden Stewart's success with satire and would soon use Stewart's example as a selling point for the *Torrents* manuscript, but Stewart was just as appalled by the book as Hadley and Dos Passos: he loathed *Torrents* "both for its bitterness and for its inept attempts at humor." He believed that parody should be amusing, but not brutal—something that he felt Hemingway did not understand.

Hemingway continued to troll for praise. He descended upon the apartment of Gerald and Sara Murphy one evening as they were getting ready for bed. Instead, they spent the night listening to Hemingway read aloud; he went through the entire manuscript. Gerald found *Torrents* "in questionable taste." Sara was in less of a position to judge the material's virtues: she slept through much of the reading, albeit "sitting bolt-upright on the sofa." Hemingway apparently didn't notice, reading until he gave himself a sore throat.

He finally found an enthusiastic backer in Pauline Pfeiffer. He and

Hadley had been seeing a good deal of her that fall. Her sister Virginia had returned to the United States after her extended Parisian holiday, leaving Pauline at loose ends — and presumably ending any sort of flirtation or affair between Virginia and Hemingway. Lonely now, Pauline had begun stopping off at the Hemingways' apartment after work; they gradually became a surrogate family to her, despite her initial horror at their living conditions and revulsion over Hemingway himself. Ostensibly Pauline's entrée to the couple was through Hadley; the two had become close albeit unlikely friends.

Yet Pauline had clearly become a creative confidante of Hemingway's as well. He inducted her into the circle of *Torrents of Spring* readers, and she found it "one of the funniest things she had ever read." Pauline urged Hemingway to push for publication — precisely the course he followed. Hadley resented the encouragement: if not for Pauline's persuasion, she felt, he might have shelved the manuscript. The episode suggested that Hadley's influence on her husband was waning and Pauline's was on the rise.

On December 7, Hemingway shipped the *Torrents* manuscript off to Horace Liveright. To keep it company, he enclosed a fairly outrageous cover letter introducing the work. He opened by delivering a short lecture about the bygone golden age of satire and reported that he had heard critics bemoaning the fact that America had no decent satirist to call its own.

"Maybe when you read this book you will think they haven't so much bewailing to do now," he wrote.

Here was a "very perfect American satire" that could stand in the company of works by greats like Donald Stewart, Robert Benchley, and Ring Lardner. If Liveright didn't want to take his word for it, Hemingway went on, F. Scott Fitzgerald would soon be dispatching a separate letter affirming its brilliance; he also reported that author Louis Bromfield agreed that *Torrents* was "one of the very funniest books he had ever read."

If Liveright wanted this book, he should be prepared to pay handsomely (here Hemingway inserted a demand for a $500 advance, even though, he added, he ought to ask for a thousand) and would have to pledge to promote the book vigorously. Hemingway reminded Liveright that he had made "no kick" about the lack of advertising surrounding *In Our Time* nor its ill-advised cover: all of those blurbs, Hemingway complained, had only put would-be readers on the defensive instead of luring them in. He instructed Liveright to release *Torrents* that upcoming spring and to hire artist Ralph Barton — whose drawings had adorned one of Donald Stewart's books and Anita Loos's best-selling 1925 satire *Gentlemen Prefer Blondes* — to illustrate the book. He predicted that *Torrents* was bound to sell up to twenty thousand copies — if the project was handled properly by its publisher, that is.

There was, of course, the bothersome matter of Sherwood Anderson, and the fact that if Boni & Liveright published *The Torrents of Spring,* the house would basically be harpooning one of its most lucrative authors. "I do not think that anybody with any stuff can be hurt by satire," Hemingway contended, implying that if Anderson took offense, he was being unduly thin-skinned.

Hemingway demanded Liveright's immediate decision. "In case you do not wish to publish it I have a number of propositions to consider," he declared. He also made sure that Liveright knew he was revising the manuscript of a completed novel, although he neglected to mention that *The Sun Also Rises* skewered Harold Loeb, another author from the Liveright stable — the very one who had campaigned so diligently for Hemingway's acceptance at the house in the first place.

Liveright's reply, he instructed, should be sent to the Hotel Taube in Schruns, where Hemingway and Hadley would be staying for the next three months. A few days later, the Hemingways departed for Austria for their second winter holiday in the little town, soon to be joined by Pauline Pfeiffer and eventually John Dos Passos.

Two feet of snow greeted the family. Once they settled in at the Taube, Hemingway read, skied, played poker, and waited for the inevitable drama to unfold.

HEMINGWAY MAY HAVE genuinely felt that *The Torrents of Spring* was a brilliant satire, yet it was more likely "a cold-blooded contract-breaker," as Hemingway friend Mike Strater put it.

"I have known all along that [Liveright] could not and would not be able to publish it as it makes a bum out of [his] present ace and best seller Anderson," Hemingway wrote to Fitzgerald from Schruns. He hastily added, "I did not, however, have that in mind in any way when I wrote it."

As Hemingway had ceaselessly reminded his associates over the past year, if Boni & Liveright failed to accept his next book for any reason, the house's option on his future works lapsed. Therefore, if Horace Liveright rejected *Torrents,* he would relinquish any claim on *The Sun Also Rises,* thus allowing Hemingway to rush into the welcoming embrace of a more prestigious publisher, namely Maxwell Perkins at Scribner's. On the one hand, his letter to Liveright could be seen as a wildly confident sales pitch by a hungry young author; on the other hand, it could be construed as a document impishly crafted to push a publisher over the edge.

F. Scott Fitzgerald may have helped Hemingway strategize an exit from Liveright. The two men had reconnected in Paris that autumn, and they began, once again, drinking champagne together (presumably on Fitzgerald's tab). They had become "very thick," as Fitzgerald informed Perkins. He resumed his own patronage of Hemingway, penning a review of *In Our Time* in an effort to help the book's chances and also "working like a beaver to get Max Perkins to take on Hemingway at Scribner's," as John Dos Passos put it. By that December, Fitzgerald had read *Torrents* and indeed sent Horace Liveright and one of his editors a letter extolling its virtues.

"To one rather snooty reader, at least, [*Torrents*] seems about the best comic book ever written by an American," he informed them. That said, he rather hoped that Liveright wouldn't like the book: "I am something of a ballyhoo man for Scribners and I'd some day like to see all my generation that I admire rounded up in the same coop."

Fitzgerald and Hemingway stayed in weekly touch while Hemingway was in Schruns. As Hemingway waited to hear back from Liveright, he was nursing an ugly cold but expended nervous energy on the slopes and playing billiards. He also began to revise *The Sun Also Rises,* which he later described as "the most difficult job of rewriting I have ever done." Some of the revising at Schruns involved an attempt to wrest the story away from Jake's first-person point of view, an effort that Hemingway would soon abandon. In any case, he was working it "over and over" and wanted it to be "darn good."

SOON EDITORIAL BACKUP arrived in the form of Pauline Pfeiffer, who materialized in Schruns around Christmastime. Earlier that month, Kitty Cannell had beheld the spectacle of tiny Pauline dragging a pair of skis along a Paris street while clad in a fashionable Louise Boulanger suit. When Pauline told Cannell that she was about to join the Hemingways on a skiing holiday, Cannell was taken aback. "I had not realized that they had been seeing that much of each other," she later wrote, adding that she worried that Pauline would break her little "bird bones" on the slopes. She probably need not have been concerned: Pauline was tougher than she looked.

Hemingway later claimed that Pauline came to Schruns not to ski but rather to "murder" his marriage. She had already begun this lengthy, insidious campaign to wrest him away from Hadley, starting with an infiltration using what he called the oldest trick in the book: "This is when an unmarried young woman becomes the temporary best friend of another young woman who is married, comes to live with the husband and wife and then unknowingly, innocently and unrelentingly sets out to marry the husband."

As a couple, he and Hadley were particularly vulnerable to such an invasion: at that time, his revisions to *The Sun Also Rises* were consuming much of his time; this meant that Hadley needed a playmate while he was working, and Pauline seemed a sensible solution. Then, at the end of each working day, there were two attractive women on hand to tempt him. "One is new and strange and if he has bad luck he gets to love them both," he later wrote.

"Then the one who is relentless wins," he added.

Seduction does, however, involve two willing parties. While Pauline has long been depicted as a predator and home wrecker, she had certain virtues that would have conceivably encouraged Hemingway to pursue her as well — namely that she was an heiress, while Hemingway remained decidedly broke. Her increased presence in the Hemingway households coincided with Hadley's waning relevance: now that Hemingway was — finally — poised to make a noisy breakthrough into the realm of literary celebrity, he may have realized that he had outgrown her. Her own diminished trust fund had proved inadequate even for the world of simple pleasures they had created, and he may also have sensed that she was not suited for life on a grander stage.

It is unclear whether Hemingway and Pauline began a physical affair at Schruns or weeks later, but by the time she left Austria, the Hemingways and Pauline were in triangle mode, at least emotionally. As with *The Torrents of Spring,* Pauline made herself essential to the revisions of *The Sun Also Rises:* each night, Hemingway read his revisions to her, and she gave him editorial feedback. She became increasingly emotionally invested in his professional goings-on.

It is also unclear whether Hadley — who had long commented on her husband's works in progress — was included in these evening manuscript sessions. At this point she appears to have been living in cheerful denial; yet that winter she may have realized that the chessboard was being rearranged around her, and that hers was not an advantageous position. When Kitty Cannell ran into Hadley back in Paris, Cannell "innocently" inquired how things had gone during Pauline's visit. Hadley replied that she was certain Cannell knew what was happening. Cannell claimed that she did not.

"She's taking my husband," Hadley told her.

HEMINGWAY'S BEST Christmas present arrived five days after the actual holiday. On December 30, a cable arrived from Horace Liveright:

REJECTING TORRENTS OF SPRING
PATIENTLY AWAITING MANUSCRIPT SUN ALSO RISES
WRITING FULLY

In the letter that followed, Liveright was measured yet merciless. The submission of *The Torrents of Spring* had thrown Boni & Liveright into an uproar over the past few weeks; nearly everyone at the office had been called upon to read it. The team had even conscripted several "entirely unprejudiced" outside readers to opine on the work. The collective impression had not been positive, to say the least.

"Who on earth do you think would buy it?" Liveright asked. "We disagree with you and Scott Fitzgerald and Louis Bromfield and Dos Passos, that it is a fine and humorous American satire."

The Torrents of Spring was, he continued, "horribly cruel," "vicious," "in extremely rotten taste," and, perhaps worst of all, "entirely cerebral." Hemingway had predicted easy sales of twenty thousand copies, but Liveright couldn't imagine that more than seven or eight hundred readers would be willing to shell out money for the book. Furthermore, he added, practically the only reason booksellers had placed any orders for *In Our Time* was thanks to the blurbs on the cover which Hemingway had criticized—a stinging reminder to Hemingway that, at least in the eyes of this publisher, his most saleable asset at this point was still the support of his better-known champions. And what was more, the lack of advertising had not killed sales of *In Our Time*. Rather, the reading public had rejected it.

"*In Our Time* will sell some day," Liveright predicted. "After your first successful novel."

As ever, it all came down to a novel. Liveright made it clear that he still expected Hemingway to submit *The Sun Also Rises* to Boni & Liveright. After all, the house had invested in him "for the long future": it had published *In Our Time* to get to the goose that laid the golden egg.

Hemingway, however, had no intention of handing over the novel.

"I'm loose," he wrote immediately to Fitzgerald, adding that it already felt great to be emancipated from the Liveright shackles. "It's up to you how I proceed next," he added.

He informed Fitzgerald that other publishers were now also interested, including Alfred Harcourt, who had been so keenly anticipating a potentially country-rocking novel; he had also, he said, been approached by an editor from rival publishing house Knopf. Hemingway thought that Harcourt in particular was a "sure thing," as Alfred Harcourt had essentially offered to take his works sight unseen. That said, Hemingway felt that he already had an understanding with Scribner's.

"I am not going to Double Cross you and Max Perkins to whom I have given a promise," he wrote.

He suggested that Fitzgerald write to Perkins about the situation and endorse *The Torrents of Spring* again, as he had to Horace Liveright. Perkins should also be informed that Hemingway was perfecting *The Sun Also Rises* and it was "damned good." The rewrites would be completed in just a couple of months, and it could be published in the fall.

"I'm certainly relying on your good nature in a lousy brutal way," he said apologetically.

Fitzgerald excitedly reported back to Perkins. Here was the moment they had been waiting for: Hemingway — now endowed with a mighty novel — was in play at last. There was, however, a small sting to impart.

"He's dead set on having the satire published first," Fitzgerald advised Perkins.

It would probably sell only a thousand copies, he speculated, but it would be worth it, for the novel promised to be "something extraordinary." There was now competition from other publishers, but Fitzgerald felt confident that Scribner's could bring Hemingway into the coop.

A week after Liveright's rejection came through, Fitzgerald contacted Perkins again, urging him to make his bid. It was now or never, for Harcourt had made a definite offer:

YOU CAN GET HEMINGWAYS FINISHED NOVEL
PROVIDED YOU PUBLISH UNPROMISING SATIRE . . .
WIRE IMMEDIATELY WITHOUT QUALIFICATIONS

Perkins sprang into action. He wired Fitzgerald back:

PUBLISH NOVEL AT FIFTEEN PERCENT AND ADVANCE IF DESIRED
ALSO SATIRE UNLESS OBJECTIONABLE OTHER THAN FINANCIALLY
HEMINGWAY'S STORIES SPLENDID

Perkins chased the cable with a letter; in it, he fretted that he might have missed his big chance to reel in Hemingway. There had been some in-house worry about commissioning the satire sight unseen, as "it is not the policy obviously of Scribners to publish books of certain types," but apparently he now felt it worth the risk. He would have wired immediately otherwise, and he feared now that the lag had been "fatal."

"If only," he wrote, "we could get the novel!"

Perkins's position seemed a peculiar one: he was vying aggressively for works that he had never read, created by a little-known writer whose only American-published book had fizzled commercially, exclusively on the strength of Fitzgerald's confidence and what Perkins had glimpsed in those *In Our Time* stories and vignettes. That said, he had found the stories "astonishingly fine" and "invigorating as a cold, fresh wind." Others felt the same way. In New York as well as Paris, Hemingway was indeed starting to look like something new under the sun, as Robert Wolf had put it.

"People are beginning to talk about his writing," Perkins informed Fitzgerald, "those who find things for themselves and appreciate aside from technical literary qualities, a true eye for reality."

News of that unfinished draft of *The Sun Also Rises* — currently being reworked in Schruns against the backdrop of a brewing love triangle — had ejected him out of man-to-watch territory into the category of major catch.

Hemingway decided to go to New York to field all offers in person. With agent-like shrewdness, he knew better than to let things cool off. If he waited in Schruns, weeks could lapse in between propositions. He was in demand now; better to materialize in the center of action and continue to stoke the fire he had lit. The news of his imminent arrival would likely create an even greater sense of drama and urgency around him and his novel. Plus, he wrote to Fitzgerald, he got the sense that Liveright intended to hold on to him (in this assumption he was correct), and preferred to settle the matter with Horace face-to-face.

The preparations for his trip to New York took on the tenor of a military team mapping out a high-stakes invasion. Hemingway wrote a stern letter to Liveright, advising him that his option on any subsequent

Hemingway works had clearly lapsed. He offered up some cutting words regarding the collective sensibilities of the Liveright team.

"Your office was also quite enthusiastic about a novel by Harold Loeb called Doodab which did not, I believe, prove to be a wow even as a *succes d'estime.*" To make Liveright fully aware of the grave shortsightedness of his decision to reject *Torrents,* he added: "As you know I expect to go on writing for some time . . . I will pay my keep to, and eventually make a great deal of money for, any publisher."

But in the meantime, he had no intention of letting Liveright sit back and reject his manuscripts while Liveright waited for him to crank out an eventual best-seller. It was all or nothing. On that note, he informed Liveright that he would be sailing for New York imminently and looked forward to meeting him there.

That same day, Fitzgerald prepped Max Perkins for Hemingway's arrival. Liveright was likely going to fight to keep Hemingway, he informed the editor, on the grounds that *The Torrents of Spring* was not really a book. It was a shaky claim, but Liveright was also apparently "crazy" to get Hemingway's novel, Fitzgerald added. That said, Hemingway was just as crazy to be rid of Liveright.

"To hear him talk you'd think Liveright had broken up his home and robbed him of millions," Fitzgerald added.

By the way, he went on, Perkins should probably know about Hemingway's somewhat volatile nature.

"He's very excitable," Fitzgerald wrote, "and I can't promise he'll know his own mind next month." In a separate missive, he warned Perkins that Hemingway could be "tempermental in business" and strongly urged him to "get a signed contract" for *The Sun Also Rises.*

Other than that, they were bound to get along famously.

"You won't be able to help liking him," Fitzgerald assured Perkins. "He's one of the nicest fellows I know."

10

Dorothy Parker's Scotch

S MAX PERKINS waited for Hemingway to cross the icy Atlantic, he must have been filled with unease. Not necessarily apprehension about Hemingway's temper—in the years to come, Perkins would prove to be especially adept at handling volatile authors—but about the inevitable fistfight that would arise in-house over bringing such a terribly modern author into Charles Scribner's Sons.

"It was the most genteel and the most tradition-encrusted of all the publishing houses that had survived from Victorian days," as writer Malcolm Cowley put it. "No word unfit for a young girl's ear could appear in a book that Scribner's published."

It was an exaggerated assessment but not an entirely unfounded one. In the early days, Scribner's had turned out religious publications: *The Puritans and Their Principles* was the first book to roll off the Scribner's presses in 1846, and subsequent lists showcased the works of the more fashionable preachers of the day. Gradually Charles Scribner's successors expanded into fiction and scored some enormously popular authors. Edith Wharton published her first work of fiction—*The Greater Inclination*—with the house in 1899 and remained one of its star writers. Her presence on the Scribner's list indicated that despite the house's puritanical roots, its editors did occasionally push the boundaries of convention. After all, Wharton was a divorcée who wrote about society scandal, adultery, and overdoses.

But by the 1920s, even Wharton no longer felt particularly modern. Among the postwar generation, she and her contemporaries were deemed "dreary" and "weary," as expat writer Kay Boyle put it. Wharton's press photo—featuring the ballroom-ready author festooned with pearls, her hair in a tidy Victorian coif—told you everything you needed to know. "The most highly respected American authors of the past century were given no quarter," Boyle added; Wharton was on that blacklist. For Boyle and her crowd of young writers, James Joyce was in; Henry James was out. Emily Dickinson was passé; William Carlos Williams was now. Sensibilities were shifting quickly.

That decade, then, had laid a particular challenge at the feet of Maxwell Evarts Perkins and his more forward-looking colleagues. It was a tightrope challenge, which involved keeping traditionalist readers happy — Wharton still sold many thousands of books each year — while bringing in a new generation of authors, most of whom openly railed against anyone who carried the scent of Victoriana.

At first glance, Max Perkins seemed an unlikely candidate to revolutionize a publishing house, much less to help usher in a new era of modern literature for mainstream readers.

"Max was a combination of extreme gentleness and feminine sensitivity and craglike obstinacy and puritanical severity — a mixture of the Puritan and the Cavalier," recalled his former Scribner's colleague John Hall Wheelock.

Like Charles Scribner's Sons, Perkins's background was marked by New England uprightness; his family — which at one point commanded fourteen pages in the *Dictionary of American Biography* — was stocked with notables from the realms of academia and public service. Born in New York in 1884, Perkins had gone to Harvard and joined the usual prestigious clubs. Understatement seemed his defining quality — that, and his distinctive way of speaking out of the side of his mouth, a tic peculiar even now to at least one of his descendants.

Despite the grandeur of his clan and résumé, Perkins had given early signs that he was a man who was interested in all walks of life. After finishing Harvard, he took a job as a junior reporter at the *New York Times;* his stories at the paper revealed a predilection for zaniness and risk. For one story, he accompanied a race car driver on his quest to break a speed record. Flames and smoke shot out of the car at one point, giving Perkins plenty to write about. For another story, he volunteered to be tied to an electric chair at Sing Sing prison. As Hemingway's reporting background gave him both material and style guidance for his stories, Perkins's time as a journalist gave him a sense of ordinary people's sensibilities; he understood the appetites of both the ivory tower and the street. Even if Perkins wasn't a daredevil himself, he relished being a close-proximity observer, and was always ready to give extraordinary, even outlandish feats a platform.

Eventually Perkins and his fiancée decided that he needed a somewhat saner existence. He first joined Charles Scribner's Sons as the firm's advertising manager — experience that would prove as invaluable as his *Times* adventure. If reporting taught Perkins how to identify a good story, this advertising savvy would help him discern a saleable one. Not only did he have "a great [editorial] instinct, like a musical ear, he had a commercial streak to him," says Charles Scribner III. After a year in advertising, Perkins became a Scribner's editor. For nearly a decade he lay low. But then an incident took place that revealed Perkins to be an agent of change.

The Scribner's editorial team held monthly meetings in which each editor would present a book that he wished to publish. Arguments of varying intensity would ensue; the final decision, of course, lay with Charles Scribner Sr. ("Old C.S.") and his son, Charles Scribner Jr. One September afternoon in 1919, Perkins brought up a book that he wanted to publish. The firm had already rejected it twice, but Perkins had worked closely with its author on revisions and the manuscript was now ready to be reconsidered. It was a highly original work, Perkins thought. The book was titled *This Side of Paradise* and its author was F. Scott Fitzgerald. Instantly, Scribner's was a house divided.

"*This Side of Paradise* seems innocent enough today, but then it was the terrifying voice of a new age," recalled writer Malcolm Cowley. One Scribner's editor who had read an earlier incarnation of the manuscript "could not stomach it at all." But another employee, who felt it had "serious flaws," saw that it was "obviously an outstanding work, something belonging to a new order."

Charles Scribner Sr. remained among the unconvinced.

"It's frivolous," he proclaimed in the meeting. "I will not have a frivolous book like that on my list."

Perkins had been standing behind him. Scribner looked up at him. "How do you feel about it?"

Perkins was silent for a moment. Then, with characteristic quietness, he responded, "My feeling, Mr. Scribner, is that if we let a book like this go, we ought to close up and go out of the publishing business."

The comment upset Scribner. "What do you mean by that?" he demanded.

Perkins replied that the firm simply could not go on publishing old guard authors such as Theodore Roosevelt, Richard Harding Davis, and Henry Van Dyke forever.

"We've got to move on with the times," he said.

Scribner was reportedly impressed by this logic, and told Perkins that he would think it over. Ultimately he allowed Perkins to publish the book, provided that certain changes were made to the manuscript. And thus Perkins let the first of the modern "bad boys of letters into one of the citadels of Victorian publishing," as Malcolm Cowley later put it.

He soon lowered the drawbridge again for "bad boy" writer Ring Lardner, a friend and former Long Island neighbor of Fitzgerald's. There was a kerfuffle in-house over Lardner's 1924 book *How to Write Short Stories,* and yet another fight broke out over the acceptance of *The Great Gatsby,* which contained the scandalous phrase "son of a bitch" and other objectionable material. Perkins prevailed in both cases.

But now a third prospective bad boy was coming his way—this time one with flagrantly modern sensibilities. Fitzgerald's fictional worlds might have disturbed the fustier editors at the house, but at least his style of writing was still reassuringly romantic. Lardner was an accessible humorist and had long been a familiar, jovial figure to readers.

Hemingway, however, was a stranger from a strange land, intent on confronting the masses with a terrifyingly modern world bereft of any comforting stylistic trimmings. His was bare, savage content rendered in a bare, savage style. There was no shelter in that writing, nary an adjective to shade readers from a harsh sun. Not to mention that Lady Brett Ashley made Fitzgerald's characters Daisy Buchanan and Jordan Baker seem chaste in comparison.

Even if Perkins could wrench Hemingway away from Horace Liveright and triumph over the rival house, he would have to face down his own house again. And if he could land this novel, he would push Charles Scribner's Sons further into the strange, hard terrain of the twentieth century than any commercial American publisher had ever ventured.

ON FEBRUARY 9, 1926, the day Hemingway's ship, the *Mauretania,* docked in New York, nearly a foot of snow fell on the city. Yet nothing would halt his mission.

The moment he set foot in Manhattan, Hemingway was deep in Fitzgerald territory. Though Fitzgerald himself had been gone for a year, his imprint was evident all over the city. A play adapted from *The Great Gatsby* had just opened on Broadway; a film adaptation would soon be brought out by Paramount. Perkins attended a preview performance of the play and reported back to Fitzgerald that he had been called a "wonder" and a "genius" by other attendees.

As with Paris, New York's social worlds carved out distinct spheres for themselves. Affluent uptown Manhattan resembled the glitzy Right Bank, with the regal Plaza standing as its patron saint hotel instead of the Ritz. Greenwich Village served as New York's Left Bank, teeming with similarly bohemian aspirations, glamour, and squalor.

Hemingway made his way to the Hotel Brevoort on lower Fifth Avenue, in the heart of Greenwich Village, whose terrace was that neighborhood's answer to the Dôme in Montparnasse. Like the Dôme, the Brevoort was often skewered as ground zero for artistic pretension and posturing; still, it was popular among the upper ranks of New York's literary crowd and visiting international luminaries. At any moment, patrons might glimpse *Vanity Fair* founder Frank Crowninshield dining in its restaurant several tables away from fashion editor Carmel Snow. Other patrons included the sexually liberated redheaded poet Edna St. Vincent Millay, playwright Eugene O'Neill, and assorted European royals and statesmen. This was definitely the right place for an ambitious young novelist to make his debut in the scene.

Hemingway's first order of business: cutting ties with Boni & Liveright. Despite the snow, he charged forty blocks north from the Brevoort to the brownstone housing Liveright's operation. Given Hemingway's hostile feelings about the *Torrents* situation, one might have expected him to challenge Horace Liveright to settle the matter with a bloody boxing round — or, at the very least, a heated confrontation. But their final meeting was almost anticlimactically civilized. A handful of house editors — presumably the same ones who had spurned *Torrents* — gave Hemingway an amicable reception.

Horace Liveright himself firmly but graciously reiterated his rejection of *Torrents*. He told Hemingway that he still wanted to publish *The Sun Also Rises* when it was done.

This, obviously, was a nonstarter. Hemingway firmly replied that Liveright had no legal claim to his other books. In his letters leading up to the meeting, Liveright had made it sound as if he intended to fight tooth and nail to keep Hemingway. Yet once he was sitting across from Hemingway in person, all of Liveright's bravado appears to have faded away. He conceded. Hemingway was officially free. The two men may even have had a few drinks together before parting.

"We're Horace and Ernest now," Hemingway wrote to Louis Bromfield afterward. "[I] told him how sorry I was etc.," without a hint of remorse.

Horace Liveright, though, would soon be very sorry indeed. On that freezing day in 1926, relinquishing Hemingway for Sherwood Anderson surely seemed like the safe—even the sane—thing for the publisher to do. It would take a decade before the gravity of the misstep was revealed. By the early 1930s, Hemingway had become a literary icon, while Anderson's stardom had shriveled to near obscurity.

Liveright's own star was destined to sink even further. In 1930, after years of reckless management and bad investments, he was forced out of his own house (which retained his name). Afterward, he devolved into a shabby spectacle.

"A poseur to the last, he could be found tapping his long cigarette holder nervously at a table at the Algonquin, a mere shadow of his former jaunty self," recalled fellow publisher Bennett Cerf.

When Liveright died three years later of pneumonia and complications of alcoholism at the age of forty-six, only a few of his former authors attended his funeral. Hemingway was not among them.

"It was," Cerf recalled, "a dismal last curtain to a spectacular career."

THE DAY AFTER his meeting with Liveright, Hemingway once again made his way uptown through the snow, this time to the offices of Charles Scribner's Sons on Fifth Avenue at 48th Street. The publishing house—like the rest of New York—was consumed with all things Fitzgerald. His third story collection, *All the Sad Young Men,* was about to be launched. As Hemingway walked into the building to meet with Perkins, the windows of the ground-floor Scribner's store were filled with Fitzgerald's books and pictures of scenes from the Broadway *Gatsby.*

Hemingway had originally planned to play Scribner's and Harcourt off against each other, but by the time he left Perkins's office, that plan had been abandoned. Perkins had read *The Torrents of Spring;* in the meeting, he offered Hemingway $1,500 for both the satire and *The Sun Also Rises* with a plush royalty rate of 15 percent.

"He wrote an awfully swell contract and was very damned nice," Hemingway wrote to Louis Bromfield.

Not only did Hemingway accept on the spot; he even offered Perkins options on future works, which the editor declined. Presumably the men did not end their meeting in a speakeasy, as the Hemingway-Liveright meeting had reportedly concluded; Hemingway was likely on his best behavior, a trait that Perkins's New England manners tended to bring out in writers.

Perkins enjoyed the meeting. His new author amused him. "He is a most interesting chap about his bull fights and boxing," he wrote to Fitzgerald. For his part, Fitzgerald was thrilled with the outcome of his latest matchmaking. "I'm glad you got Hemmingway," he replied to Perkins. He had now brought Perkins successes and failures in exactly equal numbers.

"Ernest will decide whether my opinions are more of a hindrance or a help," he added.

After sealing the deal with Perkins, Hemingway sent a jubilant missive off to Bill Smith and Harold Loeb, regaling them with details of the new arrangement with Scribner's. He still made no mention of the content of *The Sun Also Rises,* although he told his friends that he was "crazy" to share *Torrents* with them. By the way, he informed Loeb*, In Our Time* was performing quite well — as well as *Doodab,* in fact. "Neck in Neck," he wrote. "Us writers ought to stick together."

He also made a lame-duck visit to Alfred Harcourt. "I should have done the business man and tried to see what Harcourt Brace would do in opposition," Hemingway wrote to Bromfield, who had paved his way to that house, "[but instead] I just told Perkins I would take it and went over and told Mr. Harcourt the news."

Harcourt left the door open for Hemingway to come to his house should Scribner's displease him as Liveright had. The house had already championed other midwestern writers, like Glenway Wescott — whom Harcourt personally admired — and there was always room for more.

When Harcourt mentioned Wescott, Hemingway's good behavior went out the window. He had met Wescott in Paris and immediately disliked almost everything about him, especially his affected British accent. (Wescott actually hailed from Wisconsin.) In fact, Hemingway's antipathy ran so deep that it earned Wescott a cameo as an insufferable up-and-coming writer named "Robert Prescott" at the beginning of *The Sun Also Rises* — the very novel Alfred Harcourt was trying to buy. (Hemingway later, at Perkins's urging, changed the character's name to "Robert Prentiss.") Hemingway informed Harcourt that he found Wescott's work unsound.

"I felt sorry as soon as I said it," he later confessed to Bromfield. "But I know so well what a literary fake his prose is." Thus ended Hemingway's brief flirtation with Harcourt, Brace.

There was a certain irony that Hemingway abandoned a publishing house that itself was a product of modern times for a venerable old firm that got its start peddling Puritan ethics. After all, tiresome American Puritanism had helped motivate Hemingway's generation to flee to Europe in the first place.

In any case, the decision was made. Ernest Hemingway's debut novel was going to be brought out by Charles Scribner's Sons, the publisher of F. Scott Fitzgerald, Henry James, Edith Wharton, and Theodore Roosevelt.

It was rather romantic company for such a determined, self-hardened realist, but Hemingway was getting what he wanted at long last: a big advance, a big publisher, and a shot at a big future.

FATEFUL LITERARY MATTERS now concluded, Hemingway embarked on a celebration worthy of Bacchus. In the past, he had felt no great fondness for New York City. A few years earlier, he had written to Gertrude Stein about the streets rendered lightless by skyscrapers and the town's grim-faced citizens. "All the time I was there I never saw anybody even grin," he wrote. "Wouldn't live in it for anything."

Yet for a charismatic young writer who had found a top-shelf publisher for his all-important first novel, New York was a different matter entirely. The city's Prohibition-era giddiness provided the perfect backdrop to celebrate the imminent debut of *The Sun Also Rises*. That winter, everyone in town may have been drinking underground, but they appeared to be drinking a lot more than ever before, and there were suddenly twice as many places to do so. When Prohibition went into effect in 1920, New Yorkers had fifteen thousand drinking establishments to choose from; just a few years later, that number had more than doubled. Even respectable families had private bootleggers; F. Scott Fitzgerald's was said to be quite good.

Now blissfully unencumbered not only by Horace Liveright but also by his wife, mistress, and offspring, Hemingway went on a weeklong bender. "Everybody [was] cockeyed including myself," he later told a friend, adding that it had been a fog of bootleggers, cocktails, ale, champagne, and —perhaps the greatest evidence that he had gone straight to the heart of the most debauched party in town—Dorothy Parker's scotch. Just as Hemingway had arrived in Paris with entrée to its most fascinating literary lights, in New York he was immediately admitted to that city's own literary Olympus, the Algonquin crowd, thanks to his friendship with Donald Ogden Stewart and Robert Benchley. He met "hells own amount of people," as he put it, including Mrs. Parker.

Just as in Paris, clique mentality ran rampant in New York's literary crowd. The Algonquin Round Tablers—including critics Alexander Woollcott and Heywood Broun, and playwright George Kaufman—were feral wolves, but ones that couldn't stand to be apart from the pack for too long. Whether at the Algonquin, one of their favored speakeasies, or the studio of artist Neysa McMein—one of the clique's few female members—the Algonquin crowd dined, drank, and caroused together "until they dropped from exhaustion," recalled Nathaniel Benchley, son of Robert Benchley.

"There was never any need to worry or feel lonely, because the group was always there and ready to keep on going. The lonely ones were the ones who fell behind," he added.

This cabal may have stuck together out of insecurity, or perhaps disdain for the company of lesser mortals. Perhaps they just luxuriated in their ensemble wit and couldn't bear to sacrifice a minute of banter to sleep or solitude. Whatever the case, it was a tightly knit crowd, nearly impossible to penetrate.

That is, unless you were Ernest Hemingway. He gave no sign that he was intimidated by the verbal butchery demanded of its members, and during that fortnight in New York, he immediately beguiled their queen bee. Dorothy Parker may have hated half of what she saw on Broadway—producers, directors, and actors cowered in anticipation of her deliciously nasty reviews—but she adored Hemingway right away. This had been far from a predictable outcome. Among Parker and her cohorts, there was much eye-rolling about the pretension of the intellectual salons and lifestyle of the Left Bank, for which Hemingway was seen as an ambassador.

"There is something a little— well, a little *you*-know—in all of those things," Parker later wrote.

The Stein crowd simply wasn't irreverent enough for the Algonquin Round Tablers, for whom humor trumped all. According to Parker, when "Gertrude Stein . . . said, 'You're all a lost generation,' . . . we all said, Whee! We're lost."

Nor had Hemingway's inaugural American publication made a thunderous impression. In Parker's words, *In Our Time* had "caused about as much stir in literary circles as an incompleted dogfight on upper Riverside Drive." American booksellers, critics, and readers were rarely in the mood to tolerate such fare. They wanted novels.

"They feel cheated," she explained. "Literature, it appears, is here measured by a yard-stick."

Yet news spread about Hemingway's new book deal and the stir that he had shrewdly caused among New York's premier publishers. His persona fascinated Parker; all of that blunt masculinity must have stood out in stark relief among her usual cohorts, such as the plump, dandified Alexander Woollcott, with his penchant for bow ties, long cigarette holders, and reclining poses in publicity photos. Parker grilled Hemingway about his writing process and was astonished to find that they both usually found the task excruciatingly slow. Even if he boasted to her about the speed with which he had written *The Sun Also Rises,* she still felt that she had found in him a kindred spirit. Parker and the Algonquinites may have poked fun at the Paris Crowd, but some of them harbored serious literary ambitions of their own — including Parker. She had yet to publish a book of her own, and she certainly would have commiserated with Hemingway about the pressure to turn out a novel.

"Write novels, write novels, write novels — that's all they can say," she complained later to Robert Benchley. "Oh, I do get so sick and tired, sometimes."

During Hemingway's visit, she became so engrossed in his tales of the Left Bank that she shunted aside her skepticism and decided on the spot to move abroad.

It seems unlikely that Hemingway drew any inspiration from Parker in kind, although he seems to have written an amusing little homage to a now famous Dorothy Parker couplet, published in 1925:

> Men seldom make passes
> At girls who wear glasses

Later that year, when he went back to Paris, Hemingway penned his own Parker-like ditty:

> Mr. Hemingway now wears glasses
> Better to see to kiss the critics' asses —

For Hemingway, Parker would prove a strong ally. He was smart to cultivate her: she was powerful and well connected in the entertainment world, and soon it would be time to consider theatrical possibilities for *The Sun Also Rises*. In years to come, she would also pen several adoring Hemingway profiles and book reviews. By the end of his New York adventure, he was calling her "Dotty."

Other powerful critics also got a dose of Hemingway charm that week, including Herbert Gorman and Edmund Wilson. (They had even asked him for tips on other up-and-coming talent, he reported to Morley Callaghan.) He descended one evening upon the Coffee House, a club founded by *Vanity Fair*'s Frank Crowninshield. It would have been networking heaven for him, despite its no-introduction policy. (This was a pretentious anti-pretension measure: no introductions were necessary because practically all of its members were so famous or influential that they were recognizable on sight, and presumed to inhabit the same stratum anyway.) The club's membership included giants from the worlds of publishing and entertainment, among them Cole Porter, P. G. Wodehouse, Charles Scribner, Maxwell Perkins, Douglas Fairbanks, and Condé Nast. In other words, it was another major platform for Ernest Hemingway to make his presence and plans known.

He attempted some cultural outings as well, including a viewing of the *Gatsby* play on Broadway; he told a friend that he would gladly have paid to get out at several points during the performance. He also took stock of the literary landscape. Probably to his displeasure, he learned that Ford Madox Ford was quite popular among the New York literati. He grew equally indignant over the success of Anita Loos's just released blockbuster satire, *Gentlemen Prefer Blondes;* Hemingway sullenly called it "one of the dullest books I've ever read" and likened its ubiquity to an epidemic of the flu.

Hemingway also indulged in a flirtation with the literary scene's preeminent ice queen poet, Elinor Wylie. He reported to a friend that when they met, it had been "great love at first sight on both sides." To literary men, Wylie served as a formidable muse; she was also a much-emulated thinking girl's style icon, with her dark curls parted in the middle and arranged in dramatic waves around her face. John Hall Wheelock deemed her "the strikingly good-looking, disdainful type." Like Hemingway, Wylie was charismatic and had accrued an intensely devoted following, dubbed her "cultists" by writer Thomas Wolfe, who was not among them. Hemingway did not join the Wylie cult, although he apparently saw its appeal; it remains unclear whether he became her lover, although she would later accompany him to his ship back to France, stopping at several bootleggers' establishments along the way.

Before leaving New York, Hemingway signed his contract with Scribner's. The house was already creating mock-ups for *The Torrents of Spring*. He then boarded the *Roosevelt,* heading back to Europe at last, flanked by Dorothy Parker and Robert Benchley. Parker was following through on her impulsive decision to move to France; ironically, she funded the odyssey that Hemingway inspired by selling a book of poetry to Horace Liveright — so the publisher got something, at least, out of Hemingway's New York visit.

Another snowstorm engulfed the city as the group prepared to leave; ice glistened on the ship's decks. A raucous bon voyage party, fueled by bootleg champagne, included Wylie and Algonquinite Marc Connelly; one of the revelers absconded with Parker's scotch, an affront not discovered by the travelers until they were out at sea. The hilarity continued on the trip. Benchley hadn't been able to get a proper stateroom and had instead been relegated to a maid's cabin.

"[On] the 4th day out he said it was funny but he felt just like the time he had crabs," Hemingway wrote to Louis Bromfield. "And on the 6th day out he *had* crabs."

After the trip, Parker let it be known that Hemingway had taken saltpeter — supposedly an anti-aphrodisiac — during the group's meals together, notifying those present that it was necessary to keep his sexual appetite under control.

For Hemingway, it was an appropriately triumphant journey back, made in the company of one of America's most adored literary celebrities and one of its most feared critics. Both were now resolutely part of his arsenal. Benchley and Hemingway would remain friends for years, and Parker's devotion to him bordered on idolatry. This adoration would prove useful, although far from mutual.

11

Kill or Be Killed

B ACK IN SCHRUNS, Hadley waited in vain for word from Hemingway: he never once contacted her from New York. She hiked and practiced the piano during her husband's absence, but grew lonely and anxious. His trip had stretched to nearly a month.

When the *Roosevelt* group arrived in Paris, Hemingway did not rush back to his family. Rather, he lingered in the city, dining and drinking with Dorothy Parker, Robert Benchley, and the Fitzgeralds.

There were also other reasons to linger. Hemingway's affair with Pauline Pfeiffer was now officially under way. She had even offered to accompany him to New York; when he made the trip solo, she waited patiently in Paris to welcome him back with open arms. For Hemingway, remorse would eventually settle in; but at that moment, their liaison gave him "unbelievable wrenching, kicking happiness" that was at once dreadful and "un-killable." Pauline now "owned half" of him. She was also still cultivating Hadley, writing to her regularly in Schruns so she could maintain her easy entrée to the Hemingways' life, he later wrote.

After a few days, Hemingway forced himself to travel back to Schruns. Hadley met him at the train station, her face golden with a winter tan and her red hair gleaming in the sun. Bumby stood with her, looking chubby and blond and somewhat Germanic. Hemingway saw them waiting there and "wished [he] had died" before having betrayed them; yet he said nothing of the affair.

The liaison with Pauline would resume when the Hemingways returned to Paris, but for now, they settled back into their family routine at the Hotel Taube. Soon John Dos Passos and the Murphys joined them there. Everyone was in the mood to celebrate. Gerald Murphy was especially thrilled by Hemingway's news about Scribner's and *The Sun Also Rises.*

"It certainly broke prettily for him," Murphy wrote to Hadley before coming to Schruns. "My God this world of success!"

Their Austrian days were filled with roaring fires, feather beds, and cross-country skiing expeditions; the kirsch flowed so freely that "they gave it to us to rub off with when we came in from skiing," recalled Dos Passos. "Mealtimes we could hardly eat for laughing."

At Schruns, Hemingway settled down to revise *The Sun Also Rises*. He wrote to Max Perkins and promised him that the novel would be ready for fall publication. He had to rework five more chapters, but Perkins could expect to see the manuscript in May. Perkins replied that he was impatient to read it and begged Hemingway not to get himself killed "with all of this flying and bullfighting" in the meantime.

Now working on a typewriter, Hemingway began to reshape the final chapters of the book. In this draft, the Pamplona crew would finally be translated into their fictional guises: Duff Twysden now masqueraded full-time as "Brett Ashley," Pat Guthrie officially became "Mike Campbell," and so on.

Separated from the actual events and real-life characters by a gulf of eight months, seven notebooks, and hundreds of pages, Hemingway was now in full command of their on-paper behavior and destinies. They all obeyed his pen and his imagination. Cayetano Ordóñez had been receiving an elegant makeover. By March he was "Pedro Romero," and had become the book's hero. While the real Ordóñez overindulged in flamenco parties, racy women, and Spanish sherry, his more solemn fictional counterpart was steeped in inner nobility and traditional ethics, making Lady Brett Ashley's seduction of him all the more disgraceful. Like the author who created him, however, the character was capable of brutal pragmatism. Romero says:

> *"The bulls are my best friends."*
> *I translated to Brett.*
> *"You kill your friends?" she asked.*
> *"Always," he said in English, and laughed. "So they don't kill me."*

The name "Pedro Romero" would have special meaning for aficionados. Here Hemingway borrowed once more from real life, this time from bullfighting history. The real Pedro Romero was an eighteenth-century Spanish hero—painted by Goya, beloved by thousands. He and his family were said to have founded the modern art of *toreo*. Co-opting his name was the perfect way to endow Hemingway's own new hero with an air of consequence, just as designating Brett, Jake, and the others as mascots of a "lost generation" had elevated their characters.

In Schruns, the relationship between Jake and Brett also got a going-over. In the first draft, in the scene in which Jake is summoned to Madrid to rescue the fictional Lady Duff from her failed affair with Ordóñez, he bitterly frets and tortures himself for pages about the injustice of his situation and the general failings of the British aristocracy before letting the matter rest. In the Schruns revision, Hemingway chiseled Jake's tormented ponderings down to a controlled shrug. When Jake receives Brett's telegraphed plea for help, he sends her a reply informing her that he is en route. Afterward, he exudes nonchalance: "That seemed to handle it. That was it. Send a girl off with one man. Introduce her to another to go off with him. Now go and bring her back. And sign the wire with love. That was it all right. I went in to lunch."

There was also the matter of the very final scene, in which Jake and Brett drive through Madrid in the back of a taxi; Brett fantasizes about what might have been. In the first draft, Hemingway had written:

> "Oh Jake," Duff said. "We could have had such a damned good time together."
>
> Ahead was a mounted policeman in Khaki . . . directing traffic. The car slowed suddenly pressing Duff closer against me.
>
> "Yes," I said. "It's nice as hell to think so."

Hemingway had not been entirely satisfied with that final line. Now he felt that he had the answer:

> "Yes," I said. "Isn't it pretty to think so?"

It transformed a bitter, resigned statement into a cynical yet sad rhetorical question, and would leave readers with a sense of poignancy.

The revisions were minute and grueling but tightened the screws of the entire novel. In the evenings, Hemingway read the new work aloud to Dos Passos and the Murphys, as he had read to Pauline earlier that winter. If Gerald Murphy had been less than enthusiastic about *The Torrents of Spring,* he was "blown out of the water" by *The Sun Also Rises.*

Hemingway loved the praise, although he would later chide himself for reveling in the adoration. He *should* have thought to himself, "If these bastards like it what is wrong with it?" he later wrote. He cringed at the memory of the readings, which he came to regard as grossly unprofessional—and even dangerous to the writer. At the time, however, he was grateful for the encouragement and his friends were glad to give it, although they would be punished later for doing so.

"We were all brothers and sisters when we parted company," recalled Dos Passos. It was the "last unalloyed good time" he would remember having with Hemingway and Hadley during this European chapter of their lives.

BY THE END of the month, Hemingway was back in Paris and had good news for Perkins.

"I finished re-writing The Sun Also Rises," he informed him on April 1. He complained later that it had been an intensely difficult revision, but all things considered, it had not taken him very long to make the leap from frantically scribbled draft to chiseled masterpiece. The completed manuscript, which was being sent off for a professional retyping, ran nearly ninety thousand words—a far cry from *War and Peace,* but a respectable length by anyone's standards. It would reach Perkins in a couple of weeks.

Hemingway had also been deliberating the dedication, and had, for the moment, alighted upon the following:

TO MY SON
John Hadley Nicanor
This collection of Instructive Anecdotes

Even though his editor had not even seen the manuscript yet, Hemingway felt that it was time to get down to the matter of publicity. He not only furnished Perkins with pictures of himself for the Scribner's publicity team, but also included a shot of Bumby, perhaps in case there was any press potential in his family life.

A week later he sent Perkins a list of powerful reviewers and writers who should get advance copies of *The Torrents of Spring,* and even supplied their addresses and press affiliations. The roster included influencers from the Paris Crowd and some of the Algonquin Round Tablers with whom he had just rubbed elbows.

Around this time, he also engaged agent Curtis Brown to sell his works in England and Europe, and had already set up an arrangement with the British publisher Jonathan Cape to publish *In Our Time.* ("I don't think

Jonathan Cape is the best publishing house in England but they're not the worst," Hemingway wrote to Perkins.) Cape would also have the right of first refusal on both *The Torrents of Spring* and *The Sun Also Rises,* although, somewhat tellingly, Hemingway was not making the publication of *Torrents* a prerequisite for acquiring *The Sun Also Rises.* In fact, Cape didn't want *Torrents* anyway. Like Liveright and Scribner's, all the publisher really wanted was the novel.

Meanwhile, Perkins was ravenous to read *The Sun Also Rises.* He hastily sent *Torrents* off to the presses for a late May publication; all of his attention could now be turned to the novel. A mere two weeks after Hemingway had completed his revisions, Perkins informed his new author that the Scribner's team had already mocked up a cover for the book they had yet even to read. His salesmen would be ready to take out dummies on May 1.

"In fact, the book will be complete except for the text," he added. "That I shall await with great eagerness."

By late April, the wait was over. Hemingway alerted Perkins by letter that "the Sun A.R. (the pig that you bought in a poke)" was en route. As he anxiously waited for a response, he wrote morosely to Fitzgerald that he felt "low as hell," and his mood only sank from there. In another letter to Fitzgerald he confessed that he was lonesome again and signed it from "Ernest M. Shit."

The manuscript of *The Sun Also Rises* survived its ocean voyage and landed safely on Perkins's desk. Perkins read it eagerly. Like *This Side of Paradise,* it was indeed bound to cause an uproar in the house. From its liberal sprinkling of four-letter words to its characters' profligate drinking habits to the sexually emancipated, emotionally deadened female protagonist, *The Sun Also Rises* was a perfect storm of affronts to the sensibilities of the more conservative Scribner's editors.

At home, Perkins fretted about it to his wife, the writer and poet Louise Saunders. The couple hotly debated the book. Later Saunders would have no great love for Hemingway, but she came out in favor of his contentious debut novel.

"Max, you have to stand up for this, and protect its integrity by not taking out obscene words," Louise told him.

Perkins agonized over the situation. "He always staunchly defended the right of the author to write his or her own book, but he was also pragmatic," says his granddaughter Jenny Phillips. "The book was so shocking and disturbing at the time."

In fact, Perkins believed that *The Sun Also Rises* was "almost unpublishable," as he wrote to Fitzgerald that spring. But he prepared to make his case for the book anyway. When the Scribner's editors gathered to discuss the book's status, Perkins marched into the meeting, determined to defend his acquisition as important literature, not mere profanity.

"It's a vulgar book," Charles Scribner Sr. declared. "There are four-letter words in it that I never would permit on the page of any book that enters a gentleman's house."

Perkins started by making concessions.

"Well, Hemingway is willing to cut out some of these words," he ventured. (Hemingway, unaware of this discussion, was certainly *not* willing to cut words, but at this point, it was more important just to get the book greenlighted.)

"Which words?" Scribner demanded.

Unable to utter the words out loud, Perkins hustled back to his office and came back with a piece of paper. He scribbled a short list and handed the sheet to Scribner, who gave a tight smile and responded, "Max, if Hemingway knew that you didn't dare say those words in my presence, he'd disown you!"

Scribner was amused but unconvinced. Perkins tried a different approach. He reminded the team that the house's reputation needed continued renovation: despite the presence of Fitzgerald and Lardner on their list, younger writers still considered Scribner's to be "ultra conservative," and if they rejected Hemingway's book, that reputation would be set in stone.

This argument had persuaded the house to publish Fitzgerald's *This Side of Paradise,* but in the case of *The Sun Also Rises,* Scribner simply would not budge. The team reached an impasse; the atmosphere was one of "general misery," as Perkins put it later. Junior editor John Hall Wheelock was then summoned and pressed for his opinion.

Perkins must have squirmed as he awaited his colleague's feedback. Wheelock was, in Perkins's view, something of a hermit who dwelled "out of the world on that balcony of his." Despite his comparative youth, he was fairly out of touch with "modern tendencies in writing."

Wheelock entered the room and gave his verdict.

"To my amazement," Perkins later told the younger Scribner, "he thought there was no question whatever but that we should publish."

Finally—painfully—the book was accepted, but with deep misgivings among its detractors. Rumors circulated first in-house and later throughout the literary community that "Old C.S." had rejected the book and that Perkins had threatened to resign.

Yet once *The Sun Also Rises* was added officially to the Scribner's list, the house was prepared to launch Hemingway as strongly as it had backed Fitzgerald. Securing the acceptance of *The Sun Also Rises* was, of course, primarily Perkins's triumph, but the book was now the house's collective gamble. "Old C.S." has often been described as authoritarian and resistant to change, but he had also begun to see — through Perkins's eyes — where modern sensibilities were heading. The elder editors softened in their aversion to *The Sun Also Rises* as well, and even began to look at it as another experiment.

"I should think . . . we might go ahead and see what happens," wrote one of them in an internal memo about the debate surrounding the book. After all, he added, "a single mistake would not be fatal."

A couple of years later, when the book had been published and was getting some of the inevitable horrified backlash the elder editors had feared, Perkins personally responded to one of the more irate readers' letters. By then he had had time to hone and clarify the reason he and Scribner had decided to publish *The Sun Also Rises* in the first place. Not every work necessarily reflected the personal taste of the publisher, he stated.

Nevertheless, "[the publisher] is under an obligation to his profession," Perkins wrote, "which binds him to bring out a work which in the judgment of the literary world is significant in its literary qualities and is a pertinent criticism of the civilization of the time."

In other words, the publisher had a duty to advance the cause of art, and *The Sun Also Rises* represented art's next frontier.

BY MID-MAY, Hemingway had heard nothing from Perkins and stewed in anxiety; he was also feeling defensive about *The Torrents of Spring,* which would hit bookstores a few days later. When Perkins finally wrote to his new author on May 18, he kept him ignorant about the in-house row over his novel.

"'The Sun Also Rises' seems to me a most extraordinary performance," Perkins congratulated him. "No one could conceive of a book with more life in it." The reader truly felt he was there, especially in the pastoral Burguete scenes. The humor and satire, especially as expressed by Jake and Bill Gorton, were top-notch. It was an astonishing work of art, one that involved "an extraordinary range of experience and emotion, all brought

together in the most skillful manner — the subtle ways of which are beautifully concealed — to form a complete design."

He advised that edits would follow, but Perkins was light-handed in
this first missive. He did have to bring up, however, the sensitive fact
that Hemingway had managed to shoot a sharp arrow — as was now
his habit — at one of his publishing house stablemates. This time the
victim was Henry James; in the manuscript, Bill Gorton implies that
James had, like Jake Barnes, been rendered impotent by an accident. In
this case, the catalyst was a mishap with a bicycle — or maybe even a tri-
cycle, Gorton jokes — rather than a war wound. According to Perkins,
it would have to go.

"I am not raising this you must believe, because we are his publishers,"
he wrote to Hemingway. Even though James had been dead for ten years,
Perkins simply did not see how the reference could be included: "It could
not by any conception be printed while he was alive, if only for the fear of
a lawsuit; and in a way it seems almost worse to print it after he is dead."
Other than that, it was time to move forward at full speed and put the
manuscript into production.

First, however, they had to get over the speed bump of publishing *The
Torrents of Spring,* which debuted to the world on May 28 bearing the title

The Torrents of Spring
A Romantic Novel in Honor of the Passing of a Great Race

No one in-house seemed particularly invested in promoting the book.
Hemingway had predicted to Horace Liveright sales of at least 20,000 copies, but Scribner's answered that bluff with a modest first printing of 1,250
copies. The publication schedule had been so rushed that the book was not
included in the house's spring catalogue, and only a limited advertising
campaign was attempted.

The house used the book's launch, however, as an opportunity to tease
the upcoming novel and get the drumbeat going about Hemingway himself. Scribner's vigorously marketed him as a new leader of "modern tendencies in writing," as Perkins had put it. In a supplement to the spring
catalogue, the house announced that "Hemingway as a writer is in revolt
against the soft, vague thought and expression that characterizes the work
of extremists in American fiction today." His writing was "utterly direct"
and "completely fearless," and would give readers "a shock like cold water." *The Torrents of Spring* provided a hint of the "extraordinary talent of

the writer, a talent which will be even more clearly revealed when his first novel, 'The Sun Also Rises,' is published next fall."

In reality, *The Torrents of Spring* did little to showcase Hemingway's revolutionary style, as it was a satire of Anderson's, but no matter. The house's ads for *Torrents* echoed these sentiments, driving home the message that Hemingway was brilliant, promising, and young.

Most of the reviewers who did bother to write up the book did not take the bait, however. At least one of them simply seemed confused by *The Torrents of Spring:* How had Hemingway made the leap from *In Our Time,* with its terse, brutal prose, to this? Another reviewer—Harry Hansen of the *New York World*—made short work of Hemingway's attempt at satire.

"Parody is a gift of the gods," he wrote. "Few are blessed with it. It missed Hemingway."

He also called the book out as a blatant betrayal of Anderson: "When Hemingway published 'In Our Time' it was Sherwood Anderson who turned the handsprings and welcomed this newcomer to the ranks of America's great men . . . and now Hemingway pays him back."

Yet as far as Scribner's was concerned, there was positive news too: Hemingway's apparent attack on Anderson was proving good, gossipy copy—and so was Hemingway himself. The *Kansas City Star* included some colorful albeit inaccurate background about his war years: the author of this "audacious little volume" had "volunteered in the Italian army and got himself gloriously shot up." A reviewer for the *New York Herald Tribune* commented, "Mr. Hemingway's name, which one hears everywhere now, [may be] more famous than his prose." This all portended well for a major publicity push when it came time to release *The Sun Also Rises.*

Some of Hemingway's acquaintances were stunned by *The Torrents of Spring,* which had suddenly revealed his capacity for public betrayal. It was shocking even to those on the outer rings of the Paris Crowd: Hemingway had been among the privileged few admitted into the den, and now he was eating his own. Backstabbing friends and mentors on the terrace of the Dôme café was acceptable, if not de rigueur, but doing so with the backup of a major American publisher and an attentive, headline-hungry press corps was quite another affair.

The book especially displeased Gertrude Stein. Hemingway had remained in close touch with her until around 1925, but had since grown to resent her—as he would anyone with any claim on his own genesis as a stylist or public figure. She had apparently declined to review *In Our Time,* which incensed him. (Clearly she expected him to fail with his first novel, he told Pound, and didn't want to risk the public association with him.) Plus, she was "cockeyed lazy," Hemingway had decided, and her image as the creative den mother of the Left Bank irritated him now. None of the expat writers in Paris, including himself, he later reportedly stated, had been looking for a "Mommy" to lead them out of the creative wilderness. She was even too self-obsessed to be angry about *The Torrents of Spring* as an attack on Anderson, Hemingway claimed. Rather her indignation stemmed from the fact that he had "attacked someone that was a part of her apparatus." The *Torrents* affair foreshadowed a nasty public rift that would soon play out between the former teacher and student.

Of course, no one was more shocked and chagrined by *The Torrents of Spring* than Sherwood Anderson himself. A week before the book's publication, Hemingway sent Max Perkins a sealed letter for Anderson and asked him to mail it along with a copy of the book. Perkins was surprised but complied. "What did he say [in it], I wonder?" he wrote to Fitzgerald, but he duly sent it along.

Anderson deemed Hemingway's missive "the most self-conscious and probably the most completely patronizing letter ever written." Hemingway had informed Anderson that *Dark Laughter* was evidence that Anderson had been "slopping," and Hemingway was therefore honor-bound to save Anderson from himself: "When a man like yourself who can write very great things writes something that seems to me . . . rotten, I ought to tell you so," he wrote.

He felt that he was qualified to do so because he was a "fellow craftsman." He knew that Anderson's feelings would likely be hurt, but it was nothing personal. And anyway, who could be hurt by a little satire? Hemingway then trailed off into small talk about the weather in Paris and offered his best regards to Anderson's wife.

Anderson read the book. His conclusion: *The Torrents of Spring* was a failed attempt at humor. Maybe it would have worked if a more gifted satirist, like Max Beerbohm, had written it and whittled it down to, say, twelve pages. Yet Hemingway's missive had cut him more deeply than his satire did.

"There was something in the letter that was gigantic," Anderson later recalled. "It was a kind of funeral oration delivered over my grave. It was so raw, so pretentious, so patronizing that in a repellant way it was amusing."

He penned a response to Hemingway, in which he shakily tried to reestablish the old dynamic between them.

"You . . . speak to me like a master to a pupil," he wrote. "Come out of it, man. I pack a little wallop myself. I've been a middle weight champion. You seem to forget that."

He predicted that *The Torrents of Spring* would only help him and hurt Hemingway. Yet underneath this bravado, there were hints at real pain and surprise.

"You didn't sound like [this] when I knew you," he wrote. "It must be Paris — the literary life."

The publication of *The Torrents of Spring* ended their friendship. A few months later, the two men met again briefly when Anderson was visiting Paris. According to Anderson, he was in his hotel room on his last night in town when he heard a knock on his door. He opened it, and there in the hallway stood Hemingway.

"How about a drink?" he said.

The men went to a small bar across the street. Each of them ordered a beer. Hemingway raised his glass.

"Well, here's how."

"Here's how," Anderson responded.

And then Hemingway drank his beer and strode away. "He had, I dare say, proved his sportsmanship to himself," mused Anderson.

Hemingway painted a rosier picture of the reunion for Perkins. "We had two fine afternoons together," he wrote. "He was not at all sore about Torrents and we had a fine time."

Anderson was actually quite sore about *Torrents* and would be for years. He and Gertrude Stein would talk at length about their ungrateful protégé.

"Hemingway had been formed by the two of [us]," Stein later recalled, adding that they were both "a little proud and a little ashamed of the work of [our] minds." Hemingway was, they concluded, a bit of a coward and also a sham; they simply didn't buy his ultramasculine image.

"What a book, [we] both agreed, would be the real story of Hemingway," wrote Stein. "Not those he writes but the confessions of the real Ernest Hemingway."

And, finally, they didn't think that he had understood what they were up to stylistically anyway. He tried hard to seem modern, but to Stein, he "smelled of the museums."

More than a decade later, Hemingway's betrayal still weighed on Anderson. "In the case of Hemmy," he wrote to his mother in 1937, "there is the desire always to kill." This was because Hemingway couldn't "bear the thought of any other men as artists," and because of his need to dominate the whole field. But Anderson did not lose his respect for Hemingway's skill with a pen. After reading one of Hemingway's new short stories in a literary magazine called the *Quarter,* he wrote to Stein of his admiration. "It was a beautiful story," he enthused. "Beautifully done."

"Lordy," he added, "but that man can write."

THAT APRIL, when the Hemingways had returned from Schruns, Hadley received an invitation: Pauline and Virginia Pfeiffer — now back from the United States — asked her to join them on a road trip down to château country in the Loire Valley. It would be a ladies-only lark: they could stop at Versailles and swing by Chartres; there would be delicious restaurants and overnight stays at the best hotels. Wouldn't it be lovely for Hadley to have a break from her family obligations? Pauline even offered to bankroll the whole excursion.

Hadley mulled it over. It would be nice, for once, to go on a trip that didn't center on fishing or skiing. She accepted the Pfeiffers' invitation.

She quickly regretted the decision. Pauline was in a horrid mood as the three of them sped along in Virginia's car. If Hadley asked a question or made a remark, Pauline shot back a hostile, terse reply. Hadley avoided confronting the situation directly, but she must have had some sense of the root of Pauline's anger. One evening, with her customary gentleness, she approached Virginia.

"Do you think Pauline and Ernest get along awfully well?" she asked.

"Well," replied Virginia, "I think they're very fond of each other."

Virginia's tone told Hadley everything she needed to know. The atmosphere among the little group turned even blacker, and the return journey was made in tense silence. Hadley wondered if the Pfeiffer sisters had planned the whole trip as a way to break the news of the affair to her. It has been suggested that Pauline's hostility toward Hadley may have been compounded by an unwanted and soon-to-be-terminated pregnancy, courtesy of Hadley's husband, although evidence on that score is circumstantial. Whatever the case, the "fond of each other" remark made it impossible for Hadley to continue in "innocent" silence any longer. Whether or not she genuinely had been unaware of the affair before then, Pauline and Virginia had now forced the issue.

"There are two versions of life: one is turn the other cheek and the other is destroy the enemy," says Hemingway's son Patrick, implying that

Hadley was of the former camp and Pauline of the latter. Sooner rather than later, Hemingway would have to choose between the women, and Pauline apparently felt that she was in the stronger position.

Hemingway became irate when Hadley confronted him back in Paris. Yes, he was having an affair, he admitted, but then he turned the tables on Hadley: *she* was the one doing irreparable damage to the marriage by bringing it up. Everything would have been just fine if she hadn't dragged it into the open—or at least, that was Hadley's interpretation of his position. It is unclear whether he meant that the affair would simply have run its course, or that he would have been perfectly happy to continue enjoying the attentions of both a wife and a mistress. He swept out of the apartment while Hadley cried.

The couple decided to stay together. Yet it became clear that Hemingway had no intention of excising Pauline from his life. Soon after the confrontation, Pauline sent a message to Hadley through Hemingway, requesting a woman-to-woman chat. Hadley declined. She had had quite enough of Pauline Pfeiffer's invitations.

Not long after the showdown, Hemingway boarded a train to Madrid. He and Hadley had planned another Spanish summer together, but when Bumby came down with a cough, Hadley stayed with him in Paris. Hemingway made the trip alone. Once in Madrid, he checked in at the Pensión Aguilar, his usual haunt. Filled with nervous energy, he began to write at breakneck speed, as he had the summer before. In one day alone he completed three short stories.

"I had so much juice I thought maybe I was going crazy," he later recalled.

The pension's staff got into the spirit of his writing mania, sending fortifying food and wine up to his room. When Hemingway told the waiter that he was exhausted, the waiter looked at him with disapproval.

"You tired after three miserable little stories," he muttered.

Other factors may have contributed to his exhaustion: Pauline had left Paris around the same time as Hemingway, ostensibly to visit relatives in Italy. Yet it has been speculated that she may actually have joined Hemingway in Madrid to get an abortion. Whether this was true or not, Hemingway's personal life was in a state of upheaval as he anxiously waited for Perkins's response to his manuscript of *The Sun Also Rises*.

• • •

AFTER HEMINGWAY left for Madrid, Hadley took Bumby down to the Riviera: Sara and Gerald Murphy had offered to look after the child at their Antibes villa so Hadley could join Hemingway in Spain. Scott and Zelda Fitzgerald were already summering nearby.

The Murphys' fourteen-room house, Villa America, was perched on seven acres of land overlooking the "burnished blue-steel" of the Mediterranean, as Gerald Murphy put it. Terraced gardens cut across a hill that sloped gently down to the sea; the property teemed with mimosas. The sunbaked air smelled of heliotrope, eucalyptus, and tomatoes. Palms, lemon trees, and white Arabian maples rustled in the sea breezes.

At first glance, life at Villa America seemed an unrepentantly opulent and celebrity-filled existence. Sara casually wore an opera-length pearl necklace to the beach; Rudolph Valentino, Cole Porter, and Pablo Picasso were frequent presences at the house. The Murphys' sleek one-hundred-foot schooner, the *Weatherbird,* swayed in the waters offshore.

Yet simplicity and a lack of pretension defined the Murphys' existence. They avoided the ostentation of the aspiring and the nouveau riche; to their admirers, they seemed superior and thoroughbred. If the Fitzgeralds trafficked in decadence, the Murphys' life was a study in wholesome luxury. Sara's luncheons epitomized studied effortlessness: One day she might serve perfectly boiled potatoes with butter, muscadet wine, and bread. Another menu featured poached eggs with homegrown corn and tomatoes, served outdoors in the shade of a rustling linden tree. The couple could also be irreverent—especially Gerald, who liked to prepare canapés and offer them to the family's dogs on Italian china before serving his human guests.

"They would never be young again and they proposed to live well," recalled poet and Murphy friend Archibald MacLeish. "But they knew how to live without throwing money around."

Even for Hadley, who hated being apart from Bumby during her travels with Hemingway, Villa America must have seemed a guilt-free place to deposit her little son for the summer: the place was a child's paradise as well. The world of Villa America often centered on the Murphys' three young children; Sara and Gerald seemed determined to give them the chicest and most whimsical childhood possible. The children spent much of the summer on the villa's private beach, running naked under the Riviera sun. Their playmates often included some of Paris's most celebrated creative figures. Once the Murphy children staged an art show which Pi-

top

Ernest and Hadley Hemingway on their wedding day, Horton Bay, September 3, 1921. The couple originally planned to go to Italy afterward, until writer Sherwood Anderson instead convinced them that Paris was *the* place for ambitious young creatives.

left

A popular writer in the 1920s, Anderson was immediately impressed by young Hemingway when they first met in Chicago in 1921. "I think he's going to go someplace," he told mutual friends.

Hemingway's 1923 passport photo. For the young journalist and writer, his trip to Paris was just the beginning of his travels: the *Toronto Star* and other news services would soon send him all over Europe on important stories.

The newlyweds in Switzerland, 1922.

Le Dôme café in Paris's Montparnasse, the nerve center of the 1920s expatriate colony. Anyone who wanted to broadcast a salacious bit of gossip, show off a new mistress, or brag about selling a new novel did so at the Dôme; word then ricocheted through the crowd with satisfying speed.

Deemed "the acknowledged leader of the modern movement" in
the Paris expat colony, Ezra Pound first met Hemingway in early 1922
and became his mentor. "Make it new" was one of his mantras, and
he often wore a scarf stitched with the phrase.

Experimental writer and salon hostess Gertrude Stein also took Hemingway under her wing soon after he arrived in Paris. Her commanding physique and outsized persona earned her an array of nicknames around the Left Bank: "the Sumerian monument," "the great god Buddha," and perhaps most amusingly, "the Presence."

American expatriate Sylvia Beach, publisher and proprietor of Shakespeare and Company, a popular Left Bank bookstore, lending library, and salon. To her, Hemingway looked marked for success: "He seemed to me to have gone a great deal farther and faster than any of the young writers I knew," she later wrote.

Hemingway at Shakespeare and Company shortly after his arrival in Paris, in a photo taken by Sylvia Beach.

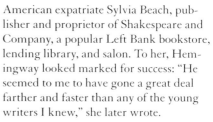

above

Robert McAlmon, proprietor of the
Contact Publishing Company, a boutique
press and Hemingway's first book publisher.
Acid-tongued and openly bisexual, McAlmon
seemed an unlikely collaborator for Hemingway; the men locked horns almost immediately
but still brought their project to fruition.

top right

Robert McAlmon and Hemingway in Spain,
1923. Hemingway had been nursing a growing
fascination with bullfighting and was eager
to behold the spectacle in person. McAlmon
footed the bill for the excursion.

bottom right

McAlmon and Bill Bird in Spain, 1923. Hemingway and McAlmon were joined on their
trip by Bird, an expat journalist and publisher
who had also just founded his own small book
press in Paris. For an ambitious new writer
in search of a publisher, these were most
promising travel companions. By the end of
the trip, both men had agreed to release books
by Hemingway.

When the Hemingways returned from their ill-fated fall 1923 foray to Toronto, they moved into a flat at 113 rue Notre-Dame-des-Champs. The apartment overlooked a lumberyard and sawmill, but anything was tolerable after the misery they had experienced in Canada. Here Hemingway stands outside the building in 1924.

Hemingway and his son Jack "Bumby" Hemingway, likely in late 1924 or early 1925.

above left

British novelist and editor Ford Madox Ford, who had just joined the Paris colony when Hemingway returned from Canada. Ezra Pound arranged for Hemingway to become deputy editor of Ford's new literary magazine, the *transatlantic review*. Ford was so taken by Hemingway's writing that he pledged to "publish everything [Hemingway] sent me," although Hemingway would prove less enthusiastic about his new colleague.

below

Café patrons at La Closerie des Lilas, which became Hemingway's de facto office. He found it sufficiently removed from the raucous, posturing crowds up the street at the Dôme. At the Closerie, "no one was on exhibition," he later wrote with approval.

Kathleen "Kitty" Cannell: American expat fashion correspondent, popular girl-about-town, and Harold Loeb's lover. She and Hemingway disliked each other upon first sight; she deemed him volatile and weak with anti-Semitic tendencies, and later claimed that she had repeatedly told Loeb about her misgivings to no avail. Hemingway would register his displeasure with her in a far more permanent way.

Harold Loeb in a portrait by Man Ray—a court photographer of the Paris expat creative elite. A descendant of two of New York City's richest and most prominent Jewish families, Loeb met Hemingway at a party in 1924 and grew to hero-worship him. "I relish[ed] his spontaneity, his zest for living," he later recalled.

A best-selling author and one of the quick-witted members of New York's notorious Algonquin Round Table, Donald Ogden Stewart met Hemingway in Paris and immediately concluded that "he seemed to be my kind of guy." He soon revised his opinion. "When Ernest was enthusiastic about something it was extremely dangerous to resist anything, especially friendliness," he learned.

Horace Liveright was not exactly a conventional publisher; his fellow publishers deemed him a glamour-seeking charlatan, a reckless upstart, and an outrageous interloper. In the year this portrait was taken — 1925 — Liveright would become Hemingway's first commercial American publisher.

In 1925, Hemingway met *Vogue* writer and heiress Pauline Pfeiffer. Unlike Hadley, Pfeiffer worshipped at the altar of fashion. At first, she and Hemingway made poor impressions on each other: he would rather have taken her sister Virginia "out in Pauline's coat," he declared, while she found him repellent and slovenly. Soon enough, however, they discovered each other's more charming qualities.

left
Wealthy and attractive hosts Sara and Gerald Murphy stood at the apex of Paris's creative scene. Their dinner guests on any given evening might include Picasso, Cole Porter, or Douglas Fairbanks. They quickly detected Hemingway's nascent genius and became enthusiastic supporters of his career. They are pictured here on the beach of their villa in Cap d'Antibes.

Hemingway's boyhood friend Bill Smith turned up empty-pocketed in Paris just in time to tag along with Hemingway and his illustrious expat friends to the fateful 1925 Pamplona fiesta. He had a gift for cynical wisecracks — an attribute that Hemingway had spent years observing and would soon advertise to much of the literate world.

Maxwell Perkins, an editor at the prestigious publishing house Charles Scribner's Sons. Perkins may have been a Harvard-educated blueblood, but he was also shrewd when it came to discerning modern publishing trends and wrangling vanguard talent. "Perkins would have been great at *Vanity Fair,*" said Charles Scribner III. "He had a commercial streak to him."

When Hemingway met F. Scott Fitzgerald and his wife, Zelda, in 1925, Fitzgerald was at the zenith of his fame. "Poor Scott was earning so much money from his books that he and Zelda had to drink a great deal of champagne in Montmartre in an effort to get rid of it," recalled Sylvia Beach. He had already become Hemingway's champion behind the scenes and would soon put more effort into boosting Hemingway's career than nurturing his own.

Hemingway and his entourage at a café, taken during the San Fermín festival in Pamplona, July 1925. Nearly everyone at the table would soon be translated into thinly veiled characters in Hemingway's break-through novel, *The Sun Also Rises*. From left to right, the individuals along with their *Sun* pseudonyms: Hemingway ("Jake Barnes"), Harold Loeb ("Robert Cohn"), Lady Duff Twysden ("Lady Brett Ashley"), Hadley Hemingway, Donald Ogden Stewart ("Bill Gorton"), and Patrick Guthrie ("Mike Campbell"). Hadley was mentioned briefly in some preamble material, but did not make the leap to the actual manuscript. Not pictured: Bill Smith.

Harold Loeb's moment of glory during the amateur fights at the 1925 Pamplona fiesta. At least one New York City newspaper ran this image, much to the amusement of Loeb's family.

Not to be outdone, Hemingway managed to catch hold of the bull's horns and wrestle it to the ground. Yet despite this Herculean feat, Loeb was the king of the ring that day: the locals were in awe of the first man (or the first foreigner, anyway) in living memory who had ridden a bull's head, and they treated Loeb like a hero.

Cayetano Ordóñez, the nineteen-year-old matador who had been thrilling aficionados throughout Spain. "He was sincerity and purity of style itself with the cape," Hemingway wrote of him later. In *The Sun Also Rises*, Hemingway translated Ordóñez into "Pedro Romero" and ultimately made him the book's hero.

Hadley Hemingway and Pauline Pfeiffer during the winter of 1925–26, when Pfeiffer had joined the Hemingways for a skiing holiday at Schruns, an Austrian mountain town. Hemingway became torn between the two women: "One is new and strange and if he has bad luck he gets to love them both," he later wrote.

Dorothy Parker: influential critic, author, poet, and barb-tongued queen bee of the Algonquin Round Table. Hemingway met her in February 1926 when he traveled to New York City to break ties with Boni & Liveright and sign with Charles Scribner's Sons. Parker was captivated by Hemingway; she even impulsively decided to join him on his ocean voyage back to Europe, and would long remain a vocal supporter of his work.

above

The 1926 Pamplona entourage. Seated at table, left to right: Gerald Murphy, Sara Murphy, Pauline Pfeiffer, Hemingway, and Hadley Hemingway. Soon after the fiesta, Hemingway and Hadley decided to separate. He would be married to Pfeiffer by the following year's fiesta.

right

An advertisement for *The Sun Also Rises* featuring an illustration of its author, whom Charles Scribner's Sons wished to promote as heavily as the book itself. A drawing was being used instead of a photograph, Maxwell Perkins explained to Hemingway, because it was easier for publications to reproduce, and the publishing house wanted Hemingway's youthful, chiseled visage to be as widely reproduced as possible.

THE NEW YORKER

Ernest Hemingway

whom Ford Madox Ford called "the best writer in America of the moment" now presents his first full novel—

The Sun Also Rises

—and with its publication Mr. Hemingway's sun also will rise. The alert reader will want to be aware of this book from the start—it will inevitably command the sharpest attention.

$2.00 at bookstores   *Scribner's*

casso judged; another time, the Fitzgeralds held an elaborate treasure hunt for the children, including their daughter Scottie.

Yet Bumby's cough had become more pronounced by the time he and Hadley turned up at Villa America. Watching him play with their children on the beach, the Murphys grew alarmed and summoned their doctor. The prognosis was grim: whooping cough.

The Murphys immediately exiled Bumby and Hadley from paradise. Luckily, they were able to move into a small house in Juan-les-Pins that the Fitzgeralds had rented but abandoned for a more lavish villa with its own beach. Gerald wrote to Hemingway in Madrid and tried to put a cheerful face on the banishment of his wife and son. Hadley would probably be far happier not having to listen to the shrieks of so many kids, he contended, and Bumby was under the care of a superlative English doctor and was getting fresh vegetables from the garden. Hemingway was not to worry; everything was under control.

Bumby's nanny hustled down to the Riviera from Paris; she, Hadley, and Bumby settled into an isolated sickroom routine in the little house. The Murphys and Fitzgerald kept "a grand distance from us poisonous ones," Hadley reported to Hemingway, although the Fitzgeralds sent them necessities such as chicken, eggs, and roses. The Murphys also dispatched their chauffeur with provisions. Loneliness and uncertainty tormented Hadley, although a walk into town and a shot of whisky sometimes helped alleviate her unhappiness and stress.

Soon, however, company arrived that likely made Hadley long for solitude again.

"Pfeiffer is stopping off here Wednesday," Hadley informed Hemingway in a letter.

Hadley later indicated that she was bemused by Pauline's sudden appearance on the Riviera, even claiming to one biographer that Hemingway had likely implored Pauline—who'd had whooping cough as a child and was immune—to go to Juan-les-Pins and alleviate the little family's isolation. But on May 21 Hadley had actually written to her husband and told him that she'd invited Pauline "to stop off here if she wants," adding that it would be a "swell joke on tout le monde if you and Fife and I spent the summer [together]" on the Riviera. She appeared to be making an effort to make light of the tricky romantic situation, although she may have invited Pauline out of fear that her rival might otherwise join Hemingway in Spain during her own absence. In any case, Pauline materialized on the

Riviera and moved into the small house, with the stated purpose of giving Hadley some relief from her sickbed duties.

"She's sorry for me," Hadley wrote to Hemingway. But the person Pauline was "really sorry for is Mr. Hemingway all alone in Madrid," she added somewhat bitterly. "I'm sure that she will go on and make Madrid a place of pleasure instead of the awful strain of a place its been to you alone."

SOON HEMINGWAY joined them in Juan-les-Pins, setting the stage for what must have been one of the odder and more claustrophobic households in literary history. The idea of sharing a two-bedroom house with his mistress, an angry wife, a sick toddler, and a hovering nanny might have brought a lesser man to his knees, but Hemingway later described the setting as "a splendid place to write."

Their collective plan was to remain on the Riviera for three weeks or so until Bumby recovered, and then take off for their usual jaunt to Spain, including the annual fiesta in Pamplona. The Murphys and Fitzgeralds welcomed Hemingway's Riviera arrival with a little champagne party at a nearby casino. After that, the Hemingway ménage remained in quarantine at their house, but the Antibes crew insisted on bringing the ongoing party to them. Not exactly to their doorstep, but close: in the early evenings, the couples parked their cars on the road and hung out in front of the fence lining the small front yard of the Hemingways' house. At the end of each outing, they mounted their empty bottles upside down on the fence spikes. By the time the Hemingways and Pauline left a few weeks later, these trophies ran the entire length of the fence, resembling a long colored-glass garland glinting in the Antibes sun. At these gatherings, the Fitzgeralds and Murphys had front-row seats to the Hemingways' unconventional arrangement—or their "domestic difficulties," as Zelda Fitzgerald put it.

Beneath the show of camaraderie, antipathies sparked within the group, recalling the tense dynamic within the Pamplona entourage the summer before. Hemingway adored Sara but was less simpatico with Gerald. "[My father] was unable to go along with [Hemingway's] 'tough-guy' lingo, as Archie MacLeish and John Dos Passos did," recalled the Murphys' daughter Honoria, describing that lingo as "consisting of short, punchy sentences and single-syllable words." Gerald was a dandy, and both Hemingway and Fitzgerald suspected he was masking a "repressed homosexual streak," as Murphy friend Calvin Tomkins puts it. Fitzgerald would needle Gerald with little barbs, asking him things like, "Why do you have such a passion for buckles?" It created an awkward distance between the men, although Gerald's support of Hemingway's talent never dwindled.

The Murphys' patience with the Fitzgeralds had also begun to fray by that summer. As their friendship progressed, the Murphys gradually realized that they had inadvertently added two more high-maintenance children to their brood. Scott's behavior that summer pushed that friendship to its limit. Months earlier, Fitzgerald had extolled the calm, restorative qualities of the Riviera to Hemingway; he promised that it would be a spare, wholesome, joyous routine of work, swimming, sunbathing, and just two aperitifs a day.

Instead, when Hemingway arrived, he found that Fitzgerald was drunk day and night. He was, another friend thought, "committing suicide on [an] installment plan." Zelda later reported that a "sense of carnival & impending disaster [had] colored [the] summer," although she was drinking a fair amount herself that season. The couple had been terrorizing the Riviera with their inebriated hijinks, which included kidnapping a bartender. Fitzgerald threatened to saw his hostage open to ascertain his contents; they would, Zelda predicted, include a jumble of pencil stubs and saucer shards, among other less choice *objets*. On another evening, driving home from dinner, the Fitzgeralds steered their car onto a train track and promptly passed out. Salvation arrived in the form of a passing peasant, who woke them up just before a train was about to plow into them. Fitzgerald's misbehavior at Hemingway's welcome party — he took to throwing ashtrays at other restaurant patrons — earned him a temporary banishment from the Murphy home. Exile was a terrible fate for Scott, who worshipped Sara.

"We *cannot* — Gerald & I — at our age — & stage of life — *be bothered* with sophomoric situations like last night," she chided him in a letter.

Fitzgerald managed to plead his way back into Eden, but matters worsened when he openly began studying the Murphys as prototypes for his own *roman à clef*. He had decided that Sara and Gerald would be the stars of his next novel, which needed to be an even greater sensation than *The Great Gatsby* to solidify his reputation as an important new literary voice. Such consolidation was, after all, as crucial a step as making a splashy debut in the novel club; it was a requisite pressure that Hemingway would also have to look forward to. Fitzgerald eventually translated the Murphys into Dick and Nicole Diver, the glamorous but doomed protagonists of his 1934 novel *Tender Is the Night,* and his interrogation of the real-life couple lasted for years beforehand. He quizzed them unabashedly about their finances, sex life, and family backgrounds. Sara and Gerald bristled under the glare of his spotlight, but still could not bring themselves to expel him permanently.

"What we loved about Scott was the region in him where his gift came from," said Gerald, adding that nothing ever managed to bury that realm completely.

In the meantime, Hemingway and Zelda Fitzgerald continued to antagonize each other. In a reversal of accusations, Zelda now blamed Hemingway for encouraging Fitzgerald's drinking and sabotaging his work. Yet Hemingway could do no wrong in Fitzgerald's eyes. Zelda's hatred did not budge him. Nor could the fact that their mutual friends were beginning to value Hemingway's talents over Fitzgerald's. To the Murphys, "Scott was a successful commercial writer," says Calvin Tomkins. "They liked *Gatsby,* but [his work] didn't hit the contemporary note in the way that Hemingway's did. Hemingway's came like a blast out of the zeitgeist."

They were not the only ones who felt that way. "People watched Hemingway and watched what Hemingway was doing and cared deeply about it, as I did, and weren't too much impressed by Scott," recalled Archibald MacLeish, who was also on the Riviera that summer. "Scott doesn't exist when you're talking at the level of Picasso and Stravinsky." But Hemingway was about to reach that stratum, and his peers sensed it.

Yet no one sensed this more keenly than Fitzgerald, who continued to champion his friend through every phase of his nascent career. Not even the alcoholism that was siphoning off Scott's precious store of vitality could change that. That summer, his skin had taken on a faintly greenish hue, despite the best efforts of the Riviera sun; dark circles ringed his eyes and nicotine stained his fingers. He had developed a paunch and a few nervous tics, and was sinking into a morass of non-productivity. While adversity seemed to spur Hemingway's creativity, Fitzgerald's was essentially grinding to a halt.

"Scott is writing an amazingly good novel which goes so slow it ought to be serialized in the Encyclopedia Britannica," Zelda complained to a friend.

When Hemingway arrived in Antibes, Fitzgerald put aside his own work and turned his attention to Hemingway's. Even Hemingway — not known for rewarding his early investors — would later remember with gratitude that Fitzgerald had, by this point, become "truly more interested in my career than his own."

By early June, Hemingway proudly reported to Perkins that Fitzgerald had read *The Sun Also Rises* and had claimed to like it, although Fitzgerald wrote privately to Perkins that his affection for the book came with "certain qualifications." He disliked the character Brett Ashley, he reported, but that was probably because he didn't "like the original"—meaning the real-life Duff Twysden. Furthermore, he felt that Hemingway had "bit off more than can yet be chewn" with Jake's impotence; he had "lost his nerve a little" with the theme. Yet Scott implored Perkins to treat Hemingway gently.

"Do ask him for the absolute minimum of necessary changes, Max," he wrote. "He's so discouraged about the previous reception of his work by publishers and magazine editors."

Fitzgerald, however, had also handed Hemingway his own critique of *The Sun Also Rises,* and it was anything but gentle. If Hemingway had chided Sherwood Anderson for "slopping," he was about to get some of his own medicine back in kind. After reading the manuscript, Fitzgerald wrote a letter to Hemingway, urging him to excise what he saw as mediocre flourishes and push himself to the next level. Parts of the book were "careless" and "ineffectual"; Fitzgerald reported that he couldn't even abide the novel until he was some thirty pages deep.

"Ernest I can't tell you the sense of disappointment that beginning with its elephantine facetiousness gave me," he wrote.

All of that preamble material skewering the Quarter was the stuff of guidebooks, not literature, he scolded. It amounted to a petulant squall. Few readers would be curious or dedicated enough to stick with a novel that limped through its introduction; Hemingway needed to sharpen the hook. As it stood, the beginning of *The Sun Also Rises* seemed an amateur effort riddled with "sneers, superiorities and nose-thumbings-at-nothing." It might have been cranked out by celebrity writer Michael Arlen—an accusation practically guaranteed to motivate Hemingway to scissor up those early chapters.

"I go crazy when people aren't always at their best," Fitzgerald added somewhat apologetically.

It was essentially a more benevolent echo of the quality-control explanation Hemingway had offered Anderson. Yet unlike *The Torrents of Spring*—an after-the-fact, disdainful public rebuke—Fitzgerald's critique lacked malice. Rather, it may have been the only tough-love missive an editor or another writer ever dared to send Hemingway, and it could not have been a more crucial element in cementing the success of

Hemingway's launch as a major author. Fitzgerald offered a detailed list of suggested edits. The instructions took on an athletic tenor, as though Fitzgerald were coaching a promising young pitcher before his major-league debut. Hemingway was not the only talented player vying for that opportunity, Fitzgerald reminded him.

"When so many people can write well + the competition is so heavy I can't imagine how you could have done these first 20 [pages] so casually," he said.

The usurped, lengthy background about Lady Brett needed to be axed. Hemingway provided everything a reader needed to know about the character later in the manuscript, Fitzgerald argued; ditto for Hemingway's "shopworn" ruminations about the postwar English aristocracy. Fitzgerald also noted that a few real-life characters still lingered in the book's pages under their real names. This was a "cheap" device, he admonished, especially if those personages were "somebod[ies]." Anything that gave the novel a feeling of "This is a true story ect." needed to disappear right away. Lest all the edits demoralize or anger Hemingway, Fitzgerald offered encouragements throughout the letter. These elements had to be shaved away, he advised, to showcase the book's inherent brilliance.

"Remember this is a new departure for you, and that I think your stuff is great," he added. "The novel's damn good."

It was a dignified, noble letter, which showed Fitzgerald's intense desire to see Hemingway succeed. It also revealed the depth of Fitzgerald's devotion to the craft of writing, and how much he wanted to see Hemingway elevate that craft in a bold new way. To his mind, the status that he and Hemingway craved must not come as a result of commercial drivel masquerading as literature, à la Michael Arlen. It must come from innovation and virtuosity. Fitzgerald had no interest in watching Hemingway make an imperfect debut and then call him out afterward. Rather, he wanted to see him soar from the beginning.

It is unclear how Hemingway felt upon receiving Fitzgerald's advice, but in any case, he immediately adopted it. Tolerating feedback from Kitty Cannell was one thing, but heeding suggestions from F. Scott Fitzgerald was another matter. The proposed edits just happened to dovetail perfectly with Hemingway's own omission theory. Right away he informed Perkins that he was cutting the first two chapters, although he implied that the edits had been his own idea.

"I think it will move much faster from the start that way," he wrote. "Scott agrees with me."

He explained that Fitzgerald had suggested various elements to cut out of those chapters, but that he himself felt it best just to lop off all of the initial material. He had never been that fond of it in the first place, he reported. The book would now begin with an introduction to Robert Cohn—Loeb's character—and his background, and dive straight into the Paris part of the narrative. Fitzgerald would probably be writing to Perkins separately, he advised, to tell him of his great excitement about "the book in general."

Fitzgerald never took any public credit for his contributions to *The Sun Also Rises* that summer in Antibes. A decade later, he downplayed his role, stating that he and Hemingway used to throw all sorts of advice at each other, some that stuck and some that did not.

"The only effect I ever had on Ernest was to get him in a receptive mood and say let's cut out everything that goes before this," he told writer John O'Hara. "And so he published it without that and later we agreed that it was a very wise cut."

With characteristic wryness, he added, "This is not literally true and I don't want it established as part of the Hemingway legend."

That said, Hemingway did privately appreciate Fitzgerald's input and told him so. Later that fall, he wrote to Fitzgerald, informing him that he had figured out an appropriate way to express his gratitude. He had instructed Scribner's to amend the title, he joked, and add a subtitle or two to reflect Fitzgerald's role in bringing the novel to its mature state. Henceforth, after the eighth printing, the cover of the book would read:

THE SUN ALSO RISES (LIKE YOUR COCK IF YOU HAVE ONE)
A greater Gatsby
(Written with the friendship of F. Scott FitzGerald
(Prophet of THE JAZZ AGE)

IT IS UNLIKELY THAT Maxwell Perkins would have appreciated the ribald joke. After all, he had been tasked with toning down the tawdrier aspects of *The Sun Also Rises*. Not only would the book's casual sex and listless drinking rustle up objections from readers, booksellers, and the generally straitlaced from coast to coast, but also certain words and phrases dotting the manuscript made it inevitable that the novel would be banned in some precincts.

Unlike Fitzgerald, however, Perkins edited the manuscript lightly and with conciliatory cheer. Toward the end of July, he sent Hemingway the proofs of the book. "I have hardly made a mark on it," he promised, but immediately voiced wariness about the Fitzgerald-mandated cuts. He understood that axing Lady Brett's unconventional background was in keeping with Hemingway's "method," but worried that it might place an unnecessary burden on readers.

"Your way of writing will be new, and in many cases strange," he reminded his author, adding that mainstream readers unfamiliar with his work might welcome the padding and hand-holding of those early chapters as they adjusted to the Hemingway world.

Hemingway stood his ground. The book was much better without all of that, he thought. "After all if I'm trying to write books without any extra words I might as well stick to it," he wrote to Perkins. He conceded in a later letter that it was a shame to lose some of that "very good dope on Brett," but added that retaining the dope would compromise the overall artistry of the novel.

The first scenes stayed on the cutting-room floor. Perkins acquiesced but remained nervous about the decision; a few months later he circled back and gingerly suggested the insertion of a foreword or prologue reinstating some of the more sympathetic material about Lady Brett, in a bid to "make one understand her better in the end." On the one hand, the inevitable stir that this character was bound to provoke would create valuable publicity around *Sun,* but on the other hand, widespread suppression of the book on moral grounds, as with James Joyce's *Ulysses,* would likely hurt sales. Hemingway demurred once again. Brett's borrowed background would filter into the novel, like clues to a riddle, and that was that. (And when it came to moral objections about Brett's carnal activities, as Hemingway pointed out later to Pound, at least "all the fucking takes place off the stage as in Shakespeare.")

On other issues Perkins was more tenacious. *The Sun Also Rises* seemed riddled with potential lawsuits, he argued. He came back to the Henry James reference: Hemingway needed to cut it.

"Henry James is . . . as dead as he will ever be," Hemingway protested to Perkins, adding that James had left no descendants to offend with this bit of dialogue; therefore a libel suit was not an issue. Anyway, it was well known that James had suffered such an accident, he argued.

Perkins would not give up. James might be dead, but he was still a living memory for many people in the literary community. "There are four right in this office who were his friends, — two his close friends," he wrote. In the end, Perkins prevailed; Hemingway offered to change the name to "Henry or Whatsisname — whichever seems best to you." In the published version, Bill Gorton would refer to him only as "Henry"; readers familiar with this supposedly ubiquitous story of the Henry James bicycle incident would know whom he was talking about.

The editor cited legal reasons for other cuts: Hemingway had included an anecdote about the Anglo-French writer Hilaire Belloc in the opening passages. "An Englishman will actually sue for libel at the slightest provocation," Perkins advised his author, adding that the British felt "a right to privacy, unknown in the U.S.A." That said, Perkins never addressed any potential violations of the privacy of Lady Duff Twysden, who was as British as one could get. Both Fitzgerald and Hemingway had alerted Perkins to the fact that Lady Brett Ashley was based on a real person. That fall, Hemingway admitted to Perkins that the biography was "not imaginary": he had drawn a "girl" he knew "so close to life that it makes me feel very badly," but added that his guilt was assuaged by the fact that he suspected she never actually read anything.

Nor did Perkins and Hemingway discuss the privacy of Harold Loeb or Donald Stewart — both of whom ran in the same New York literary circles as Perkins. Rather, the quibbles between editor and author continued to center on figures at the novel's fringes, and in the end, most were snipped away or assigned fictitious monikers. If Perkins had any concerns about the fact that the book's major characters were blatantly based on recognizable people, he did not bring it up. The pseudonyms assigned to them presumably provided sufficient legal cover for the publisher, and that was what mattered. Hemingway certainly deemed them adequately "protected," as he put it to Perkins.

Finally, there was the issue of obscenity. Perkins understood Hemingway's need to be modern and authentic, but words like "bitch" and "balls" presented a problem. Here Perkins cleverly blamed the provincial reading public.

"It would be a pretty thing if the very significance of so original a book should be disregarded because of the howls of a lot of cheap, prurient, moronic yappers," he argued.

He added that Hemingway had lived in Europe for so long that he had likely forgotten how huffy Americans could get about such things. In response, Hemingway launched into a defense of the word "bitch" that would have impressed Plato in its persuasiveness and also pleased Chaucer, for it offered up the comparative acceptability of the word "fart" in literature. "I have never once used [the] word [bitch] ornamentally nor except when it was absolutely necessary," Hemingway argued, "and I believe the few places where it is used must stand." One should never use such words simply for shock value, he added; that would be distracting. For example, he pointed out, the word "fart" would overpower any page that it graced, "unless the whole matter were entirely rabelaisian." Even though it was a "very old and classic English word for the breaking of wind," a writer simply could not use it. Hemingway would cut any profane words that he felt were gratuitous, he promised, but "bitch" was not one of them.

"Balls," however, proved negotiable. Regarding the scene in which Mike Campbell yells repeatedly at Pedro Romero, "Bulls have no balls" —retained from Hemingway's earliest draft of the novel—Hemingway made a chaste amendment: the Pamplona bulls remained virile but now had "no horns." But that was as far as Hemingway was willing to go.

"Perhaps we will have to consider it simply as a profane book and hope that the next book will be less profane or perhaps more sacred," he wrote to Perkins.

Perkins accepted these concessions and made his peace with "bitch." It was, after all, a clinical mammalian noun, despite its undeniably slangy application in the novel. He showered Hemingway with deferential apologies.

"I know you would not use a syllable except for the right purpose," he wrote, adding that he was sorry he had even brought it up. He had known Hemingway only briefly, but already he was sure of his author's writerly character.

"You would not," he stated, "stoop to sensationalism."

A CERTAIN FORMALITY prevailed between Perkins and Hemingway, who still addressed their letters to "Mr. Perkins" and "Mr. Hemingway." It is unsurprising, then, that in their summer missives about *The Sun Also Rises,* Hemingway declined to mention that his personal life had taken on the character of a tornado.

Back in Antibes, the Hemingway-Pauline ménage moved out of the Fitzgeralds' house into a hotel. Bumby and his nanny were stashed away in a little house on the grounds, while the Hemingways and Pauline took rooms in the hotel itself. The trio had settled into an odd, forced idyll, filled with group activities: bridge games (which Hadley loathed), bike rides à trois, and daily beach visits (during which Pauline gave Hadley diving lessons that nearly killed her reluctant student). Pauline's ubiquity infuriated Hadley, but she felt helplessly at a disadvantage and submitted to all sorts of intrusions. Once, when the nanny brought the Hemingways a breakfast tray in their bedroom, Pauline reportedly followed her in and crawled into bed with the couple, ready to dine as well.

Not only was she overwhelmed by Pauline's brazenness; Hadley began to feel that her enemies now extended to the Murphys, who she suspected were rooting for Pauline to prevail in the contest for her husband. Her intuition was correct. During the first part of that summer, the Murphys treated Hadley kindly and even praised the marriage.

"As for you two children: you grace the earth," Gerald informed Hemingway. "You're so right: because you're close to what's elemental. Your values are hitched up to the universe."

But weeks later, the Murphys revealed to Hemingway that they had felt all along that Hadley was "miscast" as Hemingway's wife. They liked her personally but sensed that she and Hemingway had been destined for different things.

As she observed her circumstances that summer, it must have dawned on Hadley that Hemingway had already made the choice between her and Pauline, and that the decision carried a weighty symbolism. There on the Riviera, surrounded by their new friends' beautiful villas, with her husband's fashionable mistress perpetually on hand, it must have become painfully clear that Hemingway had moved on. They were already in the physical world of his future—a glaringly bright, illustrious realm far away from the naïve, hungry aspirations of their carpenter's loft in Paris. Hemingway and Hadley were no longer allies defying the idle, ignorant rich while taking refuge in the joys of a warm bed, simple food, and uncomplicated love. Her shabbiness used to exude a certain nobility; now it just appeared unseemly and inappropriate. Suddenly she was a problematic character in the fast-paced narrative of her husband's life, one that would have to be fixed—or omitted. And Hemingway had already made other ruthless editorial cuts that summer.

Neither personal nor professional entanglements could keep Hemingway from the San Fermín fiesta. A new entourage in tow—this year consisting of the Murphys, Pauline, and Hadley—he descended upon Pamplona in early July with his usual vigor. By this time, the Hemingway-led tours of the fiesta were becoming well known in certain circles. They were now well-scripted events: the entourage stayed at the Hotel Quintana, where Hemingway communed with the bullfighters. General giddiness was mandatory, as were shenanigans involving wineskins.

Seeing the fiesta with fresh eyes, the Murphys were floored by the spectacle. Hadley, however, had seen it all before, except this year she was being eclipsed by Pauline instead of Duff Twysden. This time around, Hemingway goaded Gerald Murphy into the bullring during the morning amateur sessions. Just as Harold Loeb had taunted a bull with his ill-fated sweater the summer before, Gerald used his raincoat as a cape and narrowly evaded a charging bull.

In the previous fiestas, Hemingway had exulted in going native, melding with the masses of Basque peasants and conferring confidentially with Juanito Quintana about the merits of the latest crop of bullfighters, while disdaining other American interlopers who dared to join the festivities. This year he courted the spotlight more aggressively. He finally succeeded in becoming the star of amateur hour. One morning, when he and Gerald were in the ring, Hemingway provoked a bull into charging him.

"He had absolutely nothing in his hands," Gerald recalled. "Just as the bull reached him, he threw himself over the horns and landed on the animal's back, and stayed there, facing the tail."

The bull wobbled along and then collapsed, squashed beneath Hemingway's weight.

On another occasion, the Murphys found themselves surrounded by a crowd of Spaniards, who began chanting, *"Dansa Charles-*ton! *Dansa Charles-*ton!" Bewildered at first, the Murphys then demonstrated the new dance right there in the middle of the main square, accompanied by a brass band and a raucous crowd. They later discovered that Hemingway had put the Spaniards up to it.

Amidst the festivities, both of Hemingway's women grew increasingly unhappy. Across the table at the Café Iruña, Hadley noticed that her rival had begun to look distinctly forlorn. When the festival was over, Pauline decamped back to Paris and the world of *Vogue;* the Hemingways left for San Sebastián, where Jake Barnes, the narrator of *The Sun Also Rises,* went to lick his wounds after his own dizzy nightmare of a fiesta. If Hadley had been hoping to do the same, she was given no such respite. Pauline made sure that her presence was felt from afar. Her letters trailed the Hemingways as they moved on to Valencia.

"I am going to get everything I want," she wrote in one particularly audacious missive. "Please write to me. This means YOU, Hadley."

That letter may have struck a definitive blow. Somewhere on their post-Pamplona tour through the country, Hemingway and Hadley decided to separate. "[It is] an awfully hopeless business to lose someone you've been in love and made your life with," he wrote woefully to a friend. "It's one of the swell things especially reserved for all of us." The Hemingways planned to return to Paris and scout out separate homes.

On their way back, they stopped at the Villa America in Antibes to tell the Murphys the news. Their Riviera group had expanded: Donald Ogden Stewart had come back to Europe, a new bride at his side and flush with the successes of the past year. He was a big shot back in Los Angeles now; his bachelor party had been attended by Hollywood royalty like Charlie Chaplin and King Vidor. Yet Stewart divined an equally potent air of imminent celebrity gathering around Hemingway, foreseeing that *The Sun Also Rises* was about to make "his name known in twenty-five countries."

Everyone professed dismay about the Hemingways' breakup, although the Murphys were quick to help Hemingway jump-start the next phase of his life. Gerald offered up money and his painting studio as possible living quarters; he threw in an opinion that differed starkly from the homage to the Hemingway union he'd given earlier that summer. "Hadley's tempo is a slower and less initiative one than yours," he wrote to Hemingway. Sticking with her and Bumby would have been "a dangerous betrayal of your nature." In a later missive, he assured his friend that both he and Sara "believe in what you're doing, in the way you're doing it." Sara added at the bottom of the note how much she admired Hemingway's refusal "to accept any second-rate things places ideas or human natures."

Decades later, Hemingway would rebuke the Murphys for having abetted his "evil" decision to leave Hadley ("I had hated these rich because they had backed me and encouraged me when I was doing wrong," he wrote in *A Moveable Feast*), but at that moment, he accepted Gerald's hospitality. He and Hadley took a train back up to Paris. Afterward Hemingway would almost immediately write a story titled "Canary for One," in which a soon-to-separate couple makes a similar journey, witnessing all sorts of scenes of destruction along the way, including a telltale three-car wreck. Apparently no experience was off-limits when it came to his art. It seems symbolic that the Hemingways' last journey together as husband and wife ended at the Gare de Lyon, where Hadley had lost Hemingway's starter novel three and a half years earlier.

Hadley never returned to their sawmill apartment again. She took rooms at the Hôtel Beauvoir, across the street from her husband's home café, La Closerie des Lilas, where he had spent so much time teaching himself to write in spare, hard sentences and simmering with ambition for the moment that was finally about to arrive. Hemingway moved into Gerald Murphy's Montparnasse studio at 69 rue Froidevaux, a few blocks from the Dingo, the Select, and the Dôme.

As ever, work proved a tonic. He began his near-final revisions on *The Sun Also Rises,* which included some that Perkins had assigned and a very important one of his own. That spring, in the throes of a more buoyant mood, he had dedicated the book to Bumby and added an irreverent line describing the book as a "collection of Instructive Anecdotes." Now in a more somber frame of mind, he changed the dedication. In a letter to Perkins, Hemingway advised his editor that he wanted the dedication to read:

TO HADLEY RICHARDSON HEMINGWAY
AND TO JOHN HADLEY NICANOR HEMINGWAY

He then crossed this out and replaced it with

THIS BOOK IS FOR HADLEY
AND FOR JOHN HADLEY NICANOR

The revised dedication managed to be both poignant and brutal. At first glance, the use of first names only implied a loving intimacy between a husband and a wife who had supported him from the beginning. This was appropriate: the publication of *The Sun Also Rises* should have been Hadley's triumph as well. Besides Hemingway himself, no one had sacrificed more to help bring it to fruition. Hadley had been an unconditional stalwart since the earliest days of his career, when limitless ambition and a gift for cynical intuition were the chief items on his résumé. She had cheered her fiancé as he spun out idea after idea for the book that might someday put him in the same pantheon as someone like F. Scott Fitzgerald —then a golden-boy stranger staring out at the Hemingways from newspapers, magazines, and best-seller lists. Writers like Gertrude Stein and Ezra Pound had still been remote, fabled figures trying to incite a revolution in a faraway city across an ocean. Even as Hemingway began attracting those figures as mentors, Hadley had supported him when he gave up journalism to perfect the style that would surpass those mentors'.

Now, on the eve of the Hemingways' epic and hard-earned victory, it appeared that another woman would be taking Hadley's place at her husband's side. Suddenly Hadley was no longer even a Hemingway: all it had taken was a quick swipe of the hand to scratch a line through her surname, bringing an abrupt, symbolic end to that half decade of marriage and king-making. Unlike Fitzgerald's character Jay Gatsby, Hemingway had no interest in sentimentalizing the past, at least not at that moment. The darkest hours of the night were behind him. He would not be looking back.

A new era was dawning, and he was watching the sun rise.

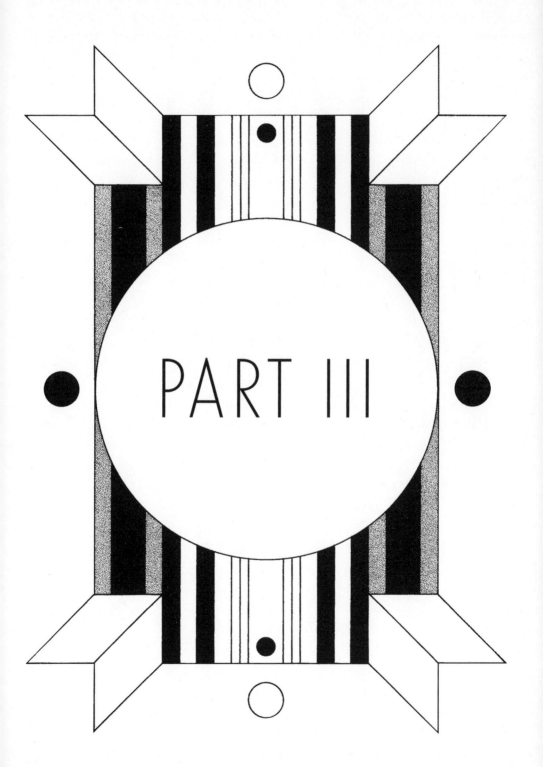

PART III

12

How Happy Are Kings

ONCE THE HEMINGWAYS returned to Paris, Hadley apparently got a second wind. Perhaps she wasn't ready to surrender her husband to Pauline after all. He was susceptible to flattery, she felt; perhaps if he spent some time away from his adoring mistress, he might come to his senses. In one last flailing effort to salvage her marriage, Hadley delivered an edict to Hemingway and Pauline: if they could stay apart for three months, and they still found themselves in love after the separation, Hadley would allow Hemingway to move forward with a divorce.

Hemingway and Pauline agreed to her terms. They decided that the best way to weather the period was for the two of them to spend those months on different continents. At the end of September, Pauline boarded an ocean liner, the *Pennland,* for New York. She was miserable, she reported back to Hemingway, but felt defiant and was determined to keep her eyes on the prize. She would even go three more months, if Hadley so decreed.

As the days passed, however, Pauline's patience thinned and despair began to sink in. While she felt bad for Hadley, she wrote to Hemingway, she was anxious to resolve the situation. The three-month separation must result in divorce. She instructed Hemingway to offer Hadley whatever she demanded in terms of a financial settlement.

Back in Paris, Hemingway went underground. The pressure of the unresolved triangle and upcoming release of *The Sun Also Rises* was clearly taking its toll. He felt as if he had fallen to pieces, he wrote to Pauline, adding, "All I want is you Pfife and oh dear god I want you so." He drank nothing, saw no one, and avoided his usual haunts in the Quarter.

"Trying unusual experiment of a writer writing," he wrote to Fitzgerald.

He added that he was in hell and had been since the previous Christmas. It was a hell of his own making, he acknowledged, but hell nevertheless. Now he was trying to break out of it.

"I'm sure we should all be as happy as kings," he wrote, quoting a poem by Robert Louis Stevenson. But then again, he wondered, "How happy are kings?"

Six weeks into the separation from Pauline, he too plunged into despair. He suspected that Hadley would stall and extend the mandated period of separation. Maybe she wouldn't give him a divorce at all. Maybe he should just commit suicide, he wrote to Pauline, to absolve her of the sin of breaking up a marriage and to spare Hadley the humiliation of a divorce.

"I'd rather die now while there is still something left of the world than to go on and have every part of it flattened out and destroyed and made hollow before I die," he told her.

Meanwhile, oblivious to his author's plummeting mood, Maxwell Perkins had begun prepping Hemingway for the big debut of *The Sun Also Rises*. He reported that sales for *The Torrents of Spring* had been modest, but added that Hemingway should not be discouraged. Anticipation about the novel was running high in New York.

"You may not realize how highly you are regarded, how seriously, by those whose opinion as a rule prevails in the end," he wrote.

By September, *The Sun Also Rises* was ready to go into print. All in all, Perkins had edited it very lightly. He was satisfied that his minor tweaks had budged the novel into the realm of acceptability without sacrificing its titillating rawness.

Hemingway instructed Perkins to place Gertrude Stein's "You are all a lost generation" quote on the title page along with the "sun also ariseth" passage from Ecclesiastes. Perkins tried to oblige him, but the title page looked cluttered and awkward with so much text. He moved the epigraphs to their own page, on the back of the newly reworked dedication page. From there, the reader dove directly into the book's text. The new arrangement nicely highlighted the quotes, Perkins thought.

"They gain an emphasis from standing alone," he told Hemingway.

Unlike Hemingway's frazzled personal relationships at the moment, the one between him and Perkins seemed mercifully uncomplicated. As *The Sun Also Rises* was being readied for the Scribner's presses, the men grew increasingly affectionate toward each other. By the middle of September, Perkins addressed a letter to "My dear Mr. Hemingway." Jocularity and excitement abounded. Nothing in their communications betrayed the state of deep depression and anxiety into which Hemingway was sinking.

DESPITE HEMINGWAY'S ANGST and self-imposed social isolation, he did make room for at least one outing during that time. Poet Archibald MacLeish and his wife gave a party one evening. Donald Ogden Stewart attended with his new wife, Beatrice; Hemingway also dropped by, a bit of his latest work in tow — a poem this time — ready to be shared with his friends. Its title: "To a Tragic Poetess." In front of this audience, he began to read aloud.

> Oh thou who with a safety razor blade
> a new one to avoid infection
> Slit both thy wrists
> the scars defy detection

Donald Stewart was aghast. The subject was clearly Dorothy Parker, who had tried to kill herself twice in the past three years. Hemingway read on, describing a recent tour of Spain taken by the tragic poetess:

> you sneered your way around
> through Aragon, Castille and Andalucia.
> Spaniards pinched
> the Jewish cheeks of your plump ass

The subject of this poem then promptly returns to Paris, her "ass intact," to turn out more poetry for *The New Yorker*. Parker had, indeed, gone to Spain after arriving in Paris with Hemingway and Benchley. Pretty much everything about the country — from its treatment of animals to the rump-pinching habits of Spanish men — had appalled her. In Barcelona, she had walked out of a bullfight after a bull gored a horse and declared that she found matadors disgusting. Once back in Paris, Parker had imparted these impressions to Hemingway, for whom such views amounted to sacrilege. The next forty-nine lines of his poem addressed the sacred scenes Parker had overlooked while sneering her way around the country. This sort of condescension and lack of talent for observation was why, the poem implied, Parker was and would remain a second-rate writer.

It remains unclear what prompted Hemingway to create this devastating portrait at this moment, but perhaps it should have surprised no one that he had little sympathy for the self-inflicted wounds of a caustic and comparatively pampered urbanite. Still, the poem shocked Don Stewart, who later called it "viciously unfair and unfunny." He could not discern a motive behind the attack, given that Hemingway was one of the few living artists who hadn't suffered from one of Parker's poison-pen reviews. He upbraided Hemingway on the spot.

"No one else did," Stewart recalled. "Not Archy [MacLeish] or anybody else. I've always been known as the easy guy, everybody's Uncle Don, but I did tell him off that time, and of course you didn't do that to Ernest." He cringed, waiting for the retort.

To Stewart's surprise, Hemingway took his reprimand in stride. "Without a murmur," actually, said Stewart, "which is some kind of record I suppose."

Still, in Stewart's view, the incident ended their friendship. Not that they ceased to be friendly; as Stewart later explained, "We were always technical friends, but it was a different kind of friendship after that." The poem had rattled him by revealing a "mean streak" in Hemingway that, to Stewart, seemed like "a booby trap kind of thing."

To the best of Stewart's knowledge, Parker never learned about the existence of the poem, which remained unpublished until after her death; unaware of its existence, she continued to write wildly enthusiastic reviews of Hemingway's work in *The New Yorker* and called him one of her favorite writers.

HEMINGWAY HAD ALWAYS been a splendid target of gossip at the Dôme and beyond, and his split from Hadley — coinciding with Pauline's sudden departure from Paris — piqued the interest of his attentive followers. Now alone, Hadley passed her mornings at La Closerie des Lilas, where she was inundated with nosy acquaintances who were "just dying of curiosity" about the whole situation. But late that October, an event across the Atlantic abruptly changed the conversation.

On October 22, 1926, Charles Scribner's Sons released 5,090 copies of *The Sun Also Rises.*

Back in New York, Maxwell Perkins and Scribner's were determined to make the novel's debut a major event. Whatever misgivings the editorial team may have had about Hemingway and *The Sun Also Rises,* the house's publicists were crazy about the project. Both novel and author gave them almost limitless material to work with; they peddled Hemingway and his book to everyone from highbrow critics to gossip columnists. Not only were they debuting another Scribner's "bad boy," but also this one was a new breed entirely: a hybrid of Parisian glamour, Alpine ruggedness, boxing-ring savagery, and yet, somehow, intellectual brilliance.

"We have three publicity men in the house and all of them were particularly wild over your book," Perkins wrote to Hemingway. "[They] have been ravenous for any kind of advertising material, and [are] anxious to go the limit."

The team quickly realized that they were onto something big. The press had an enormous appetite for Hemingway. Perkins implored his author to send the house "any kind of pictures there are of you." The publicists would use anything they could get their hands on. Three days later Perkins wrote again, begging Hemingway for additional biographical information that could be pumped out to eager news editors and columnists.

"Papers are glad to print almost anything we send about you," Perkins reported excitedly, "and we are very hard put to it."

He even admitted to culling Hemingway's letters to him for material, extracting a couple of incidents to feed the publicity beast. Hemingway obliged, sending a couple of photographs for reproduction and distribution, including an athletic shot taken in the mountains, a snowy background shimmering behind him. But he bristled at the request for more information.

"I would rather not have any biography and let the readers and the critics make up their own lies," he informed Perkins.

This reticence may have been genuine, or it may have been strategic. As a new master of a less-is-more approach to literature, perhaps Hemingway felt that a little mystery might serve to augment his allure. That approach had worked with the characters in *Sun,* in his opinion — and Fitzgerald's. Or he may have seen advantages in letting the press do its own storytelling, however embellished, when it came to presenting Hemingway the man. Publicity was publicity, after all.

If this had indeed been Hemingway's attitude, he seems to have quickly changed his mind. As a press clipping service began to send dozens of reviews and stories his way, he was unnerved to see that the papers were indeed making up their own lies. The *New York Herald Tribune* informed its readers that Hemingway had earned his way through college as a boxing instructor. ("I never went to college and have never told a living person that I went to college," he protested to Perkins.) Another paper reported enthusiastically on Hemingway's record as a star athlete in high school.

("I was a long way from being a football star," he demurred.) Yet another source exaggerated the number of Hemingway's progeny.

Most alarmingly, however, Hemingway saw far-fetched stories about his wartime experiences, and he worried that, to those in the know, he would come across "as a faker or a liar or a fool." He wanted to clarify that he had not been in the actual military; rather, he had been attached to the Italian infantry as a "very minor sort of camp follower." He demanded to know if the Scribner's machine had been responsible for any of these tall tales. If so, they needed to set the record straight, he decreed.

That said, he promised to supply any juicy anecdotes that might further pique press interest.

"If I break a leg or have my jewels stolen or get elected to the Academie Francaise or killed in the bull ring or drink myself to death I'll inform you officially," he added.

Perkins investigated the matter and wrote a not particularly apologetic letter of explanation.

First of all, he had discerned the possible source of at least some of the more outlandish Hemingway tales: apparently one of the in-house publicity men "had Scott [Fitzgerald] on the witness stand for a while." And everyone knew that Fitzgerald was an expert at crafting exciting backgrounds for his characters. Perkins would certainly try to rein in the publicity team, but only with reluctance.

"Of course it is right that they should want to do everything they possibly can to advertise an author," he explained to Hemingway. If he held them back from doing so, it would feel as though he were "restraining a naturally good impulse."

Meanwhile, the Scribner's advertising team launched a major print campaign promoting *The Sun Also Rises*. Hemingway's obscurity was over at last.

"We are preparing bigger advertisements than we have ever used on it," Perkins informed Fitzgerald, who—as ever—was being kept in the loop about Hemingway's in-house affairs.

Like Perkins and the publicity team, the admen had been excited by the book and readily foreseen its saleability. This was, Perkins reported privately to Hemingway, both fortunate and significant. The admen were supposed to work equally hard for all Scribner's titles, but the fact that they genuinely adored the book would inevitably inspire them to push it even harder. "They are not supposed to take their own predilections into consideration," Perkins said of his former department. "[But] they of course do."

Scribner's advertised the book heavily in the New York press, knowing that the city was a trendsetter for national appetites. Thanks to a half decade's experience in marketing its new and even flamboyant postwar authors, Scribner's ads were modern pitches for modern books. Conversational and irreverent, they foreshadowed the unsubtle, urgent voice of television commercials decades later. Fitzgerald's early books had been forerunners: the Scribner's ads had unrepentantly peddled both book and author as consumer products. *This Side of Paradise* was "more than a bestseller," one ad had informed readers; it was a "national tonic." The same ad advised consumers to "Make it a Fitzgerald Christmas."

The Scribner's ad team even slyly exploited bad reviews for their entertainment value. Algonquin Round Table critic Heywood Broun had claimed that *This Side of Paradise* had left him "not only cold but baffled"; in turn, the Scribner's team ran an ad blaring in oversized font that "*HEYWOOD BROUN* scoffs and snorts—" alongside five blurbs from other reviewers who found the book "cracking good stuff." Readers were implored to read the book for themselves and decide.

In both ad campaigns and publicity, Scribner's relied heavily on what would today be called "FOMO"—or fear of missing out. Anyone who didn't read the house's latest books would be left behind, covered with dust and cobwebs. "The book is timely, most timely," read one press release for another Scribner's title. "You cannot afford not to read it."

The house went to equally great rhetorical lengths on behalf of *The Sun Also Rises*. Its sales team had already alerted booksellers that this debut novel would cross a literary Rubicon: its release would permanently change literature. The book "quiver[ed] with life" and had been penned in the "spirit of literary revolt." Hemingway was clearly "disgusted" with the sentimentality of "certain popular novels." (Never mind that some of those authors may also have been published by Scribner's.) His novel was a different beast entirely.

Taking its cue from the book's epigraphs, the team pushed it as *the* tome encapsulating the voice of the "war generation too strongly dosed with raw reality . . . all illusions shattered, all reticences dissipated." The Lost Generation was being ushered down the red carpet, brought to audiences by Hemingway, sponsored by Scribner's. With unintentional irony, the house's fall catalogue noted that the book's characters were "so palpable that one . . . would recognize them upon the street." Those who knew Twysden and Loeb and the other *Sun* victims would soon confirm the accuracy of this claim.

As with the PR campaign, the advertisements rolled out Hemingway himself as an exciting character. In one ad, an image of his face (his expression pensive, intense) loomed larger than the text extolling his virtues as a writer. An illustration was being used, Perkins explained to his author, instead of a photograph because it was easier for publications to reproduce, and naturally the house wanted Hemingway's youthful, chiseled visage to be as widely reproduced as possible.

"With [this novel's] publication Mr. Hemingway's sun also will rise," the house pledged.

The ad team even trotted out Ford Madox Ford's endorsement from the jacket of *In Our Time,* assuring readers that Hemingway was "the best writer in America of the moment." Presumably the admen did not know at that point that a thinly disguised Ford was making a buffoonish appearance in the novel's pages—or else they just didn't care.

Naturally, advertisements were placed in all of the major literary publications, from the *Saturday Review of Literature* to *American Mercury* to *The Atlantic,* but the ad team expanded its campaign to lifestyle and niche publications as well, from *Christian Century* to *Golden Book* to *Town & Country.* Ads were soon placed in regional papers and magazines from Chicago to Boston to Philadelphia. Harvard, Yale, and Princeton publications were also included. No demographic was to be ignored: everyone from students to debutantes to preachers would soon know about *The Sun Also Rises* and its author.

Hemingway did not approve of all of the ways the house marketed the book. For example, he disliked the book's cover, created by an artist who went by the pen name "Cleon," whose work was featured on other popular Scribner's books—including ones put out by both Scott and Zelda Fitzgerald. The cover featured an image of a beautiful but somewhat beleaguered-looking woman, clad in golden Grecian-style garb and leaning closed-eyed, head against her knees, under a tree, an apple in one hand; a black sun rises behind her. Golden apples also flank the book's title. Her sandaled feet rest on an unfortunate typo identifying Hemingway as the author of *In Our Times* instead of *In Our Time.*

Yet Hemingway could kick up only a limited fuss: Scribner's marketing campaign was substantial by any standard, but especially compared to Boni & Liveright's tepid efforts for *In Our Time.* Perkins mailed some of the ads to Paris for Hemingway to peruse. The illustration of his face used in the ads was okay, Hemingway guessed; it was sort of how he had envisioned Jake Barnes. That said, it looked "very much like a writer who had been saddened by the loss or atrophy of certain non replaceable parts," he wrote to Perkins. "It is a pity it couldn't have been Barnes instead of Hemingway."

CRITICS ACROSS AMERICA immediately weighed in on the new novel. About a week after its release, Perkins steeled Hemingway for the first batch of reviews. The notices from the *New York Times* and the *New York Herald Tribune* were the most important, he felt. Both editor and author must have been excited, then, when the *Times* reported that there had been a great deal of anticipation surrounding the book's release: "This is the novel for which a keen appetite was stimulated by Mr. Hemingway's exciting volume of short stories, 'In Our Time.'" *The New Republic* echoed this sentiment: "No one need be afraid any more that Hemingway's power is going to be limited to episodes."

More important, even the least enthusiastic reviewers conceded that *The Sun Also Rises* represented a stylistic tour de force. If Fitzgerald's work was frequently described as "alive," Hemingway's was "fresh." This once-promising new writer had suddenly sprinted ahead of the crowd and established himself as a young master of modern writing. The *Herald Tribune* review likely would have made Ezra Pound and Gertrude Stein proud, and perhaps even envious. "It is alive with the rhythms and idioms, the pauses and suspensions and the innuendos and shorthands of living speech," wrote the reviewer, Conrad Aiken. "'The Sun Also Rises' makes it possible for me to say this of [Hemingway], with entire conviction, that he is in many respects the most exciting of contemporary American writers of fiction."

The *New York Times* exulted in the book's "lean, hard, athletic narrative prose that puts more literary English to shame." *The Sun Also Rises* was an "event," an example of magnificent writing. "No amount of analysis can convey [its] quality," the reviewer contended, adding that the narrative itself was "absorbing, beautifully and tenderly absurd, [and] heartbreaking." The *Saturday Review of Literature* called Hemingway's style "terse, precise, and aggressively fresh," and added that *The Sun Also Rises* contained "some of the finest dialogue ever written in this country." Privately, influential critic Edmund Wilson wrote to Hemingway that his book was a "knockout," and maybe even the best fiction yet conjured up by his generation of American writers.

Soon a review came in from the *Boston Evening Transcript.* Perkins deemed the publication the most conservative newspaper in the country, so the critic's response would be a litmus test. Rather than being scandalized by the book, the *Transcript*'s reviewer declared it a "beautiful and searching novel." If he had gone overboard in its praise, the critic explained, "it is only because the book called it forth." Furthermore, the review noted the debt that Hemingway's writing owed to his training as a reporter: "With what mastery Mr. Hemingway has used his rather bare, journalistic style." At first the "staccato sentences" were irritating, the reviewer warned, but one soon got used to them.

The Algonquin crowd also contributed to the fanfare. Heywood Broun might have "scoffed and snorted" over Fitzgerald's debut novel, but in his *New York World* review, he called *The Sun Also Rises* beautiful and truthful. Dorothy Parker later bolstered the growing Hemingway legend in *The New Yorker* by asserting that for weeks "you could go nowhere without hearing of 'The Sun Also Rises.'" Some in her crowd, she reported, were already declaring it the great American novel, shunting aside classics like *Huckleberry Finn* and *The Scarlet Letter.*

"The Stars and Stripes were reverentially raised over [Hemingway]," she informed her readers. "Eight hundred and forty-seven book reviewers formed themselves into the word 'welcome,' and the band played 'Hail to the Chief' in three concurrent keys." So much brouhaha surrounded the novel's debut that, she added affectionately, "I was never so sick of a book in my life." (To Hemingway, she sent a private cable, celebrating his triumph: "BABY YOUR BOOK IS KNOCKING THEM COLD HERE ISN'T IT SWELL LOVE = DOTTY.")

The *Paris Tribune*'s gossip column noted the emergence of a Hemingway "cult" on two continents, without noting that the Left Bank branch of that cult had been in the making for years.

There was, of course, blowback too — which was just as well, since controversy was, and remains, a reliable sales booster. Even Dorothy Parker conceded that members of the literary crowd either "hated [*Sun*] or they revered it." Among the publications that found the book "without excuse," as Parker put it, was the *Springfield Republican.* The "extreme moral sordidness" of *The Sun Also Rises,* contended the paper's critic, defeated any sort of "artistic purpose" the author may have had. Furthermore, he added, the novel had no structure. Allen Tate of *The Nation* accused Hemingway of sentimentality despite his best efforts to appear hard-boiled. Even critics who liked the book's style found Lady Brett and the *Sun* crowd repellent; all they ever did, complained one reviewer, was bathe, eat, and have sex—while drinking continuously. Another dubbed the cast of characters "spiritual bankrupts"; yet another called them "utterly degraded."

The New Masses ran a review that must have felt like a kick in the crotch to Hemingway. John Dos Passos reduced his friend's book to "a cock-and-bull story about a whole lot of tourists getting drunk." It had been a mistake, he added, to quote the Bible at the beginning of the book: doing so only raised readers' expectations, which were not met by the story that followed. Dos Passos did concede, however, that the cock-and-bull story was well written.

Disapproving readers and organizations also noisily responded. Some protested directly to Scribner's. A man from Sarasota called the book "coarse and uncouth as it can be," adding that it was "a disgrace to [Scribner's] good name." He predicted terrible sales. A library committee in New Hampshire deemed the book "worse than worthless" and informed Scribner's that it would be destroying its copy.

If all of this brouhaha about the immorality of *The Sun Also Rises* helped create an essential air of scandal around the book, the nastier reviews bothered Hemingway, who detested critics in general. Most of the reviews had been extremely laudatory, as Perkins pointed out to him; and they were saying all the right things about Hemingway's revolutionary style. Still, the criticism stung him.

Pauline did her best to bolster his spirits from afar, echoing Perkins when she assured her lover that he was already being written about as a legendary character. She knew that she was now sharing her life with a public persona: already he had become known as Hemingway the Bullfighter, Hemingway the Expatriate, and Hemingway the Satirist. As for Hemingway the Man and Hemingway the Artist, *that* Ernest was "perfect," she assured him.

Yet he still could not get his detractors out of his mind. Though he was "his own severest critic," as Sylvia Beach noted, he could be, she added, "hypersensitive to the criticism of others." To Fitzgerald he compared criticism in general to "horse shit" but without manure's pleasant smell. The fact that reviewers were making such a big deal about the unlikeability of his characters showed, to Hemingway, how useless and off-target most of them were. To Perkins he complained that such reactions seemed "very funny as criticism when you consider the attractiveness of the people in, say, Ulysses, the Old Testament, Judge [Henry] Fielding and other people some of the critics like." (That said, he privately agreed with some of the assessments. The characters had been "smashed" by life and were "hollow and dull," he admitted to a friend, "but that is the way they are.")

Perhaps most frustrating to Hemingway, however, was the critics' near-universal insistence on viewing the book through the prism of Gertrude Stein's "lost generation" quote. Review after review stated that Hemingway's purpose had been to depict definitively his damaged generation, which was "stumbling through life like a man lost in the forest," as one critic put it.

He quickly tried to backpedal from the "lost generation" web of his own weaving. Yes, the quote had elevated the book's material and imbued it with profundity; Hemingway had not, after all, wanted this book to be a "jazz superficial story," as he wrote to Perkins, in a barb likely aimed at Fitzgerald. But neither had he meant to create a tome detailing all that ailed his generation. Reviewers were misunderstanding his intentions, he complained crossly. Stein's "lost generation" remark was merely "bombast," and he had meant to lampoon its pomposity, not endorse it. Why weren't critics taking their cue from the "sun also ariseth" Ecclesiastes quote? To Hemingway, the whole point of the book was that "the earth abideth for ever." Wasn't that obvious enough?

"Nobody knows about the generation that follows them and certainly has no right to judge," Hemingway insisted. "I didn't mean the book to be a hollow or bitter satire but a damn tragedy with the earth abiding for ever as the hero."

Decades later, he was still protesting.

"Gertrude was a complainer," he told a friend in the 1950s. "So she labeled that generation with her complaint. But it was bullshit . . . Nobody I knew at that time thought of himself as wearing the silks of the Lost Generation, or had even heard the label. We were a pretty solid mob."

His protests notwithstanding, Hemingway was immediately anointed that contingent's new spokesman. The phrase captured the popular imagination too completely. *The Sun Also Rises* suddenly seemed to have expertly pinpointed a certain postwar malaise that others may have keenly felt but been unable to describe—until Hemingway (and Gertrude Stein) did it for them.

Therefore, from October 22, 1926, onward, Hemingway would be cloaked in the Lost Generation's silks in perpetuity—whether he had buyer's remorse about the garb or not.

• • •

BEFORE HEMINGWAY REMOVED all real-life names from the manuscript, Maxwell Perkins had feared a potential lawsuit, and eventually a complaint did cross his desk. The legal representatives of a real-life Lady Ashley had found the use of her name for "the disreputable heroine" of *The Sun Also Rises* to be libelous. Perkins wrote to Hemingway and his British publisher about the matter, although he and Scribner's attorney did not consider the complaint actionable, only amusing. This Lady Ashley's lawyers had maintained that the complainant was a comely twenty-five-year-old, although Perkins had it on good authority that she was actually a fifty-something woman who lurked on the fringes of the theater world. If anything, perhaps the publishers could use the complaint to generate further publicity for the book.

"We offered to publish a statement that the Lady Ashley of the book was not the Lady Ashley of fact," Perkins informed Hemingway, "which would make an excellent advertisement anyhow." (Hemingway's take on the matter: "She might as well try and sue Robinson Crusoe.")

That particular Lady Ashley appears to have abandoned her cause; nor did the real-life inspiration behind Lady Brett protest to Hemingway's publishers. But it did not take long for the actual prototypes—from Duff Twysden to Harold Loeb to Kitty Cannell—to learn, with red faces, of their appearance in Hemingway's incendiary new novel. Hemingway had given them no advance warning; they simply had to read it along with everyone else in their world.

It did not matter that Scribner's had not advertised in the Paris papers: *The Sun Also Rises* became an immediate scandal within the Left Bank crowd. For those who actually wanted to read the novel instead of merely gossip about it, Sylvia Beach was stocking copies at Shakespeare and Company. It became a topic of choice at many of the cafés and bars depicted in the book's pages. Guessing the real-life identities of its characters might have made a good parlor game had Hemingway not made them so transparent. A more appropriate name for the novel, some joked, would have been "Six Characters in Search of an Author—with a Gun Apiece," a riff on the title of the recent popular Pirandello play.

News of the *Sun* scandal went transatlantic as the press on two continents picked up the story. It was "the best thing that could have happened to Hemingway from the point of view of launching him into the selling brackets comparable to those of Fitzgerald," noted writer and Montparnasse memoirist Morrill Cody, who added that "everyone" had been talking about it from the moment of its debut. For Twysden and Loeb and the rest of the prototypes, "it was like somebody putting you on a billboard in Times Square," as Hemingway friend A. E. Hotchner put it. Janet Flanner informed her *New Yorker* readers back in America that the "four leading characters" in Hemingway's *"roman à clef"* were "local and easily identifiable." She declined to give the real names of these characters but pointed out that "the titled British declassée and her Scottish friend, the American Frances and her unlucky *Robert Cohn* with his art magazine which, like a new broom, was to sweep aesthetics clean" could easily be found on any given day "just where Hemingway so often placed them at the Select." Flanner did, however, state that it was safe to assume that Donald Ogden Stewart was the "stuffed-bird-loving Bill" (in reality, the character Bill Gorton harbored an affection for stuffed dogs, not birds), and that Ford Madox Ford was prancing through the book's pages "under the flimsy disguise of Braddocks."

Other press reports from the Quarter were somewhat less gleeful.

"Several well-known habitués of the Carrefour Vavin are mercilessly dragged through the pages" of the novel, noted the *Paris Herald* in its "Around the Town" column. *The Sun Also Rises* was "not very pretty reading," but its contents were probably fairly accurate: Hemingway was "noted for being an observant journalist and for not respecting the feelings of friends." The *Saturday Review of Literature* informed readers that not a single one of Hemingway's characters could be credited with being the product of the author's imagination (ditto for the events that inspired the plot), implying that the book was more an example of incisive reportage than fictional accomplishment.

There must have been a bit of schadenfreude within the colony over Hemingway's character send-ups. At least one person found the Robert Cohn portrait to be shrewdly accurate.

"Like Cohn, [Loeb] was inclined to be tense, over-serious and humorless," recalled Morrill Cody, who added that most Montparnassians thought Loeb took on "unjustified airs of superiority." Yet Hemingway's willingness to sacrifice him so publicly rattled others. "What a savage portrait!" exclaimed the *Herald* of Robert Cohn.

The Sun Also Rises stunned Harold Loeb. After the disappointing reception of his novel *Doodab,* he eventually left New York City and returned to Europe. By the time Hemingway's novel came out, Loeb had made his way to the south of France in the company of a new paramour whom he later described as a waifish Dutch runaway. The couple was living in a farmhouse surrounded by artichoke fields as Loeb worked on another novel, to be titled *Tumbling Mustard*.

One day a package arrived; a friend had sent him a copy of *The Sun Also Rises*.

"The book hit me like an upper-cut," he recalled later.

He scoured the book for passages about Robert Cohn. The "unnecessary nastiness" shocked him, as did the extensive co-opting of his personal background. It would have been just as easy, he reasoned, for Hemingway to have made changes to all of the characters' biographies so he and the others weren't so instantly recognizable. Why did Hemingway make the portraits so literal? Ritual humiliation? Yet for all the blatant similarities, Loeb found Cohn to be a gross distortion of himself, an "offensive characterization." He simply could not understand, he said, "what had led my one-time friend to transform me into an insensitive, patronizing, uncontrolled drag."

He was equally appalled that Hemingway had "travestied" the others —especially Duff Twysden, who came across as a "repugnant tramp," in Loeb's opinion. It was said that the book gave him an ulcer and also earned him nearly a decade on a shrink's couch, although he later denied both allegations.

Rumors zinged throughout the Quarter that Loeb had returned to Paris looking for Hemingway, gun in hand. The news apparently delighted Hemingway.

"I sent word around that I would be found unarmed sitting in front of Lipp's brasserie from two to four on saturday and Sunday afternoon," he wrote to Fitzgerald. Anyone who felt like shooting him could do it then and there. "No bullets whistled," he reported.

Later, Hemingway would improve on that story. In a new version of the tale, he claimed to have sent a telegram imploring Loeb to come find him at the Hole in the Wall, a notorious hangout for dope peddlers with a rear exit that supposedly led into the Paris sewers. Hemingway said that he'd selected the bar because mirrors covered its walls. "You can see whoever comes in the door and all their moves," he explained. He claimed that he hunkered down there for three days, but the cowardly Loeb never showed up.

Loeb once again found it necessary to defend his honor against a probably embellished Hemingway Version of Events. "I never threatened to kill anyone," he contended. "Nor did I get a telegram to meet him at the 'Hole in the Wall' or elsewhere."

The two men did, however, encounter each other months later. According to the Loeb Version of Events, he had been sipping a Pernod at Brasserie Lipp when Hemingway strode in. He saw Loeb but didn't approach him. Rather, he sat down at the bar with his back to Loeb and ordered a drink.

"I distinctly remember being amazed at the color of his neck," Loeb recalled. "Red gradually suffused it—and then his ears, right up to their tips." Eventually Hemingway paid for the drink and left; the men had not spoken. Loeb had been tempted to approach him but held back.

"I wanted nothing more to do with him," he recalled.

The publication of *The Sun Also Rises* caught Duff at a particularly difficult moment. Her divorce from Sir Roger Twysden had finally come through, but her ex-husband retained custody of their young son. Plus, she and Pat Guthrie were on the rocks. By the winter following the novel's release, Guthrie was living with an older woman, Margaret "Lorna" Lindsley, an American writer and journalist. Hemingway was still keeping tabs on the "demented characters out of my books," as he called them, for he reported on the breakup to Fitzgerald. Duff was free at last, but Guthrie wouldn't marry her because she had lost her looks, Hemingway claimed. Guthrie's new relationship had a somewhat compulsory tenor to it, Hemingway went on. Lindsley had spared him a bit of jail time resulting from a bad check. As a result, she now had Guthrie by the balls, as she could "let him go to jail at any time." So Guthrie was in a jail of a different variety.

By the way, Hemingway added, he had run into Duff the other night.

"She wasn't sore about the Sun," he claimed. In fact, her only objection had been that "she never had slept with the bloody bull fighter."

This was likely another bit of Hemingway revisionism: Duff was actually said to have been furious about the book and deeply hurt by his portrayal of her. In the years that followed, she reportedly called the novel "cruel" and insisted that Hemingway had played a nasty trick on her and the others. In her opinion, the book was nothing more than an example of "cheap reporting." The story Hemingway told Fitzgerald may have been accurate in one regard, however: Duff was appalled at having been romantically linked to a matador; she later told a friend that keeping company with bullfighters "would have been like being up to the arse in midgets." Yet she apparently did find some grim humor in the situation: a year later, when an acquaintance stumbled upon Duff and Guthrie at the Dôme, she was calling Guthrie "Mike"—the name Hemingway had given him in *The Sun Also Rises*.

Though Duff managed to make light of the controversy in public, the intrusion of Lady Brett Ashley into her life seems to have created real fallout in her private affairs. Hemingway had been horribly indiscreet about airing her dirty laundry before her former in-laws, she felt. The British aristocracy can tolerate all sorts of misbehavior among its own, but indiscretion is not among the forgivable sins. It was alleged that the Twysden clan attempted to buy the plates from the publisher to prevent further printings, and, when unsuccessful in its bid, tried instead to buy as many copies as possible to keep the book from wide circulation. A member of the clan later denied these allegations, but Duff became, more than ever, persona non grata within the family, and she felt certain that Hemingway's book had complicated her visitation rights. She was even said to be hatching plans to kidnap her child just to be able to see him again.

By the following summer, Duff had found new romantic company, and word went around the Quarter that her boyfriend—a slight artist named Clinton King, heir to a Texas candy fortune—had knocked Hemingway out over the Lady Brett portrait. Like the Loeb-with-a-gun story, the tale made for great retelling at the Dôme and the Dingo, but it didn't carry a lot of credibility for those who knew the parties in question.

"I would have been one of the first to learn about it," claimed Dingo barman Jimmie Charters, who joked that "Mr. Clinton King, bless his heart, [would have had] to use a hammer, or a similar weapon for that purpose," for Hemingway was so much bigger than King.

Yet another rumor went around that Kitty Cannell had procured a steely six-foot-three boyfriend to pummel Hemingway over her portrayal as Frances Clyne. She later denied this, claiming that she already had a crew of Montparnasse bartenders ready to defend her honor if Hemingway insulted her—again—in their presence. (In any case, she claimed, Hemingway went out of his way to avoid her after the book came out.) Just a year earlier, he had assured her that she would not appear in the novel that was "tearing those [other] bastards apart," but there she was, in its pages alongside those bastards. And although her appearance in *The Sun Also Rises* was briefer than most of the others', the portrait made for painful reading. For three days after perusing the book, Cannell could not scrape herself up out of bed. Like Loeb, she scrutinized Hemingway's version of her: Frances had none of her manners or looks, she concluded, but it was obvious that she was the primary inspiration behind the character.

"Hemingway gave Frances my conversation," she decided. "From family wheezes, jokes and so on I had developed practically an individual language."

Even though *The Sun Also Rises* shocked her, Cannell was not entirely surprised. After all, she had felt all along that Hemingway had a vicious streak. Loeb had been the guileless one when it came to Hemingway, not her. And now, thanks to his naïveté, they would both suffer for the rest of their lives. Furthermore, it was humiliating to be portrayed as such an inept gold digger — much less the mistress of such a weak, contemptible bore. And on a final note, Cannell thought the book was "awful" from an aesthetic point of view.

Nor was Donald Stewart particularly impressed by the book's artistic merits. Back in California, he got a copy and found himself uneasily transported back to the Pamplona misadventure.

"It was so absolutely accurate that it seemed little more than a skillfully done travelogue," he later recalled. "What a reporter, I said to myself."

He was baffled by the commotion the book was stirring up in the loftier publications and among his comrades back on the East Coast. *The Sun Also Rises* was, in Stewart's opinion, journalism with just enough fiction — such as Lady Brett's affair with Pedro Romero — to permit Hemingway to get away with calling the book a novel.

"It didn't make too much of an impression on me, certainly not as an artistic work of genius," he remembered.

Predictably, the easygoing Bill Smith seemed least perturbed about having been used by Hemingway as fiction fodder. After the Pamplona trip, he had been trying to write his own short stories, with no real success, but this did not prevent him from exulting in the accomplishment of his boyhood friend. Like Hadley, he'd had a front-row seat for Hemingway's ambitions since the early days. If Smith had been "utilized" — to borrow the word that Hemingway had borrowed from him — to help make this breakthrough possible, so be it. Furthermore, Smith did not, like Stewart, consider *The Sun Also Rises* a "complete copying" of the Pamplona events. He and Loeb and the others were just springboards for carefully crafted characters, he asserted.

"Hemingway was not a diarist," he said later. "He was an artist."

• • •

BY THE NEW YEAR, the sales statistics for *The Sun Also Rises* were looking impressive. By January 1927, the book had gone into its fourth printing. Nearly 11,000 copies had been sold.

"The Sun has risen," Perkins wrote to Hemingway, "and is rising steadily." By April, 19,000 copies had sold.

These were not blockbuster sales — at least when compared to the performance of Fitzgerald's debut novel: *This Side of Paradise* had sold 35,000 copies within the first seven months. *The Sun Also Rises* did not hit that mark in its entire first year of publication.

Yet it did not matter. For Perkins, the latest "bad boy" gamble had clearly paid off: the reception of *The Sun Also Rises* had been thunderous and portended even bigger things for his new author. Beyond the critical reception, the novel had clearly begun to capture the hearts and minds of a generation. It quickly became a "craze" among the college crowd, to whom the book had been heartily advertised. News that *Sun* had been "suppressed" in Boston likely helped its reputation with that demographic. Five years earlier, everyone had wanted to imitate well-bred Fitzgerald characters; Ivy League hijinks and cocktail adventures at the Plaza Hotel had been all the rage. Now everyone wanted to be Jake Barnes, Lady Brett Ashley, or even Hemingway himself.

"Young women of good families took a succession of lovers in the same heartbroken fashion as the heroine," recalled expat writer Malcolm Cowley. Their male counterparts tried to get "as imperturbably drunk as the hero" when they weren't shadowboxing and warding off imaginary bulls with sweaters and jackets. Both sexes soon "all talked like Hemingway characters."

For this group, the idea of being part of a "lost generation" took hold hard and fast. The epithet was quickly moving toward capitalized status: the Lost Generation. In subsequent generations, similar umbrella identities would be ascribed to each era's under-thirty crowd: the Beat Generation, Generation X, the Millennials, and so on. But the Lost Generation was the forerunner of modern youthful angst banners, and *The Sun Also Rises* was its bible. That said, no one in that demographic seemed particularly glum about being "lost." Membership in this new club had an undeniable glamour.

"Most of those who used the phrase about themselves . . . knew they were boasting," recalled Cowley. "They were like Kipling's gentlemen rankers out on a spree."

Lost Generation lifestyle became a dark, sexy alternative to Fitzgerald's fizzier vision of youth culture. Though Hemingway's and Fitzgerald's subject matter overlapped somewhat—namely, renegades from society behaving badly—Lost Generation decadence had nothing to do with dinner dances and eating clubs. Rather, it was all about purposeful dissipation. With Jake and Brett as their lodestars, self-fashioned Lost Generationers were spiritually obligated to defy convention, embrace hangovers as holy, and indulge in sexual adventures—the more ill-fated the better.

New York had been the altar at which Fitzgerald's flock had worshipped, but Paris was clearly the Lost Generation capital. Soon disciples of *The Sun Also Rises* were traveling there, descending on the cafés and bars mentioned in the novel. Veteran expats began to notice a new clientele cropping up at the Dingo: "young Americans [who] were doing their best to imitate Jake and his 'let's have another one' friends," recalled expat writer Samuel Putnam.

If tourists used to gape at literary luminaries like James Joyce and Gertrude Stein, now people tried to spot Hemingway's characters in real life. Once Kitty Cannell was sitting at La Coupole when someone approached her and exclaimed: "Why you're Kitty Cannell! I'd recognize you anywhere from [the] descriptions." It was not the only time she was thus outed.

"If I had a dollar for each person," she said, "who came up to me and demanded: 'Did you really hold Harold Loeb up for such a sum, in such a place, on such a date and in such a way?'—it would have been unnecessary to hold anyone up for years."

IN THE WEEKS that followed the book's release, Hemingway seemed uncharacteristically subdued about the excitement surrounding his novel. Here he was, at his own coronation at last. He was already discussing future projects with Perkins. Important critics had been rhapsodic about him. The literati on two continents could not stop talking about him. A growing legion of worshipful young subjects were writing him letters; he was even becoming a bit of a heartthrob among female readers. He had, in short, achieved the success and notoriety he'd hoped for.

Yet his personal affairs kept him mired in misery—until Hadley suddenly caved in. "The three months separation is officially off," she wrote to him in a mid-November missive, bereft of the usual nicknames.

Hemingway should start divorce proceedings right away, she informed him. His welfare was no longer her concern. Rather, it was in his own hands—and God's. He could see Bumby as often as he liked.

"[Come] take him out sometimes if you feel like that kind of thing," she wrote, "so that he will know you are his real papa."

Hemingway immediately agreed. Her decision was brave, unselfish, and generous, he told her, adding that they had been like "two boxers who are groggy and floating and staggering around and yet will not put over a knock-out punch." Now that Hadley had delivered that punch at last, all parties could start the process of healing and recovery.

All in all, it was a tender letter. In it Hemingway acknowledged that *The Sun Also Rises* was essentially their second child together. Accordingly, she would henceforth receive all royalties from the book.

"It is really your right and due," he told her.

He was also creating a will. Under its terms, all income from his books, past and future, would be held in trust for Bumby, under Hadley's supervision. He hoped that Bumby could help make up for some of the hurt he had caused Hadley, who was "the best and truest and loveliest person" he had ever known.

Hadley received a preliminary judgment of divorce on January 27, 1927, just as *The Sun Also Rises* was about to go into its fifth printing. She later claimed that she felt liberated.

"I didn't know what was going to happen to me, but I had lots of confidence in myself," she said. "I knew that I could get along and I knew that I could still get some fun out of music."

That April she took Bumby back to America to see her family. When she got there, she felt "like a million dollars and free as air." Pauline, she had decided, was a better fit for Hemingway after all. She had certainly shown that she had the requisite toughness for the job. As a husband, Hemingway had proven "a very difficult horse to ride," as his son Patrick would put it.

Fitzgerald offered his support from America, where he was attempting to make progress on his novel. He was delighted with the press response to "The Sun ect." Also, he had reread the novel and reported to Hemingway that he "liked it in print even better than in manuscript." (Zelda, by contrast, considered it a novel about "bullfighting, bullslinging, and bullshit.") Nevertheless, he was chagrined but unsurprised by the news of the failure of the Hemingways' marriage. "I'm sorry for you and for Hadley + for Bumby and I hope some way you'll all be content and things will not seem so hard and bad," he wrote, and promised that he would continue to look out for Hemingway's interests at Scribner's.

"I can't tell you how much your friendship has meant to me during this year and a half," he added. "It is the brightest thing in our trip to Europe for me."

Years later, Fitzgerald ruminated on the relationship between Hemingway's writing and Hemingway's wives.

"I have a theory that Ernest needs a new woman for each big book," he told Morley Callaghan over dinner in Paris. For *The Sun Also Rises* — his first big book — there had been Hadley. Hemingway had since then published his next novel, written in the company of Pauline.

"If there's another big book," Fitzgerald ventured, "I think we'll find Ernest has another wife."

13

Sun, Risen

S OON AFTER *The Sun Also Rises* was published, expat editor Samuel Putnam ran into Hemingway at Les Deux Magots in Saint-Germain. Hemingway was by this time perceived as "edging away" from Montparnasse and the world that had made him famous. High-ceilinged and airy, filled with white light, the Deux Magots was an appropriately majestic backdrop for him. It had for decades been the home café of many international literary and artistic heavyweights. Now Hemingway was joining their ranks.

He and Putnam had a few drinks together.

"It did not take me long to discover that the somewhat shy and youthful reporter whom I had met in Chicago had vanished," Putnam later recalled. "In his place was a literary celebrity."

Hemingway spoke at length about the art of writing, even giving Putnam a tip or two.

"The first and most important thing of all, at least for writers today, is to strip language clean, to lay it bare to the bone," he said. "And that takes work."

Had he been influenced by Gertrude Stein in this matter? Putnam asked.

Sure, Hemingway admitted unenthusiastically, he had learned something from her, but not *that* much. On the subject of Pound, Hemingway was "rather pleasantly, and youthfully, patronizing," recalled Putnam. He claimed to have been far more influenced by the Old Testament in the King James Version.

"That's how I learned to write," he said. "By reading the Bible."

By then, another acquaintance noted, Hemingway had — like many of his readers — begun to talk like one of his own characters. Apparently he still visited some of the old haunts in the Quarter, for when Arthur Moss ran into him at the Select, he found that Hemingway the "shy youth had become Tarzan of [the] printed page."

It's hard to say whether these were sour grapes testimonials or merely the observations of other expat writers who—like Hemingway—were shrewd chroniclers of the characters in their milieu. Hemingway was not even in Paris much that winter or the subsequent spring, once he and Hadley settled the terms of their divorce. When Pauline returned to Paris, she and Hemingway departed for a lengthy skiing holiday in Gstaad, a popular winter resort destination among chic expats. Gone were the "Black Christ" days of the humble Hotel Taube in Schruns. Instead, the couple checked in to the regal Grand Hotel Alpina. They stayed in Switzerland until March; a few days after returning to Paris, he left on a tour of Italy.

Hemingway had always evacuated Paris during the dreary winters, but now this onetime shimmering Olympus must have begun to look like the backwater playing fields of his youth. He had simply outgrown the city—along with all of the mentors, publishers, and luminaries who had backed him since he first arrived there with Hadley years earlier.

The Sun Also Rises had elicited a wide array of reactions from his discarded Paris champions. Even though Hemingway had cut the Bill Bird–inspired portion of Jake Barnes's biography, Bird still detected with amusement some of his habits in the character. Hemingway's second publisher, Robert McAlmon, had nothing kind to say about either the book or its author.

"Beginning with the 'Sun Also Rises' I found his work slick, affected, distorted characterization, himself always the hero," he later wrote. (The feeling was mutual: Hemingway had recently dismissed McAlmon as a "son of a bitch with a mind like an ingrowing toe nail" and even considered making him the subject of a punishing little short story.)

Ford Madox Ford reacted elegantly to his bumbling cameo as Braddocks. Despite Hemingway's send-up, Ford would eventually write a preface to Hemingway's next novel, in which he would note that he hadn't particularly cared for *The Torrents of Spring* or *The Sun Also Rises* but still had the highest regard for Hemingway's artistic abilities.

Gertrude Stein was another matter entirely. According to Hemingway, *The Sun Also Rises* made her despise him because it officially turned the tables on their relationship: now *he* was the teacher and she was the student. The novel had, he claimed, schooled her in the art of dialogue, and she could not abide having been surpassed by her former protégé.

"It never occurred to me until many years later that anyone could hate anyone because they had learned to write conversation from that novel that started off with the quotation from the garage keeper," Hemingway wrote, although he conceded that the breakdown in their friendship was in reality "more complicated than that."

Soon after the novel came out, he made light of his supposed debt to her in a satirical piece for *The New Yorker* titled "The True Story of My Break with Gertrude Stein"—another public announcement that he'd severed ties with a former mentor, as *The Torrents of Spring* had broadcast his repudiation of Sherwood Anderson. Even if Stein never responded to Hemingway's declarations against her, she was indignant that he had claimed the mantle of bullfighting expert for himself.

"He heard about bull-fighting from me," she later informed the public in *The Autobiography of Alice B. Toklas.* She had long loved Spanish bull-fights and dancing and had been there first; what was more, she had the photos to prove it. Also, Stein claimed, Hemingway had recounted to her conversations that he later put into *The Sun Also Rises,* and that she and Hemingway had "talked endlessly about the character of Harold Loeb," possibly implying that she had influenced Hemingway's portrayal of him in the novel. It was the beginning of an ugly feud that played out in dueling books and other publications for more than a decade.

If Stein's indignation toward her former pupil was justified, Hemingway also had a right to suspect that she was jealous. Unlike her, he didn't have to anoint himself a genius; others were bestowing that crown upon him. He was the one negotiating new projects with a major American publisher, while she had resorted to publishing her work herself.

In fact, Hemingway was now utterly in demand. Emissaries from other industries were suddenly approaching him, seeking to tap the potential earning power of Ernest Hemingway, influencer and voice of the Lost Generation. Inquiries and entreaties poured in. In February 1927 Hemingway wrote to Maxwell Perkins from Gstaad to say that he needed help fielding all of the demands. From the magazine world alone, he had received requests from *The New Yorker, Vanity Fair* (which had rejected his satirical bullfight story two years earlier), *Harper's Bazaar,* and many others. Even *College Humor* was tugging on his sleeve. He began using Scott Fitzgerald's agent, but the job would prove too big for one man. The growing Hemingway team grew confusing even to Hemingway.

"I now have two British, one each of Danish, Swedish, French and

German publishers, apparently two agents in England, another agent in Germany (all volunteers, all unsolicited and all collecting a percentage) [and] at least two agents in France (both volunteers)," he reported later that year to Perkins. "All these splendid people engaged in sending cables which have to be answered at great [crossed out] some cost and the utter disruption of a morning's work."

Broadway and Hollywood also pursued him. Within a few weeks of the book's publication, Perkins advised Hemingway that two "movie people" had contacted him about *The Sun Also Rises,* although he warned that the adaptation would likely entail extensive rewriting. He was equally wary about the outreaches made by a well-known Broadway producer.

"These people are the most eccentric and vacillating in the world next to the movie people," he warned Hemingway.

Hemingway decided that he could tolerate eccentric vacillators if the price was right.

"[I] would not care what changes they made," he informed Perkins, and directed him to investigate further. "For the movie rights I think you should <u>ask</u> a good sized sum," he advised. Around $30,000—at a minimum—sounded about right to him. "Take whatever you can get in <u>cash,</u>" he added.

Fitzgerald predicted that nothing would come of the film inquiries. "No movie in <u>Sun Also</u> unless [the] book is [a] big success of scandal," he prophesied to Hemingway. He was right. Even though *The Sun Also Rises* had indeed scandalized elite crowds in Paris, London, and New York, it would still take more than thirty years for it to reach the silver screen.

Yet the novel had made Hemingway's name so ubiquitous that he was finally invited to join a certain roster of notables that had long eluded him.

"Got a sheet to fill out from *Who's Who,*" he informed Fitzgerald, adding that his life had been so "fuckingly complicated" that he had managed to answer only two of their questions and suspected that they would be used against him anyway.

Public interest in him was now running so high that even an undignified domestic accident—in which a skylight above his toilet collapsed and gave him a wound requiring stitches—was picked up by the wire services. A flurry of concerned cables and notes arrived from two continents. It was a dubious way to earn a fresh round of headlines, but by then, Hemingway was an international celebrity. Privacy would soon be as distant and dusty a memory as that of a dark little apartment, four stories above a *bal musette.*

• • •

NOW THAT *The Sun Also Rises* was rocking the country, those who had missed out on its publication sat glumly on the sidelines. Boni & Liveright made one last desperate plea to lure Hemingway back into its stable; its tactics were a curious combination of carrot and stick. Horace Liveright dispatched an ambassador, Boni & Liveright vice president Donald Friede, to meet with Hemingway in Paris.

"His argument was that Boni and Liveright had published In Our Time when no one else would and that I had only been allowed to leave because he," meaning Friede, "wasn't there," Hemingway reported to Maxwell Perkins. Friede offered $3,000 on any new novels, and pledged to buy the rights to both *The Sun Also Rises* and *The Torrents of Spring*—clearly a sign that Hemingway was now seen as a stronger stock than Sherwood Anderson. Hemingway turned Friede down, adding that he was "absolutely satisfied" where he was.

After all, nowhere was Hemingway more in demand than at Charles Scribner's Sons. *The Sun Also Rises* hadn't even had time to cool down after being rolled off the Scribner's presses before Perkins proposed the idea of chasing the novel's release with a spring 1927 short story collection. Hemingway had ten completed short stories on hand, he reported, and he was still interested in writing a nonfiction bullfighting tome. Yet he worried that they might be cranking out Hemingway books too fast.

"Don't you think we might give them a rest?" he wrote to Perkins, arguing that what came out next would have to be "awfully good" to secure his new position. After all, "there will be a lot of people with the knife out very eager to see me slipping—and the best way to handle that is not to slip."

In the end, they decided that his next book would indeed be a collection of short stories, slated for a fall 1927 release. It would keep Hemingway's name in the press until the next big thing, and, Perkins predicted, keep *The Sun Also Rises* in circulation for several more seasons as well. Hemingway suggested calling the collection *Men Without Women*—an ironic title, considering that the author rarely was without lavishly devoted female company. Each of the stories lacked a "softening feminine influence," he explained to Perkins, adding that he was willing to come up with an alternative should Perkins find it a "punk title." Perkins deemed it "splendid."

Men Without Women received mixed reviews, with two leading ladies of letters taking opposing sides. Virginia Woolf wrote an unflattering review for the *New York Herald Tribune,* calling *Men Without Women* "self-consciously virile" and adding that Hemingway's talent was contracting, not expanding. Dorothy Parker sailed to his defense in *The New Yorker,* calling the stories "truly magnificent"; Hemingway was, in her opinion, a "genius" and "the greatest living writer of short stories."

Yet Hemingway and Perkins both knew that he would ultimately have to secure his powerful position with a second novel. Another "big book," as Fitzgerald called it, was the only way to evolve from new champion into mature master.

As usual, Hemingway was on top of it. "Once he'd finished a book, his obsession was with the next [book], not the past," according to his son Patrick. Even before *The Sun Also Rises* was released, Hemingway had already been mulling his second act and even had a possible title for a new novel: *The World's Fair.* A few months later, he informed Perkins that he intended to start another novel once "things get straightened out and my head gets tranquil." It would not have any real-life people in it, as he was not especially eager to venture down that road again.

This was most welcome news to Perkins. He had not yet begun to pressure Hemingway about beginning a new novel, but the demand was certainly there. By that spring, the International Magazine Company had approached Hemingway in a bid to serialize his next novel—whatever it might be—and offered a $30,000 option for film rights for the phantom book.

Hemingway turned them down. It was unhealthy for a writer to undertake a commissioned book. He didn't want to carry that "extra weight," he explained to Perkins.

"I can't see it doing me any good now—and I have never seen an American writer survive it," he stated. Perkins concurred. Anyway, the offer hadn't been high enough, in his opinion.

Yet by that summer, "things" had gotten straightened out. Hadley had been assigned the proceeds from *The Sun Also Rises* and was now in California with Bumby. Hemingway had married Pauline on May 10, 1927. Virginia was her sister's attendant. The Pfeiffer clan blessed the union with the bestowal of checks, some of them for as much as $1,000—nearly the amount that Perkins had given Hemingway as an advance for both *Torrents* and *The Sun Also Rises.* After their almost month-long honeymoon in a walled town in France, there was the annual jaunt to Pamplona, followed by a recuperative trip to San Sebastián.

The intensive summer travel appears to have had the usual stimulating effect on Hemingway. By October he had begun a new novel and had nearly thirty thousand words completed. He got twenty-two chapters deep into the manuscript before he shunted it aside and started working on another. At first he'd thought it would be just a story, but it was turning out to be something bigger. Now as a nascent novel, he wrote to Perkins, it was going "wonderfully."

The pressure was, once again, beginning to build. The only way to create a formidable follow-up to *The Sun Also Rises,* Hemingway concluded, was to write about what he knew. That had been his formula with *Sun,* after all. In the meantime, he wanted to assure Perkins that he wasn't stalling. He knew that there were high expectations for his sophomore effort. He also knew that there was an unspoken timetable for turning works out, and that steady output was crucial to building one's reputation. Fitzgerald, Hemingway felt, was already a year or two late in producing his follow-up to *The Great Gatsby.* He didn't want to fall into that trap, but neither did he want to turn out anything mediocre.

"This next book <u>has</u> to be good," he reiterated to Perkins.

A month later, his new novel had stretched out to fifteen thousand words. It would soon be given a title—*A Farewell to Arms*—a phrase he borrowed from a sixteenth-century George Peele poem he'd come across in the *Oxford Book of English Verse.* Once again, Hemingway had drawn his heroine from real life: Catherine Barkley bore a startling resemblance to Agnes von Kurowsky, the young American nurse who had attended to Hemingway in a Milan hospital after he had been wounded during the war. The two had fallen in love and planned to marry before von Kurowsky jilted Hemingway for an Italian officer. Perhaps she thought that she was making a clean break with Hemingway. She was wrong.

The writing of *Farewell* may have brought a sense of déjà vu to Hemingway's friends watching from the sidelines. Hemingway was again furiously working on a novel in an atmosphere of pressure and high stakes. ("I work <u>all</u> the time," he informed Perkins.) And once again he frequently supplied his friends with status reports on the novel's progress, down to the word count. There was, as before, a Hemingway wife in the background, offering funds and limitless encouragement. That wife was even now pregnant with a son.

Yet everything had changed. Hemingway's neophyte days were over. He had successfully stripped the English language down and bent it to his will, and was on his way to becoming one of the most recognizable cultural icons on the planet. All of the elements of the Hemingway persona

—which would grow to outsized proportions in years to come—were in place.

Paris, too, had been ably conquered. Hemingway would return to the city many times, but an era had ended. By 1928, he and Pauline had decided to return to America for an extensive sojourn, starting in Havana and Florida. Just as Sherwood Anderson had extolled the virtues of an exotic locale known as Montparnasse to Hemingway and Hadley seven years earlier, Hemingway had been hearing about the wonders of sultry Key West from John Dos Passos. On March 17, 1928, the Hemingways set sail across the Atlantic.

Nearly six years later, in late 1933, Hemingway returned to Paris and took a good look around. By then he was the man he had hoped to become all those years earlier. *A Farewell to Arms* had been published to great acclaim, securing his place as the leading voice of the postwar generation. It had topped best-seller lists and been dubbed "the very apotheosis of a kind of modernism." In 1932 Paramount released a major film adaptation of the novel, starring Gary Cooper and Helen Hayes. Hemingway had also published two more books: *Winner Take Nothing,* another collection of short stories, and *Death in the Afternoon,* the nonfiction tome about bullfighting that he had been mulling for years. His public persona had grown steadily with his literary reputation and sales numbers. *Vanity Fair* would soon honor him with a satirical editorial: five Ernest Hemingway paper dolls, each representing a different aspect of the Hemingway legend. Three of the five guises—Hemingway as hard-drinking Lost Generation writer, Hemingway as zealous matador, and Hemingway as wounded soldier—had been launched along with *The Sun Also Rises* and have remained permanent, essential components of that image.

Since leaving for America in 1928, he had been back in Paris many times, but on this 1933 trip he was documenting the state of the city in an article for *Esquire.* (Journalism was about to become a big part of his life once again: he would soon cover two wars that would roil Europe for the next decade.) His subsequent "Paris Letter" for the magazine can almost be seen as a grim sequel to the giddy, decadent world he had portrayed in his debut novel.

Paris remained as beautiful as ever, he thought, but it had been a "big mistake" to come back. The 1929 stock market crash had officially ended the party for thousands of expats, who had packed up and reluctantly gone home. Even Jimmie Charters, the popular bartender at the Dingo, had retreated to London. By the time of Hemingway's visit, "only a few diehards who literally could not tear themselves away from the scene of past glories" remained in Montparnasse. Now, not only had *The Sun Also Rises* distinguished itself as the vanguard of modern literature, but it had become the book of record depicting a vanished world.

Hemingway revisited his old haunts and, perhaps from some of those leftover diehards, learned the fates of various former cohorts. So-and-so had shot himself; another friend had died of an overdose; yet another had gone back to New York and plummeted to his death from a high window. No one had any money; dealers could not sell paintings; everyone was discouraged. The Quarter had become disconcertingly middle-class and bourgeois, but sinister elements were creeping into the neighborhood too. The terrace of the Dôme — once filled with champagne- and Pernod-drinking American and English expats — was now crowded with frightened German "refugees from the Nazi terror" and the Nazis who had been dispatched there to spy on them. Everywhere people talked of the inevitability of another war.

"It is accepted and taken for granted," Hemingway wrote.

The scene depressed him, but not enough to keep him from thinking with tenderness and even nostalgia about his early years in Paris. He was seeing the city with new clarity now: it was like an ageless woman who moves from lover to lover. Paris had tired of Hemingway's generation, he realized, and had taken on new lovers. And like the city, Hemingway too had moved on.

"It was a fine place to be quite young in and it is a necessary part of a man's education," he mused. "We all loved it once."

"And," he added, "we lie if we say we didn't."

Epilogue

F OR THE PEOPLE who inspired the principal characters in *The Sun Also Rises,* life was divided into two categories: "B.S." — before *Sun* — and "A.S." What follows are summaries of their post-*Sun* existences. There is more information available about some than others; but in the end, all of them received at least some documentation, in several cases exclusively because of their role in Hemingway's debut novel.

Lady Duff Twysden (Lady Brett Ashley)

In 1927 Duff met Clinton King, a soft-spoken American artist nearly a decade her junior. He had come to Paris to paint and study. One day he was invited on an outing by artists Cedric Morris and Arthur Lett-Haines, who were both friends of Duff's (and also Hemingway's models for Brett's gay sidekicks in the opening chapters of *The Sun Also Rises*). Duff's reputation had preceded her; King opted to come on the outing when he heard she would be in attendance. They fell in love and were married the following year.

Like Duff's previous marriage to a man of reputable lineage, this union became something of a low-grade scandal at first. Two days after the wedding, the *New York Times* reported that "the secret marriage of Lady Twysden, to Clinton Blair King, young artist and son of an American candy manufacturer, came to light today." King's clan owned the King Candy Company in Fort Worth (its slogan: "King's Chocolates for American Queens"); though it was a family of commerce and not aristocracy, his relations protested Duff's marriage to Clinton as vigorously as the Twysdens had her union with Sir Roger. When the King family's lawyers were unable to deter Clinton from making Duff his bride, his father is said to have withdrawn financial support, leaving Duff—once more—in the arms of a penniless scion.

Some of their contemporaries also regarded the couple with disdain. Again Duff unwittingly played muse to an artist in her circle: poet Witter Bynner penned some verses nastily immortalizing the couple. He dubbed Twysden "an Englishwoman with a worn-out title" and "a mother of liquor," while King was reduced to "a son of candy." Of their romance, Bynner wrote:

> She pounced on upon him, so they say, like Jove,
> Liking his cherub face and fleshy wings.
> And he liking her force. And then they clove
> Together, circling through the airy rings
> Of Paris, not an eagle and a boy
> But a hawk and a rabbit, or a dead balloon

At first the couple remained in Paris, subsisting on handouts from Duff's relatives in England and living briefly in an apartment of Robert McAlmon's. He did not "entertain any false hopes" of collecting rent from them, he later acknowledged, even though it cost a pittance. When he needed to resume occupancy of the space himself, "it took more than gentle suggestions to get Lady Brett and her boy friend" out of his studio.

Like Hemingway and Pauline, the Kings eventually abandoned Paris for North America, residing over the next decade in Mexico, Texas, New York, and Santa Fe. Their habits, however, remained distinctly Montparnassian: hangovers kept them in bed until afternoon, observed one acquaintance in Mexico. In New York they attempted to set up an art school, but the project faltered. The Kings—apparently broker than ever—were then bailed out by friends who lent them the use of a shack-like building on their property along with access to their vegetable garden; there the couple subsisted on the garden's offerings and one drink of gin per day, administered by their landlord's Korean servant.

Theirs was an artistic existence, and—despite the penury—apparently a happy one. Duff posed for King's paintings and made her own sketches and watercolors. They read and socialized; Duff still had a penchant for dramatic hats. Yet by all reports, they drank relentlessly. Bynner deemed Duff "the most capable drinker I ever met."

"The only trouble [was] that Clinton [tried] to keep up with her," he observed.

The Kings eventually moved to Santa Fe, which had become a Southwest alternative to Greenwich Village. That said, as an artists' colony it didn't always get the respect afforded to the Village or the Quarter. Critic Edmund Wilson once called its residents "about the worst set of artists and writers to be found anywhere"—yet it remained a popular destination. The Kings elicited mixed reactions there "on account of their drinking and lewdness," noted Bynner. (Duff was apparently virtuosic in the art of swearing and had a repertoire of indecent music hall songs.) That said, Bynner conceded that Duff was "witty and hearty on the uptake and a swell yelper over puns," and added that she had remained "lankly handsome." (Harold Loeb, by contrast, ran into her at a cocktail party in the mid-1930s and thought that his former paramour looked terrible.) It was known in the Santa Fe community that Hemingway had based Lady Brett Ashley on Duff; her neighbors occasionally referred to her as "Brett" or even "the Duff-Brett woman."

Duff would spend her final days in that city. In 1938, while in Texas, she was diagnosed with tuberculosis. The Kings returned to Santa Fe, where Duff was placed in a sanatorium. "She looks as frail as a dried sea horse but maintains the gallant sparkle," Bynner reported to a friend. He predicted that the disease would keep her hospitalized for a year and might even kill her.

She died just twenty-two days after this prediction was made, on June 27, 1938, at the age of forty-six. While Lady Brett Ashley would forever live on as the model of unconventional glamour, "Mrs. Duff Stirling King" was listed as a "housewife" on her death certificate.

News of her death filtered back to Hemingway, who once again could not resist taking liberties with her life narrative.

"Brett died in New Mexico," he told his friend A. E. Hotchner years later. "Call her Lady Duff Twysden, if you like, but I can only think of her as Brett."

All of "Brett's" pallbearers had been her former lovers, he went on; one of these gentlemen slipped while holding the coffin, which then crashed to the ground and cracked open. (In reality, Duff was cremated, and no funeral was held.) When Hotchner repeated the ghoulish story in his 1966 book *Papa Hemingway,* it created a minor sensation and added another ignoble chapter to the already notorious fictionalized life story of Lady Duff Twysden.

"Who knows if [the funeral story] is true or not?" Hotchner recently said. "What's the difference? I was presenting a portrait of Hemingway saying these things."

Clinton King died in 1979. The remnants of his estate included none of Duff's art, correspondence, or other personal effects. Therefore, after her death, she was remembered largely through the recollections of others—and faced perpetuity as the fading shadow behind Lady Brett Ashley.

Harold Loeb (Robert Cohn)

When *The Sun Also Rises* was released, Harold Loeb had been living in the south of France with a young Dutch woman. They decided to marry, although Loeb severed their brief union after discovering that she was having an affair with an officer of the French Foreign Legion. She did, however, manage before the divorce to dispose of some of Loeb's memorabilia from the Duff Twysden affair: he remembered her flinging a youthful photograph of Twysden out of a ship's porthole.

Loeb remained in Paris until he completed his third novel, *Tumbling Mustard,* released by Horace Liveright in 1929. When he returned to the States, he swapped the literary life for a career as a government economist. Before turning his attention entirely to the world of commerce, however, Loeb wrote a never-published novel, whose early chapters were set in mid-1920s Paris and featured an expat writer character that may have been inspired by Hemingway. The book's title: *Leaf of Twisted Olive.* From then on, his subject matter changed considerably: Loeb's later works bore titles such as *Life in a Technocracy* and "Report on the National Survey on Potential Product Capacity." Soon there was a third wife, two more children, and a house in Connecticut; his pastimes included "gardening with a passion" and making successful stock market investments.

Yet Loeb was never able to escape the shadow of Robert Cohn. Among his descendants, opinions are divided about the extent to which his portrayal in *The Sun Also Rises* and his permanent link to Hemingway affected him in the decades that followed. One of his daughters, Susan Sandberg, feels that "it gave him importance, in a way, and a focus"; a niece, Barbara Loeb Kennedy, thinks that Loeb was pleased by the attention the

Hemingway relationship brought him, despite the deeply unflattering nature of the Cohn portrait.

But Loeb's other daughter, Anah Pytte, believes that her father would have preferred to bury the past, but the world would not let him. The manuscript of Loeb's 1959 memoir, *The Way It Was,* originally featured more material about his own early life and illustrious family background, Pytte maintains, but "the publisher's interest was in Hemingway," and the book ended up "revolving around that incident." She recalls that "people were always looking him up because of the connection, so he couldn't totally leave it behind."

Loeb did help keep that connection to Hemingway alive through his writings and interviews about the *Sun Also Rises* period and what he publicly dubbed "Hemingway's bitterness." As late as the 1950s, he implied that there was still something of a rivalry or unspoken dialogue between the two men. For instance, Loeb maintained that Hemingway had kept a copy of *The Way It Was* open on his desk when writing *A Moveable Feast,* his memoir of Paris in the 1920s. (Hemingway's assistant from 1959 until 1961, Valerie Hemingway, calls this allegation "absolutely untrue.")

Despite the persistent presence of the *Sun Also Rises* saga, Loeb's final years were content, says his niece. By then he had a fourth wife, with whom he lived in a custom-built glass-walled house in Weston, Connecticut. Plus, "he always had a mistress," says his daughter Susan Sandberg, adding that sometimes wife and mistress both occasionally graced the same lunch table at the Connecticut house.

In early 1974, Loeb, his wife, and Sandberg were vacationing in Marrakech, Morocco. The family checked into the plush La Mamounia hotel and spent their time shopping and swimming in the hotel's pool. On January 20, Loeb's heart suddenly "gave out," recalls Sandberg, who was with her father when he died. He was buried in a local cemetery. At least two of his obituaries linked him to Robert Cohn, thus further cementing Loeb's legacy with the portrait. Hemingway had "savaged Mr. Loeb in 'The Sun Also Rises,'" the *New York Times* reminded its readers, adding that the Loeb-as-Cohn character had been depicted as a "wealthy Jewish hanger-on and social climber."

That said, Loeb had—by outward appearances—mellowed admirably about the whole situation in later years; he had been "carrying off his role as a patriarch from the twenties with stylish aplomb." Five decades later, Loeb was still being cast as an official ambassador from the Lost Generation.

Kitty Cannell (Frances Clyne)

Kitty Cannell remained in Paris longer than Hemingway, Twysden, or Loeb. She eventually married again, this time to the French surrealist playwright and poet Roger Vitrac; the marriage did not last.

In the early 1930s, Cannell became a Paris-based fashion reporter for the *New York Times;* she also contributed to *The New Yorker* and various French publications.

She remained in the city during the Second World War as an "enemy-alien parolee under police surveillance." During that time, she was arrested twice by the Gestapo and released, and was not allowed to leave the city for four years. It was, she recalled, a survival-of-the-fittest existence: the pillars of her daily wartime experience were "cold, hunger, dirt, restrictions, depressions, bombardments and boredom"—a far cry from the joyous vitriol of the Dôme-and-Dingo days.

To combat depression during one of the blacker periods, when she had just been "tipped off by the French Police" that she was "probably going to be arrested for the third time," Cannell began to write a memoir of her childhood. Its title—*Jam Yesterday: Gay, Insouciant Reminiscences of the Late Nineties of a Happy Childhood Spent Shuttling Between Canada and the U.S.A.*—seemed a not-so-distant cousin to the meandering Victorian fare spoofed by Donald Ogden Stewart and Hemingway. She was eventually allowed to leave Paris in 1944, coming first to New York and later settling in Boston.

Cannell quickly began the next chapter of her life as a mistress of all trades. She was, by all accounts, professionally fabulous; one publicity photo circulated by her agency features Cannell coiled in a lengthy fur stole. Among her various postwar professional adventures were pinch-hitting for radio gossip commentator Walter Winchell when he was on vacation, directing publicity for the Brooklyn Museum, penning ballet critiques for the *Christian Science Monitor,* and commentating on couture shows. She also became a presence on the television and radio circuit: her management agency billed her areas of expertise as "everything from Timeless glamor to prison experiences."

Her publicity material did not, however, list her as an expert on early Hemingway, although Cannell habitually made herself available to biographers to discuss the events of 1920s Paris and the *Sun Also Rises* period in general. Despite her exciting life "A.S.," she continued to be annoyed by her appearance in *The Sun Also Rises* as Frances Clyne; Hemingway's ascent and growing reputation as a heroic man of letters and admirable lifestyle irritated her. Like Harold Loeb, she eventually published an essay attempting to puncture the legend surrounding the now heavily romanticized Lost Generation era: her sarcastically titled "Scenes with a Hero" depicted Hemingway as volatile, backstabbing, and self-obsessed.

She died exactly four months after Harold Loeb, on May 19, 1974.

Donald Ogden Stewart (Bill Gorton)

For years in Hollywood, Donald Stewart's lucky streak continued unabated. Half a decade after *The Sun Also Rises* was released, he was nominated for his first Oscar for best writing and original story behind the film *Laughter;* in 1941 he won an Academy Award for his screenplay for *The Philadelphia Story.*

And then he went "in one quick step from being the highest-paid writer in Hollywood to a man without a job," as his friend Katharine Hepburn pithily put it.

This swift demotion came courtesy of the anticommunist blacklisting that targeted countless Hollywood luminaries in the 1940s and 1950s. By Stewart's own admission, during his early years in Los Angeles, he had little interest in Bolsheviks or communism and instead served the gods of humor. Yet he soon became an outspoken advocate for civil liberties. "It was said that when President Franklin D. Roosevelt got up in the morning, he ordered orange juice, coffee and his first 10 telegrams of protest from Donald Stewart," reported the *New York Times* after Stewart's death. In the 1930s, he served as president of the Hollywood Anti-Nazi League and as president of the League of American Writers, which endeavored to involve writers in combating the menace of Nazism and fascism. He was also a member of the Communist Party briefly during the 1930s.

"By 1950 I was officially on the Black List," he recalled in his memoir. He was pressured to confess to having been "'duped' into assuming a left-wing position in [his] political and personal philosophy" and clear himself by submitting the names of other "dupees." Instead, Stewart and his second wife — the writer Ella Winter, whom he had met at a political rally — went into exile in 1951 and settled in London. "Ella and I decided that we might have a go at corrupting some other country than the United States," he wrote, "so we piled our subversive thoughts and our evening clothes into the car and started to explore un-American countries such as France and Italy and England."

Once considered "one of the great wits of the late 20's, 30's, and 40's; the creator of laughter and delight in movies, plays, books, and high society," Stewart drifted out of the public spotlight. Tastes changed while he was stranded far from his professional community; by the 1970s, he realized that his particular and once highly compensated brand of humor belonged to another generation. "In the old days I didn't have to worry," he said in a 1971 interview. "I remember my secretary in Hollywood — it was in her contract that she had to laugh at my jokes."

According to Stewart's granddaughter Daneet Steffens, he was not embittered by his exile and disappearance from center stage. "He didn't sit around and feel sorry for himself," she says, although Stewart's son Donald Ogden Stewart Jr. says that he was plagued by a sense of failure at the end of his life. Stewart and his wife entertained a great deal, including large Sunday lunches attended by everyone from Katharine Hepburn and other Hollywood legends to the local family doctor. "Their friends stayed with them into old age," Steffens says.

Even though Stewart's later friendships included countless luminaries from Hollywood's creative elite, Hemingway was still very much on Stewart's mind as he wrote his 1975 memoir, *By a Stroke of Luck!* The men had been out of each other's lives for years; Hemingway had been dead more than a decade. Even at this point, Stewart still refused to grant *The Sun Also Rises* the artistic stature that others accorded it. "He would say, 'That's exactly what happened . . . it was like a photograph,'" recalls his son. "He just didn't think Hemingway had the gift. He wasn't Archibald MacLeish. He thought [Joseph] Conrad had it; he though F. Scott Fitzgerald had it. But not Hemingway."

Stewart remained upset at Hemingway until the end of his life — not just because of the vicious poem Hemingway had penned about Stewart's dear friend Dorothy Parker, but also because he felt that Hemingway had used him yet again as literary fodder decades after *The Sun Also Rises* debuted. When he first read Hemingway's 1937 novel *To Have and Have Not,* one of the characters startled him: John Hollis, described as a highly paid sellout of a Hollywood director with affected communist sympathies. He was certain that Hemingway had based Hollis on him. Even worse, Stewart's wife, Beatrice, seemed to him to be making an appearance as Dorothy Hollis, a sultry character depicted as cheating on her husband with a wealthy man.

The John Hollis cameo was fleeting, but it "was a terrible affront to him," says Stewart's son. The send-up may have stemmed from more than a decade-old grudge: Stewart felt that Hemingway was likely also punishing him for having gone to Hollywood—something that Hemingway would hold against F. Scott Fitzgerald as well. "Selling out was one thing you didn't do," says Donald Stewart Jr. "[Not] to Hollywood, to your wife, to drink, to life."

"Not," he adds, "if you were a friend of Hemingway's."

It was further evidence of "the curious bitter streak" the elder Stewart had detected in Hemingway and his writings. Hemingway had felt, he contended, a need to destroy the love that his greatest friends had for him —and in the end, Stewart maintained, there was "no one left for Hemingway to obliterate but himself."

Donald Ogden Stewart died in England on August 2, 1980, of complications following a heart attack. He was eighty-five.

Pat Guthrie (Mike Campbell)

Most of the information about the fate of Pat Guthrie comes via Jimmie "the Barman" Charters, who remained close with him in the years following the release of *The Sun Also Rises*.

According to Charters's account, Guthrie's life spiraled into a nightmare. He apparently split up with Lorna Lindsley, the wealthy American woman who had supposedly kept him a romantic hostage with her dollars. Accordingly, his financial situation took a turn for the worse. He cut a bad check to a Paris hotel; when the police tried to hunt him down, Guthrie's wealthy mother intervened and had him shipped off to South Africa, or, as Charters put it, "'to the colonies,' which English families always think a magic cure for black sheep." Once in Cape Town, he invented some sort of scheme involving a nonexistent farm and sold shares in the fictitious enterprise to friends. His activities triggered an investigation, and Guthrie once again gave authorities the slip, this time escaping to England.

He was eventually permitted to return to France: his mother had "arranged things in Paris through the English ambassador." Guthrie resumed his dissolute routine. Besides Charters, his primary company was a taxi driver friend who managed Guthrie's meager finances and a female companion with an affection for narcotics. One evening, having popped a few unspecified pills, he was deposited at a café by his taxi driver friend. Guthrie poured Veronal—a barbiturate—into a cup of soup and slipped into a coma. Because he had not paid for the soup, he was taken not to a hospital but rather to a police station, where officers left him unconscious on a cement floor. Eventually he was taken to a hospital, where he died on May 24, 1932, at the age of thirty-six.

Charters deemed it an accidental overdose, but word went around the colony that Guthrie had committed suicide. His funeral was sparsely attended. "So few people came to the funeral of this man who had been so popular," Charters later recalled, "not even the American girl for whom he had given up Brett [Duff Twysden]!"

Following Guthrie's death, his now elderly mother materialized in Paris. Determined to salvage as much of her son's legacy as possible, she made the rounds and paid off his debts. She soon approached Charters and offered to make reparations.

"I felt like waiving the debt as a token of good friendship and in respect to the memory of her beloved son," he stated, but Guthrie's mother insisted on giving him a substantial check. Charters relented. The two had a drink together and "parted company [as] good friends."

Bill Smith (Bill Gorton)

Bill Smith got into the literary spirit during his 1925 sojourn in Paris and Pamplona; after returning to the United States with Harold Loeb, he worked on his own short stories. He eventually abandoned his creative endeavors and went to work for Loeb as a government writer. Over the years he worked for several branches of the government and wrote speeches for Harry Truman on labor topics. He eventually married another Loeb employee; the couple had no children.

In the late 1960s, an interviewer caught up with Smith, who was then living with his wife in a ranch house in Arlington, Virginia, just outside Washington, D.C. Although his wife, Marion, insisted that Hemingway was "a genius about hate as much as he was about writing," Smith gave a lengthy and affectionate interview about Hemingway, still calling him "Wemedge," a nickname left over from their shared boyhood. Over the years, as Hemingway's circle of friends and associates had grown to include movie stars, generals, and presidents, the two men had fallen out of touch. Was this the result of hard feelings? asked the interviewer.

It wasn't so much "a falling out as a falling apart," Smith explained. "We simply lived a long way apart and that always causes a drift of some kind . . . Wemedge was batting about all over the world."

How had Smith's feelings about *The Sun Also Rises* evolved? the interviewer asked. Did it still seem accurate to him?

Sun was not his favorite Hemingway book, Smith admitted. That honor probably went to *A Farewell to Arms* or *For Whom the Bell Tolls.* As for the accuracy of *The Sun Also Rises,* he went on — well, the novel had just been Hemingway's take on the events during that summer of 1925.

"Every one of us would write a different book," he mused. "None would jibe exactly. That is only natural. The thing about Hemingway's account is that it caught a mood better than anyone else could."

Smith died in March 1972.

Cayetano Ordóñez (Pedro Romero)

Cayetano Ordóñez, "El Niño de la Palma," had impressed Hemingway as the potential savior of bullfighting during the mid-1920s, but in 1932 the author declared that the real-life Pedro Romero had lost his stuff. He had been gored badly a few years earlier, and "that was the end of him." After that, Ordóñez "could hardly look at a bull . . . [H]is fright as he had to go in to kill was painful to see," wrote Hemingway of his former hero in *Death in the Afternoon.* The season after this fateful goring, Ordóñez landed an avalanche of contracts and then gave the public "the most shameful season any matador had ever had up until that year in bullfighting," Hemingway reported. No other bullfighter in recent years had raised hopes higher or proved a graver disappointment.

To make matters worse, Ordóñez had begun keeping risqué company: a year after *The Sun Also Rises* was released, he married Consuelo de los Reyes, a half-Gypsy flamenco dancer. Her Gypsy mother came to live with the couple, and reportedly brought along an appetite for entertainments that went on night and day. Critics were quick to draw a connection between Ordóñez's decline and his raucous new home environment.

Ordóñez did not, however, succumb to Hemingway's summary judgment that he was finished. In 1932, the year *Death in the Afternoon* appeared, he actually had a resurgence in both popularity and passion, or *afición;* he performed so admirably in a bullfight that fall that the crowd "forgave him everything." He was awarded his bull's ears and carried out of the ring on his fans' shoulders — just like in the old days.

Years later, Hemingway exalted another member of the Ordóñez clan on paper: Cayetano's bullfighter son Antonio. In *The Dangerous Summer,* Hemingway described in reverential detail how Antonio improved on Cayetano's "absolute technical perfection." He recounted a conversation in which a wounded Antonio lies on a bed after a fight and implores Hemingway: "Tell me. Am I as good as my father?"

"I told him that he was better than his father and I told him how good his father was," Hemingway wrote.

By this time Antonio was too good to compete even against his contemporaries; rather, he was, as Hemingway put it, in a competition with history.

His father, Cayetano, by contrast, had long been out of the public eye. Unlike the real-life inspirations behind the other characters in *The Sun Also Rises,* Ordóñez might have been better served if his *Sun* avatar, Pedro Romero, had soldiered on as his sole representation to posterity. Unfortunately, other competing portraits were painted. One was especially devastating. In 1955 a young American student named Sam Adams, then studying at the University of Madrid, was asked by the owner of his pension if he would mind sharing his bedroom with an older man who was down on his luck. The student reluctantly agreed. A repellent old drunk who referred to himself as Niño de la Palma soon arrived to occupy the room's second bed. When Adams realized that he was in the presence of a one-time Hemingway hero, he carefully observed his new roommate and later published a *Sports Illustrated* account of their three weeks together.

By this time, the man Hemingway described in *The Sun Also Rises* as "the best-looking boy I have ever seen" had degenerated into a balding, pockmarked mess: purple lines spattered his nose; his mouth sported swollen gums and two yellow front teeth. According to Adams, Ordóñez drank heavily and would wake up his roommate nightly with the sound of "almost unhuman retching." His now illustrious offspring, he claimed, paid him to stay away.

"I'm just an old drunk and my family are all high society now and live where there are trees, while I stay in this whore of a pension in this whore of a town," he reportedly told Adams.

Ordóñez also talked about Hemingway. His appearance in *The Sun Also Rises* had apparently been a great honor to him.

"He wrote about me in a book once," he informed Adams. "In this book Ernesto called me Pedro Romero after Spain's greatest matador . . . [A]nd it all occurs at the Feria de San Fermín in Pamplona and I make love to the English woman."

He was predictably less enthusiastic about Hemingway's *Death in the Afternoon* portrait of him. "What does this American writer know about being afraid and alone out there with the bull and sometimes having to find your nerve again to please the animals in the expensive seats in the shade so they'll give you contracts for another season? What does Don Ernesto Hemingway have to say about that?"

"What fear I had," he added wistfully. "What magnificent fear. Sometimes I shook so bad I could hardly control my legs."

He died six years later on October 30, 1961, at the age of fifty-seven.

Ernest Hemingway (Jake Barnes)

Following the publication of *The Sun Also Rises,* Ernest Hemingway published during his lifetime four more novels, a novella, several collections of short stories, and many works of nonfiction, including two books. As a reporter, he covered the Spanish civil war — an experience that greatly informed his 1940 novel *For Whom the Bell Tolls* — and later World War II; other assignments over the years took him from Africa to China. (F. Scott Fitzgerald had been accurate in his prediction that for each major Hemingway book, there would be a new woman at his side: *For Whom* was dedicated to war correspondent Martha Gellhorn, who became Hemingway's third wife in 1940; his novella *The Old Man and the Sea* was written during his fourth marriage, to Mary Welsh Hemingway.)

Although he was prolific, his career seemed to be veering into twilight in the 1940s. His 1950 novel *Across the River and into the Trees* — first serialized in *Cosmopolitan* magazine that year — was widely regarded as a failure at the time; critics felt that Hemingway had become a parody of himself. Some took the opportunity to parody the unintentional parody. *The New Yorker*'s E. B. White wrote a story called "Across the Street and into the Grill" sending up the book: "'Schrafft's is a good place and we're having fun and I love you,' Pirnie said. He took another swallow of the 1926, and it was a good and careful swallow. 'The stockroom men were very brave,' he said, 'but it is a position where it is extremely difficult to stay alive.'" ("Parody is the last refuge of the frustrated writer," Hemingway privately grumbled.)

If the role of earnest, poor, and unpublished young writer hadn't suited him back in the 1920s, neither did he care for the part of passé aging champion. In 1952 he staged his comeback with the publication of *The Old Man and the Sea*. Although he had been mulling the subject matter for years, he wrote the book in a mere eight weeks, recalling the fervor with which he had written *The Sun Also Rises* decades earlier. Advance sales of the

American edition reached fifty thousand copies, and when *Life* magazine published *Old Man* in its entirety that September, the magazine sold over 5 million copies in the first forty-eight hours alone.

H. R. Stoneback, president of the Hemingway Society, remembers how the story resonated around the country and across all demographics. While traveling that September, he had stopped at a West Virginia truck stop. Behind the counter stood a waitress, bent over a copy of *Life*. A truck driver hollered for more coffee. "She says, 'Shut up and listen,'" Stoneback recalls. "And in the middle of the night, in this truck stop, she starts reading *The Old Man and the Sea*." A truck driver unplugged a blaring jukebox by ripping its cord out of the wall so everyone could hear better. At that moment, Stoneback realized how pervasive Hemingway's influence and allure were. As with *The Sun Also Rises,* Hemingway's high-low formula had held fast once again.

Hemingway seemed almost taken aback by the story's instant success. "This five million (or however many it is) readers at a time is spooky," he wrote to Scribner's editor Wallace Meyer. "It is very bad for a man to read so much shit pleasing or not about himself."

The book won the Pulitzer Prize the following year; by 1954, Hemingway's stature was beyond dispute. That year he was awarded the Nobel Prize in Literature for his "mastery of the art of narrative, most recently demonstrated in *The Old Man and the Sea,* and for the influence that he has exerted on contemporary style."

Hemingway did not attend the awards ceremony but sent a characteristically brief speech to be read for him. "A true writer," he wrote, "should always try for something that has never been done or that others have tried and failed. Then sometimes, with great luck, he will succeed."

Seven years later, after struggling with depression, Hemingway killed himself with a shotgun at his Ketchum, Idaho, home. At first, the death was not reported as a suicide. Hemingway's fourth wife — now his widow — Mary, issued the following statement to the press: "Mr. Hemingway accidentally killed himself while cleaning a gun this morning at 7:30 a.m. No time has been set for the funeral services, which will be private." She had not been "consciously lying," she later recalled. "It was months before I could face the reality."

In the final years of his life, the Paris of Hemingway's youth had been on his mind again. He had been working on what he called his "Paris sketches" — a series of stories about his life there in the 1920s and the people he had known. In 1964 they would be published posthumously in book form as *A Moveable Feast*, a title suggested by A. E. Hotchner to Mary Hemingway. Hotchner had been sitting with Hemingway at the bar of La Closerie des Lilas in 1950 when Hemingway told him, "If you are lucky enough to have lived in Paris as a young man, then wherever you go for the rest of your life it stays with you, for Paris is a moveable feast."

He was happy while working on the Paris manuscript, according to Valerie Hemingway, who, as Hemingway's assistant in fall 1959, accompanied him around Paris as he fact-checked the book. They revisited the sites that he was bringing to life in the manuscript's pages. Once again he drank at the Closerie and the Dôme and the Select, where Jake Barnes and Lady Brett Ashley had caroused on paper. They revisited the apartments where he had lived with Hadley, but they did not go inside, Valerie says, because Hemingway wanted to preserve the frozen-in-time images of these places he had in his mind. Standing in front of his old building on rue du Cardinal Lemoine, he recounted stories about the long-gone ground-floor *bal musette* and those early years in that cold, tiny flat without plumbing.

"He shrugged off the lack of bathrooms and other inconveniences," Valerie recalls. "This [was] where they were happiest. He still had tremendous affection for the place. This building represented the beginning of everything."

Hotchner says that he talked with Hemingway about those Paris years and the people who had dwelled in the world of *The Sun Also Rises*. Hemingway spoke about Fitzgerald with great affection, although in *A Moveable Feast* he would depict Fitzgerald as a jejune mediocrity and drunken basket case. Gertrude Stein received less than a rave review: her book *The Autobiography of Alice B. Toklas* had been "full of lies," Hemingway asserted. Plus, she always exaggerated her role as den mother to all of the young writers who flocked to the city. And Harold Loeb's affair with Duff Twysden, Hemingway went on, had "ruined poor Loeb for the rest of his life."

If Hemingway felt remorse about the anguish that *The Sun Also Rises* may have caused Loeb, Twysden, and the others, he appears to have kept it to himself.

"I once asked him: so, if you had it to do over, would you have been softer?" Hotchner recalled.

"Oh, hell no," Hemingway replied.

Acknowledgments

Like the novel this book documents, *Everybody Behaves Badly* has been an ensemble production, and I am grateful to the many people who helped me realize this group portrait.

My debt to my editor, Eamon Dolan, is so great that it requires top billing. From my first meeting with him, he challenged and advanced my thinking on the material, and later patiently helped me chisel this book out of a 1,400-page outline. He makes streamlining into a high art, and delivers often brutal edits with such a gallant, humorous bedside manner that I rarely despaired of losing all of that hard-earned material. And like Hemingway, Eamon has a genius for making complicated subjects accessible and enjoyable. I could not have asked for a more incisive collaborator nor a truer stalwart.

My gratitude to Charles Scribner III and Valerie Hemingway runs just as deep. Both devoted hours of their time to this project, and I cannot adequately express my appreciation for their patience, knowledge, insights, encouragement — and above all, their friendship. My profound thanks also to Patrick Hemingway for his two wonderful, spirited interviews, and to his wife, Carol, for paving the way for these talks and tolerating my follow-up queries. Angela Hemingway Charles was also very generous in releasing to me the recordings of the Hadley Hemingway interviews conducted by Alice Hunt Sokoloff. In addition, I am grateful to the Hemingway Society presidents — past and present — who lent their support to this book, including James Meredith, H. R. "Stoney" Stoneback, and Allen Josephs.

Other descendants of the principal figures in this book granted interviews and gave me access to family files and photographs, and their knowledge greatly informed my work. Heartfelt thanks to John Sanders, Jenny

Phillips, Frank Phillips, Eleanor Lanahan, Anah Pytte, Susan Sandberg, Keith Sandberg, Roger Loeb, Barbara Loeb Kennedy, Karole Vail, Donald Ogden Stewart Jr., Daneet Steffens, Laura Donnelly, Robin Rowan Clark, and Noel Osheroff. I am also very grateful to Hemingway's friends A. E. Hotchner, Nancy Dryer, and Joseph Dryer for welcoming me into their homes; they spent hours discussing their memories of Hemingway and helping me understand the nuances of his complex character. Kendall Conrad, Barnaby Conrad II, Winston Conrad, and Maria Cooper Janis also generously shared insightful memories and anecdotes of their families' experiences with Hemingway.

I also thank the biographers and scholars who helped guide me through various aspects of this story, including A. Scott Berg, Gioia Diliberto, Scott Donaldson, Lois Gordon, Ruth Hawkins, Lois Palken Rudnick, and Calvin Tomkins. Sandra Spanier was especially supportive and generously gave me early access to the not-yet-released third volume of Hemingway's letters, many of which were previously unpublished.

Many knowledgeable editors and writers also generously spoke with me about the workings of the historical New York publishing scene and the colorful luminaries within that world, including Nelson Aldrich, Roger Angell, Jay Fielden, Lewis Lapham, Nicholas Lemann, and Nan Talese. Adam Gopnik, Lorin Stein, and Gay Talese made themselves repeatedly available to me and helped me make further inroads in the community, and for that I am profoundly grateful. My thanks also to Hamish Bowles and Valerie Steele for their insights into the world of 1920s fashion and fashion publications. Robert Evans spoke with me at length about the making of the 1957 film *The Sun Also Rises;* Julian Fellowes kindly shared a wealth of information with me about the interwar British aristocracy. They have all of my appreciation.

Research for this book required many hours in the Princeton University Library's Rare Books and Special Collections division, which houses the archives of pioneering Hemingway biographer Carlos Baker, the Archives of Charles Scribner's Sons, the F. Scott Fitzgerald Papers, the Sylvia Beach Papers, the Patrick Hemingway Papers, the Broom Correspondence of Harold Loeb, and more. I am deeply indebted to Don C. Skemer and the Princeton team, including Gabriel Swift, Sandra Calabrese, Brianna Cregle, AnnaLee Pauls, and Christa Cleeton, for their help, enthusiasm, and kindness to me during my months at the university. I am equally grateful to Susan Wrynn of the Ernest Hemingway Collection at the John F. Kennedy Presidential Library and Museum, who tolerated my ubiquitous presence since the earliest days of my research. Others on the JFK team who provided great and deeply appreciated support include Stacey Chandler, Abigail Malangone, Amna Abdus-Salaam, Melissa Taing, Laurie Austin, Aubrey Butts, Maryrose Grossman, and Kyla Ryan. My thanks also to Ingrid Lennon-Pressey and Stephen R. Young of Yale's Beinecke Rare Book and Manuscript Library, and Susan Halpert at Harvard's Houghton Library. The New York Public Library played an important role as well by giving me access to rare first editions of Hemingway's earliest works and other related material; I am especially grateful to Isaac Gerwitz and Joshua McKeon of the Berg Collection and to Amy Geduldig for their help. John Pollack at the University of Pennsylvania Libraries, which house the Horace Liveright Papers, also delved into that archive on my behalf.

Several people were crucial to expanding my understanding of the final years of Lady Duff Twysden. Matt Kuhn and Fred Kline helped handle the Clinton King estate and successfully found material remainders of Duff Twysden's life for me; William Butler led me to important correspondence within the Santa Fe community about the Kings' existence there. Chris Webster and Gerald Rodriguez also have my thanks for providing details of Twysden's last days and death.

Dozens of other people lent crucial support in various ways, and I am grateful to each of them, including Nan Graham, Brant Rumble, and Roz Lippel of Scribner's; Case Kerns of the Harvard University Department of English; Luisa Gilardenghi Stewart; Sanford J. Smoller; Ian von Franckenstein; Michael Katakis; Yessenia Santos; Lore Monig of the New York City Club Taurino; Jeffrey Lyons; Anthony Ahern and Allan Cramer; my original team of editors at *Vanity Fair,* including Punch Hutton, Katherine Stirling, Lenora Jane Estes, and Cat Buckley; Mark Rozzo; Jay Fielden and Ben Howe of *Town & Country,* who sent me on a tour of Hemingway's Paris — in April, no less; Lili Rosenkranz; Lilah Ramzi; Sadie Stein; Claire Fentress, Tucker Morgan, and Anna Heyward of the *Paris Review;* Alexa Cassanos; Susan Morrison; Cressida Leyshon; Jeannie Rhodes; Fabio Bertoni; Shelley Wanger; Ben Adler; Elizabeth Frank; Marilyn Sarason; Carol Cheney; the Manchester Historical Society; Rebecca Potance at the New Mexico Museum of Art; Joan Livingston of *Taos News;* Maggie Van Ostrand; Libby Willis of the Oakhurst Neighborhood Association; Stefan Rak and Bill Ray of the Coffee House Club; Sara Racine and Abigail Dennis of *The Madisonian;* Richard Layman and Giesela Lubecke of Layman Poupard Publishing, LLC; Sam Farrell of the

WGBH Educational Foundation; Giles Tremlett of *The Economist;* Joy Day of the Twin Bridges Historical Association; Dawn Youngblood, Tarrant County archivist in Fort Worth; Gail Stanislow of the Brandywine Museum; Amanda Davis and Sheryl Woodruff of the Greenwich Village Society for Historic Preservation; Jennifer Joel of International Creative Management; Paul Morris of the PEN/Faulkner Foundation; Kevin Fitzpatrick of the Dorothy Parker Society; Vivian Shipley; Patricia Adams; Craig Tenney of Harold Ober Associates, Inc.; Anna Bond and Rachel Ewen of Cambridge University Press; Eric Sandberg; Michael Sandberg; Anders Pytte; Mimi Levitt; Ray Chipault; Holly Van Buren of New York City's Film Forum; Chip Lorenger of the Horton Bay General Store; Jeff Sanderson; Alex Bier; Jill Quasha; Julia Masnik; Marianne Merola; Dave Miller; David Meeker; Karaugh Brown; Brooke Geahan; Ashley Wick; Dora Militaru; Emily Arden Wells; Tenzing Choky; Karen Seo; Claiborne Swanson Frank; Sarah Rosenberg; Oberto Gili; Frances McCarthy; Jenna Blum; Judy Blum; and Rick and Monica Macek.

As *Everybody Behaves Badly* was an international tale that spanned two continents and many countries, I relied on several talented people for assistance in translating works, phrases, and slang from French, Spanish, and Italian: Sophie Capéran, Jean-Luc Giai Piancera, Chiara de Rege, Alex Dickerson, and Ana Herrero. Brooke Wall and Jason Cannon also helped me navigate fishing terminology. I am grateful to each of them.

I could not have undertaken this intensive research effort without the assistance of my A-team of research associates, who tracked down documents, rare and out-of-print books, magazine and newspaper articles, obituaries, unpublished poems, and other materials of that ilk. Alison Forbes — my right-hand woman from the earliest incarnation of this project, a proposed magazine feature — and Abigail Crutchfield Arzoumanov never came back empty-handed, and each always managed to track down the most elusive of contacts. I could not have asked for better bloodhounds. My Harvard-based associate Alexander Creighton made many trips to the Kennedy Library and Museum and Harvard's Houghton Library, where he transcribed countless letters and manuscripts; no request was too daunting or too minute, nor was any handwriting too idiosyncratic for him to decipher. I am deeply in debt to all three researchers, and I am very proud of their contributions to this work. Melissa Goldstein also has my thanks for helping us to track down elusive, decades-old photos in libraries and archives.

Nor would this project have been possible without my formidable literary agent Molly Friedrich and her team, including Lucy Carson, Molly Schulman, Nichole LeFebvre, and Alix Kaye. From the earliest days of this project, they championed the idea of a young(ish) female reporter taking on the most masculine of subjects, and were unflagging sources of support, counsel, and encouragement throughout every step of the research and writing process. I would also like to thank Glynnis MacNicol, who has been my co-reporter on many assignments and first introduced me to this team; her deeply appreciated contributions to this book are myriad.

I am also extremely grateful to Rosemary McGuinness, Mary Dalton-Hoffman, Margaret Anne Miles, and Lisa Glover of Houghton Mifflin Harcourt in helping me with the often tricky administrative, legal, and permissions aspects of this project. I owe many thanks also to our astute and patient copyeditor, Amanda Heller.

Everybody Behaves Badly belongs as much to my adored husband, Gregory Macek, as it does to me. No aspect of this book lacks his imprint: he has been my first-wave editor, my vigilant lawyer, and my most crucial pillar of support. Every night he dutifully listened to the latest snippet from Lost Generation Paris; after each edit to the manuscript was completed, he always had two tumblers and a bottle of Pappy Van Winkle at the ready. We essentially raised a baby daughter and this book together from scratch at the same time — not unlike the coinciding of Jack "Bumby" Hemingway and *The Sun Also Rises* — and I will long remember this period with fierce poignancy.

Notes

Introduction

page

ix   *"Ernest Hemingway, America's"*: "Vanity Fair's Own Paper Dolls—No. 5," *Vanity Fair,* March 1934, 29.

      "The rejection slip": A. E. Hotchner, *Papa Hemingway* (New York: Random House, 1966), 57.

x   "The Sun Also Rises": Lorin Stein, interview with the author, January 28, 2013.

xi   *"Fitzgerald was"*: Charles Scribner III, interview with the author, March 11, 2014.

      "primitive modern idiom": Paul Rosenfeld, *The New Republic*, November 25, 1925, 22–23.

      trains bearing magazines: Literary editor Lewis Lapham says that his father—a Yale student in the 1920s—waited at the station for trains bearing the latest editions of the *Saturday Evening Post* with new Fitzgerald stories. By the time he was at Yale himself a few decades later, he and his fellow students were waiting at the station for the latest J. D. Salinger story in *The New Yorker.* Lewis Lapham, interview with the author, February 22, 2014.

xii   *"Scott gave the"*: Zelda Fitzgerald to Sara and Gerald Murphy, 1940, quoted in Honoria Donnelly, *Sara & Gerald: Villa America and After* (New York: Times Books, 1984), 150.

      "wanted very much": Archibald MacLeish, *Reflections* (Amherst: University of Massachusetts Press, 1986), 44.

xiii *"[He] wanted to be"*: Omitted passage from "Big Two-Hearted River" by Ernest Hemingway, quoted in Carlos Baker, *Ernest Hemingway: A Life Story* (New York: Charles Scribner's Sons, 1969), 132.

      "bitched" his writing: In "Birth of a New School," a chapter in *A Moveable Feast,* Hemingway would describe his chagrin at being disturbed at

work during those early years. Anyone who interfered with him at Close-rie could expect to be treated to this sort of boilerplate response: "You rotten son of a bitch what are you doing in here off your filthy beat?" Ernest Hemingway, *A Moveable Feast,* restored ed. (New York: Scribner, 2009), 170.

"family life [was]": Patrick Hemingway, interview with the author, July 30, 2014.

his wicked wit: Email from Valerie Hemingway to the author, May 26, 2015.

"If you knew": Joseph Dryer, interview with the author, May 16, 2014.

xiv   *"Limelight Kid":* Robert McAlmon, quoted in John Glassco, *Memoirs of Montparnasse* (New York: New York Review Books Classics, 2007), 43–44.

"He made men": Morley Callaghan, *That Summer in Paris: Memories of Tangled Friendships with Hemingway, Fitzgerald, and Some Others* (New York: Coward-McCann, 1963), 26.

"When he met": Valerie Hemingway, interview with the author, December 20, 2013.

xv   *"Hemingway's first novel":* Alfred Harcourt to Louis Bromfield, fall 1925, quoted in Ernest Hemingway to F. Scott Fitzgerald, December 31, 1925–January 1, 1926, reprinted in *The Letters of Ernest Hemingway,* vol. 2, *1923–1925,* ed. Albert Defazio III, Sandra Spanier, and Robert W. Trogdon (Cambridge: Cambridge University Press, 2013), 459. Bromfield apparently transcribed the contents of the Harcourt letter in a missive to Hemingway.

"I knew I": Hemingway, *A Moveable Feast,* 71.

"I would put": Ibid.

xvi   *"the country that":* Ernest Hemingway, *The Dangerous Summer* (New York: Touchstone/Simon & Schuster, 1997), 43.

"It is a": Ernest Hemingway to Jane Heap, ca. August 23, 1925, reprinted in Defazio, Spanier, and Trogdon, *Letters of Ernest Hemingway,* 2:383.

xvii   *"When I first":* Donald Ogden Stewart, *By a Stroke of Luck! An Autobiography* (New York: Paddington Press, 1975), 156.

"I'm writing a": Kathleen Cannell, "Scenes with a Hero," reprinted in *Hemingway and the* Sun *Set,* ed. Bertram D. Sarason (Washington, D.C.: NCR/Microcard Editions, 1972), 149.

"that kike Loeb": Baker, *Ernest Hemingway: A Life Story,* 154, citing an interview with Kathleen Cannell, October 13, 1963.

"But, of course": Cannell, "Scenes with a Hero," 150.

xviii   *"alcoholic nymphomaniac":* Ernest Hemingway, *Death in the Afternoon* (New York: Charles Scribner's Sons, 1932), 383.

"He had a": Patrick Hemingway, interview with the author, July 30, 2014.

"a lot of": Ernest Hemingway, *The Sun Also Rises,* early handwritten draft, item 193, Ernest Hemingway Collection, John F. Kennedy Presidential Library and Museum.

xix   *"later [became] known"*: Cannell, "Scenes with a Hero," 145.

eighteen translation markets: Email from Scribners representative to the author, April 25, 2014; *shocked:* Charles Scribner III, interview with the author, April 23, 2014.

"Everybody behaves badly": Ernest Hemingway, *The Sun Also Rises,* Hemingway Library ed. (New York: Scribner, 2014), 145.

1. Paris Is a Bitch

3   *"I want to"*: F. Scott Fitzgerald to Edmund Wilson, quoted in Edmund Wilson, *Classics and Commercials: A Literary Chronicle of the Forties* (New York: Farrar, Straus and Giroux, 1999), 110.

4   *"glorious faith in"*: Alice Hunt Sokoloff, *Hadley: The First Mrs. Hemingway* (New York: Dodd, Mead & Company, 1973), 19.

to be his "helper": For example, in one missive to Hemingway, Hadley writes: "I really value your ambition so much . . . I want to be your helper — not your hinderer — wouldn't for anything have your ambitions any different." Hadley Richardson to Ernest Hemingway, January, 13, 1921, quoted ibid., 21–22.

"the kind of": F. Scott Fitzgerald, *The Last Tycoon* (New York: Penguin Classics, 2010), 23.

fallen victim to shelling: In a droll commentary on the unglamorous incurring of his wounds, Hemingway depicts the hero of his second novel, *A Farewell to Arms,* getting shelled while eating a piece of cheese.

"227 marks": "Had 227 Wounds, but Is Looking for Job," *New York Sun,* January 22, 1919, reprinted in *Conversations with Ernest Hemingway,* ed. Matthew J. Bruccoli (Jackson: University Press of Mississippi, 1986), 1.

"Men loved him": Agnes von Kurowsky, quoted in Baker, *Ernest Hemingway: A Life Story,* 49.

"the next best": Ernest Hemingway to his family, August 18, 1918, reprinted in *The Letters of Ernest Hemingway,* vol. 1, *1907–1922,* ed. Sandra Spanier and Robert W. Trogdon (Cambridge: Cambridge University Press, 2011), 130.

5   *"It'll be wonderful"*: Hadley Richardson to Ernest Hemingway, August 18, 1921, quoted in Sokoloff, *Hadley,* 27–28.

"eliminated everything": Hadley Hemingway to Ernest Hemingway, date

unspecified but said to be in response to an April 1921 missive from Ernest Hemingway, quoted in Raymond Carver, "Coming of Age; Going to Pieces," *New York Times,* November 17, 1985.

a meager living: According to Carlos Baker (*Ernest Hemingway: A Life Story,* 76), Hemingway was paid $40 a month, or around $530 today.

"Cicero is a": Ernest Hemingway, quoted ibid., 21.

6   *"awful dope":* Ernest Hemingway to Maxwell Perkins, May 30, 1942, quoted ibid., 38.

"I saw some": Donald St. John, "Interview with Hemingway's 'Bill Gorton,'" *Connecticut Review* 1, no. 2 (1968), and 3, no. 1 (1969), reprinted in Sarason, *Hemingway and the* Sun *Set,* 174–75.

hundred rejection slips: Malcolm Cowley, *A Second Flowering: Works and Days of the Lost Generation* (New York: Viking Press, 1973), 22.

stories of fishing and hunting: Hadley Richardson Hemingway Mowrer to Carlos Baker, quoted in Gioia Diliberto, *Paris Without End: The True Story of Hemingway's First Wife* (New York: Harper Perennial, 2011), 133. Hemingway's starter novel may have been fairly romantic, at least according to its author: decades later, in *A Moveable Feast,* Hemingway cast a gauzy glow around the ill-fated work, stating that he had written it when he had the "lyric facility of boyhood" (*A Moveable Feast,* 71). A maddeningly vague clue about the book's possible plot resides in a 1921 letter in which Hemingway informed Hadley that the novel contained "real people, talking and saying what they think." Quoted in Peter Griffin, *Along with Youth: Hemingway, The Early Years* (Oxford: Oxford University Press, 1987), 169.

"all treading on": Hadley Richardson to Ernest Hemingway, undated but estimated late August 1921, Ernest Hemingway Collection, John F. Kennedy Library and Museum. There is no way of ascertaining the exact content of Hemingway's letters to Hadley from this period. She is said to have burned them following the collapse of their marriage. Diliberto, *Paris Without End,* xix. The volume of letters between the two would likely have been sizable: Hadley alone wrote nearly two hundred letters to Hemingway between November 1920 and early September 1921, which Hemingway kept. Sandra Spanier, "General Editor's Introduction to the Edition," in Spanier and Trogdon, *Letters of Ernest Hemingway,* 1:xxiii–xxiv.

7   *"hulky, bulky something":* Hadley Hemingway Mowrer, quoted in Baker, *Ernest Hemingway: A Life Story,* 75.

"bold penniless dash": Hadley Richardson to Ernest Hemingway, January 13, 1921, quoted in Sokoloff, *Hadley,* 21.

"my sweet little": Hadley Richardson to Ernest Hemingway, April 1, 1921, quoted ibid., 25.

$2,000 to $3,000: In 1921 dollars, $3,000 would have amounted to roughly $40,000 today.

"filthy lucre": Ernest Hemingway, quoted in Baker, *Ernest Hemingway: A Life Story,* 78.

"There are those": St. John, "Interview with Hemingway's 'Bill Gorton,'" 160.

8   *"on the side":* Ernest Hemingway to Grace Quinlan, July 21, 1921, quoted in Spanier and Trogdon, *Letters of Ernest Hemingway,* 1:290.

"Think of how": Hadley Richardson to Ernest Hemingway, undated, quoted in Sokoloff, *Hadley,* 27–28.

"the best things": Hadley Richardson to Ernest Hemingway, April 1921, quoted in Carver, "Coming of Age."

"strangely poor": Hemingway, *A Moveable Feast,* 60.

9   *polite, quiet attentiveness:* According to Charles Fenton, who interviewed former Chicago friends and colleagues of Hemingway's for his 1954 landmark biography of Hemingway. See Charles Fenton, *The Apprenticeship of Ernest Hemingway: The Early Years* (New York: Viking, 1965), 103–4.

"never spoke of": Robert Emmett Ginna, "Life in the Afternoon," *Esquire,* February 1962, reprinted in Bruccoli, *Conversations with Ernest Hemingway,* 155.

"Thanks for introducing": Fenton, *Apprenticeship of Ernest Hemingway,* 104.

"knew Hem was": St. John, "Interview with Hemingway's 'Bill Gorton,'" 179.

"At this point": Y. K. Smith to Donald St. John, excerpted ibid., 179.

"thoroughly hostile": Fenton, *Apprenticeship of Ernest Hemingway,* 104.

"You couldn't let": Ibid.

"That's foolish": Hadley Richardson to Ernest Hemingway, date unidentified, quoted in Sokoloff, *Hadley,* 41.

10   *"I saw him":* Sylvia Beach, *Shakespeare and Company* (Lincoln: University of Nebraska Press, 1980), 30.

"Sherwood's deference": Ibid., 31.

"You see, dear friend": Sherwood Anderson to Gertrude Stein, spring 1923, reprinted in *Letters of Sherwood Anderson,* ed. Howard Mumford Jones (New York: Kraus Reprint Co., 1969), 95.

11   *"I remember his":* Sherwood Anderson, *Sherwood Anderson's Memoirs* (New York: Harcourt, Brace, 1942), 473.

12   *twelve francs a day:* Ernest Hemingway, "Living on $1,000 a Year in Paris," *Toronto Star Weekly,* February 4, 1922, reprinted in *Ernest*

Hemingway: Dateline: Toronto: The Complete Toronto Star Dispatches, 1920–1924, ed. William White (New York: Charles Scribner's Sons, 1985), 88.

"Vicki Baum's Grand Hotel": Robert McAlmon, *Being Geniuses Together, 1920–1930,* rev. with supplementary chapters and an afterword by Kay Boyle (San Francisco: North Point Press, 1984), 31.

expat "inmates": Hemingway, *A Moveable Feast,* 83.

"We've been walking": Ernest Hemingway to Sherwood Anderson, ca. December 23, 1921, reprinted in Spanier and Trogdon, *Letters of Ernest Hemingway,* 1:313.

"I do not": Ernest Hemingway, "Notes and Fragments," version two of *A Moveable Feast,* item 186, Ernest Hemingway Collection, John F. Kennedy Presidential Library and Museum.

"I watched to": Hemingway, *A Moveable Feast,* 74.

"marvelous strange city": Hadley Hemingway, interview with Alice Sokoloff, November 27, 1971, quoted in Sokoloff, *Hadley,* 43.

13   *unfathomably affordable:* On the affordability of Paris life during this period, lawyer turned expatriate poet and Hemingway friend Archibald MacLeish would later memorably describe the situation: "We were beneficiaries of the inflation that was murdering the French." He added, "You could practically count on the franc to drop two points against the dollar every month," leaving Americans with dollars "two points better off" every thirty days. MacLeish, *Reflections,* 26.

poules: The literal translation of *poule* is "hen." A particularly expensive prostitute was amusingly called *une poule deluxe.*

"treated like a": Alfred Kreymborg, *Troubadour: An Autobiography* (New York: Boni and Liveright, 1925), 372.

Editors back home: Press services with Paris bureaus during the 1920s included Reuters, the United Press, and the Associated Press; local papers also established offices, including the *Philadelphia Ledger,* the *Chicago Tribune,* and the *Brooklyn Eagle.* The *Paris Herald* was especially prone to hiring journalists who were also aspiring novelists.

"Around the Studios": William Wiser, *The Crazy Years: Paris in the Twenties* (New York: Thames and Hudson, 1983), 24.

"Paris is, perhaps": "All Paris for the Asking: When to Come, What to See, Where to Conquer," *Vogue,* January 1, 1925, 68. *Vogue's* information bureau was located in the magazine's Paris office at 2 rue Édouard VII; readers were invited to stop by if "there is anything they want in Paris or out of Paris that they are unable to find." Ibid., 100

14   *"Paris is the":* Ernest Hemingway, "The Mecca of Fakers," *Toronto Daily Star,* March 25, 1922.

"The scum of": Ernest Hemingway, "American Bohemians in Paris," *Toronto Star Weekly,* March 25, 1922.

"sour-faced, scurvy swine": McAlmon, *Being Geniuses Together,* 38.

15   *"Many [expats]"*: Jimmie Charters, *This Must Be the Place: Memoirs of Montparnasse,* ed. Hugh Ford (New York: Collier, 1989), 102.

suicidal patron: Ibid., 119.

"dinners, soirees, poets": Hart Crane, postcard to a friend, quoted in Tony Allan, *Americans in Paris* (Chicago: Contemporary Books, 1977), 95.

Paris was like cocaine: Malcolm Cowley to Harold Loeb, July 14, 1922, Broom Correspondence of Harold Loeb, Princeton University Library.

"[At first] I": McAlmon, *Being Geniuses Together,* 114.

16   *"the town best"*: Hemingway, *A Moveable Feast,* 156.

"Your hair, Henri!": Ernest Hemingway, "Wives Buy Clothes for French Husbands," *Toronto Star Weekly,* March 11, 1922.

"drifting along in": Ernest Hemingway, "Paris Is Full of Russians," *Toronto Daily Star,* February 25, 1922.

17   *"They are nearly"*: Hemingway, "American Bohemians in Paris."

2. Storming Olympus

19   *"He was an"*: Hearst correspondent Basil Swoon to Charles Fenton, quoted in Fenton, *Apprenticeship of Ernest Hemingway,* 143.

"some sort of": *New York Tribune* reporter Wilbur Forrest to Charles Fenton, quoted ibid., 144.

an exceptional life ahead: Biographer Charles Fenton tracked down a handful of Hemingway's former press corps colleagues, who told him that Hemingway was deemed an alien in their world and often recognized as exceptional. Ibid., 143.

"I've been earning": Ernest Hemingway to Sherwood Anderson, ca. December 23, 1921, reprinted in Spanier and Trogdon, *Letters of Ernest Hemingway,* 1:313.

worn through his: Ernest Hemingway to Howell G. Jenkins, March 20, 1922, reprinted ibid., 334.

"On the Star": George Plimpton, "The Art of Fiction: Ernest Hemingway," *Paris Review* 18 (Spring 1958): 70.

"This goddam newspaper": Ernest Hemingway to Sherwood Anderson, March 8, 1922, reprinted in Spanier and Trogdon, *Letters of Ernest Hemingway,* 1:331.

20   *"slow, rain-soaked"*: Ernest Hemingway, "A Silent, Ghastly Procession,"

Toronto Daily Star, October 20, 1922; *plodding along:* Ernest Hemingway, "Refugees from Thrace," *Toronto Daily Star,* November 14, 1922.

"black-shirted, knife-carrying": Ernest Hemingway, "Italy's Blackshirts," *Toronto Star Weekly,* June 24, 1922.

"Europe's Prize Bluffer": Ernest Hemingway, "Mussolini, Europe's Prize Bluffer," *Toronto Daily Star,* January 27, 1923.

"launching a flock": Ernest Hemingway to Sherwood Anderson, ca. December 23, 1921, reprinted in Spanier and Trogdon, *Letters of Ernest Hemingway,* 1:313.

21   *literary gods of Olympus:* Cowley, *A Second Flowering,* 54.

"the Crowd": Beach, *Shakespeare and Company,* 25. Beach actually borrowed the term from expat writer and publisher Robert McAlmon, but she uses the phrase throughout her memoir to describe the inner circle of expat creative figures in 1920s Paris.

"sort of royalty": F. Scott Fitzgerald, "Babylon Revisited," in *Babylon Revisited and Other Short Stories* (New York: Simon & Schuster, 2008), 213.

"didn't count": Harold Stearns, *Confessions of a Harvard Man: Paris and New York in the 1920s & 30s* (Santa Barbara: Paget Press, 1984), 209.

declined to introduce: Beach recalled the George Moore–James Joyce incident with sheepish amusement in her memoir *Shakespeare and Company.* She noted that her protectiveness of Joyce in this case had been a "mistake" and that the two writers eventually managed to meet up in London. Moore magnamiously "didn't hold the incident in the bookshop against me," she added. Beach, *Shakespeare and Company,* 72–73.

"Who is your": Gertrude Stein, *The Autobiography of Alice B. Toklas* (New York: Vintage Books, 1990), 13. Stein explained, "The idea was that anybody could come but for form's sake and in Paris you have to have a formula, everybody was supposed to be able to mention the name of somebody who had told them about it."

"To be 'done'": Beach, *Shakespeare and Company,* 112. Hemingway would eventually be among those thus anointed: Man Ray, amusingly dubbed the Crowd's "court photographer" by one biographer, took a formal portrait of him in August 1923.

largely an American movement: For many, the Americans' insularity went beyond the creative realm. "I am puzzled by the persistence with which these fluently French-speaking English and American artists of the quarter for the most part kept to themselves," observed English art critic Clive Bell. "Some of them had French mistresses—kept mistresses; but very few had French friends." Allan, *Americans in Paris,* 7.

"America in Europe": Kreymborg, *Troubadour,* 364.

"I never met": MacLeish, *Reflections,* 66.

22   *"There was no":* McAlmon, *Being Geniuses Together,* 336.

"Fame was what": Archibald MacLeish, "Years of the Dog" (1948), reprinted in *Archibald MacLeish: Collected Poems, 1917–1982* (New York: Mariner Books, 1985), 376.

"In 1922 it burst": Janet Flanner, introduction to *Paris Was Yesterday: 1925–1939* (New York: Harvest/HBJ, 1988), x.

"just when Joyce": John Chamberlain, "Books of the Times," *New York Times,* January 25, 1934.

23   *"a young fellow":* Sherwood Anderson to Lewis Galantière, November 28, 1921, in Jones, *Letters of Sherwood Anderson,* 82.

box a few rounds: Hadley's recollection of the boxing match is recounted in Sokoloff, *Hadley,* 44–45. Hemingway would soon become known for subjecting prospective friends and acquaintances to bravery-proving tests such as these, whether those rites of passage entailed impromptu boxing sessions, being shamed into staring down ornery bulls in Spanish bullrings, or even indulging in little knife rituals. Maria Cooper Janis — daughter of actor Gary Cooper, with whom Hemingway had a decades-long friendship — recalled a certain dinner-table ritual that involved putting "your hand . . . on the table and he'd take a hunting knife and throw the knife and hopefully it would hit between the fingers." Then they upped the ante: in the next round the knife was aimed at the lap area. Luckily, blood was never drawn, she recalled. Maria Cooper Janis, interview with the author, May 20, 2014.

"the acknowledged leader": Beach, *Shakespeare and Company,* 26.

willing mentors: Both Stein and Pound "encouraged younger artists to despise the old forms and the old stuff, to rebel, break away and dare," as journalist Lincoln Steffens later put it. Lincoln Steffens, *The Autobiography of Lincoln Steffens* (Berkeley: Heyday Books, 2005), 833.

"the leading review": Nicolas Joost, *Scofield Thayer and* The Dial: *An Illustrated History* (Carbondale: Southern Illinois University Press, 1964), 47. Pound served as a commissioned agent from early 1920 until April 1923, after which point he remained a contributor to the magazine. Ibid., 166.

24   *seventeen cups of tea:* Sokoloff, *Hadley,* 49.

"Don't be viewy": For these and other tenets of Pound's doctrine, see Ezra Pound, "A Few Don'ts by an Imagiste," March 1913, *Poetry* magazine, reprinted on the website of the Poetry Foundation, October 30, 2005, http://www.poetryfoundation.org/poetrymagazine/article/335.

"in full": Ezra Pound, *How to Read/The Serious Artist,* reprinted in Ezra Pound, *Literary Essays of Ezra Pound* (New York: New Directions Publishing, 1968), 38.

25   *Pound parody:* The anecdote was relayed by Lewis Galantière to Heming-

way biographer Carlos Baker in a March 1963 interview and described in Baker, *Ernest Hemingway: A Life Story,* 86.

"Ernest was always": Flanner, introduction to *Paris Was Yesterday,* xviii.

"risk his dignity": Ernest Hemingway to Sherwood Anderson, March 9, 1922, reprinted in Spanier and Trogdon, *Letters of Ernest Hemingway,* 1:331.

"an American writer": Sherwood Anderson to Gertrude Stein, December 3, 1921, reprinted in Jones, *Letters of Sherwood Anderson,* 85.

26 *"little piece of"*: Sokoloff, *Hadley,* 50.

"I think about": Ibid.

"Sumerian monument": The nickname came courtesty of editor Robert McAlmon. Hemingway dubbed Stein "the great god Buddha" (according to Hadley Hemingway, quoted in Sokoloff, *Hadley,* 50), and Harold Stearns, onetime editor of *The Dial* and eventual fodder for a character in *The Sun Also Rises,* amusingly referred to Stein as "the Presence." Stearns, *Confessions of a Harvard Man,* 151.

one of her favorite chairs: Stein, *Autobiography of Alice B. Toklas,* 202. Speaking of herself in the third person, Stein added that she first met Pound at a dinner party and "liked him but did not find him amusing. She said he was a village explainer, excellent if you were a village, but if you were not, not." Ibid., 200.

"steerage" motif: Hemingway, *A Moveable Feast,* 26. Poet John Glassco described Stein as a "rhomboidal woman dressed in a floor-length gown apparently made of some kind of burlap." Quoted in Anton Gill, *Art Lover: A Biography of Peggy Guggenheim* (New York: Harper Perennial, 2003), 96. That said, the gown apparently hadn't been carelessly stitched together. Journalist Lincoln Steffens claimed that at least one of Stein's rough-hewn ensembles had actually been carefully, thoughtfully constructed by a great designer: "Yvonne Davidson, one of the most creative of the famous French *couturières* of the day, made for Gertrude Stein, at her behest, a great flowing fat gown to wear" (*Autobiography of Lincoln Steffens,* 834).

"would come to": Beach, *Shakespeare and Company,* 29.

"monologue, and pontificate": McAlmon, *Being Geniuses Together,* 205.

"Don't frighten her": Ibid., 228–29.

"Megalomaniac": Ibid., 206.

"Nobody has done": Ibid., 228.

27 *"the Jews have"*: Ibid.

"I may say": Stein, *Autobiography of Alice B. Toklas,* 5.

"wife-proof technique": Beach, *Shakespeare and Company*, 31. Beach claimed that women who were not wives were welcome at Stein's chats, although other testimony counters this assertion. Admission to these chats was apparently administered on a case-by-case basis. Writer Kay Boyle recalled being relegated to the wife stash during a visit to Stein's salon later in the 1920s. Brought along by a male friend, she was usurped by Alice Toklas, who "immediately started to talk of cooking, and to exchange recipes." Apparently Boyle had not favorably impressed either Toklas or Stein; her escort, she reported, later informed her that Stein had banned her from returning, having decided that Boyle was "as incurably middle-class as Ernest Hemingway." McAlmon, *Being Geniuses Together,* 295–96. Pablo Picasso's girlfriend Françoise Gilot, by contrast, claimed that on her first visit, not only was she granted an audience with Stein, but also Picasso sat apart from the two women while they talked. Françoise Gilot and Carlton Lake, *Life with Picasso* (New York: McGraw-Hill, 1964), 68–71.

a private museum: The apartment at 27 rue de Fleurus where Stein lived with Toklas was a lavish shrine to modern art. Janet Flanner, once instructed by Stein in the 1930s to tally the collection, estimated that it then included "one hundred and thirty-one canvases, including five Picassos . . . hung in the china closet." The "salon alone contain[ed] four major masterpieces," including a Cézanne and Picasso's portrait of Stein, "and nineteen smaller Picassos." Janet Flanner, "Letter from Paris" (1938), reprinted in Flanner, *Paris Was Yesterday,* 187. Picasso and Matisse themselves, among countless other artists of many nationalities, had been frequent Stein guests—although after the war more writers than artists turned up on her doorstep.

"rather foreign looking": Stein, *Autobiography of Alice B. Toklas,* 212.

"Rose is": Gertrude Stein, "Sacred Emily" (1913), reprinted in Gertrude Stein, *Geography and Plays* (Madison: University of Wisconsin Press, 2012), 187.

few people felt neutral: "Most of us balk at her soporific rigmaroles, her echolaliac incantations, her half-witted-sounding catalogues of numbers," opined Edmund Wilson, then a highly influential critic, about Stein's writing style. Fellow salon hostess and writer Natalie Barney wanted to believe that "Stein's brain is an innovation mill," but instead Barney suspected that Stein had merely imposed on herself "the infirmity of the stutterer." Natalie Clifford Barney, *Adventures of the Mind* (New York: University Press, 1992). To newspaper editors, her writing style sometimes made great fodder for caricature. One newspaper—reporting the news of Stein's arrival for an American tour—ran the headline: GERTY GERTY STEIN STEIN IS BACK HOME BACK HOME. Allan, *Americans in Paris,* 66. Stein, of course, had her staunch admirers as well. Lincoln Steffens thought of her "not only as a genius, but as a wise woman" and a prophetess who "gave you glimpses of what a Buddha can see by sitting still and quietly looking" (*Autobiography of Lincoln Steffens,* 834). Janet Flanner reported back to her *New Yorker* readers that "no American writer is taken more seriously than Miss Stein by the Paris modernists" (*Paris Was Yesterday,* 9).

28   *fewer than seventy-five:* According to Tony Allan, Stein's first book sold a mere seventy-three copies during the first eighteen months (*Americans in Paris,* 64). Her only best-seller — *The Autobiography of Alice B. Toklas* — wasn't published until 1933 and was written in traditional prose.

"nobody's idea of ": Ibid.

"You musn't write": Hemingway, *A Moveable Feast,* 25. The story was indeed so overtly sexual — for its time, anyway — that Hemingway's friend Bill Smith recalled "kidding him about it and saying your next story should be called 'Even Further up in Michigan.'" St. John, "Interview with Hemingway's 'Bill Gorton,'" 175.

"There is a": Stein, *Autobiography of Alice B. Toklas,* 213.

"cutting up the": Ibid., 90.

"Cézanne came closer": Gilot and Lake, *Life with Picasso,* 284.

"I was learning": Hemingway, *A Moveable Feast,* 23.

29   *"She took little":* Beach, *Shakespeare and Company,* 28.

"weakness" for him: Stein, *Autobiography of Alice B. Toklas,* 216.

"Gertrude Stein and": Ernest Hemingway to Sherwood Anderson, March 9, 1922, reprinted in Spanier and Trogdon, *Letters of Ernest Hemingway,* 1:330.

"please, without speaking": Sokoloff, *Hadley,* 48.

reading something behind: Ibid., 51.

30   *"The people that go":* Ernest Hemingway, "Wild Night Music of Paris," *Toronto Star Weekly,* March 25, 1922.

"Pound thinks I'm": Ernest Hemingway to Sherwood Anderson, March 9, 1922, reprinted in Spanier and Trogdon, *Letters of Ernest Hemingway,* 1:331.

Thayer did not: Joost, *Scofield Thayer and* The Dial, 248.

"Isn't writing": Ernest Hemingway to Gertrude Stein and Alice B. Toklas, August 15, 1924, reprinted in Defazio, Spanier, and Trogdon, *Letters of Ernest Hemingway,* 2:141.

many of her manuscripts: Hemingway, *A Moveable Feast,* 26.

31   *"Liz liked Jim":* Ernest Hemingway, "Up in Michigan," reprinted in *The Complete Short Stories of Ernest Hemingway* (New York: Scribner, 2003), 59.

"Down through the": Ernest Hemingway, unpublished fragment (1923),

reprinted in Michael Reynolds, *Hemingway: The Paris Years* (New York: W. W. Norton, 1999), 38.

"all her unpublished": Stein, *Autobiography of Alice B. Toklas,* 197.

knew he *could get:* As Hemingway scholar H. R. Stoneback put it: "Hemingway knew that he wanted commercial success. Stein wanted it, but you're not going to get it with her stuff. She was a crucial part of modernism, but do you pick up [her books] for pleasure? And Pound—well, he's a poet. He knows he's not going to sell twenty thousand copies of a Canto." H. R. Stoneback, interview with the author, June 2, 2014.

"rhythm and tones": Hadley Hemingway to Ernest Hemingway, 1921, quoted in Carver, "Coming of Age."

3. Fortuitous Disasters

33   *"the end of"*: Ernest Hemingway, "The Greek Revolt," *Toronto Daily Star,* November 3, 1922, reprinted in White, *Ernest Hemingway: Dateline: Toronto,* 244.

"dawned upon me": Steffens, *Autobiography of Lincoln Steffens,* 834.

"KEMAL INSWARDS UNBURNED": Fenton, *Apprenticeship of Ernest Hemingway,* 187.

"vivid, detailed picture": Steffens, *Autobiography of Lincoln Steffens,* 834.

34   *"I asked him"*: Ibid.

"He could": Ibid.

"travelly": Cable from Ernest Hemingway to Hadley Hemingway, November 25, 1922, reprinted in Spanier and Trogdon, *Letters of Ernest Hemingway,* 1:369.

"singing high praises": This was what Hadley Hemingway later told biographer Charles Fenton. Fenton, *Apprenticeship of Ernest Hemingway,* 196. Yet the exact motive has long been a source of debate. Some accounts state that Hemingway had instructed her to send all his work down so he could share it with Steffens, and not trusting the mails, she decided to deliver it personally. But in *A Moveable Feast,* Hemingway laid the blame at Hadley's feet, claiming that she had lugged the manuscripts to Lausanne "as a surprise . . . so I could work on them on our holidays in the mountains" (*A Moveable Feast,* 69); he mentions no letters praising Steffens or asking her to bring the material. Steffens may have asked Hadley himself: on November 28, 1922, Hemingway informed Hadley, "Steffens wrote you a letter." If so, that letter may have contained such a request—but Steffens makes no mention of it in his autobiography, and the Steffens-to-Hadley letter itself is believed to have gone missing. Hadley biographer Gioia Diliberto states that "Steffens's letter to Hadley hasn't survived" (*Paris Without End,* 129). What has especially baffled biographers is Hadley's decision

to bring the carbon copies as well, although Diliberto points out that such reasoning "made some sense": if Hemingway was to make changes to the various works, he would want to make those changes in the copies as well (*Paris Without End,* 130).

"She had cried": Hemingway, *A Moveable Feast,* 70.

35   *"I remember what"*: Ibid. The timing of this trip to Paris is unclear. It has been widely assumed that it took place immediately after Hadley's pitiful arrival in Lausanne, although a January 23, 1923, letter from Hemingway to Ezra Pound indicates that the trip took place several weeks later: "I went up to Paris last week to see what was left." Ernest Hemingway to Ezra Pound, reprinted in Defazio, Spanier, and Trogdon, *Letters of Ernest Hemingway,* 2:6. The mysterious activity to which Hemingway alludes may have been nothing terribly tawdry. If Hemingway's fictionalized account of the theft and his return trip to Paris to confirm the total loss in his posthumously published short story "The Strange Country" can be trusted as an accurate representation of what actually happened, then Hemingway merely crawled into his bed and lay there cradling two pillows in despair. After that, the bereaved writer character relates what happened with the apartment building's unwashed concierge, who sobs on his chest in commiseration and then sends him out to dinner at a local café. Ernest Hemingway, "The Strange Country," in *Complete Short Stories,* 648–49. An editor's note explains that "'The Strange Country' comprises four chapters of an uncompleted novel that Hemingway worked on at intervals in 1946–1947 and 1950–1951. These scenes represent preliminary material for an early version of [Hemingway's novel] *Islands in the Stream,* which was published posthumously in 1970" (*Complete Short Stories,* 605). An editor's endnote in *The Sun Also Rises* identifies "The Strange Country" as a "posthumously published short story." Hemingway, *The Sun Also Rises,* 287.

"No amount of": Fenton, *Apprenticeship of Ernest Hemingway,* 196.

"the Great Train Robbery": St. John, "Interview with Hemingway's 'Bill Gorton,'" 175.

"lovely and loyal": Ernest Hemingway, introduction to *A Hemingway Check List,* ed. Lee Samuels (New York: Charles Scribner's Sons, 1951), 6.

"she had not": Hotchner, *Papa Hemingway,* 160.

"Das Kapital": Hemingway, introduction to Samuels, *A Hemingway Check List,* 6. In January 1923, Hemingway indicated to Ezra Pound that not even this material still existed: all that he had been able to recover at that point was "three pencil drafts of a bum poem," some correspondence, and a few journalism carbons. Ernest Hemingway to Ezra Pound, January 23, 1923, reprinted in Defazio, Spanier, and Trogdon, *Letters of Ernest Hemingway,* 2:6.

"in a drawer": Hemingway, *A Moveable Feast,* 69.

"I suppose you": Ernest Hemingway to Ezra Pound, January 23, 1923, reprinted in Defazio, Spanier, and Trogdon, *Letters of Ernest Hemingway*, 2:6.

"act of Gawd": Ezra Pound, undated reply, excerpted in *Ernest Hemingway: Selected Letters, 1917–1961*, ed. Carlos Baker (New York: Scribner, 2003), 77.

"it was probably": Hemingway, *A Moveable Feast*, 70. At least one of his contemporaries deemed the loss of Hemingway's "Juvenilia" to be a fortuitous event; some experts today agree. The theft was "the best thing that ever happened to him," states Hemingway Society co-founder Allen Josephs (interview with the author, April 1, 2014). Hemingway scholar H. R. Stoneback believes that if the material hadn't been lost, Hemingway's early work "would all look like 'My Old Man,' which really sounds like Sherwood Anderson" (interview with the author, June 2, 2014).

36   *"I know what"*: Ernest Hemingway to Ezra Pound, November 8, 1922, reprinted in Spanier and Trogdon, *Letters of Ernest Hemingway*, 1:369.

"I could see already": Hemingway, "The Strange Country," 650.

He was working hard: Ernest Hemingway to Gertrude Stein, February 18, 1923, reprinted in Defazio, Spanier, and Trogdon, *Letters of Ernest Hemingway*, 2:11.

happiest in bed: Biographer Carlos Baker quotes from an "undated fragment on sheets" but designates it a "ca. Feb., 1923" Rapallo writing (*Ernest Hemingway: A Life Story*, 106, 580). The fragment is also excerpted in Reynolds, *Hemingway: The Paris Years*, 104.

"He came to": Stein, *Autobiography of Alice B. Toklas*, 213.

37   *relayed her amusement*: Sokoloff, *Hadley*, 61.

salary of $125: In 1923 dollars, $125 a week is equal to around $1,700 today —a salary of $88,000 a year.

"I want, like": Ernest Hemingway to Edward O'Brien, May 21, 1923, reprinted in Defazio, Spanier, and Trogdon, *Letters of Ernest Hemingway*, 2:21. O'Brien, the editor of *The Best Short Stories* anthologies, published annually, obliged Hemingway's wish to "get published" by including "My Old Man" in *The Best Short Stories of 1923*.

"who seem not": McAlmon published an announcement detailing the press's mission in the expat publication the *transatlantic review*, which Sylvia Beach reproduced in her memoir. He added: "Three hundred only of each book will be printed. These books are published simply because they are written, and we like them well enough to get them out." Beach, *Shakespeare and Company*, 130–31.

literary luminaries: There were also less lofty names associated with Contact Publishing, and some of McAlmon's authors were found via admittedly casual means. According to Sylvia Beach, "manuscripts were submitted to McAlmon at the Dôme Café, and he told me that he discovered most of his writers at one café or another." Ibid., 132.

"small-boy, tough-guy swagger": McAlmon, *Being Geniuses Together,* 157.

Like Pound, McAlmon: The Kansas-born McAlmon had a reputation on two continents for being, as writer Kay Boyle put it, "wild and daring and as hard as nails." Ibid., 23. He was, Sylvia Beach recalled, "certainly the most popular member of the Crowd . . . [W]hatever café or bar McAlmon patronized at the moment was the one where you saw everybody" (*Shakespeare and Company,* 403).

"When Bob McAlmon": Callaghan, *That Summer in Paris,* 132.

a British heiress: McAlmon's wife was Winifred Ellerman, a poet and novelist who wrote under the pen name "Bryher." She was the daughter of a wealthy shipping magnate, Sir John Ellerman. Like McAlmon, she was homosexual; it was well known that she had a long-term relationship with the poet H.D. (Hilda Doolittle). Another source of McAlmon's income, at least according to expat writer John Dos Passos, was writing "smutty poems" for a German magazine called *Der Querschnitt.* John Dos Passos, *The Best Times* (New York: Signet Books, 1968), 163.

38 *"an older person"*: McAlmon, *Being Geniuses Together,* 158.

"given us the": Ernest Hemingway to Ezra Pound, March 10, 1923, reprinted in Defazio, Spanier, and Trogdon, *Letters of Ernest Hemingway,* 2:14.

"sneers and open": Callaghan, *That Summer in Paris,* 81; *universally liked:* Karen L. Rood, "William Bird," in *Dictionary of Literary Biography,* vol. 4, *American Writers in Paris, 1920–1939,* ed. Karen Lane Rood (Detroit: Bruccoli Clark, 1980), 39.

"I called [it]": Alice B. Toklas, *What Is Remembered* (New York: Holt, Rinehart and Winston, 1963), 70–71.

39 *"The first matador"*: Ernest Hemingway, *in our time* (Paris: Three Mountains Press, 1924), chap. 2.

"Beery-poppa": McAlmon, *Being Geniuses Together,* 160.

"He tenderly explained": Ibid.

"in hysteria: Ibid., 161.

40 *"It's a great"*: Ernest Hemingway to William Horne, July 17–18, 1923, reprinted in Defazio, Spanier, and Trogdon, *Letters of Ernest Hemingway,* 2:36.

an instant expert: Bill Bird to Carlos Baker, June 1962, quoted in Baker, *Ernest Hemingway: A Life Story,* 110.

"If there's ever": Ernest Hemingway to Clarence Hemingway, June 20, 1923,

reprinted in Defazio, Spanier, and Trogdon, *Letters of Ernest Hemingway,* 2:24.

he insulted him: Bill Bird told Carlos Baker that Hemingway was actually "outrageously insulting" in a June 1962 interview, quoted in Baker, *Ernest Hemingway: A Life Story,* 111. Others from the Paris Crowd would also voice indignation over Hemingway's reported treatment of McAlmon. "All the bills were paid by Bob, of course," wrote Kay Boyle, "but when a choice of seats came up at a bullfight, Hem would . . . have to have the one good seat left, down by the ring, because he was 'studying the art of it,' while Bob[,] . . . not knowing anything, I suppose, about art in any shape or form, could just as well sit in the bleachers." She added that the Johnnie Walker scotch Hemingway consumed had also gone on McAlmon's tab. McAlmon, *Being Geniuses Together,* 313.

a poseur: Hemingway would write in his 1932 book *Death in the Afternoon* that McAlmon clearly believed that his love of bullfighting was feigned.

"If the writer": Hemingway, *Death in the Afternoon,* 192.

41   *near-literal translation:* Ernest Hemingway to F. Scott Fitzgerald, December 24, 1925, reprinted in Defazio, Spanier, and Trogdon, *Letters of Ernest Hemingway,* 2:455.

"drunk of a": Ibid.

"didnt think the": Ibid.

"Your ear is": Ibid.

Three Mountains Press: The three peaks referenced in the name of Bill Bird's publishing house were the three "mountains" of Paris: Sainte-Geneviève, Montparnasse, and Montmartre.

"uglyish wads of": Ford Madox Ford, quoted in Rood, "William Bird," 39. In Three Mountains' Quai d'Anjou printing headquarters, there was room for only the handpress and printer-editor himself, Sylvia Beach recalled, requiring Bird to take all meetings outside on the sidewalk (*Shakespeare and Company,* 132). Writer and editor Ford Madox Ford, who later shared this space — recalled that Bird stashed his printed books in a makeshift kitchen. Ford Madox Ford, *It Was the Nightingale* (Philadelphia: J. B. Lippincott, 1933), 322.

42   *teamed up with:* According to one source, Hemingway had played a role in making the Bird-Pound match. Bird had first mentioned his new press to Hemingway when they met while traveling to the Conferenza Internazionale Economica de Genova in April 1922, and "Hemingway suggested that Ezra Pound might allow Bird to print out part of a long poem he was writing. Bird went to see Pound, and Pound suggested instead that Bird publish a series of six books. As Bird wrote to one biographer in 1956, 'He said the thing to do was to have a series of books that went

together, and not just print things as they came along.'" Rood, "William Bird," 39–40. Bird later claimed that he, not McAlmon, was to have been Hemingway's first book publisher, but Hemingway had grown too impatient about being the final installment of the "inquest" series and prioritized giving material to McAlmon, who promised a quicker turnaround. Ibid., 40.

series of vignettes: Neither McAlmon nor Bird appears to have tried to talk Hemingway into writing a novel or other long-form work for these initial collaborations.

"We were in": Hemingway, *in our time,* chap. 4.

43   *"5 days of":* Ernest Hemingway to William Horne, July 17–18, 1923, reprinted in Defazio, Spanier, and Trogdon, *Letters of Ernest Hemingway,* 2:36.

"embroidering in the": Sokoloff, *Hadley,* 63.

"I like the": Ernest Hemingway to Robert McAlmon, August 5, 1923, reprinted in Defazio, Spanier, and Trogdon, *Letters of Ernest Hemingway,* 2:39.

44   *"It couldn't be":* Ernest Hemingway to Ezra Pound, ca. September 6–8, 1923, reprinted ibid., 45.

"He couldn't walk": Callaghan, *That Summer in Paris,* 26.

"I've discovered a": Ernest Hemingway, quoted in Baker, *Ernest Hemingway: A Life Story,* 121; *"Ezra Pound says":* Callaghan, *That Summer in Paris,* 30.

"I can still": Callaghan, *That Summer in Paris,* 26.

"driven to break": Ibid., 23.

"busy galloping around": Ibid., 25.

"piddling, just junk": Morley Callaghan, quoted in Fenton, *Apprenticeship of Ernest Hemingway,* 246.

45   *"greatly overworked":* Hadley Hemingway to Grace Hemingway, September 27, 1923, quoted in Sokoloff, *Hadley,* 63.

"You may save": Ernest Hemingway to Ezra Pound, ca. September 6, 1923, reprinted in Defazio, Spanier, and Trogdon, *Letters of Ernest Hemingway,* 2:46.

"hated all things": Kreymborg, *Troubadour,* 369; *"Tomato, Can":* Fenton, *Apprenticeship of Ernest Hemingway,* 246.

killed off ten years: According to biographer Carlos Baker, Hemingway reportedly made this remark to "the paper's girl reporter" Mary Lowrey (*Ernest Hemingway: A Life Story,* 119).

"kill my Tiny": Hadley Hemingway to Isabel Simmons, October 13, 1923, quoted in Sokoloff, *Hadley,* 67.

"go through the": Ernest Hemingway to Gertrude Stein and Alice B. Toklas, October 11, 1923, reprinted in Defazio, Spanier, and Trogdon, *Letters of Ernest Hemingway,* 2:54; *"utter contempt"*: Ernest Hemingway to Ezra Pound, October 13, 1923, reprinted ibid., 58.

named their seven-pound baby: Had the baby been a girl, Hemingway informed Sylvia Beach, she would have been named Sylvia. Ernest Hemingway to Sylvia Beach, November 6, 1923, box 22, Sylvia Beach Papers, Princeton University Library.

"As it includes": Hadley Hemingway to Grace Hemingway, October 5, 1923, quoted in Sokoloff, *Hadley,* 66.

"just when we": Hadley Hemingway to Isabel Simmons, October 13, 1923, quoted ibid., 67.

a shot stomach: Ernest Hemingway to Ezra Pound, October 13, 1923, reprinted in Defazio, Spanier, and Trogdon, *Letters of Ernest Hemingway,* 2:58.

a waking nightmare: Ernest Hemingway to Gertrude Stein and Alice B. Toklas, ibid., 54–55.

46 *"I'll get on"*: Ernest Hemingway to Sylvia Beach, November 6, 1923, box 22, Sylvia Beach Papers, Princeton University Library.

"dry inside his": Ernest Hemingway, sketch published fall 1923, quoted in Baker, *Ernest Hemingway: A Life Story,* 120.

revenge novel: For an account of this "abortive novel," see Fenton, *Apprenticeship of Ernest Hemingway,* 242. Charles Fenton, who interviewed some of Hemingway's *Star* colleagues from this period, writes that Hemingway "discussed on several occasions the possibilities of a satiric novel" about Hindmarsh and adds that Hemingway later discussed his reasoning behind abandoning the novel with another unnamed "Toronto colleague."

"too fussy": Hadley Hemingway to Sylvia Beach, November 1923, box 22, Sylvia Beach Papers, Princeton University Library.

"if it hadn't": Callaghan, *That Summer in Paris,* 22–23.

4. Let the Pressure Build

47 *"very gentle buzzing"*: Hadley Hemingway to Grace Hemingway, February 20, 1924, quoted in Sokoloff, *Hadley,* 69.

"The marble-topped tables": Hemingway, *A Moveable Feast,* 169.

"Nobody ever threw": MacLeish, *Reflections,* 26–27.

48 *"blind pig"*: Hemingway, *A Moveable Feast,* 81.

"You rotten son": Ibid., 170.

"marvelous": Cowley, *A Second Flowering,* 58.

"Burton Rascoe said": Ernest Hemingway to Ezra Pound, July 19, 1924, reprinted in Defazio, Spanier, and Trogdon, *Letters of Ernest Hemingway,* 2:135.

49   *"It was my"*: Hotchner, *Papa Hemingway,* 38.

Bumby slept: The baby-in-the-dresser-drawer rumor comes courtesy of Honoria Donnelly (née Murphy), daughter of expats Sara and Gerald Murphy, who were to become a vital presence in the Hemingways' lives the following year: "The Hemingways' son, John, or Bumby, I was told, had to sleep in a dresser drawer." Donnelly, *Sara & Gerald,* 15.

"The one who": Hemingway, *A Moveable Feast,* 42.

Hadley burst into: Sokoloff, *Hadley,* 73. Sokoloff reports that Hadley had become "self-concious" about her clothes but not to the point of accepting such gifts.

50   *"short-lived, alas!"*: Beach, *Shakespeare and Company,* 137.

transatlantic review: Lowercase titles were apparently something of a vogue among the literary set during this time, although Ford later claimed that he had "merely seen the name of a shop somewhere on the Boulevard without capital letters and had rather liked the effect." The fact that it coincided with the lowercase poetry of E. E. Cummings was a coincidence, Ford said, although he claimed that a "great sensation" was made of it: "We were suspected of beheading initial letters as if they had been kings." Ford, *It Was the Nightingale,* 324.

"I had never": McAlmon, *Being Geniuses Together,* 116.

"Oh Canada": Ernest Hemingway to Ezra Pound, December 9, 1923, reprinted in Defazio, Spanier, and Trogdon, *Letters of Ernest Hemingway,* 2:82.

shadowboxing: Ford actually recalled that Hemingway "shadowdanced," but that has usually been interpreted by biographers as shadowboxing. Ford, *It Was the Nightingale,* 323; *finest prose stylist:* Baker, *Ernest Hemingway: A Life Story,* 123.

wicked Hemingway parody: Ford would, in the decades to follow, be sent up in at least two Hemingway books, *The Sun Also Rises* and *A Moveable Feast,* once under a pseudonym and once under his own name; the latter is the far crueler of the two portrayals.

"the toast under": Rebecca West, quoted in Elizabeth Mahoney, "Radio Review: Ford Madox Ford and France," *The Guardian,* August 25, 2010.

51   *"He was always"*: Anderson, *Sherwood Anderson's Memoirs,* 479.

espouse his own genius: "On one occasion Ford assured me that he was a genius, that he was born of a family of geniuses and [raised] in the tradition of a genius," recalled Robert McAlmon (*Being Geniuses Together,* 116).

"Publishers and editors": Anderson, *Sherwood Anderson's Memoirs,* 479.

"Ford was blessed": Harold Loeb, *The Way It Was* (New York: Criterion Books, 1959), 203. Furthermore, Ford's asthma apparently made him almost impossible to understand even when he was telling the truth. Bartender and "father confessor" of the Left Bank, Jimmie Charters, recalled that once, while presenting a poetry award, "Ford made a speech of presentation that was completely unintelligible, sounding something like 'woof-woof and . . . aaaah . . . woof-woofus . . . who . . . whhhhhh . . . aaaaaah . . . whoof-whhhhhhhhhh!'" Charters, *This Must Be the Place,* 39.

"He described the": Anderson, *Sherwood Anderson's Memoirs,* 479–80.

lied about money: Hemingway, *A Moveable Feast,* 199.

"fouler . . . than the": Ibid., 201.

"He comes and": Stein, *Autobiography of Alice B. Toklas,* 220.

"I did not": Ford, *It Was the Nightingale,* 323.

52   *"a figure in":* Dos Passos, *The Best Times,* 172.

"I was finally": Hotchnher, *Papa Hemingway,* 57.

"That attitude": Baker, *Ernest Hemingway: A Life Story,* 126.

"I knew": Hemingway, *A Moveable Feast,* 71.

53   *"I would put":* Ibid.

"it was more": Beach, *Shakespeare and Company,* 137.

"Famished beginners": Kathleen Cannell, "Essay II on Ford Madox Ford," *Providence Sunday Journal,* September 20, 1964, reprinted in Sarason, *Hemingway and the* Sun *Set,* 263.

an amusing portrait: Sokoloff, *Hadley,* 72.

"had a shy": Loeb, *The Way It Was,* 190.

"poverty-stricken Bohemian": Ibid., 10.

54   *"Harold," he said:* Ibid., 18.

"seemed to burn": Ibid., 4. In 1912, $50,000 was the equivalent of around $1.2 million today.

"tended to repeat": Ibid., 6.

"disapproval of the": Harold Loeb, untitled essay, Broom Correspondence of Harold Loeb, Princeton University Library.

55   *"with a newly":* Loeb, *The Way It Was,* 229. Loeb was quick to point out that he was not a mega-rich Guggenheim, for he had blossomed on a poor-relation branch of the family tree, meaning that his mother Rose Guggenheim's "pearls were smaller than those of her sisters-in-law, her dresses less numerous, her horses not so thoroughly bred," as he put it. Ibid., 20. That said, according to one of her granddaughters, Rose still "slept in satin

sheets under a portrait of herself." Barbara Loeb Kennedy, interview with the author, May 7, 2014.

"spoiled man [who]": Susan Sandberg, interview with the author, May 30, 2014.

"no more personality": McAlmon, *Being Geniuses Together,* 86.

"did stupid things": Morrill Cody quoted in Sarason, *Hemingway and the Sun Set,* 45.

"The more I saw": Loeb, *The Way It Was,* 194.

"a jiggling of": Harold Loeb, "Hemingway's Bitterness," *Connecticut Review* 1 (1967), reprinted in Sarason, *Hemingway and the Sun Set,* 114–15.

56   *"What you've got"*: Loeb, *The Way It Was,* 219–20.

57   *"certainly didn't want"*: Ibid., 217.

"relish[ed] his spontaneity": Ibid.

"great capacity for": Ibid., 215; *Paris suddenly felt empty:* Ibid., 209.

lady of the stage: Decades later, Cannell's publicity bureau would assert that she had been a mime during her early career, although neither Cannell nor Loeb mentioned this stint in their memoir material about this period. "Kathleen Cannell: Fashions from Paris to Main Street, [a] Sparkling Talks Feature," undated press release and biography sheet issued by Lordly & Dame, Boston.

"The mistress of": Malcolm Cowley to Kenneth Burke, September 10, 1922, reprinted in *The Long Voyage: Selected Letters of Malcolm Cowley, 1915–1987,* ed. Hans Bak (Cambridge: Harvard University Press, 2014), 79.

58   *"alimony gang"*: Charters, *This Must Be the Place,* 19.

"There is a": Loeb, *The Way It Was,* 78.

"I instantly felt": Cannell, "Scenes with a Hero," 145, 147.

"Her clothes are": Loeb, *The Way It Was,* 207.

"All the in-girls": Cannell, "Scenes with a Hero," 145.

"bad example to": Baker, *Ernest Hemingway: A Life Story,* 124.

59   *"Feather Puss"*: Biographer Bertram Sarason reported that decades later, Cannell and Loeb would bicker about the origin of the cat, with Loeb recalling that they had rescued it in Rome and Cannell asserting that it had belonged to her mother. Sarason, *Hemingway and the Sun Set,* 19. Hemingway would immortalize Feather Puss as Bumby's dutiful babysitter in *A Moveable Feast.*

"I have just": Cannell, "Scenes with a Hero," 148.

5. Bridges to New York

61   *"wonderful and beautiful":* Ernest Hemingway to the Hemingway family, ca. May 7, 1924, reprinted in Defazio, Spanier, and Trogdon, *Letters of Ernest Hemingway,* 2:120.

mistaken for smugglers: Hemingway jokes about smugglers in a letter to his parents, Ernest Hemingway to Clarence and Grace Hall Hemingway, May 26, 1924, reprinted ibid., 125.

a "compromise": Ernest Hemingway to Ezra Pound, May 2, 1924, reprinted ibid., 113. Regarding Ford's publishing praise of his own works under a pseudonym, Hemingway scholar Sandra Spanier points out that Ford also published in the magazine under the names R. Edison Page and Daniel Chaucer, and that in some Chaucer items—titled "Stocktakings"—there are "brief positive mentions of Ford's work." Ibid., 116, n. 18.

62   *Madame Lecomte's:* Hemingway would later put this boîte and its owner in *The Sun Also Rises.* Characters Jake Barnes and Bill Gorton dine there; once quaint and intimate, the restaurant was depicted as having become overrun by tourists, one of the ways that Hemingway intimated what a scourge the influx of visiting Americans had become to pioneering expatriates.

"I didn't know": Stewart, *By a Stroke of Luck!* 116.

"insisted, with characteristic": Ibid., 116.

"Conversation in the": Dos Passos, *The Best Times,* 157.

"dog-eat-dog": Stewart, *By a Stroke of Luck!* 106.

63   *"Bring plenty of pesetas":* Ernest Hemingway to Donald Ogden Stewart, ca. early July 1924, reprinted in Defazio, Spanier, and Trogdon, *Letters of Ernest Hemingway,* 2:127.

"I was to": Stewart, *By a Stroke of Luck!* 116.

"[Hemingway] had an": Dos Passos, *The Best Times,* 160–61.

"[The town] was ours": Donald St. John, "Interview with Donald Ogden Stewart," in Sarason, *Hemingway and the Sun Set,* 191.

64   *"From every alley":* Dos Passos, *The Best Times,* 173.

"sweated through one's": McAlmon, *Being Geniuses Together,* 243.

thrown up all over: Ernest Hemingway to John Dos Passos, April 22, 1925, reprinted in Defazio, Spanier, and Trogdon, *Letters of Ernest Hemingway,* 2:323. Stewart's son claims that Hemingway's presence made his father "more aggressive" and made him drink more than he usually did. Donald Ogden Stewart Jr., interview with the author, January 26, 2015.

Down the corridor: In the nineteenth century, according to James Michener, those permitted to run ahead of the beasts included "only butchers and those who worked with cattle," yet those regulations had been loosened. Michener himself reported sighting "incredible accumulations in which several dozen men have formed a mad pile in front of the flying animals," who trampled over the human barricade. James Michener, *Michener's Iberia: Spanish Travels and Reflections,* vol. 2 (New York: Corgi Books, 1983), 505–6.

65   *"[He] had been":* McAlmon, *Being Geniuses Together,* 244–45.

jumped into the ring: Hemingway reported in a December 1924 letter to *Vanity Fair* editor Frank Crowninshield that he and his friends had gone into the ring five times in front of a crowd of twenty thousand. He wrote to his mother, however, that they had entered the ring six times. Ernest Hemingway to Grace Hall Hemingway, July 18, 1924, reprinted in Defazio, Spanier, and Trogdon, *Letters of Ernest Hemingway,* 2:133.

"ran away bellowing": McAlmon, *Being Geniuses Together,* 245.

"practicing coward": St. John, "Interview with Donald Ogden Stewart," 193.

"Ernest was somebody": Stewart, *By a Stroke of Luck!* 131.

"ass over teakettle": St. John, "Interview with Donald Ogden Stewart," 194.

"I felt as": Stewart, *By a Stroke of Luck!* 133.

souvenir postcards: Hemingway sent one postcard to Stein and Toklas, identifying entourage members in the image; Hadley sent one to Sylvia Beach, exclaiming on the back, "Cogida of Hemingway Stewart and Mc Almon also in the ring . . . [T]he valiant Stewart was carried out by the aficionados." Postcard from Hadley Hemingway to Sylvia Beach, box 22, Sylvia Beach Papers, Princeton University Library. The Hemingway entourage may have taken a film camera into the ring and captured Stewart's tossing exploit, as well as some footage of Hemingway in the ring, although the film appears to have been lost. Ernest Hemingway to Maxwell Perkins, December 6, 1926, Archives of Charles Scribner's Sons, Princeton University Library, and Ernest Hemingway to Grace Hall Hemingway, July 18, 1924, reprinted in Defazio, Spanier, and Trogdon, *Letters of Ernest Hemingway,* 2:133.

BULL GORES 2: "Bull Gores 2 Yanks Acting as Toreadores," *Chicago Tribune,* July 29, 1924.

66   *"They must have":* St. John, "Interview with Donald Ogden Stewart," 194.

Hemingway wrote a letter: A former editor from the *Star* told Stewart interviewer Donald St. John that "the letter was tossed out many years ago —they didn't know their reporter 'Hemmy' was scheduled for fame." Ibid., 196. Yet biographer Carlos Baker summarizes its contents, calling the letter "boastful" and adding: "Ernest immodestly reported that he and Don performed each day before 20,000 fans. It was all very fine" (*Ernest Hemingway: A Life Story,* 129).

"sight of a crowd": Dos Passos, *The Best Times,* 174.

"He stuck like a": Ibid., 173–74.

67   *"He was so":* McAlmon, *Being Geniuses Together,* 246.

"Stop acting like": Ibid., 247.

"meazly and shitty": Ernest Hemingway to Ezra Pound, July 19, 1924, reprinted in Defazio, Spanier, and Trogdon, *Letters of Ernest Hemingway,* 2:135.

68   *"re-assume its international":* Ford Madox Ford, editorial, *transatlantic review* (August 1924), quoted in Reynolds, *Hemingway: The Paris Years,* 207.

"could be an": Email from Valerie Hemingway to the author, September 21, 2014.

Ford and his wife: Baker, *Ernest Hemingway: A Life Story,* 128, 584.

"They tried as often": Ernest Hemingway, "Mr. and Mrs. Elliot," in *Complete Short Stories,* 123.

"[Nick] wanted to": Deleted ending to "Big Two-Hearted River," quoted in Baker, *Ernest Hemingway: A Life Story,* 132.

69   *"right away put":* Ibid., 159–60.

"why Hem was": Ibid., 219.

70   *"Lord Roseberry":* Walker Gilmer, *Horace Liveright, Publisher of the Twenties* (New York: David Lewis, 1970), 2.

ended disastrously: One Liveright biographer calls the Pick-Quick adventure a "fiasco." Ibid., 4.

Boni would swiftly exit: The two men had different visions for the firm: Liveright wanted big names and Americans; Boni preferred politically minded Continentals. The partners flipped a coin to see who would buy the other out. Liveright won. Boni subsequently went off to Europe, and then the U.S.S.R. to observe the revolution in person. In 1920 he was imprisoned on spying charges there; he later was released, returned to the United States, and started another publishing concern, this time with his brother. Ibid., 19.

"When you went": Anderson, *Sherwood Anderson's Memoirs,* 356.

"the most noisome": Gilmer, *Horace Liveright,* 10.

$100 weekly allowance: One hundred dollars a week in 1925 would be the rough equivalent of a $62,000 annual salary in today's dollars.

71   *anti-Semitic tendencies:* Hemingway biographer Carlos Baker writes: "Be-

neath that attractive exterior, she thought, ran a streak of vicious cruelty . . . [but] Harold could not rest until Ernest had met Leon. Kitty was again doubtful, having noticed Hem's occasional anti-Semitic outbursts." Baker does not elaborate on the content and timing of these "outbursts"; he cites a personal interview with Cannell (October 13, 1963) as the source of the information about her forebodings and observations. Baker, *Ernest Hemingway: A Life Story,* 586.

"I tended at": Loeb, "Hemingway's Bitterness," 119.

"It's the maid's": Loeb, *The Way It Was,* 226.

72 *"In the street":* Cannell, "Scenes with a Hero," 148. In his memoir, Loeb writes that Hemingway "said, 'The low — —!'" leaving out the actual word (*The Way It Was,* 227). In a later essay, pointedly titled "Hemingway's Bitterness," Loeb claimed that Hemingway "muttered: 'That damned kike'" ("Hemingway's Bitterness," 117).

"See what I": Loeb, *The Way It Was,* 227.

"He likes to": Ibid.

"used the word": Loeb, "Hemingway's Bitterness," 117.

"Well, Baby there's": Cannell, "Scenes with a Hero," 148.

Doran and Liveright: Harold Loeb recalled that even though Hemingway had taken such violent exception to Leon Fleischman at their meeting, he nonetheless sent Fleischman a manuscript of *In Our Time.* Fleischman eventually forwarded it on to the New York office of Boni & Liveright. Liveright's biographer Walker Gilmer states that it's unclear whether this copy actually landed on Liveright's desk: it may well have been the one sent over to Donald Stewart to peddle to Doran, who rejected it. What is clear, however, is that for Hemingway, Liveright was a distant second to Doran in desirability.

"ever so god damn": Ernest Hemingway to Donald Ogden Stewart, November 3, 1924, reprinted in Defazio, Spanier, and Trogdon, *Letters of Ernest Hemingway,* 2:173.

a book coming out: Ernest Hemingway to Howell G. Jenkins, November 9, 1924, reprinted ibid., 176.

"Doran are going": Ernest Hemingway to William B. Smith, December 6, 1924, reprinted ibid., 186.

73 *"Same old shit":* Ernest Hemingway to Robert McAlmon, ca. December 18, 1924, reprinted ibid., 196.

"I wanted to": Loeb, *The Way It Was,* 229.

"difficult and painful": Ibid., 233.

74 *"Bring my book":* Ernest Hemingway to Harold Loeb, December 29, 1924,

reprinted in Defazio, Spanier, and Trogdon, *Letters of Ernest Hemingway,* 2:197.

morale-boosting Christmas present: Despite Stewart's generosity, it is unclear how enthusiastic his advocacy may have been. "I liked [Hemingway], and I wanted to help a friend," he wrote later. "[But] actually, I didn't have any idea that Ernest was a very good writer." As for Hemingway's story submission to *Vanity Fair,* "I had decided that written humor was not his dish and had done nothing about it." Stewart, *By a Stroke of Luck!* 135.

"They were all": Ernest Hemingway to Harold Loeb, January 5, 1925, reprinted in Defazio, Spanier, and Trogdon, *Letters of Ernest Hemingway,* 2:199. Stewart had then given the rejected manuscript to "that shit," as Hemingway called him, critic H. L. Mencken, who might recommend it to Knopf. Hemingway was less than hopeful on this front: Mencken didn't even like his writing, he said, and predicted that this outreach would "probably end in horsecock too." Ibid.

"You'll live to": Loeb, *The Way It Was,* 238. In his later accounts, Loeb changed the content of his monologue to Kaufman slightly in each retelling, but it was always the same in essence.

apparently did the trick: In later years, no fewer than four Hemingway friends claimed to have played a part in persuading Horace Liveright to publish *In Our Time.* In addition to Loeb's accounts of salvaging the manuscript from the slush pile, John Dos Passos wrote that he had "played some part in inducing Horace Liveright to publish *In Our Time*" (*The Best Times,* 176). Sherwood Anderson contended that he had also gone "personally to Horace Liveright to plead for the books," although it's unclear what other book or books he was referring to (*Sherwood Anderson's Memoirs,* 476). Expat writer and editor Harold Stearns—who had given up an intellectual literary career to author a racetrack column in the *Paris Herald* under the pseudonym "Peter Pickem"—wrote that he too "contrive[d] to sell [Liveright] Ernest Hemingway's first book of short stories, called 'In Our Time'" (*Confessions of a Harvard Man,* 251). And lastly, in 1927 Hemingway told his Scribner's editor Maxwell Perkins that editor Edward O'Brien had also helped persuade Liveright to accept the manuscript.

"Anderson [was] then": Loeb, "Hemingway's Bitterness," 118.

"Hurray for you": Ernest Hemingway to Harold Loeb, February 27, 1925, reprinted in Defazio, Spanier, and Trogdon, *Letters of Ernest Hemingway,* 2:259–60.

75   *"it had taken":* Loeb, *The Way It Was,* 246.

DELIGHTED ACCEPT = HEMINGWAY: Cable from Ernest Hemingway to Horace Liveright, March 6, 1925, reprinted in Defazio, Spanier, and Trogdon, *Letters of Ernest Hemingway,* 2:272.

6. The Catalysts

79   *"Now everybody seemed"*: Loeb, "Hemingway's Bitterness," 119.

five thousand Americans: Allan, *Americans in Paris,* 131.

"Too much advertising": Charters, *This Must Be the Place,* 4.

"overwhelming prize": Nathan Asch, quoted in Cowley, *A Second Flowering,* 60.

"Ernest did have": Ibid., 61.

80   *"He's the original"*: Ibid.

"That year the": Hemingway, *A Moveable Feast,* 214.

"international birds of": Gilot and Lake, *Life with Picasso,* 149.

"[He] was telling": Dos Passos, *The Best Times,* 163.

"They were both": Stewart, *By a Stroke of Luck!* 117.

"closed circle": Stewart, *By a Stroke of Luck!* 117–18.

"He almost put": Dos Passos, *The Best Times,* 163.

81   *"They were the parents"*: Calvin Tomkins, interview with the author, September 10, 2014.

"wanted them to": Ibid. The Murphys, points out their granddaughter Laura Donnelly, were not just "the ones that fed you and listened to you and bought you records"; they also "loaned you a hundred dollars when you were strapped. It was always, 'Don't pay us back; our pleasure.'" Laura Donnelly, interview with the author, September 22, 2014.

"He seemed to": Dos Passos, *The Best Times,* 164.

"all the amenities": Sokoloff, *Hadley,* 78–79.

82   *"eyed each other"*: Loeb, *The Way It Was,* 247.

"did not let": Ibid., 245–47.

83   *Japanese dolls:* Cannell, "Scenes with a Hero," 146. This is just one version of how the introductory meeting happened. Loeb maintained that he had invited the Hemingways over for a drink to celebrate the *Doodab* and *In Our Time* book deals. When the Hemingways arrived chez Loeb, Cannell was there too, entertaining two American sisters, Pauline and Virginia Pfeiffer.

doting wealthy father: The Pfeiffers' father owned vast swaths of real estate in Piggott, Arkansas, and surrounding areas; their fiscally generous uncle Augustus "Gus" Pfeiffer co-owned a substantial international pharmaceutical firm and also the popular Richard Hudnut perfumery, which was just expanding into Europe in the 1920s.

long emerald earrings: Kay Boyle, in McAlmond, *Being Geniuses Together,* 180.

"*beneath her*": Callaghan, *That Summer in Paris,* 112.

"*ambrosial*": Cannell, "Scenes with a Hero," 146.

"*Handkerchiefs and reputations*": Pauline Pfeiffer, "Handkerchiefs a Lady Loses," *Vogue,* July 1, 1922, 72.

"*Pauline, nearing thirty*": Cannell, "Scenes with a Hero," 146. For years, biographers have perpetuated Cannell's rather dated assessment, portraying Pauline as a mantrap driven by a ticking biological clock; Carlos Baker even described her as "small and determined as a terrier" (*Ernest Hemingway: A Life Story,* 165). As trite as the aging mantrap description might seem, there is some evidence that a clock may have been ticking in Pfeiffer's mind, just as the publication-of-a-novel clock haunted Hemingway. Three years earlier, for example, Pauline had gamely offered herself up as a guinea pig for an almost violent regime of anti-aging remedies and documented the amusingly demeaning process in the pages of *Vogue.* Studying her face, she reported: "Around the eyes and on the forehead — those were the places where I ran down the ravages of time. And my hair seemed suddenly thin and worn." Pauline Pfeiffer, "Madame in Search of Her Youth," *Vogue,* January 1, 1922, 51.

84 *Virginia, by contrast:* Pauline Pfeiffer's biographer Ruth Hawkins reports that "as the more athletic of the sisters, Virginia found his stories interesting and followed him into the kitchen, where she spent much of the evening pumping him for more information — much to Ernest's delight." Ruth A. Hawkins, *Unbelievable Happiness and Final Sorrow: The Hemingway-Pfeiffer Marriage* (Fayetteville: University of Arkansas Press, 2012), 3.

"*I'd like to*": Cannell, "Scenes with a Hero," 146.

"*They remarked with*": Ibid.

"*See, here is*": Sokoloff, *Hadley,* 82.

possibly even an affair: Making a case for this possible liaison, Pauline Pfeiffer's biographer Ruth Hawkins cites a "suggestive" incident in which Virginia joined Hemingway at a dinner with Gertrude Stein and Alice Toklas soon after these first meetings. At the end of the meal, Virginia and Hemingway were said to have left together; he allegedly squired her back to her home. Decades later, Hawkins interviewed several of Virginia's surviving friends, who claimed that she had indicated to them that she and Hemingway had become involved with each other shortly after they met, and that the Pfeiffers' wealth had motivated his initial interest in her and eventually in Pauline. Ruth Hawkins, *Unbelievable Happiness and Final Sorrow.* One friend recalled a conversation in which he asked Virginia, "So, you could have been Mrs. Ernest Hemingway?" Her response: "I also had an Uncle Gus, didn't I?" Uncle Gus was the Pfeiffers' generous and wealthy uncle Augustus Pfeiffer. Ruth Hawkins, interview with the author, October 13, 2014. Hemingway and Pauline's second son, Patrick Hemingway, says that he finds the idea of an early relationship between his father and his aunt plausible, stating that in the case of two attractive, close-knit sisters, "it's almost too much to expect a man" to marry one and "not be attracted to the sister." Patrick Hemingway, interview with the author, September 26, 2014. He also pointed out that "there wasn't much future in that relationship" despite its purported early romantic tenor, as it later became clear that Virginia was gay — or "preferred the company of women," as Hawkins puts it.

85   *"I heard a":* Loeb, *The Way It Was,* 249.

long, lean woman: Although it has generally been implied that Duff Twysden towered over her suitors, one friend recalled that she actually stood about five foot seven. Yet she was fetchingly long-limbed: expat heiress Nancy Cunard once described her as having *"beaucoup de cran* [guts] and *beaucoup de branche* [branches, that is, arms and legs]." Baker, *Ernest Hemingway: A Life Story,* 144, 588. Not to be confused with a flapperish bob, Twysden's haircut was known as an Eton crop — a boyish cut recalling the playing fields of Eton. It had become a modish look around that year. Hamish Bowles, interview with the author, April 16, 2015; and Valerie Steele, interview with the author, March 6, 2014. Twysden was said to have always worn a jauntily angled masculine hat. One Twysden admirer described it as "a cross between a Basque beret and a Scotch tam-o'-shanter." James Charters, "Pat and Duff: Some Memories," *Connecticut Review* 3, no. 2 (1970), reprinted in Sarason, *Hemingway and the* Sun *Set,* 243. Others recalled that she was more closely associated with a man's fedora. Whether it was "a man's felt hat, or a matador's hat, maybe even a lamp shade . . . she had a kind of style sense that allowed her to wear with dignity and chic almost anything," contended Donald Stewart. St. John, "Interview with Donald Ogden Stewart," 197.

"certain aloof splendor": Loeb, *The Way It Was,* 250. In his memoir, Loeb assigned her a transparent pseudonym: "Lady Duff Twitchell." Her lover Pat Guthrie was given the name "Pat Swazey."

"I wondered how": Ibid.

"We were all": St. John, "Interview with Donald Ogden Stewart," 70–71.

didn't bother to bathe: On the subject of Twysden's personal hygiene, Carlos Baker cites testimony given to him in the early 1960s by Donald Ogden Stewart, W. B. Smith, and Mr. and Mrs. John Rogers (*Ernest Hemingway: A Life Story,* 588).

her ensembles: Twysden's wardrobe of jersey sweaters would have proved exciting to her suitors in the mid-1920s. At that time, the jersey for women was a new and controversial garment, then being popularized by French designer Coco Chanel. "She took it very much from menswear," states fashion historian Valerie Steele. Before the 1920s, she adds, "sweaters were still associated with being a man's garment, and jersey in particular was a man's material." It was a defiant, sexy attempt to co-opt elements from the masculine realm. Valerie Steele, interview with the author, March 6, 2014.

86 *"listening to her"*: Morrill Cody, *"The Sun Also Rises* Revisited," *Connecticut Review* 4, no. 2, 1971, reprinted in Sarason, *Hemingway and the* Sun Set, 267.

"darling": Loeb, *The Way It Was,* 274.

Iris Storm: Nancy Cunard's biographer Lois Gordon contends that Iris Storm was based exclusively on Cunard. "Arlen . . . was blind with adoration for her; she was his heroine, his goddess," she says. Email from Lois Gordon to the author, April 4, 2014; and Lois Gordon, interview with the author, April 25, 2014.

"it won't shape": Mary Butts, journal entry, June 24, 1932, in *The Journals of Mary Butts,* ed. Nathalie Blondel (New Haven: Yale University Press, 2002), 390.

"She was not": Loeb, *The Way It Was,* 250–51.

"Poor Pat": Cody, *"The Sun Also Rises* Revisited," 267.

87 *"[Duff] was really"*: St. John, "Interview with Donald Ogden Stewart," 195.

the Twysden-Guthrie union: Bartender Jimmie Charters, who was close with both Twysden and Guthrie, maintained that their relationship was the "most famous love affair and romance of the Quarter." Charters, "Pat and Duff, Some Memories," 246. Writer Morrill Cody called it a "romance of the gods which everyone knew about and everyone enjoyed." Cody, *"The Sun Also Rises* Revisited," 267.

"handsome in a": Loeb, *The Way It Was,* 250.

"a kind of": St. John, "Interview with Donald Ogden Stewart," 195.

Ritz benders: Loeb, *The Way It Was,* 270. Jimmie Charters often stepped in when Twysden and Guthrie were broke: "I could never say no or refuse Pat or Duff drink, food, or cigarettes, in that order, though it was a strain on me as I had to bear most of the credit out of my own pocket." Charters, "Pat and Duff, Some Memories," 244. He claimed that Guthrie owed him eight thousand francs at one point. Even Charters's patience wore thin sometimes; when he threatened to cut off Guthrie's credit, Guthrie would fill his pockets with toilet paper and rustle it "to make it sound like five-pound bank notes" and proclaim, "James, I feel frightfully rich!" Presumably Charters then succumbed to his charm, but landlords may have been less gullible: a few years later, Guthrie reportedly became homeless; another bar proprietor gave him shelter in her boîte, where he used a loaf of bread as a pillow. Guthrie and Twysden were far from being the only ornamental deadbeats in town. Charters contended that "the unpaid bills over a nine-year period in the Dingo totaled half a million francs, despite efforts at care," and that nightlife impresario "Zelli" had "whole drawers full of bad checks." Charters, *This Must Be the Place*, 68, 13, 24.

"I made my way": Loeb, *The Way It Was*, 248, 253.

88   *"Her early memories"*: Ibid., 254.

ignoble whisperings: Twysden's former sister-in-law Aileen Twysden told biographer Bertram Sarason that Duff Twysden's father "kept a wine shop in Darlington," County Durham, and later amended its location to Richmond, Yorkshire. Sarason investigated further and found a local who recalled a wine store owned by a family named Smurthwaite — Duff Twysden's maiden name — but Sarason ultimately concluded that the evidence was suggestive rather than conclusive. Bertram Sarason, "Hemingway and the *Sun* Set," in Sarason, *Hemingway and the* Sun *Set,* 34.

"I made a": Loeb, *The Way It Was,* 254.

"I'll get the": Ibid., 255.

89   *"I [introduced] Hemingway"*: Robert McAlmon to Norman Holmes Pearson, quoted in Sarason, *Hemingway and the* Sun *Set,* 227. Various people claimed to have introduced Hemingway and Twysden, including writer Michael Arlen. His son described an incident in which, years later, he and his father ran into Hemingway at the 21 Club in New York City. "I still owe you a favor, Michael," Hemingway said. When Arlen's son queried his father about the favor, Arlen replied: "One autumn in Paris, I introduced Ernest to a girl I was with, Duff Twysden. Ernest later made that book around her." Michael Arlen, *Exiles* (New York: Farrar, Straus and Giroux, 1970), 226.

"[It] looked like love": Robert McAlmon to Norman Holmes Pearson, quoted in Sarason, *Hemingway and the* Sun *Set,* 227.

"We are fond": Ernest Hemingway to Sherwood Anderson, May 23, 1925, reprinted in Defazio, Spanier, and Trogdon, *Letters of Ernest Hemingway,* 2:340.

"written so tight": Ernest Hemingway to Horace Liveright, March 31, 1925, reprinted ibid., 295.

90   *"I've always felt"*: Gilot and Lake, *Life with Picasso,* 73.

"no one who": Ernest Hemingway to Horace Liveright, March 31, 1925, reprinted in Defazio, Spanier, and Trogdon, *Letters of Ernest Hemingway,* 2:295.

"Your method is": Maxwell Perkins to Ernest Hemingway, February 21, 1925, Archives of Charles Scribner's Sons, Princeton University Library.

91   *"would likely have"*: Maxwell Perkins to Ernest Hemingway, February 26, 1925, Archives of Charles Scribner's Sons, Princeton University Library.

"It makes it": Ernest Hemingway to Maxwell Perkins, April 15, 1925, Archives of Charles Scribner's Sons, Princeton University Library.

"rotten luck": Maxwell Perkins to Ernest Hemingway, April 28, 1925, Archives of Charles Scribner's Sons, Princeton University Library.

unofficial talent scout: Fitzgerald was certainly not the only author to scout on behalf of his house; publishers fairly regularly treated their authors as field men, especially those abroad, and relied on them for leads. Both Harold Stearns and Sherwood Anderson introduced authors to Liveright, for example. But Fitzgerald proved an especially enthusiastic introducer; he would even try to pave the way for actor Leslie Howard (soon to be made world famous as Ashley Wilkes in the 1939 film *Gone with the Wind*) to enter the world of letters, telling Perkins that Howard had "considerable writing talent also which he is turning, at present toward short stories." F. Scott Fitzgerald to Maxwell Perkins, May 1926, Archives of Charles Scribner's Sons, Princeton University Library.

"most humorous man": Groucho Marx, "My Poor Wife," *Collier's,* December 20, 1930, reprinted in *The Essential Groucho Marx: Writings By, For, and About Groucho Marx,* ed. Stefan Kanfer (New York: Vintage, 2000), 138.

92   *"[He] was selflessly"*: Dos Passos, *The Best Times,* 176. Fitzgerald's granddaughter Eleanor Lanahan describes his impulse to promote others as stemming from his "broad spirit of inclusion and wanting to bringing out the best in people" (interview with the author, September 15, 2014).

"E[a]rnest Hemmingway": F. Scott Fitzgerald to Maxwell Perkins, ca. October 10, 1924, Archives of Charles Scribner's Sons, Princeton University Library.

"intelligable at all": F. Scott Fitzgerald to Maxwell Perkins, ca. December 27, 1924, Archives of Charles Scribner's Sons, Princeton University Library.

"the reader who": Maxwell Perkins to F. Scott Fitzgerald, October 18, 1924, Archives of Charles Scribner's Sons, Princeton University Library.

"Ernest seemed on": Callaghan, *That Summer in Paris,* 31.

three movies: The films adapted from Fitzgerald short stories were *The Chorus Girl's Romance* (from "Head and Shoulders"), *The Husband Hunter* (from "Myra Meets His Family"), and *The Offshore Pirate* (from a story of the same name). Matthew J. Bruccoli, Scottie Fitzgerald Smith, and Joan P. Kerr, eds., *The Romantic Egoists: Scott and Zelda Fitzgerald* (New York: Charles Scribner's Sons, 1974), 74. *The Beautiful and Damned* was made into a 1922 film by Warner Brothers. *This Side of Paradise* was optioned but not produced. Ibid., 98.

"[He] was making": MacLeish, *Reflections,* 60.

93   *"the recognized spokesman"*: "Fitzgerald, Flappers and Fame: An Interview with F. Scott Fitzgerald," *The Shadowland* (January 1921), reprinted in Bruccoli, Smith, and Kerr, *The Romantic Egoists,* 79.

"My point of": F. Scott Fitzgerald, "Early Success," quoted ibid., 76.

"They were celebrities": Dos Passos, *The Best Times,* 147.

"I want to": F. Scott Fitzgerald to Maxwell Perkins, July 1922, quoted in Bruccoli, *Fitzgerald and Hemingway,* 10.

"something really NEW": F. Scott Fitzgerald to Maxwell Perkins, May 1, 1925, reprinted in *F. Scott Fitzgerald: A Life in Letters,* ed. Matthew Bruccoli (New York: Charles Scribner's Sons, 1994), 108.

"[He] wrote me": F. Scott Fitzgerald to Maxwell Perkins, February 20, 1926, Archives of Charles Scribner's Sons, Princeton University Library.

94 *"one of the"*: Edmund Wilson, foreword to F. Scott Fitzgerald, *The Last Tycoon* (New York: Penguin Classics, 2010), ix.

"made a special": Flanner, introduction to *Paris Was Yesterday,* xviii.

"Poor Scott was": Beach, *Shakespeare and Company,* 116.

"a Negress with": Ibid., 116–17.

"We liked him": Ibid., 116.

"some completely worthless": Hemingway, *A Moveable Feast,* 125.

95 *"It was all"*: Ibid., 126.

"Don't talk like": Ibid., 127.

"looked up Hemminway": F. Scott Fitzgerald to Edmund Wilson, May 1925, reprinted in Bruccoli, *F. Scott Fitzgerald: A Life in Letters,* 110. Hemingway's published version of their first meeting was likely embellished or even invented by its author. For one thing, Fitzgerald's friend Dunc Chaplin—who supposedly accompanied him at this first encounter—later asserted that he hadn't even been in Paris in 1925, and furthermore, that he never met Hemingway at any time. Bruccoli, *Fitzgerald and Hemingway,* 1. Sara Mayfield—a friend of the Fitzgeralds during this time—recalled that the Fitzgerald and Hemingway meeting was actually prearranged by Donald Stewart. Sara Mayfield, *Exiles from Paradise: Zelda and Scott Fitzgerald* (New York: Delacorte Press, 1971), 105. Fitzgerald expert Matthew Bruccoli reportedly uncovered several different accounts of the meeting in Hemingway's *Moveable Feast* draft material. In one version, Hemingway and Hadley are dining at the Dingo when Fitzgerald imposes on them. In another version, Zelda Fitzgerald is also in attendance; Hemingway finds her unattractive in person but has an erotic dream about her that night and duly tells her about it. She was supposedly pleased. Bruccoli, *Fitzgerald and Hemingway,* 23, footnote. It is unclear what material Bruccoli is citing, as he does not provide further information on his sources, but no alternative versions of the meeting appear to have been included in the definitive *Moveable Feast* files in the Ernest Hemingway Collection at the John F. Kennedy Presidential Library and Museum, which houses draft and fragment material pertaining to the

manuscript. Valerie Hemingway—Hemingway's assistant when he was working on *Moveable Feast*—says that she does not recall these alternative versions, but she does remember Hemingway recounting the Zelda dream story later without specifying when the event took place (email to the author, September 21, 2014). Even though questions surround the veracity of the published *Moveable Feast* account, some parts of the story did ring true to Fitzgerald's and Hemingway's contemporaries, especially Fitzgerald's alleged inquisition about Hemingway's sex life. "Scott had an outrageous way of asking the wrong (actually the right) questions about one's most private feelings—questions which one just didn't ask," remembered Donald Stewart (*By a Stroke of Luck!* 87). Also, no one ever appears to have denied that drinking often brought out the worst in Fitzgerald. "Alcohol turned him foolish, destructive, truculent, [and] childish," as Bruccoli puts it (*Fitzgerald and Hemingway,* 12).

"quite a lot": Ernest Hemingway to Maxwell Perkins, June 9, 1925, reprinted in Defazio, Spanier, and Trogdon, *Letters of Ernest Hemingway,* 2:348.

96 *"the company of":* Hemingway, *A Moveable Feast,* 131.

"he looked like": Ibid., 141. Fitzgerald's inability to maintain his composure—or even his consciousness—when drinking appears to have particularly appalled Hemingway. "He saw it as weakness," says Valerie Hemingway, "and Ernest hated weakness" (interview with the author, December 20, 2014).

"hate at first": Sheila Graham, *College of One: The Story of How F. Scott Fitzgerald Educated the Woman He Loved* (Brooklyn: Melville House Publishing, 2013), 178.

"as silently as": Mayfield, *Exiles from Paradise,* 108.

"I learned to": Hemingway, *A Moveable Feast,* 154. This portrayal of Zelda still unnerves her descendants today. "It was a character smear," says the Fitzgeralds' granddaughter Eleanor Lanahan (interview with the author, September 15, 2014).

97 *"Zelda is crazy":* Hemingway, *A Moveable Feast,* 163.

"should have swapped": Ernest Hemingway to Maxwell Perkins, July 27, 1932, reprinted in Baker, *Ernest Hemingway: Selected Letters,* 364–65.

"phony he-man": Zelda Fitzgerald quoted in Matthew J. Bruccoli, *Scott and Ernest: The Authority of Failure and the Authority of Success* (New York: Random House, 1978), 21.

"Ernest . . . was an": F. Scott Fitzgerald to Zelda Fitzgerald, summer 1931, reprinted in Bruccoli, *F. Scott Fitzgerald: A Life in Letters,* 187.

"literary crush": Dos Passos, *The Best Times,* 176.

to meet Gertrude Stein: Unlike Hemingway, Fitzgerald may have been indifferent to Stein's art collection and deemed her work unsaleable, but he was intrigued by Stein's literary theories. Fitzgerald pleased and impressed Stein in return; he would "be read when many of his well known contemporaries are forgotten," she declared later, and credited his debut novel, *This Side of Paradise,* with "creat[ing] for the public the new generation." Stein, *Autobiography of Alice B. Toklas,* 218.

"a fine, charming fellow": F. Scott Fitzgerald to Maxwell Perkins, ca. May 22, 1925, reprinted in Bruccoli, *F. Scott Fitzgerald: A Life in Letters,* 113.

7. Eve in Eden

99   *"must write":* Ernest Hemingway, *Along with Youth* manuscript, item 239a, Ernest Hemingway Collection, John F. Kennedy Presidential Library and Museum.

100   *"perpetual drunk":* Ernest Hemingway to Ezra Pound, ca. June 8–10, 1925, reprinted in Defazio, Spanier, and Trogdon, *Letters of Ernest Hemingway,* 2:346. In the end, neither Benchley nor Fisher came on the trip. The complete entourage included Hemingway, Hadley, Harold Loeb, Bill Smith, Donald Ogden Stewart, Duff Twysden, and Pat Guthrie.

"Hemingway and his": Cannell, "Scenes with a Hero," 148–49.

"damned good": Ernest Hemingway to Harold Loeb, June 21, 1925, reprinted in Defazio, Spanier, and Trogdon, *Letters of Ernest Hemingway,* 2:353.

"We made love": Loeb, *The Way It Was,* 276. One of Loeb's friends later recalled that Loeb had been suffering from a "shocking toothache" throughout the week, which may have hampered his amorous activities, but Loeb did not mention the affliction in his memoirs. Cody, *"The Sun Also Rises* Revisited," 267.

101   *"[He's] a good":* Loeb, *The Way It Was,* 272.

"Should we go": Ibid., 275.

"with all [her]": Ibid., 280–81.

"Pat has sent": Ernest Hemingway to Harold Loeb, June 21, 1925, paraphrased in Loeb, *The Way It Was,* 281, and reprinted in Defazio, Spanier, and Trogdon, *Letters of Ernest Hemingway,* 2:353.

"low feeling which": Loeb, *The Way It Was,* 281.

"I expect I": Lady Duff Twysden to Harold Loeb, 1925, reprinted ibid., 282.

102   *a question that:* Various Hemingway contemporaries have weighed in over the years on the topic of a possible sexual relationship between Hemingway and Twysden. Hadley maintained to biographers that she believed the

relationship had remained platonic. Bill Smith later told a biographer that he felt Twysden was "wild about Ernest," but he did not think they had a sexual relationship (quoted in Baker, *Ernest Hemingway: A Life Story,* 150). Donald Ogden Stewart told a different biographer that it seemed the two were having an affair, but he wasn't certain either way (paraphrased in Sarason, *Hemingway and the* Sun *Set,* 70). Twysden's third husband, Clinton King, claimed Twysden had told him that she and Hemingway never had sex: first of all, he stated, "Hemingway was not her type," and second, she demurred out of consideration for Hadley and Bumby (Clinton King to Bertram Sarason, quoted in Sarason, *Hemingway and the* Sun *Set,* 42–43). Kitty Cannell would scoff that this was just Twysden's polite way of holding Hemingway at bay without offending him (Cannell to Sarason, paraphrased in Sarason, *Hemingway and the* Sun *Set,* 54). Hemingway's friend A. E. Hotchner asserts that they came close to consummation but never had intercourse (interview with the author, December 11, 2013). The bottom line, as Valerie Hemingway puts it, is that "we just don't know" (interview with the author, December 20, 2013).

"By all means": Loeb, *The Way It Was,* 281.

103 *"I did not"*: Loeb, "Hemingway's Bitterness," 120.

"Oh, you're here": Loeb, *The Way It Was,* 283.

"Pat broke the": Ibid., 284.

"cluttered and ordinary": St. John, "Interview with Donald Ogden Stewart," 191; *"Pamplona seemed to"*: Stewart, *By a Stroke of Luck!* 144.

"Someone had left": Ibid., 143–44.

104 *"Evidently Duff was"*: Loeb, *The Way It Was,* 286.

Hemingway, Loeb, and Smith: The memory of the broken ribs earned in the previous year's adventure prevented Stewart from following them; Guthrie also declined. "Old Pat would have been too tight [drunk] for that kind of thing," Stewart later said. St. John, "Interview with Donald Ogden Stewart," 194.

"Perhaps he felt": Loeb, *The Way It Was* 289, 294.

105 *"too keen on"*: Ibid., 290.

"Hem seems to": Ibid., 290, 291.

106 *"For an instant"*: Ibid., 292.

Even the barber: Ibid.

"Why don't you": Ibid., 293.

"Obstinacy kept me": Ibid.

107 *"there was too"*: Ibid., 294.

"He was sincerity": Hemingway, *Death in the Afternoon,* 88–89. Heming-

way adds that he had tried "to describe how [Ordóñez] looked and a couple of his fights in a book one time," a reference to his translation of Ordóñez into the character Pedro Romero in *The Sun Also Rises*. In his later book *The Dangerous Summer,* he further stated that he had "written a portrait" of Ordóñez and "an account of his bullfighting in *The Sun Also Rises*. Hemingway, *The Dangerous Summer,* 50.

"very small and": Barnaby Conrad, interview with the author, November 12, 2012.

"He did everything": Ernest Hemingway to Gertrude Stein and Alice B. Toklas, July 16, 1925, reprinted in Defazio, Spanier, and Trogdon, *Letters of Ernest Hemingway,* 2:360–61.

trying to cultivate Ordóñez: Reynolds, *Hemingway: The Paris Years,* 304.

108　　*"I was amazed"*: Juanito Quintana, quoted in Michener, *Michener's Iberia,* 2:493.

"[She] wrapped it": Ernest Hemingway to Gertrude Stein and Alice B. Toklas, July 15, 1925, reprinted in Defazio, Spanier, and Trogdon, *Letters of Ernest Hemingway,* 2:360.

"One would have": Loeb, "Hemingway's Bitterness," 121.

"I suppose you'd": Loeb, *The Way It Was,* 294–97. This was not the only time Hemingway would bring someone to the brink of violence and then make a jarring attempt to smooth things over before the situation spiraled out of control. Morley Callaghan recalled a ghoulish Paris sparring session in which Hemingway took repeated punches on the mouth: "His mouth kept on bleeding. He loudly sucked in all the blood . . . [S]uddenly he spat at me; he spat a mouthful of blood; he spat in my face. I was so shocked I dropped my gloves . . . We stared at each other. 'That's what the bullfighters do when they're wounded. It's a way of showing contempt,' he said solemnly . . . [S]uddenly he smiled. Apparently he felt as friendly as ever . . . but I was wondering out of what strange nocturnal depths of his mind had come this barbarous gesture." And yet, as with Loeb, Hemingway would somehow succeed in retaining the loyalty of the other man. Callaghan recalled that later that evening, as the two sat in a bar, "I felt closer than ever to him" (*That Summer in Paris,* 125–27).

109　　*"I was terribly"*: Ernest Hemingway to Harold Loeb, ca. July 12, 1925, reprinted in Defazio, Spanier, and Trogdon, *Letters of Ernest Hemingway,* 2:359–60.

"But I knew": Loeb, *The Way It Was,* 297.

110　　*"camaraderie fell to"*: Stewart, *By a Stroke of Luck!* 144.

"overdid the heartiness": Loeb, *The Way It Was,* 297–98.

"it occurred to": Stewart, *By a Stroke of Luck!* 144.

8. The Knock Out

111   *"the intensive sun-tanning"*: Ibid., 145.

"Let the pressure": Hemingway, *A Moveable Feast*, 71.

The story almost: It has been speculated that Hemingway may even have begun writing the story that would become *The Sun Also Rises* while still in Pamplona. Carlos Baker thought that the earliest material — the book's first two scenes — had "possibly [been] set down in Pamplona as early as July 6–12," but conceded that this view was "conjectural" (*Ernest Hemingway: A Life Story,* 589).

112   *events onto paper:* The exact date on which Hemingway began the novel remains unclear. Hemingway maintained in later accounts that he had first put pen to paper on his twenty-sixth birthday — July 21 — but this was most likely an embellishment meant to dramatize further the already theatrical sprint writing of the novel. He later wrote to his mother that he had been working on the novel for up to five hours a day since leaving the fiesta on July 13, "including days on the train" as he and Hadley traveled around the country to attend various bullfights and *ferias*. Ernest Hemingway to Grace Hemingway, September 11, 1925, reprinted in Defazio, Spanier, and Trogdon, *Letters of Ernest Hemingway,* 2:388.

"Have been working": Ernest Hemingway to William B. Smith, July 21, 1925, reprinted ibid., 364.

"Some of it's": Ernest Hemingway to William Smith, July 27, 1925, reprinted ibid., 365. In an August 5 missive to Smith, Hemingway would inflate the 1,200 words a day figure to 2,000.

a "story": It is not certain that Hemingway knew he was drafting a novel when he first started working. Hemingway's friend A. E. Hotchner says that Hemingway told him that he had originally begun the novel "as a journal of what had happened," but then turned it into fiction (interview with the author, December 11, 2013). Or he may have originally conceived of the work as an extended short story. By midsummer, however, it had become clear that Hemingway was on his way to penning a novel at last.

"I've written six": Ernest Hemingway to Sylvia Beach, August 3, 1925, reprinted in Defazio, Spanier, and Trogdon, *Letters of Ernest Hemingway,* 2:368.

thirty-three-page draft: In different biographies, this loose-leaf preamble has variously been described as being thirty-one or thirty-two pages. The surviving manuscript in the Ernest Hemingway Collection at the John F. Kennedy Presidential Library and Museum (item 193) numbers thirty-three pages total. The first page contains an epigraph, the second a typed list of characters. The remaining thirty-one pages are the handwritten manuscript, with the title "Cayetano Ordonez, Niño de la Palma" written at the top and underlined. This page is what Hemingway called page one; he wrote the page numbers at the upper left and circled them, all the way through his page thirty-one.

"[Harold] was in": Ernest Hemingway, early handwritten draft of *The Sun Also Rises,* item 193, Ernest Hemingway Collection, John F. Kennedy Presidential Library and Museum.

113 *"Pat stood wobbly"*: Ibid.

everyone was badly behaved: That is, except for Hadley, whose brief appearances were innocuous filler, and Bill Smith, who at this point had little presence and functioned mostly as a silent sidekick to "Hem."

"bulls have no": Ibid.

"I will not": Ernest Hemingway, first draft of *The Sun Also Rises,* Notebook I, item 194, Ernest Hemingway Collection, John F. Kennedy Presidential Library and Museum.

"There is a": Ernest Hemingway, early handwritten draft of *The Sun Also Rises,* item 193, Ernest Hemingway Collection, John F. Kennedy Presidential Library and Museum.

French school notebook: That first notebook featured grid-lined pages and a tan cover — not blue, as often reported. The entire manuscript for the novel would be written in seven notebooks like these, some of French origin, others Spanish (probably acquired in Valencia). Notebooks I, V, VI, and VII were of French origin: their covers proclaimed "L'Incroyable, 100 Pages, Cahier" and measured 8.8 inches by 6.8 inches. The back covers displayed helpful "Tables de Multiplication" and "Division du Temps" ("Siècle = 100 ans," for example) and guides to Roman numerals. Notebooks II, III, and IV were Spanish. The following information was printed on their covers: Papeleria, E. Bort Pellicer, Libros Rayados, Zaragoza, 18 — Valencia. Like the French notebooks, the Spanish notebooks featured tobacco- or caramel-colored covers and were roughly the same size as the French books: 6.5 inches by 8.6 inches. Color images of the notebook covers and information about their dimensions provided by the Ernest Hemingway Collection, John F. Kennedy Presidential Library and Museum. The seven notebooks together make up item 194 of the collection.

114 *"to understand what"*: Ernest Hemingway, first draft of *The Sun Also Rises,* Notebook I, item 194, Ernest Hemingway Collection, John F. Kennedy Presidential Library and Museum.

"There is nothing": Ibid.

"the best-known person": Charters, *This Must Be the Place,* 72.

"Jake Barnes": During the writing and editing of the manuscript, Hemingway went back and forth about whether to render Jake in the first or third person; in a later draft, Jake drolly informs the reader, "I did not want to

tell this story in the first person but find that I must . . . so it is not going to be splendid and cool and detached after all." Ernest Hemingway, *The Sun Also Rises,* final galley, chap. 2, item 202, Ernest Hemingway Collection, John F. Kennedy Presidential Library and Museum.

"the novel will": Ibid.

115   *borrowed a line:* First-draft material later deleted from the manuscript reveals that Hemingway likely co-opted other biographical details from the life of Bill Bird, the publisher of Hemingway's book of vignettes, *in our time.* Jake gave the reader a formal introduction to his own background: he was a war veteran (discharged from a British hospital in 1916) and a newspaperman, and had co-founded a syndication service called the Continental Press Association, of which he was now European director. Ibid. Bill Bird had co-founded the Consolidated Press Service in 1920 and then taken over its Paris bureau.

"magnificent": Sokoloff, *Hadley,* 82.

"hated newspaper work": Jack Goodman, John Milton, Alan Graber, and Bill Tangney, "Hemingway Tells of Early Career; States That He 'Won't Quit Now,'" *Daily Princetonian,* April 14, 1955, reprinted in Bruccoli, *Conversations with Ernest Hemingway,* 100.

"To damn people": Ernest Hemingway to Ezra Pound, ca. November 14, 1926, reprinted in Sanderson, Spanier, and Trogdon, *Letters of Ernest Hemingway,* 3:143.

"When you are": Ernest Hemingway to Ernest Walsh, January 2, 1926, reprinted ibid., 10.

"Lady Brett Ashley": When it came to conjuring up a name for his leading lady, Hemingway appears to have fretted a bit. While she largely remained "Duff" up through the very last passages of the novel's first full draft, the book's author knew he would eventually have to assign her an alias. "Lady Doris" was one rejected possibility. He came up with a long pearl necklace of a name: "Elizabeth Neil Brett Murray," from which "Brett" would be extracted to replace "Duff." The matter of her married name also seems to have caused some consternation. Her titled husband would go through various iterations as well: Lord "Durham" (crossed out), Lord "Lambert" (also rejected), Lord "Henry Marlowe" (nixed), and finally "Robert Ashley"—although he would be referred to several times in the book's first draft as "Sir Joseph Anthony." (Getting to "Anthony" may not have required a huge stretch of the imagination: it was the name of Twysden's son.) Hemingway ultimately made a note to himself that the "name generally used" for Duff would be "Brett Ashley," although she would have to wait for revisions to appear under that alias. Ernest Hemingway, first draft of *The Sun Also Rises,* item 193, Ernest Hemingway Collection, John F. Kennedy Presidential Library and Museum.

"Duff had been": Ernest Hemingway, first draft of *The Sun Also Rises,* Notebook I, item 194, Ernest Hemingway Collection, John F. Kennedy Presidential Library and Museum.

"too expensive for": Ibid.

116   *"clean bred, generous"*: Ibid.

"Brett was damned": Hemingway, *The Sun Also Rises,* 18.

forty-nine words: Hemingway's four-line description of Brett also revealed him to be an astute fashion journalist by calling attention to her jersey sweater — which had only recently been appropriated by women's wear designers. It was one of many 1920s sartorial badges of the independent New Woman, according to Valerie Steele, director and chief curator of the Museum at the Fashion Institute of Technology (interview with the author, March 6, 2014).

"[He] had various": Ernest Hemingway, first draft of *The Sun Also Rises,* Notebook I, item 194, Ernest Hemingway Collection, John F. Kennedy Presidential Library and Museum.

"Mike Campbell": Pat Guthrie would ultimately be assigned the name "Mike Campbell" in a later version of *The Sun Also Rises,* although he is referred to alternately as "Patrick" or "Pat Guthrie" as well as "Michael Gordon" in the first draft.

"Gerald Cohn": It has been speculated that Hemingway co-opted the name "Gerald" from Gerald Murphy, although it would prove perhaps a bit too Irish for a Jewish New Yorker.

117   *"How that kike"*: Ernest Hemingway, first draft of *The Sun Also Rises,* Notebook I, item 194, Ernest Hemingway Collection, John F. Kennedy Presidential Library and Museum.

"Frances Clyne": Unlike the other characters drawn from real-life proto-types, Cannell's character was never referred to by her actual name even in the draft. Hemingway assigned her the moniker "Frances Clyne" in the very first notebook. "Clyne" may have been a derivation from "Cannell," with their four shared letters.

"lived on gossip": Ernest Hemingway, first draft of *The Sun Also Rises,* Notebook I, item 194, Ernest Hemingway Collection, John F. Kennedy Presidential Library and Museum.

"Why did he": Hemingway, *The Sun Also Rises,* 42.

118   *"Well, it was"*: Ibid., 25.

"I got the": Fraser Drew, "April 8, 1955 with Hemingway: Unedited Notes on a Visit to Finca Vigia," *Fitzgerald/Hemingway Annual, 1970,* reprinted in Bruccoli, *Conversations with Ernest Hemingway,* 95.

"poor bastards": Hotchner, *Papa Hemingway,* 48.

"*capable of all*": Plimpton, "The Art of Fiction: Ernest Hemingway," 77.

"*Good advice, anyway*": Hemingway, *The Sun Also Rises*, 26.

"*Impotence is a*": Ernest Hemingway to Maxwell Perkins, December 7, 1926, reprinted in Sanderson, Spanier, and Trogdon, *Letters of Ernest Hemingway*, 3:179.

119   *proceeds to snub:* This last transaction would be cut from the published version and later repurposed for a vicious portrait of Ford in *A Moveable Feast;* John Dos Passos's cameo would also be edited out. Before being cut entirely, however, Dos Passos would be assigned a draft alias: "Alex Muhr."

"*liable to have*": Hemingway, *The Sun Also Rises*, 15.

name-dropped: F. Scott Fitzgerald is mentioned in passing as Hem/Jake discusses the war wound that has rendered him impotent; he states that he has been advised by Fitzgerald that the issue of impotence should be treated only "as a humorous subject." Ernest Hemingway, first draft of *The Sun Also Rises*, Notebook I, item 194, Ernest Hemingway Collection, John F. Kennedy Presidential Library and Museum.

"*Duff's gone off*": Ernest Hemingway, first draft of *The Sun Also Rises*, Notebook IV, item 194, Ernest Hemingway Collection, John F. Kennedy Presidential Library and Museum.

120   "*How long is*": Ernest Hemingway to Barklie McKee Henry, August 12, 1925, reprinted in Defazio, Spanier, and Trogdon, *Letters of Ernest Hemingway*, 2:371.

"*Don't for Chrise*": Ernest Hemingway to Ezra Pound, ca. August 19–20, 1925, reprinted ibid., 378.

"*going like wild fire*": Ernest Hemingway to William Smith, August 5, 1925, reprinted ibid., 369.

"*ought to be*": Ernest Hemingway to Morley Callaghan, August 13, 1925, reprinted ibid., 373.

"*suppressed the day*": Ernest Hemingway to Ernest Walsh, August 17, 1925, reprinted ibid., 377.

Perhaps the most: Ernest Hemingway to Jane Heap, ca. August 23, 1925, reprinted ibid., 383–84.

121   *$1,000 advance:* In 1925 dollars, $1,000 equals roughly $13,500 today.

"*Of course [I]*": Ernest Hemingway to Grace Hemingway, September 11, 1925, reprinted in Defazio, Spanier, and Trogdon, *Letters of Ernest Hemingway*, 2:388.

"*I want to*": Ernest Hemingway to Gertrude Stein and Alice B. Toklas, August 20, 1925, reprinted ibid., 381.

122   *unpolluted, idyllic counterpoint:* The portrait clearly revealed Hemingway's own preferences on urban versus country living. Here was the world that "he really loved," says his son Patrick Hemingway: "The mountains and getting away and fishing. And there's no question about which he preferred" (interview with the author, July 30, 2014).

      "We walked on": Hemingway, *The Sun Also Rises,* 94.

      "Bill gestured with": Ibid., 98.

123   *"I remember it":* St. John, "Interview with Hemingway's 'Bill Gorton,'" 183.

      "that kike": Hemingway, *The Sun Also Rises,* 131; *"superior and Jewish":* Ibid., 77. Bill Gorton is not the only character to indulge in anti-Semitic remarks: Mike Campbell instructs Cohn to "take that sad Jewish face away" (ibid., 142); Jake Barnes comments on Cohn's "hard, Jewish, stubborn streak" (ibid., 9).

      "I have no": St. John, "Interview with Donald Ogden Stewart," 201.

      "The fiesta was": Hemingway, *The Sun Also Rises,* 124.

      "They wanted her": Ibid.

      "haute monde from": Ernest Hemingway, early handwritten draft of *The Sun Also Rises,* item 193, Ernest Hemingway Collection, John F. Kennedy Presidential Library and Museum.

124   *"People would wreck":* Ibid.

      sallow, hemorrhoidal sellout: Ibid.

      modern-day Circe: Circe is a mythological sorceress with the power to turn men into swine.

      "He claims she": Hemingway, *The Sun Also Rises,* 115.

      beats the hell: Juanito Quintana later contended that a fight between Harold Loeb and Cayetano Ordóñez had indeed broken out in real life, though it was not as bad as the pummeling Cohn gives to Ordóñez in the book. Such an incident was reported by no one else in the entourage. Leah Rice Koontz, "'Montoya' Remembers *The Sun Also Rises,*" reprinted in Sarason, *Hemingway and the* Sun *Set,* 210.

125   *"like a wonderful":* Hemingway, *The Sun Also Rises,* 177.

9. Breach Season

127   *"tired as hell":* Ernest Hemingway to Ernest Walsh, ca. September 21, 1925, reprinted in Defazio, Spanier, and Trogdon, *Letters of Ernest Hemingway,* 2:390–91.

      "let [his] head": Ibid.

      "He wanted me": Ernest Hemingway, first draft of *The Sun Also Rises,*

Notebook VI, item 194, Ernest Hemingway Collection, John F. Kennedy Presidential Library and Museum.

"Oh, Jake": Ernest Hemingway, first draft of *The Sun Also Rises,* Notebook VII, item 194, Ernest Hemingway Collection, John F. Kennedy Presidential Library and Museum. Hemingway was clearly tinkering with alternate final lines; farther down the page he wrote a variation: "Isn't it nice to think so."

128   *"I want 3000"*: Duff Twysden to Ernest Hemingway, undated, series 3, Incoming Correspondence, "Twsyden, Lady Duff," Ernest Hemingway Collection, John F. Kennedy Presidential Library and Museum.

"I knew that": Stewart, *By a Stroke of Luck!* 145–46. Stewart's excitement abated, however, when he reported for duty at the MGM studios in Los Angeles and no one there, he reported, "seemed to have the faintest idea who I was." Ibid., 146.

129   *club hostesses:* In his memoir Loeb dubbed the ladies—hostesses at a club run by White Russians—"Comtesse Vera and the Princess Cléopatre"; it was the beginning of a two-week caviar-and-vodka-fueled "grand party." Loeb, *The Way It Was,* 299. Just as San Fermín would give Hemingway the idea for *The Sun Also Rises,* Loeb would later transcribe the happenings of this fortnight into another novel of his own, *The Professors Like Vodka*—released in 1927 by Boni & Liveright.

"It was now": Ibid., 300.

"The things one": Loeb, "Hemingway's Bitterness," 125.

"I'd rather he": Ernest Hemingway to Howell Jenkins, August 15, 1925, reprinted in Defazio, Spanier, and Trogdon, *Letters of Ernest Hemingway,* 2:374.

130   *" full of Madrid"*: Loeb, *The Way It Was,* 300.

"If only you'd": Cannell, "Scenes with a Hero," 149.

"And that kike": Baker, *Ernest Hemingway: A Life Story,* 154.

"But not you": Cannell, "Scenes with a Hero," 149–50.

131   *The Lost Generation:* Ernest Hemingway, foreword to *The Sun Also Rises,* "The Lost Generation: A Novel," item 202c, Ernest Hemingway Collection, John F. Kennedy Presidential Library and Museum.

"I thought you": Ibid.

"That's what you": Hemingway: *A Moveable Feast,* 61.

This anecdote: Hemingway claimed in the Chartres foreword that Stein did not tell him the lost generation garage story until after he had completed the first draft of *Sun* on September 21, 1925, and it is difficult to know whether he conceived of his material through this sort of prism beforehand. Ernest Hemingway, foreword to *The Sun Also Rises,* "The Lost

Generation: A Novel," item 202c, Ernest Hemingway Collection, John F. Kennedy Presidential Library and Museum.

132   *unsuccessfully sought solace:* "Communism" had originally been included in this roster of rejected ideologies, but he changed his mind and crossed it out. Ibid.

"This is not": Ibid.

"I thought of": Hemingway, *A Moveable Feast,* 62.

133   *the concept would resonate:* Decades later, in *A Moveable Feast,* Hemingway returned to the theme again, writing of the passage of seasons and regeneration. A portion of the Ecclesiastes passage would even be read aloud at Hemingway's funeral. Gregory H. Hemingway, M.D., *Papa: A Personal Memoir* (Boston: Houghton Mifflin Company, 1976), 119.

"just disgust with": Ernest Hemingway to Ezra Pound, ca. late September 1925, reprinted in Defazio, Spanier, and Trogdon, *Letters of Ernest Hemingway,* 2:396.

"[I] am calling": Ernest Hemingway to Harold Loeb, ca. early November 1925, reprinted ibid., 407.

"Reading it over": Ernest Hemingway to Horace Liveright, May 22, 1925, reprinted ibid., 339.

134   *published in New York:* Biographers tend to identify the release date of *In Our Time* as October 5, 1925, but an early official Hemingway bibliography, issued in book form by Charles Scribner's Sons in 1951, gives the publication date as September 15, 1925. Samuels, *A Hemingway Check List,* 9. Hemingway told Ezra Pound and his father in separate late September 1925 missives that the publication date was October 1; he later advised his father that the release date had been October 10.

"obvious": Reviews noting the "obvious" link between Hemingway and Gertrude Stein include those published in *The New Republic* and the *Saturday Review of Literature.* Reynolds, *Hemingway: The Paris Years,* 328; *"fine bare effects": The New Republic,* quoted ibid.

"Ernest Hemingway is": Robert Wolf, review of *In Our Time, New York Herald Tribune,* February 14, 1926.

"stupid but well meaning": Ernest Hemingway to Maxwell Perkins, April 8, 1926, Archives of Charles Scribner's Sons, Princeton University Library.

135   *"Hemingway is his":* Alfred Harcourt to Louis Bromfield, late fall 1925, quoted in Ernest Hemingway to F. Scott Fitzgerald, December 31, 1925– January 1, 1926, reprinted in Defazio, Spanier, and Trogdon, *Letters of Ernest Hemingway,* 2:459. Bromfield apparently transcribed the contents of Harcourt's letter in a missive to Hemingway, who relayed the information to Fitzgerald.

"I didn't get": Harold Loeb to Ernest Hemingway, undated, series 3, Incoming Correspondence, "Loeb, Harold," Ernest Hemingway Collection, John F. Kennedy Presidential Library and Museum.

"Being a simple": Ernest Hemingway to Horace Liveright, June 21, 1925, reprinted in Defazio, Spanier, and Trogdon, *Letters of Ernest Hemingway,* 2:352. For Liveright's request that Hemingway act as a scout, see Gilmer, *Horace Liveright,* 122.

"up to them": Ernest Hemingway to Harold Loeb, ca. early November 1925, reprinted in Defazio, Spanier, and Trogdon, *Letters of Ernest Hemingway,* 2:407–8.

136   *22,000 copies: Dark Laughter* was released on September 15, 1925. For the release date and sales figures, see Gilmer, *Horace Liveright,* 114–15.

"The sales climbed": Anderson, *Sherwood Anderson's Memoirs,* 363.

"This whole novel": Sherwood Anderson to Horace Liveright, April 18, 1925, reprinted in Jones, *Letters of Sherwood Anderson,* 141–42.

"I dare say": Anderson, *Sherwood Anderson's Memoirs,* 474–75.

"Anderson's last two": F. Scott Fitzgerald to Maxwell Perkins, December 30, 1925, Archives of Charles Scribner's Sons, Princeton University Library. Hemingway's and Fitzgerald's feelings about Anderson's latest works may have been symptomatic of a larger Sherwood Anderson backlash. Although Kay Boyle claimed that Anderson had been something of a literary hero and inspiration to the expat creatives, Sylvia Beach later recalled that "Sherwood Anderson [was] judged harshly by the young writers; and suffered considerably from the falling-off of his followers." That said, "he was a forerunner, and, whether they acknowledge it or not, the generation of the twenties owes him a considerable debt." Beach, *Shakespeare and Company,* 32.

"so terribly bad": Hemingway, *A Moveable Feast,* 60.

137   *only about a week:* In the text of *Torrents,* Hemingway informs the reader that he wrote the book in ten days. Yet in a letter to a friend, he claimed that he had actually written the book in six days. Ernest Hemingway to Isidor Schneider, June 29, 1926, reprinted in Sanderson, Spanier, and Trogdon, *Letters of Ernest Hemingway,* 3:91.

It enraged him: Hemingway explained his thinking on Anderson in a March 30, 1926, letter to Edwin L. Peterson, reprinted ibid., 44–45.

"the last refuge": Hotchner, *Papa Hemingway,* 70.

"Hemingway, you have": Ernest Hemingway, *The Torrents of Spring: A Romantic Novel in Honor of the Passing of a Great Race* (New York: Scribner, 2004), 68.

"And you're not": Ibid., 76–77.

"Gertrude Stein . . . Ah": Ibid., 75.

138   *"detestable":* Baker, *Ernest Hemingway: A Life Story,* 159.

"wasn't quite good": Dos Passos, *The Best Times,* 176–77.

"both for its": Stewart, *By a Stroke of Luck!* 157.

He descended: The Murphys were apparently regularly targeted for readings by members of the Crowd. Fitzgerald was said to crave Sara's approval in particular; Donald Stewart would also arrive on their doorstep with material. While he was writing *The Haddocks,* he often presented them with drafts. "Every evening I would take the day's pages over to the Murphys' apartment and after dinner would read to them," he wrote later. "I can still hear Sara's marvelously raucous laughter." Ibid., 130.

"in questionable taste": Tomkins, *Living Well Is the Best Revenge,* 25.

139   *seeing a good deal:* Ernest Hemingway to Harold Loeb, ca. early November 1925, reprinted in Defazio, Spanier, and Trogdon, *Letters of Ernest Hemingway,* 2:408.

had begun stopping off: Hawkins, *Unbelievable Happiness and Final Sorrow,* 44.

"one of the": Ibid.

Pauline's persuasion: Sokoloff, *Hadley,* 83.

"Maybe when you": Ernest Hemingway to Horace Liveright, December 7, 1925, reprinted in Defazio, Spanier, and Trogdon, *Letters of Ernest Hemingway,* 2:434.

140   *"a cold-blooded contract-breaker":* Baker, *Ernest Hemingway: A Life Story,* 160.

"I have known": Ernest Hemingway to F. Scott Fitzgerald, December 31, 1925–January 1, 1926, reprinted in Defazio, Spanier, and Trogdon, *Letters of Ernest Hemingway,* 2:459.

141   *drinking champagne:* Ernest Hemingway to Harold Loeb, ca. early November 1925, reprinted in Defazio, Spanier, and Trogdon, *Letters of Ernest Hemingway,* 2:407; *"very thick":* F. Scott Fitzgerald to Maxwell Perkins, ca. December 30, 1925, reprinted in Bruccoli, *F. Scott Fitzgerald: A Life in Letters,* 133.

"working like a": Dos Passos, *The Best Times,* 176.

"To one rather": F. Scott Fitzgerald to Horace Liveright and T. R. Smith, December 1925, reprinted in Bruccoli, *Scott and Ernest: The Authority of Failure and the Authority of Success,* 29–30.

"the most difficult": Hemingway, *A Moveable Feast,* 118.

"over and over": Ernest Hemingway to Isabelle Simmons Godolphin, December 3, 1925, reprinted in Defazio, Spanier, and Trogdon, *Letters of Ernest Hemingway,* 2:426.

"I had not": Cannell, "Scenes with a Hero," 146.

142   *"murder"*: Hemingway, *A Moveable Feast,* 215–16.

"One is new": Ibid., 216.

an heiress: Around this time, Pauline's trust fund had just been fattened up to $60,000 by her uncle Gus, a figure that amounts to approximately $815,000 today. Ruth A. Hawkins reports that Pauline's monthly yield from that fund was around $250, or about $3,400 today (*Unbelievable Happiness and Final Sorrow,* 47).

not suited for life: As Valerie Hemingway put it, "Hadley didn't like the limelight. She didn't want to be out every night. She had nurtured [Hemingway], but then he grew beyond it. When Pauline came along, she said, 'I'll go out with Ernest.' She was the person with the money. There would be nannies, that sort of thing" (interview with the author, December 20, 2013).

editorial feedback: Hawkins, *Unbelievable Happiness and Final Sorrow,* 46. Although the content of Pauline's feedback is unclear, Hawkins says that "the book probably benefited not only from Pauline's editorial skills, but from the fact that she had not yet become a part of the Pamplona bullfight crowd, so she would have been able to read it from somewhat of an outsider's perspective" (email to the author, March 7, 2015).

"innocently": Cannell, "Scenes with a Hero," 146.

143   *REJECTING TORRENTS:* Cable from Horace Liveright to Ernest Hemingway, December 30, 1925, reprinted in Gilmer, *Horace Liveright,* 123.

"entirely unprejudiced": Horace Liveright to Ernest Hemingway, December 30, 1925, reprinted ibid., 123–25.

144   *"I'm loose"*: Ernest Hemingway to F. Scott Fitzgerald, December 31, 1925–January 1, 1926, reprinted in Defazio, Spanier, and Trogdon, *Letters of Ernest Hemingway,* 2:459–61.

"He's dead set": F. Scott Fitzgerald to Maxwell Perkins, ca. December 30, 1925, reprinted in Bruccoli, *F. Scott Fitzgerald: A Life in Letters,* 134.

YOU CAN GET: Cable from F. Scott Fitzgerald to Maxwell Perkins, January 8, 1926, F. Scott Fitzgerald Files, Archives of Charles Scribner's Sons, Princeton University Library.

145   *PUBLISH NOVEL AT:* Cable from Maxwell Perkins to F. Scott Fitzgerald, January 8, 1926, F. Scott Fitzgerald Files, Archives of Charles Scribner's Sons, Princeton University Library.

"it is not": Maxwell Perkins to F. Scott Fitzgerald, January 13, 1926, F. Scott Fitzgerald Files, Archives of Charles Scribner's Sons, Princeton University Library.

"If only": Maxwell Perkins to F. Scott Fitzgerald, February 3, 1926, F. Scott

Fitzgerald Files, Archives of Charles Scribner's Sons, Princeton University Library.

"astonishingly fine": Ibid.

"People are beginning": Maxwell Perkins to F. Scott Fitzgerald, February 3, 1926, F. Scott Fitzgerald Files, Archives of Charles Scribner's Sons, Princeton University Library.

146 *"Your office was":* Ernest Hemingway to Horace Liveright, January 19, 1926, reprinted in Sanderson, Spanier, and Trogdon, *Letters of Ernest Hemingway,* 3:22.

"crazy": F. Scott Fitzgerald to Maxwell Perkins, ca. January 19, 1926, Archives of Charles Scribner's Sons, Princeton University Library.

"tempermental in business": F. Scott Fitzgerald to Maxwell Perkins, ca. March 1, 1926, Archives of Charles Scribner's Sons, Princeton University Library.

"You won't be": Ibid.

10. Dorothy Parker's Scotch

147 *"It was the":* Malcolm Cowley, "Unshaken Friend — II," *The New Yorker,* April 8, 1944, 30.

fashionable preachers: As noted by former Scribner's editor John Hall Wheelock: "Scribners had made its great success, originally, when it was founded in 1846, in the field of theology. It published books of sermons. A book of sermons had the popularity in those days that perhaps a mystery would have today." He adds that his own grandfather's sermons were published by Scribner's, and added: "The fashionable preachers of the day always had books of their sermons published." John Hall Wheelock, *The Last Romantic: A Poet Among Publishers* (Columbia: University of South Carolina Press, 2002), 77.

"dreary": Kay Boyle, afterword to McAlmon, *Being Geniuses Together,* 336.

148 *"Max was a":* Wheelock, *The Last Romantic,* 66.

149 *"a great [editorial] instinct":* Charles Scribner III, interview with the author, June 20, 2014.

"This Side of": Cowley, "Unshaken Friend — II," 30.

"could not stomach": A. Scott Berg, *Max Perkins: Editor of Genius* (New York: Berkley Books, 2008), 12.

"serious flaws": Wheelock, *The Last Romantic,* 58.

"It's frivolous": Ibid. Another account of the meeting states that there was an on-the-spot vote about the book's acceptance, resulting in a tie between

the more innovation-oriented editors and the house elders. Berg, *Max Perkins,* 16.

150   *"bad boys of"*: Cowley, "Unshaken Friend—II," 30.

a kerfuffle: Ibid.

"wonder": Maxwell Perkins to F. Scott Fitzgerald, January 28, 1926, F. Scott Fitzgerald Files, Archives of Charles Scribner's Sons, Princeton University Library. The play adapted from *The Great Gatsby,* staged by George Cukor, opened at the Ambassador Theater on February 2, 1926; the film adaptation was released by Paramount in August of that year, with Warner Baxter in the title role.

151   *an amicable reception:* Two Liveright employees, Donald Friede and Edith Stern, later told Liveright biographer Walker Gilmer that they had given Hemingway a "friendly reception," and that Liveright was "gracious but firm" when rejecting *Torrents* but still vied for *The Sun Also Rises.* Gilmer, *Horace Liveright,* 125.

"[I] told him": Ernest Hemingway to Louis and Mary Bromfield, ca. March 8, 1926, reprinted in Sanderson, Spanier, and Trogdon, *Letters of Ernest Hemingway,* 3:36.

152   *"A poseur to":* Gilmer, *Horace Liveright,* 236.

"It was": Ibid., 235.

the windows of: Maxwell Perkins to F. Scott Fitzgerald, February 6, 1926, F. Scott Fitzgerald Files, Archives of Charles Scribner's Sons, Princeton University Library.

"He wrote an": Ernest Hemingway to Louis Bromfield, March 8, 1926, reprinted in Sanderson, Spanier, and Trogdon, *Letters of Ernest Hemingway,* 3:36.

Not only did: Maxwell Perkins to F. Scott Fitzgerald, March 4, 1926, F. Scott Fitzgerald Files, Archives of Charles Scribner's Sons, Princeton University Library.

153   *"He is a":* Ibid.

"I'm glad you": F. Scott Fitzgerald to Maxwell Perkins, February 25, 1926, F. Scott Fitzgerald Files, Archives of Charles Scribner's Sons, Princeton University Library.

"crazy": Ernest Hemingway to William Smith and Harold Loeb, February 28, 1926, reprinted in Sanderson, Spanier, and Trogdon, *Letters of Ernest Hemingway,* 3:30.

"I should have": Ernest Hemingway to Louis and Mary Bromfield, ca. March 8, 1926, reprinted ibid., 36.

"I felt sorry": Ibid.

154   *"All the time":* Ernest Hemingway to Gertrude Stein and Alice B. Toklas,

reprinted in Defazio, Spanier, and Trogdon, *Letters of Ernest Hemingway,* 2:55.

more than doubled: According to one source, the number doubled from 15,000 to 32,000 "within a few years." Pete Hamill, introduction to *The Speakeasies of 1932,* ed. Gordon Kahn and Al Hirschfeld (Milwaukee: Glenn Young Books/Applause, 2003), 11.

Fitzgerald's was said: John Dos Passos attested that "Scott had good bootleggers" (*The Best Times,* 145).

"Everybody [was] cockeyed": Ernest Hemingway to Isabel Simmons Godolphin, February 25, 1926, reprinted in Sanderson, Spanier, and Trogdon, *Letters of Ernest Hemingway,* 3:32.

"hells own amount": Ernest Hemingway to Louis and Mary Bromfield, ca. March 8, 1926, reprinted ibid., 37.

155   *"until they dropped":* Nathaniel Benchley, *Robert Benchley* (New York: McGraw-Hill, 1955), 162.

"There is something": Dorothy Parker, "Reading and Writing: A Book of Great Short Stories—Something About Cabell," *The New Yorker,* October 29, 1927, 92.

"Gertrude Stein . . . said": Marion Capron, "Dorothy Parker: The Art of Fiction No. 13," *Paris Review* 13 (Summer 1956), http://www.theparis review.org/interviews/4933/the-art-of-fiction-no-13-dorothy-parker.

"caused about as": Parker, "Reading and Writing," 92.

156   *kindred spirit:* Marion Meade, *Dorothy Parker: What Fresh Hell Is This?* (New York: Penguin Books, 2006), 163–64.

harbored serious literary ambitions: For example, despite his success and celebrity, Robert Benchley "brooded over the fact that he was making no substantial contribution to Progress." Benchley, *Robert Benchley,* 81.

"Write novels": Dorothy Parker to Robert Benchley, November 7, 1929, reprinted in *Letters from the Lost Generation: Gerald and Sara Murphy and Friends,* ed. Linda Patterson Miller (New Brunswick, N.J.: Rutgers University Press, 1991), 46.

decided on the spot: Meade, *Dorothy Parker,* 164.

calling her "Dotty": Hemingway refers to Parker thus in a ca. March 8, 1926, letter to Louis and Mary Bromfield recounting the goings-on during his New York trip; reprinted in Sanderson, Spanier, and Trogdon, *Letters of Ernest Hemingway,* 3:37.

157   *Other powerful critics:* Hemingway claimed that he was asked for references to other young talent by Gorman and Wilson. Ernest Hemingway to Morley Callaghan, March 5, 1926, reprinted ibid., 34.

the Coffee House: In a ca. March 8, 2015, letter to Louis Bromfield,

Hemingway mentions that he had run into an acquaintance at the Coffee House one evening; reprinted ibid., 36.

no-introduction policy: "Custom was they never introduced because it was assumed [everyone] knew each other . . . Because everyone was at a high level of fame . . . that was the club conceit. Introductions were frowned on." Club member and historian Bill Ray, interview with the author, October 2, 2014. Early membership lists provided to the author by Ray and the club.

"one of the": Ernest Hemingway to Louis and Mary Bromfield, ca. March 8, 1926, reprinted in Sanderson, Spanier, and Trogdon, *Letters of Ernest Hemingway,* 3:37.

"great love at": Ernest Hemingway to Isabel Simmons Godolphin, February 25, 1926, reprinted ibid., 32.

"the strikingly good-looking": Wheelock, *The Last Romantic,* 94.

"cultists": Thomas Wolfe, quoted in Stanley Olson, *Elinor Wylie: A Biography* (New York: Dial Press/James Wade, 1979), 246.

158 *funded the odyssey:* Meade, *Dorothy Parker,* 165.

"[On] the 4th": Ernest Hemingway to Louis and Mary Bromfield, ca. March 8, 1926, reprinted in Sanderson, Spanier, and Trogdon, *Letters of Ernest Hemingway,* 3:37.

had taken saltpeter: Edmund Wilson, *The Twenties: From the Notebooks and Diaries of the Period,* ed. Leon Edel (New York: Farrar, Straus and Giroux, 1975), 347. Parker biographer Marion Meade notes that Parker "continue[d] to giggle" about the saltpeter episode to friends for months to come (*Dorothy Parker,* 166).

11. Kill or Be Killed

159 *waited in vain:* Ernest Hemingway to Isabel Simmons Godolphin, February 25, 1926, reprinted in Sanderson, Spanier, and Trogdon, *Letters of Ernest Hemingway,* 3:32.

"unbelievable wrenching, kicking": Hemingway, *A Moveable Feast,* 217–18.

still cultivating Hadley: Ibid., 217.

"wished [he] had": Ibid., 218.

160 *"It certainly broke":* Gerald Murphy to Hadley Hemingway, March 3, 1926, reprinted in Miller, *Letters from the Lost Generation,* 15.

"they gave it": Dos Passos, *The Best Times,* 177–78.

ready for fall publication: Ernest Hemingway to Maxwell Perkins, March 10, 1926, reprinted in Sanderson, Spanier, and Trogdon, *Letters of Ernest Hemingway,* 3:40.

"with all of": Maxwell Perkins to Ernest Hemingway, March 24, 1926, Archives of Charles Scribner's Sons, Princeton University Library.

"The bulls are": Hemingway, *The Sun Also Rises,* 149.

The real Pedro Romero: Allen Josephs, "Toreo: The Moral Axis in *The Sun Also Rises,*" *Hemingway Review* 6 (Fall 1986): 88–99; Allen Josephs, interview with the author, April 1, 2014.

161 *"That seemed to"*: Hemingway, *The Sun Also Rises,* 192; Ernest Hemingway, typewritten revision of *The Sun Also Rises,* item 198, Ernest Hemingway Collection, John F. Kennedy Presidential Library and Museum.

"Oh Jake": Ernest Hemingway, draft 1 of *The Sun Also Rises,* item 194, Ernest Hemingway Collection, John F. Kennedy Presidential Library and Museum.

"Yes," I said. "Isn't": Hemingway, *The Sun Also Rises,* 198.

"blown out of": Gerald Murphy to Hadley Hemingway, March 3, 1926, reprinted in Miller, *Letters from the Lost Generation,* 16.

"If these bastards": Hemingway, *A Moveable Feast,* 215.

162 *"We were all"*: Dos Passos, *The Best Times,* 177–78.

"I finished re-writing": Ernest Hemingway to Maxwell Perkins, April 1, 1926, reprinted in Sanderson, Spanier, and Trogdon, *Letters of Ernest Hemingway,* 3:46.

TO MY SON: In a ca. April 20, 1926, letter to F. Scott Fitzgerald, Hemingway wrote that he had been thinking about including that particular dedication; reprinted ibid., 56.

reviewers and writers: The list included Robert Woolf, Edmund Wilson, Herman Gorman, Burton Rascoe, and many other important critics. Ezra Pound, Robert Benchley, Donald Ogden Stewart, James Joyce, and Sinclair Lewis were also to get copies. He asked that one be sent to Elinor Wylie, too, with whom he had enjoyed such a flirtation during his New York trip. Ernest Hemingway to Maxwell Perkins, April 8, 1926, Archives of Charles Scribner's Sons, Princeton University Library.

Jonathan Cape: Sylvia Beach stated in her memoirs that she made the first connection between Hemingway and Cape: "I remember Jonathan Cape's enthusiasm over his first Hemingway [reading.] Mr. Cape, Colonel Lawrence's and Joyce's publisher in England, asked me, on one of his visits to Paris, what American he should publish. 'Here, read Hemingway!' I said —and that is how Mr. Cape became Hemingway's English publisher." Beach, *Shakespeare and Company,* 82.

"I don't think": Ernest Hemingway to Maxwell Perkins, April 24, 1926, Archives of Charles Scribner's Sons, Princeton University Library. Hemingway later became frustrated with Cape's handling of *The Sun Also Rises,* released in the U.K. as *Fiesta* in 1927. After its release, he com-

plained bitterly to Cape about the house's marketing and editing of the book.

163   *right of first refusal:* Jonathan Cape would decline to publish *Torrents* later that year. L. E. Pollinger, manager of the Department of American Books for Curtis Brown, would write to Charles Scribner, "As you rather thought, Cape has decided to let '*The Torrents of Spring*' by Ernest Hemingway pass him by, and I have written direct to Hemingway telling him this . . . news." L. E. Pollinger to Charles Scribner, August 31, 1926, Archives of Charles Scribner's Sons, Princeton University Library.

"In fact, the": Maxwell Perkins to Ernest Hemingway, April 12, 1926, Archives of Charles Scribner's Sons, Princeton University Library.

"the Sun A.R.": Ernest Hemingway to Maxwell Perkins, April 24, 1926, Archives of Charles Scribner's Sons, Princeton University Library.

"low as hell": Ernest Hemingway to F. Scott Fitzgerald, May 4, 1926, reprinted in Sanderson, Spanier, and Trogdon, *Letters of Ernest Hemingway,* 3:70.

"Ernest M. Shit": Ernest Hemingway to F. Scott Fitzgerald, ca. May 15, 1926, reprinted ibid., 76.

"Max, you have": Louise Saunders, quoted by her granddaugher Jenny Phillips, interview with the author, September 9, 2014. Phillips states that her mother and aunt overheard the conversation and recounted it to her.

"He always staunchly": Ibid.

164   *"almost unpublishable":* Maxwell Perkins to F. Scott Fitzgerald, May 26, 1926, F. Scott Fitzgerald Files, Archives of Charles Scribner's Sons, Princeton University Library. Fitzgerald relayed this assessment to Hemingway, who mentioned it verbatim — and proudly — to a friend in a letter around a month later. Ernest Hemingway to Isidor Schneider, June 29, 1926, reprinted in Sanderson, Spanier, and Trogdon, *Letters of Ernest Hemingway,* 3:92.

"It's a vulgar": Wheelock, *The Last Romantic,* 59.

"ultra conservative": Maxwell Perkins to Charles Scribner Jr., May 27, 1926, Archives of Charles Scribner's Sons, Princeton University Library.

"general misery": Ibid.

Rumors circulated: Malcolm Cowley recounted the anecdote in his profile of Perkins in *The New Yorker,* quoting a letter written by an unnamed former Scribner's employee to a mutual friend. Cowley, "Unshaken Friend — II," 33. Charles Scribner III does not believe that the debate over the acquisition of *The Sun Also Rises* ever escalated to this level, calling a dramatic resignation threat "totally out of character" for Perkins. He says: "Perkins was a patient man; he wasn't into showdowns. He would have advocated . . . [and] lobbied strong." Charles Scribner III, interview with the author, June 20, 2014.

165 *"I should think"*: William Cary Brownell, "Report by Brownell on Hemingway's 1st book," undated but filed under 1926, Archives of Charles Scribner's Sons, Princeton University Library.

 "[the publisher] is": Maxwell Perkins to M. J. Levey, May 4, 1927, Archives of Charles Scribner's Sons, Princeton University Library.

 "'The Sun Also Rises' seems": Maxwell Perkins to Ernest Hemingway, May 18, 1926, Archives of Charles Scribner's Sons, Princeton University Library.

166 *"I am not"*: Ibid.

 limited advertising campaign: The advertising campaign for *The Torrents of Spring* began in March 1926 and concluded the following October. Scribner's ran ads in major publications, such as the *Saturday Review of Literature,* the *New York Times,* the *New York Herald Tribune,* and *The Atlantic Monthly*—and, of course, the house's own publication, *Scribner's Magazine*—yet did not expand its campaign beyond New York and Boston. Advertising Records, "Hemingway, E: The Torrents of Spring," Archives of Charles Scribner's Sons, Princeton University Library.

 "Hemingway as a writer": "Charles Scribner's Sons Supplement to List of Spring Publications—1926," reprinted in Robert W. Trogdon, *The Lousy Racket: Hemingway, Scribners, and the Business of Literature* (Kent, Ohio: Kent State University Press, 2007), 33–34.

167 *seemed confused:* On June 13, 1926, the *New York Times Book Review* ran an unsigned piece calling *Torrents* "not precisely what might have been expected of the author of *In Our Time.*"

 "Parody is a gift": Harry Hansen, review of *The Torrents of Spring, New York World,* May 30, 1926.

 "audacious little volume": Review of *The Torrents of Spring, Kansas City Star,* excerpted in Leonard J. Leff, *Hemingway and His Conspirators* (Lanham, Md.: Rowman & Littlefield, 1997), 40.

 "Mr. Hemingway's name": Margery Latimer, review of *The Torrents of Spring, New York Herald Tribune Books,* July 18, 1926.

168 *"cockeyed lazy"*: Ernest Hemingway, "The Autobiography of Alice B. Hemingway," unpublished manuscript, folder 265.a, Ernest Hemingway Collection, John F. Kennedy Presidential Library and Museum.

 "Mommy": Hotchner, *Papa Hemingway,* 49.

 "attacked someone that": Hemingway, *A Moveable Feast,* 60.

 "What did he": Maxwell Perkins to F. Scott Fitzgerald, June 18, 1926, F. Scott Fitzgerald Files, Archives of Charles Scribner's Sons, Princeton University Library.

 "the most self-conscious": Anderson, *Sherwood Anderson's Memoirs,* 475.

"slopping": Ernest Hemingway to Sherwood Anderson, May 21, 1926, reprinted in Sanderson, Spanier, and Trogdon, *Letters of Ernest Hemingway,* 3:81–83.

"There was something": Anderson, *Sherwood Anderson's Memoirs,* 475.

169   *"You . . . speak to":* Sherwood Anderson to Ernest Hemingway, ca. June 1926, Incoming Correspondence, Ernest Hemingway Collection, John F. Kennedy Presidential Library and Museum.

"How about": Anderson, *Sherwood Anderson's Memoirs,* 476.

"We had two": Ernest Hemingway to Maxwell Perkins, January 20, 1927, Archives of Charles Scribner's Sons, Princeton University Library.

"Hemingway had been": Stein, *Autobiography of Alice B. Toklas,* 216.

"In the case": Sherwood Anderson to Laura Lou Copenhaver, November 9, 1937, reprinted in Jones, *Letters of Sherwood Anderson,* 392.

170   *"It was a beautiful":* Sherwood Anderson to Gertrude Stein, April 25, 1926, box 16, Carlos Baker Collection of Ernest Hemingway, Princeton University Library.

"Do you think": Sokoloff, *Hadley,* 86. The quote is a slight elaboration on the one in Sokoloff's book: "One night [Hadley] asked Jinny, whom she knew was very close to her sister, whether she thought that 'Pauline and Ernest got along awfully well,' or some such."

soon-to-be-terminated pregnancy: Biographer Ruth Hawkins contends that Pauline may have discovered that she was pregnant while on the trip, which would have accounted for her uncharacteristic lack of restraint and moodiness. Hawkins, *Unbelievable Happiness and Final Sorrow,* 66. Also, the following autumn, when Pauline and Hemingway were undertaking a three-month separation from each other, per Hadley's mandate, Pauline wrote to Hemingway, "I've thought very hard and what I think is four months is a . . . lot tighter than nine," indicating that the pair may at some point have been contemplating a separation of nine months, perhaps while Pauline left Paris for the duration of a pregnancy. Pauline Pfeiffer to Ernest Hemingway, October 2, 1926, series 3, Incoming Correspondence, box IC15, Hemingway, Pauline Pfeiffer, Ernest Hemingway Collection, John F. Kennedy Presidential Library and Museum.

"innocent": Hadley told Alice Sokoloff that up until this point she was still ignorant of the affair, adding that she had been either "'terribly innocent' about it all or 'just plain dumb.'" Sokoloff, *Hadley,* 86.

"There are two": Patrick Hemingway interview with the author, September 26, 2014.

171   *Hadley's interpretation:* Hadley Hemingway to Carlos Baker, August 1962, paraphrased in Baker, *Ernest Hemingway: A Life Story,* 168; Sokoloff, *Hadley,* 86.

woman-to-woman chat: Hadley Hemingway to Alice Sokoloff, November 29, 1970, quoted in Sokoloff, *Hadley,* 86–87.

three short stories: Hemingway later claimed that on May 16, the bullfights were snowed out, so he stayed at the pension and wrote "The Killers," "Today Is Friday," and "Ten Indians." Plimpton, "The Art of Fiction: Ernest Hemingway," 79.

"You tired after": Ibid.

to get an abortion: Ruth Hawkins speculates, on the basis of compelling yet circumstantial evidence, that Pauline may have joined Hemingway in Madrid and gotten the procedure done then. Hawkins, *Unbelievable Happiness and Final Sorrow,* 65–66. Pauline and Hemingway's son Patrick doesn't find the idea of an abortion plausible or in keeping with his mother's character and background: "I really don't believe it. Pauline was brought up with a very strict Catholic education at the Sacred Heart convent in St. Louis and it stuck for a long time. My mother didn't give up her religion until she was in her late forties . . . [H]er Catholicism was one of the things that made the marriage complicated, according to my father." Some of Hawkins's circumstantial evidence supporting the possibility of a pregnancy and abortion involves a story Hemingway later penned — titled "Hills Like White Elephants," in which a couple struggles with an unwanted pregnancy and the specter of an abortion — and presented to Pauline on their eventual honeymoon, but Patrick Hemingway remains unconvinced: "People are always trying to hang Christmas ornaments on what my father wrote in stories" (interview with the author, September 26, 2014). Hawkins, however, points out that if Pauline had found herself pregnant that spring, her choices would have been limited; having the baby would have been as much of an affront to her Catholicism as an abortion: "To have had a baby out of wedlock with a man who was married to someone else . . . would have been a public admission that she had sinned." It may have been a question of which route was the lesser sin (interview with the author, October 13, 2014).

172   *their Antibes villa:* Just as madcap New York City belonged to the Fitzgeralds, the Murphys have often been credited with "inventing" and then epitomizing the Riviera lifestyle — or at the very least popularizing the area as a summertime destination for wealthy expats. In the early 1920s, Antibes was still a glorious little backwater; the Biarritz crowds that Hemingway so loathed stayed away. "Summer on the Mediterranean was regarded as unhealthy and no one would go down there," recalled Archibald MacLeish, adding that one could rent "almost anything for nothing" (*Reflections,* 43).

"burnished blue-steel": Honoria Donnelly, *Sara & Gerald,* 18; *heliotrope, eucalyptus, and tomatoes:* Dos Passos, *The Best Times,* 168.

opera-length pearl necklace: The Murphys' granddaughter Laura Donnelly recalls a jewelry inventory that belonged to her grandfather, which included details of the 104-pearl strand. F. Scott Fitzgerald later immortalized the necklace in his *Tender Is the Night* character Nicole Diver — inspired by Sara — who also wore a pearl necklace to the beach, draped down her back. Picasso painted Sara wearing those pearls. Laura Donnelly says that the pearls immortalized by greats of the literary and art worlds have since "disappeared," although she still possesses other jewelry once belonging to her famous grandparents. Laura Donnelly, interview with the author, September 23, 2014.

offer them to: Roger Angell, interview with the author, October 7, 2014.

"They would never": MacLeish, *Reflections,* 46.

173   *"a grand distance":* Hadley Hemingway to Ernest Hemingway, two letters, both May 1926, Incoming Correspondence, Hadley Richardson Hemingway Mowrer, 1926 folder, Ernest Hemingway Collection, John F. Kennedy Presidential Library and Museum; *sent them necessities:* ibid.

shot of whisky: "Yesterday I . . . got so low I went downtown and spent 8 frcs. on some whiskey and felt repentant." Hadley Hemingway to Ernest Hemingway, May 1926, Incoming Correspondence, Hadley Richardson Hemingway Mowrer, 1926 folder, Ernest Hemingway Collection, John F. Kennedy Presidential Library and Museum. On her loneliness, she reported in the same letter, "I don't talk to a soul except Marie [the nanny] all day."

"Pfeiffer is stopping": Hadley Hemingway to Ernest Hemingway, May 1926, Incoming Correspondence, Hadley Richardson Hemingway Mowrer, 1926 folder, Ernest Hemingway Collection, John F. Kennedy Presidential Library and Museum.

alleviate the little: Hadley told biographer Alice Sokoloff that she thought Hemingway had drafted a "pathetic letter" depicting her and Bumby's loneliness, thus prompting a Good Samaritan visit from Pauline. Sokoloff, *Hadley,* 88. For speculation that Hadley accepted Pauline's visit out of fear that she'd otherwise join Hemingway in Spain, see Hawkins, *Unbelievable Happiness and Final Sorrow,* 53.

"to stop off": Hadley Hemingway to Ernest Hemingway, May 21, 1926, Incoming Correspondence, Hadley Richardson Hemingway Mowrer, 1926 folder, Ernest Hemingway Collection, John F. Kennedy Presidential Library and Museum.

174   *"She's sorry for":* Hadley Hemingway to Ernest Hemingway, May 1926, Incoming Correspondence, Hadley Richardson Hemingway Mowrer, 1926 folder, Ernest Hemingway Collection, John F. Kennedy Presidential Library and Museum.

"a splendid place": Hemingway, *A Moveable Feast,* 159.

colored-glass garland: Sokoloff, *Hadley,* 87.

"domestic difficulties": Zelda Fitzgerald paraphrased in Mayfield, *Exiles from Paradise,* 112.

"[My father] was unable": Donnelly, *Sara & Gerald,* 152.

"Why do you": Calvin Tomkins, interview with the author, September 10, 2014.

175   *"committing suicide on"*: Mayfield, *Exiles from Paradise,* 116.

"sense of carnival": Zelda Fitzgerald to Maxwell Perkins, September 1926, quoted in Miller, *Letters from the Lost Generation,* 5.

their inebriated hijinks: Mayfield, *Exiles from Paradise,* 114–16.

"We cannot": Sara Murphy to F. Scott Fitzgerald, ca. summer 1926, reprinted in Miller, *Letters from the Lost Generation,* 18.

176   *"What we loved"*: Tomkins, *Living Well Is the Best Revenge,* 109.

"Scott was a": Calvin Tomkins, interview with the author, September 11, 2014. Gerald Murphy once told Tomkins: "The one we took seriously was Ernest, not Scott. I suppose it was because Ernest's work seemed contemporary and new, and Scott's didn't." Tomkins, *Living Well Is the Best Revenge,* 117.

"People watched Hemingway": MacLeish, *Reflections,* 60–61.

his skin had: As recounted by Sara Mayfield, who spent time with the Fitzgeralds during this period, in *Exiles from Paradise,* 113.

"Scott is writing": Zelda Fitzgerald to Madeline Boyd, July 2, 1926, transcribed on the website of Sotheby's, which auctioned the letter in 2004 (http://www.sothebys.com/en/auctions/ecatalogue/lot.pdf.N07980.html/f/65/N07980-65.pdf), and also partly quoted in Bruccoli, *Fitzgerald and Hemingway,* 63.

"truly more interested": Hotchner, *Papa Hemingway,* 55.

177   *"certain qualifications"*: F. Scott Fitzgerald to Maxwell Perkins, ca. June 28, 1926, F. Scott Fitzgerald file, Archives of Charles Scribner's Sons, Princeton University Library.

"careless": The entire contents of the ca. June 1926 letter are reprinted in Sarason, *Hemingway and the* Sun Set, 256–59.

179   *"I think it"*: Ernest Hemingway to Maxwell Perkins, June 5, 1926, Archives of Charles Scribner's Sons, Princeton University Library.

"The only effect": F. Scott Fitzgerald to John O'Hara, July 25, 1936, reprinted in Bruccoli, *F. Scott Fitzgerald: A Life in Letters,* 303.

THE SUN ALSO: Ernest Hemingway to F. Scott Fitzgerald, ca. November 24, 1926, reprinted in Sanderson, Spanier, and Trogdon, *Letters of Ernest Hemingway,* 3:164.

180   *"I have hardly"*: Maxwell Perkins to Ernest Hemingway, July 20, 1926, Archives of Charles Scribner's Sons, Princeton University Library.

"After all if": Ernest Hemingway to Maxwell Perkins, August 26, 1926, Archives of Charles Scribner's Sons, Princeton University Library.

"very good dope": Ernest Hemingway to Maxwell Perkins, November 16, 1926, Archives of Charles Scribner's Sons, Princeton University Library.

"make one understand": Maxwell Perkins to Ernest Hemingway, October 30, 1926, Archives of Charles Scribner's Sons, Princeton University Library.

"all the fucking": Ernest Hemingway to Ezra Pound, February 13, 1927, reprinted in Sanderson, Spanier, and Trogdon, *Letters of Ernest Hemingway,* 3:202.

"Henry James is": Ernest Hemingway to Maxwell Perkins, June 5, 1926, Archives of Charles Scribner's Sons, Princeton University Library.

181   *"There are four"*: Maxwell Perkins to Ernest Hemingway, July 20, 1926, Archives of Charles Scribner's Sons, Princeton University Library.

"Henry or Whatsisname": Ernest Hemingway to Maxwell Perkins, August 21, 1926, Archives of Charles Scribner's Sons, Princeton University Library.

"An Englishman will": Maxwell Perkins to Ernest Hemingway, July 20, 1926, Archives of Charles Scribner's Sons, Princeton University Library.

"not imaginary": Ernest Hemingway to Maxwell Perkins, November 16, 1926, Archives of Charles Scribner's Sons, Princeton University Library.

"protected": Ernest Hemingway to Maxwell Perkins, November 16, 1926, Archives of Charles Scribner's Sons, Princeton University Library.

"It would be": Maxwell Perkins to Ernest Hemingway, July 20, 1926, Archives of Charles Scribner's Sons, Princeton University Library.

182   *"I have never"*: Ernest Hemingway to Maxwell Perkins, July 24, 1926, Archives of Charles Scribner's Sons, Princeton University Library.

"Perhaps we will": Ernest Hemingway to Maxwell Perkins, August 21, 1926, Archives of Charles Scribner's Sons, Princeton University Library.

183   *group activities:* Sokoloff, *Hadley,* 88.

crawled into bed: Diliberto, *Paris Without End,* 219.

rooting for Pauline: Sokoloff, *Hadley,* 88.

"As for you": Gerald Murphy to Ernest Hemingway, July 14, 1926, reprinted in Miller, *Letters from the Lost Generation,* 19.

"miscast": Gerald Murphy to Ernest Hemingway, September 6, 1926, reprinted ibid., 22. According to Calvin Tomkins, the Murphys nevertheless felt affection for Hadley as a person (interview with the author, September 10, 2014).

Hemingway-led tours: By the following year, even comedian Harpo Marx would make a bid to be included in Hemingway's Pamplona excursions.

In 1927 Gerald Murphy sent Hemingway a postcard proclaiming, "Harpo Marx wants to go to Pamplona." The Murphys were friends with Marx and had told him of their memorable time in Pamplona with the Hemingways in 1926. Donnelly, *Sara & Gerald,* 166.

184   *"He had absolutely":* Gerald Murphy to Calvin Tomkins, quoted in Tomkins, *Living Well Is the Best Revenge,* 115.

"Dansa Charles-*ton!":* Ibid., 114.

to look distinctly forlorn: Baker, *Ernest Hemingway: A Life Story,* 172.

"I am going": Pauline Pfeiffer to Ernest and Hadley Hemingway, July 15, 1926, quoted ibid., 172.

185   *"[It is] an awfully":* Ernest Hemingway to Henry Strater, ca. July 24, 1926, reprinted in Sanderson, Spanier, and Trogdon, *Letters of Ernest Hemingway,* 3:101.

"his name known": Stewart, *By a Stroke of Luck!* 155. For Stewart's bachelor party attendees, see ibid., 156.

"Hadley's tempo is": Gerald Murphy to Ernest Hemingway, September 6, 1926, reprinted in Miller, *Letters from the Lost Generation,* 21–22.

"believe in what": Gerald and Sara Murphy to Ernest Hemingway, ca. fall 1926, reprinted ibid., 23.

"evil": Hemingway, *A Moveable Feast,* 219.

186   TO HADLEY RICHARDSON: Ernest Hemingway to Maxwell Perkins, August 26, 1926, Archives of Charles Scribner's Sons, Princeton University Library.

12. How Happy Are Kings

191   *three more months:* Pauline Pfeiffer to Ernest Hemingway, October 2, 1926, Incoming Correspondence, Pauline Pfeiffer Hemingway, Ernest Hemingway Collection, John F. Kennedy Presidential Library and Museum.

financial settlement: Pauline Pfeiffer to Ernest Hemingway, October 25, 1926, Incoming Correspondence, Pauline Pfeiffer Hemingway, Ernest Hemingway Collection, John F. Kennedy Presidential Library and Museum.

"All I want": Ernest Hemingway to Pauline Pfeiffer, November 12, 1926, reprinted in Sanderson, Spanier, and Trogdon, *Letters of Ernest Hemingway,* 3:141.

"Trying unusual experiment": Ernest Hemingway to F. Scott Fitzgerald, ca. September 7, 1926, reprinted ibid., 118. Hemingway was quoting from and deliberating the poem "Happy Thought" by Robert Louis Stevenson. During this period, somewhat astonishingly, Hemingway even penned a

desperate letter to Sherwood Anderson, describing his relentless insomnia and complaining about feeling burdened. Ernest Hemingway to Sherwood Anderson, ca. September 7, 1926, reprinted ibid., 115.

192 *"I'd rather die"*: Ernest Hemingway to Pauline Pfeiffer, November 12, 1926, reprinted ibid., 140.

"You may not": Maxwell Perkins to Ernest Hemingway, August 20, 1926, Archives of Charles Scribner's Sons, Princeton University Library.

"They gain an": Maxwell Perkins to Ernest Hemingway, September 8, 1926, Archives of Charles Scribner's Sons, Princeton University Library.

193 *had appalled her:* Meade, *Dorothy Parker,* 167–68. Hemingway had mentioned Parker's trip to Spain in a missive to Fitzgerald earlier that year, adding that "of course [she] hated it." Ernest Hemingway to F. Scott Fitzgerald, May 4, 1926, reprinted in Sanderson, Spanier, and Trogdon, *Letters of Ernest Hemingway,* 3:71.

194 *"viciously unfair"*: Stewart, *By a Stroke of Luck!* 157. Hemingway was not the only person who was unsympathetic to and callous about Dorothy Parker's suicide attempts. Zelda Fitzgerald would write to a friend, "Dorothy Parker is here [in Paris] showing her wounds." Zelda Fitzgerald to Madeline Boyd, July 2, 1926, reprinted on Sotheby's website, http://www.sothebys.com/en/auctions/ecatalogue/lot.pdf.N07980.html/f/65/N07980-65.pdf.

"No one else": St. John, "Interview with Donald Ogden Stewart," 199.

one of her favorite: Meade, *Dorothy Parker,* 170.

"just dying of": Sokoloff, *Hadley,* 91.

195 *"We have three"*: Maxwell Perkins to Ernest Hemingway, March 2, 1927, Archives of Charles Scribner's Sons, Princeton University Library.

"any kind of": Maxwell Perkins to Ernest Hemingway, January 25, 1927, Archives of Charles Scribner's Sons, Princeton University Library.

"Papers are glad": Maxwell Perkins to Ernest Hemingway, January 28, 1927, Archives of Charles Scribner's Sons, Princeton University Library.

"I would rather": Ernest Hemingway to Maxwell Perkins, February 14, 1927, Archives of Charles Scribner's Sons, Princeton University Library.

"I never went": Ernest Hemingway to Maxwell Perkins, February 19, 1927, Archives of Charles Scribner's Sons, Princeton University Library.

196 *"If I break"*: Ibid.

"had Scott [Fitzgerald]": Maxwell Perkins to Ernest Hemingway, March 2, 1927, Archives of Charles Scribner's Sons, Princeton University Library.

"We are preparing": Maxwell Perkins to F. Scott Fitzgerald, January 6, 1927, F. Scott Fitzgerald Files, Archives of Charles Scribner's Sons, Princeton University Library.

"They are not": Maxwell Perkins to Ernest Hemingway, September 8, 1926, Archives of Charles Scribner's Sons, Princeton University Library.

197   *"more than a best-seller"*: Advertisement reprinted in Bruccoli, Smith, and Kerr, *Romantic Egoists,* 62.

"not only cold": Heywood Broun in the *New York Herald Tribune,* quoted ibid., 59; *"HEYWOOD BROUN scoffs"*: Advertisement quoted ibid.; *"cracking good stuff"*: Harry E. Dounce in the *New York Sun,* quoted ibid.

"The book is": Press release, Publicity and Promotion Files, Archives of Charles Scribner's Sons, Princeton University Library.

"quiver[ed] with life": Charles Scribner's Sons, fall 1926 catalogue, excerpted in Trogdon, *The Lousy Racket,* 44–45.

198   *easier for publications:* Maxwell Perkins to Ernest Hemingway, November 26, 1926, Archives of Charles Scribner's Sons, Princeton University Library.

"With [this novel's] publication": See, for example, advertisement for *The Sun Also Rises*, *The New Yorker,* October 23, 1926, 82.

No demographic was: For a full list of publications in which *The Sun Also Rises* was advertised, see advertising records, 1917–1965, "Howard — Hemingway" folder, box 3, Archives of Charles Scribner's Sons, Princeton University Library.

"Cleon": The artist's full name was Cleonike Damianakes Wilkins; she created cover art for books by a handful of seminal inner-circle Paris Lost Generation expats, including *All the Sad Young Men* by F. Scott Fitzgerald and *Save Me the Waltz* by Zelda Fitzgerald. Scribner's used her for two later Hemingway covers: *A Farewell to Arms* and a reissue of *In Our Time*. Hemingway detested the cover for *Farewell*. Ernest Hemingway to Maxwell Perkins, October 4, 1929, Archives of Charles Scribner's Sons, Princeton University Library. Cleon was paid a mere $50 "wrap design" fee to create the now famous image that adorned the first American edition of *The Sun Also Rises* — around $700 today. She eventually fell out of fashion. According to her niece Noel Osheroff, Cleon's career went into decline when abstract art came into vogue — "and that wasn't her thing," says Osheroff. Noel Osheroff, interview with the author, May 1, 2014. For more information, see the collection of Scribner's cover cards, Brandywine Conservancy and Museum of Art, Chadd's Ford, Pa.

"very much like": Ernest Hemingway to Maxwell Perkins, November 16, 1926, Archives of Charles Scribner's Sons, Princeton University Library.

199   *"This is the"*: "Marital Tragedy," *New York Times*, October 31, 1926, 7; *"No one need"*: *The New Republic,* review of *The Sun Also Rises,* December 22, 1926.

"It is alive": Conrad Aiken, review of *The Sun Also Rises, New York Herald Tribune,* October 31, 1926.

"lean, hard, athletic": "Marital Tragedy"; *"terse, precise"*: C. B. Chase, review of *The Sun Also Rises, Saturday Review of Literature,* December 11, 1926.

"knockout": Edmund Wilson to Ernest Hemingway, January 7, 1927, Ernest Hemingway Collection, John F. Kennedy Presidential Library and Museum.

200   *"beautiful and searching"*: Review of *The Sun Also Rises, Boston Evening Transcript,* November 6, 1926.

"you could go": Parker, "Reading and Writing," 92.

"BABY YOUR BOOK": Telegram from Dorothy Parker to Ernest Hemingway, November 23, 1926, Ernest Hemingway Collection, John F. Kennedy Presidential Library and Museum.

a Hemingway "cult": "Latin Quarter Notes," *Paris Tribune,* December 9 and December 28, 1926.

"hated [Sun]": Parker, "Reading and Writing," 93.

"extreme moral sordidness": Review of *The Sun Also Rises, Springfield Republican,* November 28, 1926.

accused Hemingway of sentimentality: Allen Tate, "Hard-Boiled," *The Nation,* December 15, 1926.

201   *"spiritual bankrupts"*: Review of *The Sun Also Rises, Boston Evening Transcript,* November 6, 1926; *"utterly degraded"*: Review of *The Sun Also Rises, Chicago Daily Tribune,* quoted in James R. Mellow, *Hemingway: A Life Without Consequences* (Boston: Da Capo Press, 1993), 335.

"a cock-and-bull story": John Dos Passos, "A Lost Generation," *The New Masses,* December 1926.

"coarse and uncouth": M. J. Levey to Charles Scribner's Sons, April 28, 1927, Archives of Charles Scribner's Sons, Princeton University Library.

"worse than worthless": Edward M. Smith to Charles Scribner's Sons, undated, Archives of Charles Scribner's Sons, Princeton University Library.

"perfect": Pauline Pfeiffer to Ernest Hemingway, December 18, 1926, Incoming Correspondence, Pauline Pfeiffer Hemingway, Ernest Hemingway Collection, John F. Kennedy Presidential Library and Museum.

"his own severest": Beach, *Shakespeare and Company,* 83.

"horse shit": Ernest Hemingway to F. Scott Fitzgerald, April 16, 1926, reprinted in Sanderson, Spanier, and Trogdon, *Letters of Ernest Hemingway,* 3:56. Charles Scribner's Sons kept an eye on Hemingway's general attitude toward criticism. In autumn 1927, Wallace Meyer—one of the admen who lauched *The Sun Also Rises*—lunched with Hemingway in Paris and reported back to Perkins that "literary criticism has very little value for him, and adverse criticism I think does nothing but unsettle him

a little bit . . . [T]hey put all reviews, he says, on a hook in the bathroom —as reading matter they run to just about the right length and they're not too much honored by the occasion." Regarding an unflattering October 9, 1927, review that Virginia Woolf had written about *The Sun Also Rises* and Hemingway's subsequent book, *Men Without Women,* Meyer added: "[It] really threw him off his stride a bit. He seemed to me really perturbed about her remarks about his overuse of dialogue—which the good woman can't use at all herself and probably knows it. After all, Hemingway is an original and must go his own way. And it's equally true that he's a limited person, more limited, let's say, than Scott Fitzg., but he must work freely and easily within those limits; if he does, I think they'll broaden out. The extent to which he can develop will depend on the degree to which he can be kept unselfconscious." Wallace Meyer to Maxwell Perkins, November 27, 1927, Archives of Charles Scribner's Sons, Princeton University Library. Perkins shared these impressions with Charles Scribner as they collectively monitored their new author. Maxwell Perkins to Charles Scribner, December 29, 1927, Archives of Charles Scribner's Sons, Princeton University Library.

"very funny as": Ernest Hemingway to Maxwell Perkins, December 21, 1926, Archives of Charles Scribner's Sons, Princeton University Library.

202 *"smashed":* Ernest Hemingway to Isidor Schneider, ca. January 18–20, 1927, reprinted in Sanderson, Spanier, and Trogdon, *Letters of Ernest Hemingway,* 3:189–90.

"stumbling through life": Review of *The Sun Also Rises, The New Republic,* December 22, 1926.

"jazz superficial story": Ernest Hemingway to Maxwell Perkins, November 16, 1927, Archives of Charles Scribner's Sons, Princeton University Library.

"bombast": Ernest Hemingway to Maxwell Perkins, November 19, 1926, Archives of Charles Scribner's Sons, Princeton University Library.

"Gertrude was a": Hotchner, *Papa Hemingway,* 49–50.

203 *"We offered to":* Maxwell Perkins to Ernest Hemingway, May 24, 1928, Archives of Charles Scribner's Sons, Princeton University Library.

"She might as": Ernest Hemingway to Maxwell Perkins, May 31, 1928, Archives of Charles Scribner's Sons, Princeton University Library. In this note, Hemingway explained that when he was working on proofs of *The Sun Also Rises,* he had consulted both *Burke's Peerage* and *Debrett's Peerage,* and in neither "studbook" did the name "Lady Ashley" appear.

Beach was stocking copies: Copies of *The Sun Also Rises* arrived at Shakespeare and Company on November 29, 1926. Sylvia Beach Papers, Inventories, Order Records, Clients, 1926, box 65, Princeton University Library.

The book was also available at another Paris-based English-language bookstore, the Sign of the Black Mannikin, from November 7.

"Six Characters in": This jest-title was a takeoff on the 1921 play by Luigi Pirandello, *Six Characters in Search of an Author.*

"the best thing": Cody, *"The Sun Also Rises* Revisited," 269.

204 *"it was like":* A. E. Hotchner, interview with the author, December 11, 2013.

"four leading characters": Janet Flanner, "Letter from Paris," *The New Yorker,* December 4, 1926, 90. This item—sandwiched between ads for bedding and finger-wave permanents—was ironically tagged onto another item announcing Michael Arlen's presence in Paris for the winter.

"Several well-known habitués": "Around the Town," *Paris Herald,* November 17, 1926.

incisive reportage: Cleveland Chase, "Out of Little, Much" *Saturday Review of Literature,* December 11, 1926, excerpted in Sarason, "Hemingway and the *Sun* Set," 5.

"Like Cohn": Cody, *"The Sun Also Rises* Revisited," 267.

"What a savage": "Around the Town," *Paris Herald,* November 17, 1926.

205 *"The book hit":* Loeb, "Hemingway's Bitterness," 126.

"unnecessary nastiness": Ibid., 126–27.

"travestied": Ibid., 127.

It was said: The Cohn portrait was "absolutely something that colored the rest of his life," recalled Valerie Hemingway, who knew Loeb in later years. Even decades later, she remembered, Loeb still "literally cried on my shoulder, saying, 'Why did Ernest do this to me?'" Valerie Hemingway, interview with the author, December 20, 2013. Up through his final years, he wrote essays and gave interviews on the subject, and even devoted much of his memoir to the Hemingway betrayal. He pored over Hemingway's later works and studied Hemingway's own family background, searching for clues to his former friend's "incapacity for either remorse or pity." He eventually concluded that Hemingway had been, during their time together in Paris, "already too sick for friendship"; he just hadn't heeded the warnings. Loeb, "Hemingway's Bitterness," 126, 133.

"I sent word": Ernest Hemingway to F. Scott Fitzgerald, March 31, 1927, reprinted in Sanderson, Spanier, and Trogdon, *Letters of Ernest Hemingway,* 3:222.

"You can see": Hotchner, *Papa Hemingway,* 48.

"I never threatened": Loeb, "Hemingway's Bitterness," 128.

206 *"I distinctly remember":* Ibid.

"demented characters out": Ernest Hemingway to F. Scott Fitzgerald, March 31, and ca. September 15, 1927, reprinted in Sanderson, Spanier, and Trogdon, *Letters of Ernest Hemingway,* 3:222.

furious about the book: Charters, *This Must Be the Place,* 38.

"cruel": Sarason, *Hemingway and the* Sun *Set,* 43.

"would have been": Ibid., 100.

207   *"Mike"*: This according to Matthew Josephson, who recounted having witnessed this exchange in 1927. Bertram Sarason, "Lady Brett Ashley and Lady Duff Twysden," in *Hemingway and the* Sun *Set*, 232.

rumors about the Twysdens: Sarason states that he heard the plates-buying story from photographer Berenice Abbott, who had been thus apprised by Twysden herself. The denial of the plates story was related to Sarason by Aileen Twysden. See Sarason, *Hemingway and the* Sun *Set,* 35. Duff Twysden may have believed that Hemingway had jeopardized or complicated her visitation rights with the Twysdens. Sarason, "Lady Brett Ashley and Lady Duff Twysden," 100. In fall 1927, Hemingway claimed to Fitzgerald that Twysden actually *had* kidnapped the child and sent him, accompanied by a nurse, down to the south of France, although it is unclear whether this actually happened. Ernest Hemingway to F. Scott Fitzgerald, ca. September 15, 1927, reprinted in Sanderson, Spanier, and Trogdon, *Letters of Ernest Hemingway,* 3:292.

"I would have": Charters, "Pat and Duff: Some Memories," 245.

Yet another rumor: For the boyfriend and bartenders, see Sarason, "Hemingway and the *Sun* Set," 24. For Cannell unable to get out of bed, see Baker, *Ernest Hemingway: A Life Story,* 179.

208   *"Hemingway gave Frances"*: Cannell, "Scenes with a Hero," 150.

"awful": Sarason, "Hemingway and the *Sun* Set," 95.

"It was so": St. John, "Interview with Donald Ogden Stewart," 202.

"It didn't make": Ibid.

"complete copying": St. John, "Interview with Hemingway's 'Bill Gorton,'" 155.

"Hemingway was not": Ibid., 185.

209   *"The Sun has"*: Maxwell Perkins to Ernest Hemingway, January 25, 1927, Archives of Charles Scribner's Sons, Princeton University Library.

35,000 copies: Berg, *Max Perkins,* 41.

hit that mark: The Sun Also Rises sold 23,000 copies in its first year. Baker, *Ernest Hemingway: A Life Story,* 186.

became a "craze": Malcolm Cowley, who studied the social effects of *The Sun Also Rises,* noted that "it was a good novel and became a craze" in the college age group. Malcolm Cowley, *Exiles Return: A Literary Odyssey of the 1920s* (New York: Viking, 1965), 3; *"suppressed"*: On June 8, 1927, Perkins wrote to Hemingway with the news that "the book . . . has been suppressed in Boston." Archives of Charles Scribner's Sons, Princeton University Library.

"Young women of": Cowley, *Exiles Return,* 3.

"Most of those": Ibid.

210 *"young Americans [who]"*: Samuel Putnam, *Paris Was Our Mistress: Memoirs of a Lost and Found Generation* (London: Plantin Publishers, 1987), 69.

"Why you're Kitty": Cannell, "Scenes with a Hero," 150.

"The three months": Hadley Hemingway to Ernest Hemingway, November 16, 1926, Incoming Correspondence, Hadley Richardson Hemingway Mowrer, Ernest Hemingway Collection, John F. Kennedy Presidential Library and Museum. A few days later Hadley wrote to Hemingway again: "Haven't I yet made it quite plain that I want to start proceedings for a divorce from you—right away? Thus the three months separation between you and Pauline is nil as far as I am concerned—whether you communicate with her about any or all of your and my arrangements makes no difference to me." She told him that she was willing to start the procedure herself and advised him to get a "good lawyer." Hadley Hemingway to Ernest Hemingway, November 19, 1926, ibid.

211 *"two boxers who"*: Ernest Hemingway to Hadley Hemingway, November 18, 1926, reprinted in Sanderson, Spanier, and Trogdon, *Letters of Ernest Hemingway,* 3:151–53. Hadley accepted Hemingway's offer. Hemingway duly wrote to Perkins, informing him that he had given her the British and American royalties for the book and added that he hoped "they will be considerable." The Charles Scribner's Sons archives contain an untitled document noting the official transfer of proceeds, which was filed along with Hemingway's contract for *The Sun Also Rises* (Archives of Charles Scribner's Sons, Princeton University Library). Hadley began receiving royalty payments in August 1927. In the months that followed, Hemingway advertised this transfer of royalties in correspondence with friends and acquaintances, usually adding that those royalties were substantial and that Hadley was getting along well.

The Hemingways' divorce: The preliminary judgment went through on January 27, 1927, and was finalized on April 14. Michael Reynolds, *Hemingway: The Homecoming* (New York: W. W. Norton, 1999), xi.

"I didn't know": Sokoloff, *Hadley,* 92–93.

"a very difficult": Patrick Hemingway, interview with the author, September 26, 2014.

"The Sun ect.": F. Scott Fitzgerald to Ernest Hemingway, December 1926, reprinted in Bruccoli, *F. Scott Fitzgerald: A Life in Letters,* 148.

"bullfighting, bullslinging, and": Mayfield, *Exiles from Paradise,* 112.

"I'm sorry for": F. Scott Fitzgerald to Ernest Hemingway, December 1926, reprinted in Bruccoli, *F. Scott Fitzgerald: A Life in Letters,* 148.

212   *"I have a"*: Callaghan, *That Summer in Paris,* 161.

13. Sun, *Risen*

213   *"edging away"*: Putnam, *Paris Was Our Mistress,* 69, 128. Putnam's description of his Deux Magots conversation with Hemingway appears in a passage titled "Hard-Boiled Young Man Going Places (Ernest Hemingway)."

214   *"shy youth had"*: Arthur Moss, quoted in Carlos Baker's notes on an unpublished manuscript of Moss's, "Time of the Expatriates: A Reporter's Recollections of the Lost Generation," Carlos Baker Collection of Ernest Hemingway, Princeton University Library.

Gone were: Despite the security that his association and eventual marriage with Pauline would give Hemingway, he frequently complained in letters that spring of money problems, and asked for (and received) a $750 advance on his next book from Maxwell Perkins to help make ends meet.

"Beginning with the": Robert McAlmon to Norman Holmes Pearson, quoted in Sarason, *Hemingway and the* Sun *Set,* 225.

"son of a": Ernest Hemingway to F. Scott Fitzgerald, December 24, 1925, reprinted in Defazio, Spanier, and Trogdon, *Letters of Ernest Hemingway,* 2:455. In this letter Hemingway told Fitzgerald that he planned to "write a Mr. and Mrs. Elliot on him" — referring to the story in which he had portrayed a thinly veiled Chard Powers Smith in a less than flattering light.

215   *"It never occurred"*: Hemingway: *A Moveable Feast,* 93.

a satirical piece: "The True Story of My Break with Gertrude Stein" came out in *The New Yorker* on February 12, 1927.

"He heard about": Stein, *Autobiography of Alice B. Toklas,* 217.

"talked endlessly about": Ibid., 219.

he needed help: Ernest Hemingway to Maxwell Perkins, February 19, 1927, Archives of Charles Scribner's Sons, Princeton University Library.

"I now have": Ernest Hemingway to Maxwell Perkins, October 1, 1927, Archives of Charles Scribner's Sons, Princeton University Library.

216   *"movie people"*: Maxwell Perkins to Ernest Hemingway, December 3, 1926, Archives of Charles Scribner's Sons, Princeton University Library.

"[I] would not": Ernest Hemingway to Maxwell Perkins, December 6, 1926, Archives of Charles Scribner's Sons, Princeton University Library;

"For the movie": Ernest Hemingway to Maxwell Perkins, December 15, 1926, Archives of Charles Scribner's Sons, Princeton University Library.

"No movie in": F. Scott Fitzgerald to Ernest Hemingway, December 1926, reprinted in Bruccoli, *F. Scott Fitzgerald: A Life in Letters,* 148.

more than thirty years: A film adaptation of *The Sun Also Rises* was released in 1957 by Twentieth Century–Fox, starring Tyrone Power as Jake Barnes and Ava Gardner as Brett Ashley.

"Got a sheet": Ernest Hemingway to F. Scott Fitzgerald, ca. September 15, 1927, reprinted in Sanderson, Spanier, and Trogdon, *Letters of Ernest Hemingway,* 3:292.

undignified domestic accident: Baker, *Ernest Hemingway: A Life Story,* 189–90.

217   *"His argument was"*: Ernest Hemingway to Maxwell Perkins, May 27, 1927, Archives of Charles Scribner's Sons, Princeton University Library.

"Don't you think": Ernest Hemingway to Maxwell Perkins, December 6, 1926, Archives of Charles Scribner's Sons, Princeton University Library.

"softening feminine influence": Ernest Hemingway to Maxwell Perkins, February 14, 1927, Archives of Charles Scribner's Sons, Princeton University Library; *"punk title"*: Ernest Hemingway to Maxwell Perkins, February 19, 1927, Archives of Charles Scribner's Sons, Princeton University Library.

"splendid": Maxwell Perkins to Ernest Hemingway, February 28, 1927, Archives of Charles Scribner's Sons, Princeton University Library. Perkins may have liked the title, but Fitzgerald had a wonderful time poking fun at it in letters to Hemingway, alternately calling it *All the Sad Young Men Without Women* (combining its name with the title of his own latest short story collection, *All the Sad Young Men*) and *All the Sad Young Men Without Women in Love* (rolling in the title of D. H. Lawrence's 1920 novel for good measure). F. Scott Fitzgerald to Ernest Hemingway, October 1927 and December 1927, Archives of Charles Scribner's Sons, Princeton University Library.

"self-consciously virile": Virginia Woolf, "An Essay in Criticism," *New York Herald Tribune,* October 9, 1927.

218   *"truly magnificent"*: Parker, "Reading and Writing," 93–94.

"Once he'd finished": Patrick Hemingway, interview with the author, July 30, 2014.

The World's Fair: Hemingway wrote to F. Scott Fitzgerald weeks before *The Sun Also Rises* was released and informed him that he had "a swell hunch for a new novel" and told him about the possible title. *The World's Fair* had also been an early possible title for Fitzgerald's novel *Tender Is the Night.* Hemingway did not offer any additional details about his possible new project. Ernest Hemingway to F. Scott Fitzgerald, ca. September 8, 1926, reprinted in Sanderson, Spanier, and Trogdon, *Letters of Ernest Hemingway,* 3:117.

"things get straightened": Ernest Hemingway to Maxwell Perkins, December 6, 1926, Archives of Charles Scribner's Sons, Princeton University Library.

"extra weight": Ernest Hemingway to Maxwell Perkins, June 24, 1927, Archives of Charles Scribner's Sons, Princeton University Library.

219 *"wonderfully":* Ernest Hemingway to Maxwell Perkins, March 17, 1928, reprinted in Sanderson, Spanier, and Trogdon, *Letters of Ernest Hemingway,* 3:375. This abortive novel had been tentatively titled *New Slain Knight,* although this title was crossed out in pencil on the manuscript. Reynolds, *Hemingway: The Homecoming,* 247. Hemingway informed Perkins that it was meant to be a "modern Tom Jones." By the following March (in the letter just cited), he informed Perkins that he had gotten twenty-two chapters and 45,000 words down, but was putting it aside to work on a new story — which would develop into *A Farewell to Arms.*

"This next book": Ernest Hemingway to Maxwell Perkins, March 17, 1928, reprinted in Sanderson, Spanier, and Trogdon, *Letters of Ernest Hemingway,* 3:375.

phrase he borrowed: Carlos Baker states that Hemingway informed his family of the title's origin. Baker, *Ernest Hemingway: A Life Story,* 199.

"I work all": Ernest Hemingway to Maxwell Perkins, March 17, 1928, reprinted in Sanderson, Spanier, and Trogdon, *Letters of Ernest Hemingway,* 3:374.

220 *"the very apotheosis":* The Nation, October 30, 1929.

"big mistake": Ernest Hemingway, "A Paris Letter," *Esquire,* February 1934, 22.

"only a few": Charters, *This Must Be the Place,* 197.

221 *"refugees from the":* Hemingway, "A Paris Letter," 156.

Epilogue

223 *"B.S.":* Cannell, "Scenes with a Hero," 145.

a decade her junior: King was born in 1901, according to John Powers and Deborah D. Powers, *Texas Painters, Sculptors, and Graphic Artists: A Biographical Dictionary of Artists in Texas Before 1942* (Austin: Woodmont Books, 2000). If we can rely on the birth date provided on Twysden's death certificate — 1892 — that makes her nine years older.

"the secret marriage": "Lady Twysden Secretly Weds Clinton King, Amer-

ican Artist, in England, Records Reveal," *New York Times,* August 23, 1928.

his relations protested: For the family's reaction to King's marrying Twysden, see Sarason, "Lady Brett Ashley and Lady Duff Twysden," 236.

224 *"an Englishwoman with":* Witter Bynner, "Expatriates," in *The Selected Witter Bynner: Poems, Plays, Translations, Prose, and Letters,* ed. James Kraft (Albuquerque: University of New Mexico Press, 1995), 110.

"entertain any false": McAlmon, *Being Geniuses Together,* 271, 273.

until afternoon: Sarason, "Hemingway and the *Sun* Set," 47.

bailed out by friends: Sarason, "Lady Brett Ashley and Lady Duff Twysden," 238.

"the most capable": Witter Bynner to Gladys Ficke, November 12, 1930, Witter Bynner Papers, Houghton Library, Harvard College Library.

225 *"about the worst":* Edmund Wilson, *The Thirties: From Notebooks and Diaries of the Period,* ed. Leon Edel (New York: Farrar, Straus and Giroux, 1980), 92.

"on account of": Witter Bynner to Gladys Ficke, November 12, 1930, Witter Bynner Papers, Houghton Library, Harvard College Library.

"the Duff-Brett woman": Russell Cheney to F. O. Matthiessen, November 29, 1929, F. O. Matthiessen Papers, Bienecke Rare Book and Manuscript Library, Yale University Library.

placed in a sanatorium: Duff took up residence in St. Vincent Hospital, which specialized in the treatment of tuberculosis. Clarke Kimball, *The Hospital at the End of the Santa Fe Trail* (Sante Fe: Rydal Press, 1977), 100.

"She looks as": Witter Bynner to Arthur Davison Ficke, June 5, 1938, Arthur Davison Ficke Papers, Bienecke Rare Book and Manuscript Library, Yale University Library.

"Mrs. Duff Stirling King": Sayre Andrew Funeral Home, Case 787. These records are kept by Berardinelli Family Funeral Services in Santa Fe, which would not release the records to the author, but a representative confirmed the details of their contents in a telephone conversation. The records have also been summarized in David Harrell, "A Final Note on Duff Twysden," *Hemingway Review* 5, no. 2 (Spring 1986): 45–46.

"Brett died in": Hotchner, *Papa Hemingway,* 48. A representative of Berardinelli Family Funeral Services confirmed that Duff's records include a cremation charge; the body was transported to Albuquerque for the service. Her records do, however, include a charge for a casket, but the representative maintains that it was likely just used to transport the body. Gerald Rodriguez, interview with the author, August 2014.

226   *"Who knows if"*: A. E. Hotchner, interview with the author, December 11, 2013.

Loeb's second wife: Sarason, "Hemingway and the *Sun* Set," 9–10.

Leaf of Twisted Olive: Bertram Sarason claims that Loeb showed the manuscript to him. Loeb's writer character, "Hank," was, Sarason thought, reminiscent of Hemingway, although Loeb instructed him that Hemingway was "not to be identified with Hank." At the very least, Sarason concluded, the character "represents the quintessence of Hemingway." Sarason, "Hemingway and the *Sun* Set," 12. None of the Loeb family members consulted for this book have seen the manuscript among Loeb's surviving papers.

"gardening with a passion": Anah Pytte, interview with the author, July 29, 2014.

"it gave him": Susan Sandberg, interview with the author, May 30, 2014; *pleased by the attention:* Barbara Loeb Kennedy, interview with the author, May 7, 2014.

227   *"the publisher's interest"*: Anah Pytte, interview with the author, July 29, 2014.

"absolutely untrue": Email from Valerie Hemingway to the author, April 15, 2014.

"he always had": Susan Sandberg, interview with the author, May 30, 2014.

"savaged Mr. Loeb": "Harold A. Loeb Is Dead at 82; 'Lost Generation' Figure in Paris," *New York Times,* January 23, 1974.

228   *marriage did not last:* Cannell's marriage to Vitrac was left out of her *New York Times* obituary but is mentioned in passing by Malcolm Cowley in *The Long Journey* and cited in M. C. Rintoul, *Dictionary of Real People and Places in Fiction* (Abingdon, U.K.: Routledge, 1993).

fashion reporter: Cannell's *New York Times* obituary states that she acted as Paris-based fashion correspondent for the newspaper between 1931 and 1941. Her biography included in her 1945 book *Jam Yesterday* says that she contributed for two years to *The New Yorker,* "until the Occupation." Kathleen Cannell, *Jam Yesterday: Gay, Insouciant Reminiscences of the Late Nineties of a Happy Childhood Spent Shuttling Between Canada and the U.S.A.* (New York: William Morrow & Company, 1945).

"enemy-alien parolee": Ibid., 1.

"cold, hunger, dirt": Ibid., 2.

"tipped off by": Ibid.

"everything from Timeless": "Kathleen Cannell, Sparkling Talks Feature Fashions from Paris to Main Street," undated press material issued by Lordly & Dame, Boston. Additional information about Cannell's career comes from Bertram D. Sarason, "Kathleen Cannell," in Rood, *Diction-*

ary of Literary Biography, 4:68; and "Kathleen Cannell, 82, Dies; Covered Fashion for Times," *New York Times,* May 23, 1974.

229   *She died exactly four months:* "Kathleen Cannell, 82, Dies.

"in one quick": Katharine Hepburn, "A Note from Katharine Hepburn," in Stewart, *By a Stroke of Luck!* 7.

"It was said": "Donald O. Stewart, Screenwriter, Dies," *New York Times,* August 3, 1980.

"By 1950 I": Stewart, *By a Stroke of Luck!* 295, 297.

230   *"one of the":* Hepburn, "A Note from Katharine Hepburn," 7.

"In the old": St. John, "Interview with Donald Ogden Stewart," 190.

"He didn't sit": Daneet Steffens, interview with the author, August 6, 2014.

"He would say": Donald Ogden Stewart Jr., interview with the author, January 26, 2015.

"was a terrible": Ibid.

231   *"the curious bitter":* Stewart, *By a Stroke of Luck!* 157.

"no one left": Donald Ogden Stewart to Bertram D. Sarason, June 14, 1971, quoted in Sarason, "Hemingway and the *Sun* Set," 107.

"'to the colonies'": Charters, *This Must Be the Place,* 69.

"arranged things in": Ibid.

232   *Guthrie's overdose and death:* Ibid., 70. For his death date and age, see "Patrick Stirling Guthrie," "The Peerage: A Genealogical Survey of the Peerage of Britain as Well as the Royal Families of Europe," entry no. 54807, http://thepeerage.com/p5481.htm.

"So few people": Charters, *This Must Be the Place,* 70.

"I felt like": Charters, "Pat and Duff: Some Memories," 244.

Smith's career and marriage: St. John, "Interview with Hemingway's 'Bill Gorton,'" 187–88.

"a genius about": Ibid., 158.

It wasn't so: Ibid., 155–56.

233   *"Every one of":* Ibid., 156.

"that was the": Ernest Hemingway, *Death in the Afternoon* (New York: Charles Scribner's Sons, 1932), 89–90.

raucous new home: Shay Oag, *In the Presence of Death* (New York: Coward-McCann, 1969), 68–70.

"forgave him everything": Ibid., 73.

234   *"absolute technical perfection":* Ernest Hemingway, *The Dangerous Summer* (New York: Touchstone/Simon & Schuster, 1997), 50.

"Tell me": Ibid., 52.

"almost unhuman retching": Sam Adams, "The Sun Also Sets," *Sports Illustrated,* June 29, 1970, 57–60, 62–64.

235   *"Schrafft's is a"*: E. B. White, "Across the Street and into the Grill," *The New Yorker,* October 14, 1950, 28.

"Parody is the": Hotchner, *Papa Hemingway,* 70.

Advance sales: Early sales statistics for *The Old Man and the Sea* come from Baker, *Ernest Hemingway: A Life Story,* 504.

236   *"She says, 'Shut'"*: H. R. Stoneback, interview with the author, June 2, 2014.

"This five million": Ernest Hemingway to Wallace Meyer, September 26, 1952, reprinted in Baker, *Ernest Hemingway: Selected Letters,* 783.

"mastery of the": "The Nobel Prize in Literature 1954," Nobelprize.org, accessed July 30, 2015, http://www.nobelprize.org/nobel_prizes/literature/laureates/1954/.

"A true writer": Ernest Hemingway, "Ernest Hemingway — Banquet Speech," December 10, 1954, Nobelprize.org, accessed July 30, 2015, http://www.nobelprize.org/nobel_prizes/literature/laureates/1954/hemingway-speech.html.

"Mr. Hemingway accidentally": "Hemingway Dead of Shotgun Wound; Wife Says He Was Cleaning Weapon," *New York Times,* July 2, 1961.

"consciously lying": Mary Welsh Hemingway, *How It Was* (New York: Alfred A. Knopf/Borzoi, 1976), 503.

237   *"If you are"*: Hotchner, *Papa Hemingway,* 57.

"He shrugged off": Valerie Hemingway, interview with the author, April 28, 2015.

"full of lies": Hotchner, *Papa Hemingway,* 53, 48.

"I once asked him": A. E. Hotchner, interview with the author, December 11, 2013.

Text Permission Credits

"To a Tragic Poetess" by Ernest Hemingway, © 1992, printed with the permission of The Ernest Hemingway Foundation. • "News Item," copyright 1926, renewed © 1954 by Dorothy Parker, from *The Portable Dorothy Parker* by Dorothy Parker, edited by Marion Meade. Used by permission of Viking Books, an imprint of Penguin Publishing Group, a division of Penguin Random House LLC. The author wishes to thank the National Association for the Advancement of Colored People for authorizing use of Dorothy Parker's work. • Excerpts from *Papa Hemingway: A Personal Memoir* by Aaron Edward Hotchner used with permission of Mr. Hotchner. • Excerpt from "Sacred Emily" by Gertrude Stein used by permission of the Estate of Gertrude Stein, through its Literary Executor, Stanford G. Gann Jr. of Levin and Gann, P.A. • Excerpts from the letters and interviews of Hadley Richardson Hemingway Mowrer used with permission of Angela Hemingway Charles. • Excerpt from "Expatriates" by Witter Bynner and quotes from Mr. Bynner's letters reprinted with permission from The Witter Bynner Foundation for Poetry. • Excerpts from "The Best Times" by John Dos Passos, copyright © 1966 by John Dos Passos, used with permission of Brandt & Hochman Literary Agents, Inc. • Excerpts from *By a Stroke of Luck* by Donald Ogden Stewart used with permission by Luisa Gilardenghi Stewart. • Letters of Maxwell Perkins from the Charles Scribner's Sons Archives at the Princeton University Library are quoted with permission. • Excerpt from Janet Flanner's *Paris Was Yesterday* is used with permission from *The New Yorker*. • Excerpts from *Archibald Macleish: Reflections,* edited by Bernard A. Drabeck and Helen E. Ellis, are used with permission from the University of Massachusetts Press. • Excerpts from Robert McAlmon's *Being Geniuses Together,* edited by Kay Boyle, are used with permission from the Boyle Estate. • Excerpts from Harold Loeb's *The Way It Was* and *Hemingway's Bitterness* are used with permission from the Loeb Estate. • Excerpts from the letters of Sherwood Anderson are used with permission from Harold Ober Associates. • Excerpts from the letters of Sara and Gerald Murphy are used with permission from the University Press of Florida.

Excerpts, F. Scott Fitzgerald: Reprinted with the permission of Scribner, a division of Simon & Schuster, Inc., from *A Life in Letters* by F. Scott Fitzgerald. Edited by Matthew Bruccoli. Copyright © 1994 by The Trustees under agreement dated July 3, 1975, created by Frances Scott Fitzgerald Smith. All rights reserved. • Reprinted with the permission of Scribner, a division of Simon & Schuster, Inc., from *Dear Scott, Dear Max: The Fitzgerald-Perkins Correspondence,* and edited by John Kuehl and Jackson Bryer. Copyright © 1971 by Charles Scribner's Sons. All rights reserved.

Prose excerpts, Ernest Hemingway: Reprinted with the permission of Scribner, a division of Simon & Schuster, Inc., from *A Moveable Feast* by Ernest Hemingway. Copyright © 1964 by Ernest Hemingway. Copyright renewed © 1992 by John H. Hemingway, Patrick Hemingway, and Gregory Hemingway. All rights reserved. • Reprinted with the permission of Scribner, a division of Simon & Schuster, Inc., from *The Sun Also Rises* by Ernest Hemingway. Copyright © 1926 by Charles Scribner's Sons; copyright renewed © 1954 by Ernest Hemingway. All rights reserved. • Reprinted with the permission of Scribner, a division of Simon & Schuster, Inc., from *The Dangerous Summer* by Ernest Hemingway. Copyright © 1960 by Ernest Hemingway. Copyright renewal © 1985 by Mary Hemingway, John Hemingway, Patrick Hemingway and Gregory Hemingway. All rights reserved. • Reprinted with the permission of Scribner, a division of Simon & Schuster, Inc., from *In Our Time* by Ernest Hemingway. Copyright © 1925, 1930 by Charles Scribner's Sons. Copyright renewal © 1958 by Ernest Hemingway. All rights reserved. • Reprinted with the permission of Scribner, a division of Simon & Schuster, Inc., from *The Short Stories of Ernest Hemingway* by Ernest Hemingway. Copyright © 1925, 1927, 1938 by Ernest Hemingway. Copyright renewal © 1953, 1955, 1966 by Ernest Hemingway and Mary Hemingway. All rights reserved.

Letter excerpts, Ernest Hemingway: Reprinted with the permission of Scribner, a division of Simon & Schuster, Inc., from *Hemingway Letters* as published by Cambridge University Press under *The Letters of Ernest Hemingway: Volume 2.* Copyright © Hemingway Foreign Rights Trust. All rights reserved.

Photo Credits

Ernest and Hadley Hemingway on their wedding day: Ernest Hemingway Collection, John F. Kennedy Presidential Library and Museum, Boston. • *Sherwood Anderson:* Chicago History Museum/Getty Images. • *Hemingway's 1923 passport photo:* Ernest Hemingway Collection, John F. Kennedy Presidential Library and Museum, Boston. • *The newlyweds:* Ernest Hemingway Collection, John F. Kennedy Presidential Library and Museum, Boston. • *Le Dôme café:* Apic/Getty Images. • *Ezra Pound:* Hulton Archive/Getty Images. • *Gertrude Stein:* Jewish Chronicle Heritage Images/Getty Images. *Sylvia Beach:* Berenice Abbott/Getty Images. • *Hemingway at Shakespeare and Company:* Sylvia Beach Papers, Box 168, Folder 23; Manuscripts Division, Department of Rare Books and Special Collections, Princeton University Library. • *Robert McAlmon:* Sylvia Beach Papers, Box 170, Folder 1; Manuscripts Division, Department of Rare Books and Special Collections, Princeton University Library. • *Robert McAlmon and Hemingway:* Sylvia Beach Papers, Box 168, Folder 25; Manuscripts Division, Department of Rare Books and Special Collections, Princeton University Library. • *Robert McAlmon and Bill Bird:* Sylvia Beach Papers, Box 168, Folder 25; Manuscripts Division, Department of Rare Books and Special Collections, Princeton University Library. • *Rue Notre-Dame-des-Champs:* Sylvia Beach Papers, Box 169, Folder 2; Manuscripts Division, Department of Rare Books and Special Collections, Princeton University Library. • *La Closerie des Lilas:* Branger/Roger Viollet/Getty Images. • *Ford Madox Ford:* E. O. Hoppe/Getty Images. • *Hemingway and his son Jack "Bumby" Hemingway skiing:* Sylvia Beach Papers, Box 169, Folder 3; Manuscripts Division, Department of Rare Books and Special Collections, Princeton University Library. • *Harold Loeb:* © Man Ray Trust/Artists Rights Society (ARS), NY/ADAGP, Paris 2015. • *Kathleen "Kitty" Cannell:* National Archives and Records Administration, Record Group 59, Archives II Branch, College Park, Maryland. • *Donald Ogden Stewart:* The Granger Collection, New York. • *Horace Liveright:* Courtesy of George Eastman House, International Museum of Photography and Film; © Nickolas Muray Photo Archives. • *Pauline Pfeiffer:* Apic/Getty Images. *Sara and Gerald Murphy:* © Estate of Honoria Murphy Donnelly/Licensed by VAGA, New York, NY. • *F. Scott Fitzgerald and Zelda:* Mondadori Portfolio/Getty Images. • *Maxwell Perkins:* Archives of Charles Scribner's Sons, Manuscripts Division, Department of Rare Books and Special Collections, Princeton University Library. • *Bill Smith and Hemingway fishing:* Sylvia Beach Papers, Manuscripts Division, Department of Rare Books and Special Collections, Princeton University Library. • *Hemingway and entourage at a café in Pamplona:* Ernest Hemingway Collection, John F. Kennedy Presidential Library and Museum, Boston. • *Harold Loeb at the 1925 Pamplona fiesta:* Reproduced with permission of the Loeb Estate. • *Hemingway in the bullring*: Ernest Hemingway Collection, John F. Kennedy Presidential Library and Museum, Boston. • *Cayetano Ordóñez:* Photo by M. Martin/© ullstein bild/The Image Works. • *Hadley Hemingway and Pauline Pfeiffer:* Patrick Hemingway Papers, Box 2, Folder 9; Manuscripts Division, Department of Rare Books and Special Collections, Princeton University Library. • *Dorothy Parker:* Hulton Archive/Getty Images. • *Gerald Murphy, Sara Murphy, Pauline Pfeiffer, Hemingway, and Hadley Hemingway:* Ernest Hemingway Collection, John F. Kennedy Presidential Library and Museum, Boston. • *Advertisement for* The Sun Also Rises: *The New Yorker,* October 1926. Reproduced with permission from *The New Yorker.*

Index